# Inside Web Dynpro for Java

 **PRESS**

SAP PRESS is a joint initiative of SAP and Galileo Press. The know-how offered by SAP specialists combined with the expertise of the publishing house Galileo Press offers the reader expert books in the field. SAP PRESS features first-hand information and expert advice, and provides useful skills for professional decision-making.

SAP PRESS offers a variety of books on technical and business related topics for the SAP user. For further information, please visit our website: *www.sap-press.com*.

Ganz, Gürtler, Lakner
Maximizing Web Dynpro for Java
2006, 497 pp., hardcover
ISBN 978-1-59229-077-2

Karl Kessler et al.
Java Programming with SAP NetWeaver
2008, 2nd, revised and extended edition
approx 650 pp., hardcover, with DVD
ISBN 978-1-59229-181-6

Ulli Hoffmann
Web Dynpro for ABAP
2006, 359 pp., hardcover
ISBN 978-1-59229-078-9

Horst Keller, Sascha Krüger
ABAP Objects
ABAP Programming in SAP NetWeaver
2007, 2nd, completely new edition
1276 pp., hardcover, with DVD
ISBN 978-1-59229-079-6

Chris Whealy

# Inside Web Dynpro for Java

**Galileo Press**

Bonn • Boston

ISBN    978-1-59229-092-5

2nd, revised and expanded edition 2007

**Editor** Florian Zimniak
**Copy Editor** Ruth Saavedra, Saratoga, CA
**Cover Design** Silke Braun
**Layout Design** Vera Brauner
**Production** Iris Warkus
**Typesetting** SatzPro, Krefeld
**Printed and bound in** Germany

© 2007 by Galileo Press
SAP PRESS is an imprint of Galileo Press,
Boston, MA, USA
Bonn, Germany

*Out of intense complexities,*
*intense simplicities emerge.*

Sir Winston Churchill

*The voice of ignorance speaks loud and long,*
*but the words of the wise are quiet and few.*

Ancient Proverb

*There are 10 kinds of people in the world:*
*Those who understand binary*
*and those who don't.*

Anonymous

# Contents at a Glance

# Contents

## Part II: The Fundamental Concepts

## 4　Web Dynpro Phase Model ................................................... 141

## Part III: Basic Development

## 5　The Context at Design Time ............................................. 163

## 7    UI Elements .................................................................. 237

## 8 Writing Multilanguage Applications ... 287

## Part IV: Advanced Development

## 9 Dynamic Context Manipulation ... 297

## 10 Advanced Use of the UI ......................................................... 311

## Appendix ............................................................. 497

# Author's Apology[1] — Preface to the Second Edition

Having been a professional software developer since 1986 and technical SAP consultant since 1993, I have learned (by attending the school of hard knocks) that forming a rigid set of *rules* about how problems should be solved has a fundamental weakness. That is, the rules formed for solving problem A often cannot be applied to solving problem B, even though problems A and B are similar.

Instead, I have found that many diverse and seemingly unrelated problems can be solved by understanding and then applying a common set of problem-solving *principles*. The problem-solving process then starts with an analysis of the particular situation to identify which of these principles are applicable.

This process of problem-solving is much like the process of abstraction that takes place during the design of an object-oriented program — that of condensing a problem down to its most fundamental, often abstract, elements — and I have spent much of my professional career developing these principles.

In writing this book, I do not wish to lay down an inflexible set of rules to which all developers should conform. Instead, I aim to equip the reader with an understanding of the fundamental principles that must be understood to build powerful and efficient Web Dynpro applications.

Since Web Dynpro is a programming toolset, it is not immune to abuse, and in the areas in which problems could arise, it may appear that I am laboring the point. If I have described the same concept in several different ways, it is because I am stressing its importance. I trust that this approach will communicate the necessary understanding to all readers and not be too tedious for those who "always grasp things the first time."

As with any set of tools, the results obtained from the use of Web Dynpro are determined by the skill of the operator, not the brand name on the handle. Therefore, to achieve the best results from the Web Dynpro toolset, each developer must have a thorough grasp of the principles that underpin its design and operation.

---

1  Some people have wondered why an author would "apologize" for writing a book. The word *apology* is being used here in its literary sense and means "the reason why the book was written." Although some would like me to, I am not saying sorry for writing the book!

I leave it to each developer to apply these principles to his or her own situation. Using this approach, no two solutions will ever be the same, yet all will be derived from a common set of fundamental principles.

It is these principles that I aim to communicate in this book.

### Note to Readers with ABAP Development Experience

For those readers experienced with classical SAP software design, the design concepts used by Web Dynpro represent an entirely new way of thinking, the mastery of which will require a significant shift in your thinking. For this category of reader (in which I include myself), it is even more important that these principles are fully grasped and understood.

Please allow this book to alter and expand your thinking and guide you through the mental transition that is required to move from classical R/3 design to Web Dynpro design. Failure to realize that such a mental transition is required will cause you to become frustrated by the fact that Web Dynpro does not meet your established expectations. This, in turn, can lead to all sorts of erroneous conclusions about the quality of the product.

### The "Number One" Problem with Web Dynpro Implementations

Since the first edition of this book was published in November 2004, I have performed many code reviews of Web Dynpro implementations that were experiencing "performance problems." After analysis, it was easy to see why the software was performing badly — in all cases, the developers lacked the basic training in the concepts of Web Dynpro — and in some cases, even basic knowledge of ABAP efficiency.

As a result, the Web Dynpro applications they wrote functioned as required but operated inefficiently and were difficult to maintain due to their excessive internal complexity.

### The "Number Two" Problem with Web Dynpro Implementations

In the cases where Web Dynpro implementations have suffered from both development difficulties and runtime performance problems, the developer had assumed that because Web Dynpro uses the Model–View–Controller (MVC) design pattern, it must therefore be similar to other Web development toolsets that also use MVC (e.g., Struts).

This is not a logical conclusion. Let's apply the same type of logic to a different situation. It is like saying:

- A cat is a mammal.
- A dog is a mammal.
- Therefore a cat is a dog.

I will go into this topic in greater detail in Chapter 3, but to give a brief explanation, the MVC design concept is just that — a concept. It has not been patented or copyrighted by any one or any company. Therefore no two implementations of the MVC design pattern are the same — and Web Dynpro is no exception.

## Contents

This book is focussed on the core functionality found within the Web Dynpro development and runtime environments. Please consult the standard SAP literature for information on integrating Web Dynpro with other products such as the Adobe® Document Service, the SAP NetWeaver Portal, the Business Graphics Server, or Microsoft® Office.

In addition to this preface, this book is divided into the following five parts:

- **Part I — Background**
  Chapter 1 goes right back to the original concepts found in the MVC design pattern, and from there explains the various influences that shaped the product called Web Dynpro. There are two reasons for having this chapter in the book:

  - Many people have started Web Dynpro development with the assumption that runs something like this: "I understand the MVC design pattern, and therefore I understand Web Dynpro". Unfortunately, this line of reasoning has produced quite a few disasters.

  - I want to avoid causing the reader to have to make any leaps of understanding. Any form of documentation that is "written by experts, for experts" is, in my opinion, pretty much useless. Therefore, I have taken the "smooth transition" approach that guides the reader from the basic concepts into the more complex concepts in gradual steps, rather than massive leaps.

- **Part II — The Fundamental Concepts**
  Now that you know how Web Dynpro came to be the way it is, and that it is not an exact implementation of the MVC design pattern, Chapter 2 takes a look at the fundamental building block from which all Web Dynpro applications are constructed — the Web Dynpro Component. After this, Chapter 3 takes a non-technical look at many of the issues involved in the actual implementation of Web Dynpro software. The information in this chapter has been condensed from two years of Web Dynpro implementation reviews of customer projects. I

have seen many implementations where things have gone wrong for entirely avoidable reasons, and these are shared here so that you can avoid falling into the same traps.

Some people have questioned the logic of putting Chapter 4 at this early stage of the book, but I have found that once people understand how Web Dynpro handles their business application, they will immediately understand why their business applications need to be structured in the manner shown. Again, I'm taking the smooth transition approach, rather than firing off disjointed details at you and then assuming that because I understand how they all hang together, then "of course the reader will understand".

▶ **Part III — Basic Development**
This section deals with the basics of getting a Web Dynpro application running. Here you will find all the information needed for putting data on the screen.

Chapters 5 and 6 look at how the Web Dynpro Context functions, both at design time and runtime. Chapter 7 deals with getting your business data from the locations in memory where Web Dynpro stores it (the Context) and putting it onto the screen using things called "UI Elements." Finally, Chapter 8 deals with the increasingly common requirement of making a business application multilingual.

▶ **Part IV — Advanced Development**
The Advanced Development section contains six chapters. Chapters 9 and 10 revisit the Web Dynpro Context and UI Elements in greater detail. Then Chapters 11 and 12 take another look at the design topics that were mentioned back in Chapter 3 — but this time from a technical point of view.

Finally, Chapters 13 and 14 look at an area of Web Dynpro programming that is frequently misunderstood; namely, obtaining data from a backend SAP system and how to ensure that your Web Dynpro applications achieve this in the most efficient manner.

▶ **References & Appendices**
The final part of the book contains a short reference section on the various classes generated by the NetWeaver Developer Studio (NWDS) at design time. This is followed by various appendices explaining the Web Dynpro naming nomenclature and conventions and some exercises that can be performed to put into practice the information learned in this book.


**Target Audience**

This book has been written for people who have:

▶ Java programming experience
▶ Attended at least the standard SAP training course for Web Dynpro for Java programming JA310 (Introduction to Web Dynpro for Java)

This book is not a tutorial of "how to" style exercises and answers, but rather it discusses the design and coding principles required for the development of successful Web Dynpro applications. The focus of this book is the core of Web Dynpro technology. If you want to read a book that contains worked examples of Web Dynpro development in Java, then please get the SAP Press book *Maximizing Web Dynpro for Java* by Bertram Ganz, Timo Lakner, and Jochen Gürtler.

Certain Web Dynpro–related subjects are not covered in this edition because they are not fundamental to an understanding of the subject. This book is designed to lay a foundation upon which other publications can then build.

Knowledge of SAP's ABAP programming language would be beneficial (particularly when reading Chapters 13 and 14) but is not essential.

## Conventions

### Use of Terminology

Certain words such as *component*, *element*, *context*, and *interface* have specific meanings within Web Dynpro. Therefore, to avoid ambiguity, such words will be used only when their Web Dynpro meaning is intended.

### Screenshots

For the sake of brevity, various graphical figures in this book have been cropped or resized. Therefore, when you look at the corresponding screen in your installation of the SAP NWDS, it may be larger than the image displayed in this book.

### Errata

For readers with access to SAP's Note System on the SAP Service Market (*http://service.sap.com*), please check note number 699531 for any corrections to errors or omissions discovered after publication. The note contains the errata for both the first and second editions of this book.

For readers who do not have access to the SAP Note System, please check the SAP PRESS websites *www.sap-press.com* and *www.sap-press.de/1243* for corrections, omissions, or additional content that may be delivered after the publication of this book.

### Downloads

Any time an example application is used in this book, reference will be made to Web Dynpro projects. These projects can be downloaded from the SAP PRESS website at the following addresses: *www.sap-press.com* or *www.sap-press.de/1243*.

## Acknowledgments

The author thanks everyone on the SAP Web Dynpro development team for their enthusiastic help and support while this document was being written. They all managed to find a few spare clock cycles in their very busy schedules to proofread and correct the many iterations through which this document passed before finally ending up on the printed page.

These are Andreas Wesselmann, Stephan Ritter, Johannes Knöppler, Markus Cherdron, Jens Ittel, Uwe Reeder, Harry Hawk, Thomas Chadzelek, Bertram Ganz, Arnold Klingert, Patric Ksinsik, Malte Wedel, Harry Hawk, Timo Lakner, Jörg Singler, Thorsten Dencker, Stefan Beck, Armin Reichert, and Harry Hawk.

I also thank Masoud Aghadavoodi Jolfaei, Marco Ertel, Karin Schattka, Stephanie Bachter, Svetlana Stancheva, Kerstin Hoeft, Markus Tolksdorf, and Marion Schlotte for their input and support during the writing of this book.

Chris Whealy

# PART I
# Background

# 1    Introduction

The purpose of this introduction is to provide the background concepts that were involved in the design and implementation of Web Dynpro. This information will provide you with valuable insight into the reasoning behind the architecture found in Web Dynpro. This, in turn, will help you understand how to use Web Dynpro in the most effective way.

## 1.1    Why Did SAP Decide to Build Their Own Web Development Framework?

When Web Dynpro was first postulated — in late 2000 — SAP was looking for a development toolset that would be robust enough to use as its standard development platform for browser-based business applications. A review of the then-available products revealed that none would sufficiently meet SAP's design requirements to make it worth taking the closest-fit and bending it into the product SAP required. Therefore, the decision was made to create both a development toolset and a runtime environment that would exactly meet SAP's requirements.

Like every other software vendor in the Web space, SAP needed a long-term, strategic solution to the many problems faced by Web developers. These problems were not only those experienced during the implementation of browser-based business applications, but also those experienced during the maintenance phase when functionality must be modified or extended.

Anyone who has written a Web application of any complexity has faced the pain of dealing with situations like:

- The web application that works perfectly with one browser but then develops "unexpected features" when run in a browser from a different vendor.
- Alterations in the interface to the backend system affect the presentation of the business data.
- The developer who was in a hurry and took some shortcuts during the design phase to get a quick result — only for you to find that the costs "saved" during development come back to bite you during the maintenance phase.[1]

---

1   This problem affects software developments in general and is not just confined to Web based applications.

In addition to these problems and in spite of the availability of many different client and server-side libraries, developers invariably had to write and rewrite the same blocks of code for every implementation they performed. In other words, the level of code reuse is not as good as it could be. This could be because code reuse either was not a major goal during development (perhaps because of aggressive delivery deadlines), or the code reuse existed at too low a level.

Whatever the reasons, SAP recognized that if the efficiency of application development and maintenance is to improve, the development toolset itself must have a strong focus on code reuse at a *business* level, not at some lower *technical* level.

All of these factors were brought together in the design process, the result of which is Web Dynpro.

## 1.2    What Is Web Dynpro?

This is a question I am frequently asked, and I usually answer by asking the questioner what they believe Web Dynpro to be. It's at this point that I receive a wide spectrum of opinions, ranging from:

> *"Isn't it something to do with Master Data Management or Exchange Infrastructure?"*

to

> *"Oh, it's just another Java Server Page based Web development toolset."*

These two answers come from opposite ends of the spectrum of understanding — and both are wrong. I'll explain why.

Having found out what the questioners think Web Dynpro is, I can start from their position of (mis)understanding and tell them what Web Dynpro actually is. Essentially, it is SAP's answer to the need for a reliable, functional, and powerful development environment[2] for Web-based business applications.

If we look at the answers cited above, the first opinion is typical of someone from a business background. Consequently (and often unconsciously), they regard Web Dynpro as either another business application or some sort of tool for handling business data.

The second opinion is typical of someone from a development background, and is definitely the more dangerous of the two opinions for the simple reason that it is being expressed by someone who will probably use Web Dynpro to develop a business application.

---

2  When I use the word *environment*, I am referring to the software used both at design time *and* at runtime.

The danger lies in the fact that if they develop an application while thinking that Web Dynpro is "like some other Web development toolset" with which they are already familiar, then their coding may be functional, but it will:

▶ At best, be inefficient and difficult to maintain.

▶ At worst, need to be thrown away and rewritten.

Either way, both the business user and the developer have assumed that Web Dynpro is similar to something with which they are already familiar. Since Web Dynpro is quite unlike any toolset SAP has ever released before, this assumption is both false and potentially dangerous.

A couple of mental traps are all too easy to fall into. The first goes something like this:

▶ First thought: "I know lots about hammers."

▶ Second thought: "I've never seen this problem before."

▶ Conclusion: "This new problem must be a nail."

In other words, you convince yourself that although you have no experience with solving this new type of problem (assumed to be a nail); its solution can't be too different from the solutions you've implemented in the past (use of a hammer). Therefore, you decide (possibly against all the odds) that your current experience is sufficient to solve this new problem.

The dangers this line of thinking can introduce cannot be stressed enough.

The second mental trap goes something like this:

▶ First thought: "I don't understand things that are really complex."

▶ Second thought: "I don't understand Web Dynpro."

▶ Conclusion: "Web Dynpro is really complex."

Whilst the first and second thoughts may well be true, they cannot be combined to arrive at the stated conclusion. Consequently, the conclusion is incorrect.

Unfortunately, many consultants are faced with implementing a Web Dynpro solution without having had the proper training (or they are expected to learn on the job), and as a result, they arrive at the above conclusion. This creates a way of thinking that assumes nothing will be easy, and consequently, they assume that complex coding needs to be written — because of course, Web Dynpro is complex.

I am pleased to inform you that this is not the case, and that once you have grasped the simple design principles, you'll be able to write efficient, low-maintenance Web Dynpro applications.

## 1.3 Causes of Poor Web Dynpro Implementations

The number one cause of poor Web Dynpro implementations is a lack of specific developer training. There are a variety reasons developers lack this training, but whatever those reasons are, the end result is Web Dynpro applications that:

▶ Contain excessively complex logic that leads to an extended and therefore more costly maintenance time frame

▶ Do not scale to the expected or required user load

▶ Consume excessive resources from:

   ▷ The SAP NetWeaver Application Server Java

   ▷ A backend SAP system

All in all, the resulting applications are highly inefficient.

The purpose of this book is to provide you with sufficient knowledge and understanding that you will be able to avoid the pitfalls and traps that would result in the development of inefficient applications.

## 1.4 How Web Dynpro Differs from Other Web Development Tools

Strictly speaking, Web Dynpro is not a "Web" development toolset. It has been designed as toolset for developing business applications that are aimed at a wide or generic audience. To distinguish Web Dynpro as being a product development toolset instead of a Web development toolset may seem like a pedantic point, but it has important implications when examining the features available (or not available) in Web Dynpro.

The Web Dynpro toolset is designed to create applications that will meet the following criteria:

▶ Be used by a generic target audience

▶ Place a higher priority on the stability and reliability of the business process than on the specific details of the user interface's (UI's) appearance

▶ Have a medium- to long-term life span

For instance, Web Dynpro has not been designed to give the developer pixel-perfect control over the alignment of UI elements. This is for the simple reason that if your application is being run in 15 languages, the width of the text on the screen will vary greatly from language to language (the text direction could also vary). This would mean that UI element alignment would need to be made language specific, which in turn would greatly increase the development workload.

The concept behind Web Dynpro is to reduce development workload — particularly in the area of the UI. Therefore, a task such as UI element alignment is handled automatically by Web Dynpro's screen rendering functionality. This comes at a certain price, but within the design criteria set out for Web Dynpro, this price is considered acceptable.

A Web development toolset, on the other hand, is designed to create applications that usually meet the following criteria:

▶ Be used by a specific, well-known target audience
▶ Place a higher priority on the appearance of the UI, than the stability and reliability of the business process.
▶ Have a short-term life span

For instance, if a customer wants to develop a browser-based application that will be run in only one language and used by a well-defined set of users (i.e., a specific, not generic target audience), then many of the features he expects from a Web development toolset will not be available in Web Dynpro.

Web Dynpro is both a development tool for building business applications *and* a runtime environment. It has been designed in such a way that, when used correctly, it can cut the development time scale of a complex business application by as much as 50%. The bulk of the time saving is achieved by automating the generation of the UI based on declarations made at design time[3] and a strong emphasis on code reuse. The declarative aspect of Web Dynpro software design results in the fact that all the UI coding can be generated. The only code developers need to write is that related to the core business process.

Isn't there a "but" coming ...?

As for all other technologies, you must understand the principles of Web Dynpro and then apply them to your situation to reap its rewards. The flip side of this situation has been described above: if you don't understand the principles of good Web Dynpro design, then you will end up writing a business application that contains many coding workarounds — not for any functional gaps in Web Dynpro, but to work around the gaps in your own understanding.

This explains the origin of the excessively complex code found in many Web Dynpro applications written by untrained developers. It also explains why such applications experience significant maintenance difficulties after the software has gone live.

---

3  If necessary, you can write the coding that generates the UI layer yourself. However, the typical situation is that the UI is generated for you as a direct result of your design time declarations.

## 1.5    The Fundamental Difference Between Web Dynpro and Other Web Development Tools

Many differences could be mentioned here, but the most fundamental is this: In other Web development tools (e.g., Java Server Pages), the unit of development is the web page, and your application consists of a set of connected pages[4] that, together, supply the required business functionality. In Web Dynpro, however, the unit of development is something called a *Component*.

A component is a set of independent but interrelated programs that together form a reusable unit of *business* functionality. Within this unit of code, you could have multiple web pages, although the term *web page* is not used in Web Dynpro development.

All Web Dynpro applications are built using declarative programming techniques based largely on the Model–View–Controller (MVC) design pattern. Using a combination of the MVC design pattern and declarative programming techniques, the entire UI for your application can be defined without the need to write any HTML, JavaScript, or Cascading Style Sheets.

This is achieved by first declaring the UI elements you want to have on the screen and then binding the properties of those UI elements to memory locations that will act as suppliers of the required property data. The coding written by the developer then need not be concerned with the specific UI elements used to visualize the data; instead, the coding operates on the memory locations that supply data to the UI elements. This principle creates a significant degree of decoupling between the business processing layer and the data presentation layer.

Since the business processing is strictly decoupled from the data presentation layer, the developer is not required to write the coding that renders the UI. Instead, this coding is generated automatically by the NetWeaver Developer Studio (NWDS) on the basis of the UI element declarations. This relieves the developer of the repetitive tasks of writing the actual form-based interface and then making it interactive with some scripting language such as JavaScript. The only manual coding required is that necessary to interact with the backend business system and to prepare the resulting information for presentation.

In addition to this frontend independence, there is no particular requirement to have an SAP system to provide your backend business processing. In fact, Web Dynpro has been designed to act as an independent processing layer that sits between the user's client device (e.g., a browser, a BlackBerry®, etc.) and the backend business system (e.g., an SAP system or a custom written Java database connectivity (JDBC) database or some server delivering Web services).

---

4  These pages are usually connected by some persistence layer existing in the Web server.

## 1.6    A Quick History Lesson

The initial ideas for Web Dynpro were first conceived in late 2000. During the design process, SAP had to consider a wide range of design criteria and combine them into a single toolset that was capable of meeting all their needs. The result of this development program is what we now call Web Dynpro.

In early 2001 when the designers at SAP were laying out the fundamental concepts for Web Dynpro, the following criteria were uppermost in their minds:

▶ Create a UI programming paradigm that would become the de facto standard for all future SAP software. Ease of use should be a key consideration.

▶ Eliminate the repetitive coding tasks currently experienced by Web developers. The fewer lines of handwritten code there are in the UI, the better.

▶ Make full use of abstract modeling. The Web Dynpro application should not need to care about:

  ▶ The communication technology required to access a backend business system

  ▶ The client technology being used to render the screens

▶ Make full use of generic services. Functionality that is frequently required should be made available from a standard library of services. For example, if the user is asked to enter a date, then a date picker should open automatically next to the input field without requiring any extra coding effort on the part of the developer.

▶ Use a declarative approach to application design. This is where the developer tells the Web Dynpro development toolset *what* should be done, but not *how* to do it. This approach should be extended into all areas of application design (e.g., screen flow and component reuse).

▶ Create a fundamental unit of software reuse that exists at a business level. This would fundamentally change the unit of software reuse from the individual web page or server-side persistency object to a unit of coding that represents an atomic step of a business process.

These design concepts have been followed very closely, and the result is a UI development environment strong enough in its functional capability and wide ranging enough in its scope to be adopted by SAP for *all* its future application UIs.

### 1.6.1    The Original Design Concept

The original concept for designing a Web Dynpro application was that there should be a single development tool in which an abstract description of the application's functionality is built (known as the metamodel). The metamodel would be constructed using a technique known as *declarative programming*, in which you describe the relationships that exist between the various elements within the program. The metamodel specifies such things as:

▶ Which UI elements are to be used to display information on the screen

▶ What data structures are to be used to hold the displayed data

▶ The various navigation paths from one screen to another

▶ How the various coding entities within the program are to share information between themselves

▶ How you would reuse smaller units of coding within the larger application

▶ How interaction with a business backend system is to take place

The metamodel description of the application would be stored in a language-independent format (XML) so that it could later be fed into the language-specific (Java or ABAP) code generator that would create the bulk of the UI coding automatically (see Figure 1.1). In other words, almost all the program code needed to display your business data would be generated simply on the basis of the declarations held in the metamodel.

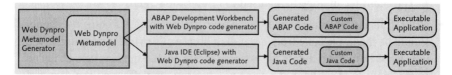

**Figure 1.1** Original Web Dynpro Design Concept

Once all these tasks had been handled declaratively, the only code the developer would need to write would be that required to implement the business logic.

There is another subtle, but very significant, benefit here. Now that all the UI coding has been generated on the basis of declarations, the developer has been relieved of the task of writing all the repetitive (and tedious) UI coding that has to be aware of, and account for, all the technical foibles of the various browsers in common use. Now the developer is free to give his full attention to how the information is flowing through the business process. Consequently, the developer is now paying attention to the most important task at hand and not being sidetracked by the technicalities of UI-specific coding. This point alone is responsible for cutting development time scales by as much as 50%.

### 1.6.2    The Web Dynpro Implementation

As the development of Web Dynpro started, it rapidly became clear that it would be far more economical to have all the Web Dynpro metamodel tools and code generator within a single development environment. Consequently, all the tools for developing a Web Dynpro for Java application can be found within the Java development environment,[5] and all the tools for developing a Web Dynpro for ABAP application can be found within the ABAP Workbench.[6] The result is that there are two independent Web Dynpro development environments: one for Java and one for ABAP.

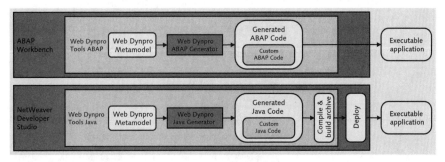

**Figure 1.2** The Web Dynpro Development Process

Figure 1.2 shows that irrespective of whether you are developing in ABAP or Java, both development environments contain the necessary tools for creating a Web Dynpro metamodel, generating the required coding, and allowing the developers to write their own custom code within the framework provided by the generated code. The end result is an executable Web Dynpro application that performs the required business task — and the end user is none the wiser as to the technology that was used to create it.

The only difference in the development process between Web Dynpro for Java and Web Dynpro for ABAP are the extra *Compile & build archive* and *Deploy* steps needed for Java. This is necessary because a Java program is written on the developer's local PC but executed by an SAP NetWeaver Application Server Java (AS Java) running (typically) on a different machine. It is possible that the PC on which the developer wrote the Web Dynpro for Java application has no AS Java installed and is therefore incapable of actually executing it. In other words, Web Dynpro for Java uses separate and independent development and runtime environments, whereas the development and runtime environments for Web Dynpro for ABAP are one and the same (the SAP system).

Therefore, before a Web Dynpro for Java program can be executed, all the files that make up the program need to be compiled and packaged together into something known as an Enterprise Archive (an .ear file). This archive file is then physically copied (or *deployed*) to the machine on which the AS Java has been installed.

---

5  The development of Web Dynpro programs in Java is performed in the NWDS. This is the standard Eclipse development tool to which SAP has added a large number of plug-ins.

6  The ABAP Workbench (transaction code SE80) in a system with a 7.00 or higher kernel.

The diagrams in Figure 1.2 can now be extended to show how the relationship between the development environment and the execution environment differs between the Java case and the ABAP case (see Figure 1.3).

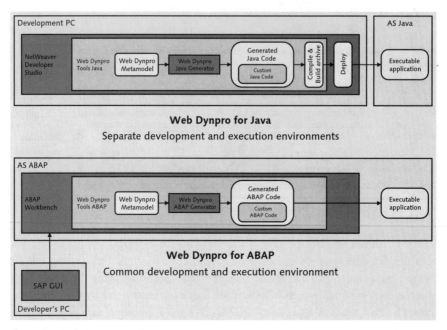

**Figure 1.3** Web Dynpro Development Environments

## 1.7 The Design Philosophy Behind Web Dynpro

In this section, we will examine the influences that helped shape Web Dynpro.

### 1.7.1 Design Influences

Web Dynpro architecture was not derived from any single design philosophy; instead, it is a union of various philosophies that were brought together to satisfy all of the stated design requirements (see Section 1.6 above). The following design philosophies exerted roughly the following level of influence on Web Dynpro design:

▶ 75 % Trygve Reenskaug's MVC

▶ 20 % SAP's own requirement to decouple a Web Dynpro application from both the client interface layer and the backend business system

▶ 5 % Karen Holtzblatt's concept of Focus Groups

The manner in which each of these design philosophies or requirements influenced the final Web Dynpro architecture are discussed in the next section.

### 1.7.2 Why Do I Need an SAP-Supplied Server To Run a Web Dynpro Application?

Good question. The "Executable Application" shown on the right of Figure 1.3 would seem to indicate that the end product of the Web Dynpro development process is some kind of self-contained, ready to run application, but this is not exactly the situation. Web Dynpro applications are perfectly executable, but they have been designed to maintain complete neutrality toward both the client software used to display the business information and the backend system from which the business data and functionality are obtained. Therefore, the Web Dynpro application itself must sit inside an abstraction layer that is responsible for:

1. The generation of any client-specific UI coding (e.g., HTML, JavaScript, or Cascading Style Sheets [CSS])

2. The low-level communication between the Web Dynpro runtime environment on the AS Java and the backend system (e.g., calling a Web service via the Service-oriented Architecture Protocol (SOAP, formerly known as Simple Object Access Protocol) or calling an ABAP function module via the Remote Function Call (RFC) protocol)

A Web Dynpro application has been designed in such a way that the developer need only declare *how* the information should be rendered on the client. They are not required to write the actual coding that implements the final frontend rendering. In fact, a Web Dynpro application is incapable of generating any type of client-specific UI coding: This task has been removed from the application and is implemented behind the abstraction layer known as the Web Dynpro Framework.[7]

The Web Dynpro Framework is the runtime environment that acts as a container for your Web Dynpro application, and it provides all the functionality required to make your Web Dynpro application interact with both the client and backend system layers.

Therefore, the presence of the Web Dynpro Framework is essential for the execution of a Web Dynpro application. Consequently, attempts to run a Web Dynpro application on another vendor's Java 2 Platform, Enterprise Edition (J2EE) engine will be doomed to failure.

---

7  You may also see the term *Web Dynpro Runtime*. This is synonymous with the term *Web Dynpro Framework*.

## 1.8    The Influence of MVC on Web Dynpro

The strongest influence on Web Dynpro architecture was the design pattern called MVC. This design pattern is not at all new; it was invented in 1978 by Norwegian software designer Trygve Reenskaug[8] while he was working as a visiting scientist with Xerox at their Palo Alto Research Center (PARC) in California.

Reenskaug proposed a solution to the problem he was working on as follows:

> There are ... indications that an object based modelling language is acceptable to people. ... [In a]n experiment at Xerox PARC in 1978 ... we developed a planning system for a new semiconductor production facility. The facility manager was thinking in terms of silicon wafers, processes and equipment, while the Smalltalk developer was thinking in terms of interacting Smalltalk objects. The communication between manager and developer went very smoothly and confirmed our belief that an object model can give users effective control over their information systems.[9]

### 1.8.1    The User's Mental Model

Reenskaug realized that the success of an object-based approach to system design was based on the fact that they had created an object model in which the data structures in the software matched the structure of the information in the user's mental model of the business process.

Now turn this situation around and think what would happen if a software product represented the data in structures *completely different* from the ones perceived by the user? The user would experience all manner of problems when trying to operate the software simply because they perceive the data to be structured one way, but the software has structured it in a completely different way.

Reenskaug then set about to define a design paradigm that would result in the user seeing a reflection of his mental model on the computer screen. The design requirement here was to create a modeling specification that must:

▶ Be intelligible to the end user. Therefore, it must use terminology with which the user is familiar.

▶ Be rigorous enough that an accurate definition of the functionality can be created, and from this description, software written.

▶ Result in a software system that reflects the user's mental model without needing to show details that are of no importance to the user.

---

8  Pronounced "TRIG-vuh RAINS-cow."
9  Accessed January 31, 2006. From page 6 of *http://heim.ifi.uio.no/~trygver/2003/javazone-jaoo/MVC_pattern.pdf*.

### 1.8.2  A Top-Down Approach

Reenskaug started by assuming that the process of recreating the user's mental model in a computer is best done by considering it as a network of object interactions.[10] For instance, at the highest level, you can regard everything done in a factory as some combination of interactions between two basic categories of object:

▶ Resources (e.g., raw materials, semi-finished goods, or employees)

▶ Activities (e.g., tasks performed by employees)

For instance, the task of building a ship is a complex and iterative set of activities performed on and by a very large number resources (see Figure 1.4).

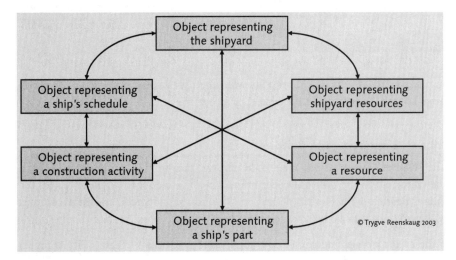

**Figure 1.4** Object Interaction

### 1.8.3  Interacting with Business Objects

Since business objects are complex entities, it is often necessary to decompose them further into simpler objects before the user's mental model can be represented accurately within a computer. This amounts to examining how a user interacts with a business object. Reenskaug realized that to achieve a successful design, there must be a separation between the part of the business object capable of user interaction and the part that performs the actual business processing.

Reenskaug named the user's mental model of the business information (logically enough) the *Model*, and the interface by which the information is accessed and manipulated, he called the *Editor* (see Figure 1.5).

---

10  This process has many similarities to what is now known as Mind Mapping®, developed by Tony Buzan.

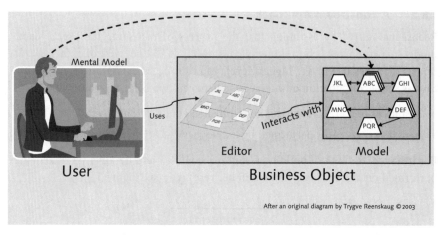

**Figure 1.5** Editor–Model Separation

In other words, the model represents what the user knows, and the editor represents how the user works with what they know.

### 1.8.4 Simplifying the Editor

The Business Object has now been split into two independent units: the model and the editor. Since the user only ever interacts with a model through an editor, the model needs no further simplification. The editor, however, is still a complex object and needs to be broken down further.

If the editor were implemented as a single object, it would become very complex very quickly; therefore, it made good sense to separate the presentation of data from the processing of data. Here's how Reenskaug assessed the problem of designing the editor:

| Problem |
| --- |
| The input and output aspects of the Editor are technically very different with few interdependencies. Their combination in a single object tends to make this object unnecessarily complex.[11] |

| Solution |
| --- |
| Let the Editor contain two objects; a View object responsible for presentation, and a Controller object responsible for taking and interpreting input from the user.[12] |

---

11  This is precisely the situation faced by SAP's classical Dynpros because the input processing (Process After Input) and the output processing (Process Before Output) are merged together into a single unit.

12  Accessed January 31, 2006. From page 10 of *http://heim.ifi.uio.no/~trygver/2003/javazone-jaoo/MVC_pattern.pdf*.

This was the first time the idea of separating data presentation from data processing had been stated as an explicit design requirement. Nowadays, this idea is common place, but in 1978, Reenskaug was making a significant conceptual leap by stipulating that this feature was a fundamental design requirement.

The net result of all this separation was that there must now be at least three independent (but interrelated) programs involved in a business application. Each part plays a very distinct role, and the designer should ensure that the functional boundaries between these program types are neither blurred nor allowed to become ambiguous.

Together with the model, the view and the controller define the three fundamental building blocks from which a robust business application can be constructed.

To use Reenskaug's own words again in summary:[13]

### Models

Models represent knowledge.

A model could be a single object (rather uninteresting), or it could be some structure of objects. ... The nodes of a model should therefore represent an identifiable part of the problem ... .

### Views

A view is a (visual) representation of its model. It would ordinarily highlight certain attributes of the model and suppress others. It is thus acting as a presentation filter ... .

### Controllers

A controller is the link between a user and the system. It provides the user with input by arranging for relevant views to present themselves in appropriate places on the screen. It provides means for user output by presenting the user with menus or other means of giving commands and data ... .

This architecture is represented in Figure 1.6.

### 1.8.5    The Essence of the MVC Design Concept

Many people consider MVC to be a design pattern that separates data presentation from data processing, and this is certainly true. However, the separation of data presentation from data processing is simply one use-case of a more fundamental concept: namely, the separation of those parts of the program that generate data from those parts that consume data, and it is this fundamental principle that you will see popping up time and time again within the Web Dynpro architecture.

---

13 Accessed January 31, 2006. From page 1 of *http://heim.ifi.uio.no/~trygver/1979/mvc-2/1979-12-MVC.pdf*.

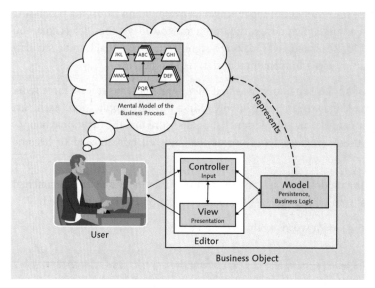

**Figure 1.6** Original MVC Structure

Those parts of a Web Dynpro application that generate data (the models) are strictly separated from those parts of the application that consume the generated data (the views). The controllers, however, sit between the models and the views, and their role as generator or consumer varies depending on which entity they are communicating with.

This principle has been applied in different areas of Web Dynpro design and at different scales. The exact role (generator or consumer) played by the different parts of a Web Dynpro component can (and will) vary depending on the specific relationship.

### Models are Generators of Data

A model is *always* a generator of data. Even though models must receive data as input, that data serves only to cause the model to perform its function — namely to perform some step of a business process — which necessarily results in the generation of data.

### Views Are Consumers of Data

A view is *always* a consumer of data; whether raw data from the user via the keyboard and mouse or processed data from a controller. Said a different way, a view is not responsible for generating the data it displays. This statement must be clearly understood as it is the most frequently violated design principle seen in Web Dynpro coding.

**Controllers Are Generators and Consumers of Data**

A controller plays a dual role. When receiving data from a model, it is acting as a consumer. However, after it has consumed data from the model and performed some processing on it, it passes that data on to the view for display. Now the controller is acting as the generator, and the view as the consumer.

So with respect to a model, a controller is a consumer, but with respect to a view, a controller is a generator.

### 1.8.6    The Data Consumer-Generator Concept in Web Dynpro

This fundamental principle has been implemented within the Web Dynpro architecture at different locations and at different scales. As the architecture of a Web Dynpro component is explained in the next chapter, you will see how this principle is fundamental to Web Dynpro's ability to decouple itself not only from the external software layers that surround it, but also to allow the various entities within a Web Dynpro application to maintain sufficient decoupling from each other to create a powerful reuse paradigm.

## 1.9    The Influence of SAP's Requirements on Web Dynpro

One of the most important design criteria required by SAP was that the Web Dynpro development environment automatically generate as much of the repetitive "plumbing code" as possible. The rationale behind this thinking was that since UI coding often consumes a significant part of an implementation project's time scale, any reduction of effort in this area would be reflected in decreased implementation costs.

In addition, if a corporate look and feel is required across all the applications in a business suite, then any mechanism that can generate the UI layer will also be able to generate the required visual appearance. This eliminates the issues created by each UI developer having his own favorite set of graphical widgets or his own web page architecture.

### 1.9.1    The Consequences of a Declarative Approach to UI Design

If the UI layer is to be generated, then there must be an effective means of declaring what appearance the UI should have, and then from those declarations, generating the required coding.

The nature of a declarative approach to UI specification is that the developer is required to declare not only the type of UI element to be used, but also the memory locations from which the various UI element properties will obtain their data. This immediately detaches the UI layer from the data processing layer. Thus, by using a declarative approach to UI design, SAP was able to create a development toolset in which the UI layer coding is both generated and decoupled from the underlying data processing layer.

The next step was to standardize the mechanism for transferring data from the UI elements in a view to the data processing contained in the underlying controller. This is the origin of a concept in Web Dynpro known as *data binding*. Data binding is the name given to the two-way connection that exists between the various properties of a UI element and the memory areas that supply the data.

Can you see the data supplier–generator principle at work here? The UI element property acts as a consumer of data, and the memory location in the controller acts as the data generator. This is just one of several situations in which this principle can be seen working.

### 1.9.2    Decoupling Data Presentation from Data Processing

In the previous section, we saw that as a result of a declarative approach to UI design, it is possible to achieve an immediate decoupling of the UI layer in the view from the data processing layer found in the controller. However, the following problem remains: Where do the UI elements live?

Reenskaug's original MVC specification is typically achieved by implementing each view as a Java Server Page, and having each controller implemented as a persistent, server-side object. Unfortunately, this type of implementation violates another of SAP's stated design criteria — namely, that the Web Dynpro application should be client neutral. If the UI layer is implemented using a Java Server Page, then by definition, it is client specific, or at least limited to a few browser types and versions.

Thus, the problem to be solved was how to create a container for the UI elements that remained client neutral. The solution was first to create a controller that would act as a container for the UI elements and second to manage the memory areas that supply data to those UI elements. However, this special controller still knows nothing about the specific client device to which the data will ultimately be sent.

In fact, there is nothing in a Web Dynpro application that needs to know the specific details of the client device. For any Web Dynpro application to be truly client neutral, the task of UI-specific rendering must be delegated to the runtime framework in which all Web Dynpro applications are executed.

The actual implementation now seen in Web Dynpro components is one in which there are essentially two types of controller: the normal controller defined by Reenskaug and SAP's special view controller that exists to act as a client-neutral processing container for the UI elements.

This situation can be summarized by saying that within a Web Dynpro component there are visual controllers (i.e., those that have a visual interface), and non-visual controllers (i.e., those that do not have a visual interface).

This subject will be expanded on greatly in the next chapter.

## 1.10    The Influence of Focus Groups on Web Dynpro

Karen Holtzblatt is the originator of the concept in UI design of *Focus Groups*.[14] Her concept is one in which information on the user's screen should be gathered together according to its logical relationship. These logical groupings are known as Focus Groups.

A Focus Group does not make any requirements for how information should be presented; it merely states that for data such as a sales order to be entered (for example), the address of the sold-to party is required. The address is regarded as a Focus Group because it forms a coherent unit of logically related data, which in turn is related to the data describing a sales order.

This concept is much the same as Reenskaug's concept of a model, but it approaches the situation from the perspective of what the user *sees* on the screen rather than what the user *knows*.

Focus Groups are not featured as distinct entities in any of the Web Dynpro tools seen in the NWDS; however, they are mentioned here because they had an influence on the way Web Dynpro views are structured within a component.

## 1.11    What Do I Need To Understand To Be Successful with Web Dynpro?

Two fundamental principles need to be understood very clearly to obtain the best results from Web Dynpro:

▶ How Web Dynpro can be used to reproduce the mental model of the data with which the user works

▶ The data generator–consumer concept and how it has been implemented in Web Dynpro

---

14  H. Beyer, and K. Holtzblatt, *Contextual Design: Defining Customer-Centered Systems* (San Francisco, CA: Morgan Kaufmann, 1998).

### 1.11.1 Using Web Dynpro to Reproduce the User's Mental Model of the Data

This is a key point when designing a large Web Dynpro application. During the design phase, the Web Dynpro architect must be in close communication with the users to establish exactly how they perceive their business information. Once a picture has been established that describes how the users perceive their business information, then the Web Dynpro design can start by mimicking this structure as closely as possible.

This topic will be discussed in much greater detail in the next chapter.

### 1.11.2 Understanding the Data Generator-Consumer Concept

Not only do the developers need to understand the difference between those parts of the program that consume data and those parts that generate data, but they need to understand where the boundaries lie and make sure they are not crossed or blurred.

In far too many Web Dynpro implementations, the developers (for a variety of reasons) did not have a good understanding of this principle. The typical symptom here is that the developers put all the business logic (i.e., the coding that acts as a generator of data) into those parts of the Web Dynpro application that should act only as consumers of data (i.e., the view controllers).

The resulting application may be functional, but during its life cycle, it will suffer from the following problems:

▶ Poor performance under heavy user load.
▶ If the Web Dynpro application connects to a backend SAP system, then it is likely that more connections will be opened to that SAP system than are necessary. This, in turn, leads to the backend SAP system working under a heavier workload than is necessary.
▶ Excessively complex coding due the implemented business logic not fitting in with the natural processing sequence found in the Web Dynpro Framework.
▶ Increased time required to perform maintenance and enhancements.

## 1.12 Is Writing a Web Dynpro Program Just a Matter of Writing Models, Views, and Controllers?

Well, yes and no ...

There's a very important fact to remember about the MVC design pattern that is frequently overlooked or simply not realized: MVC is just a concept.

No one has copyrighted or trademarked it. There is no such thing as "Fred in the Shed's patented MVC methodology." MVC is just a design concept (or pattern), in the same way that object orientation is just a design concept that describes both how units of code should be organized and how they should interact with each other within a program.

Consequently, every software vendor that implements an MVC-based design tool, does so in a slightly different way and with a slightly different interpretation of the principles. SAP is no exception here. In fact, SAP has modified Reenskaug's original design pattern by replacing the editor (see Figure 1.6) concept with a completely new entity known as a component. Without this new entity, the Web Dynpro designers found they could not correctly implement one of their key design requirements, namely, reusability at a business process level (refer back to the bulleted list in the Section 1.6.1).

In the next chapter, we shall examine the whole concept of the Web Dynpro component and you will come to see that it is the fundamental building block for all Web Dynpro applications.

Once you have defined how the users thinks about their business information, you can start writing Web Dynpro components that correspond to the steps in the user's mental model of the business process.

# PART II
## The Fundamental Concepts

# 2    The Web Dynpro Component Concept

To have a solid understanding of Web Dynpro development, it is necessary to understand the fundamental building block from which all Web Dynpro applications are constructed. This building block is known as the Web Dynpro Component.

Before diving into an explanation of the component itself, it is worth seeing how the concepts of Web Dynpro software architecture differ from the classical MVC pattern.

## 2.1    A Typical MVC Architecture

Many MVC-based development tools use an architecture similar to that shown in Figure 2.1. Notice that the diagram is divided into three areas. The model is part of the Business Interaction Layer because it contains the interface to the backend system. The view and the controller are part of the User Interaction Layer because they are responsible for communication with the user. This includes both presenting the information on the screen and then reacting to user actions taking place on the client.

You might be wondering why the third area, called the communication layer, has been identified on the left of the diagram; after all, the software to implement this functionality is not part of the MVC design pattern.

Normally a Web server would supply this part of the process, but it has been added here because SAP found it necessary to include this area of functionality in the Web Dynpro design.

In most cases, however, the editor is not implemented as a specific unit of software and has largely been forgotten. Hence, the design pattern is called Model-View-Controller, not Model-Editor-View-Controller.

However, when SAP was looking to implement a unit of code reuse that represented a discrete step of the business process, this unit needed to fit neatly (or as neatly as possible) into the existing MVC pattern. Therefore, attention turned to the editor, because it represents how the user works with what they know.

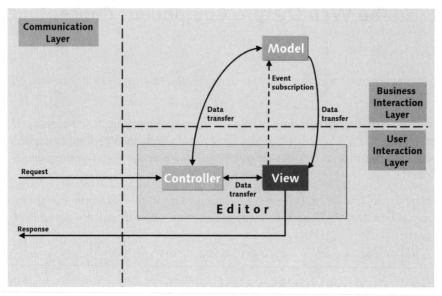

**Figure 2.1** The Architecture of a Typical MVC Implementation

In SAP's modification to MVC, we can see that several new areas have been added. If you compare the position of the Web Dynpro component in Figure 2.2 with the position of the editor in Figure 2.1, you can see that they occupy the same place in the architecture. However, there are some important differences:

▶ The view and the controller are now reimplemented as visual and non-visual controllers respectively.

▶ Communication with the model takes place at the component level, not the individual view or controller level.

Also, the view and controller are no longer responsible for direct communication with the client. Remember that SAP wanted to achieve client abstraction, so it was necessary to decouple the view from the specific details of the client device. This is why there is a client abstraction layer (CAL). This layer shields the Web Dynpro component from all the technical communication and rendering details of a specific client and means the application developer no longer needs to care about how a particular UI element should be rendered in a particular type of browser.

Inside the CAL is another area known as server-side rendering (SSR). This is where the functionality to generate the rendered output is located. The views in the component hold only an abstract representation of the UI elements, and the SSR then takes care of creating the correct mark-up for the specific client that is executing the application.

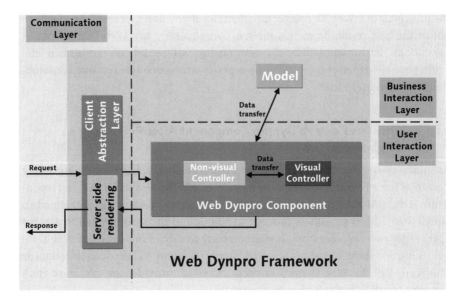

**Figure 2.2** SAP's Modification to the MVC Concept

Finally, all the Web Dynpro functionality is enclosed within the Web Dynpro Framework. Notice that the Web Dynpro Framework crosses over onto the communication side of the diagram. It is responsible not only for the execution of your Web Dynpro application, but also for the communication between the client and the server.

It is not important for you to have any detailed knowledge of how the CAL or the SSR work, other than to know that they are a fundamental part of the Web Dynpro Framework and that without them, your Web Dynpro application would not be able to function.

## 2.2 The Web Dynpro Component Concept

When you write a Web Dynpro program, you will need to write models, views, and controllers. However, these units of code are bundled together into a larger unit that SAP has called a *component*.[1] It is absolutely fundamental that you understand

---

1 The only context in which Reenskaug used the term *Component* was the following. A company-wide business process was referred to as a "Domain Service" and was seen as crossing several departmental divisions within the company. The unit of functionality performed by a single department during the execution of such a company-wide business process was referred to as a "domain Component." (For more information see *http://heim.ifi.uio.no/~trygver/2003/java-zone-jaoo/MVC_pattern.pdf.*) Reenskaug's definition of the word *Component* is very different from SAP's definition, and the two should not be thought of as bearing any similarity.

the principles of a Web Dynpro component, for if you don't, you will be unable to obtain the best results from this toolset. Consequently, any Web Dynpro implementations you attempt will be of a poor quality, will be difficult to maintain, and could possibly experience poor runtime performance due to excessive consumption of backend resources.

### 2.2.1 How Does a Web Dynpro Component Alter Reenskaug's Original Design?

As shown above, the Web Dynpro component corresponds fairly well to the entity known as the editor in Reenskaug's original design. The reason for this correspondence is that SAP needed a fundamental unit of software reuse that implemented an atomic step within a business process. In addition to this, SAP needed to achieve client independence; therefore, it was necessary to extend the design of Web Dynpro to include communication with the client. The result of these modifications is the creation of the Web Dynpro Framework, which provides the execution environment for all Web Dynpro components.

To understand why the Web Dynpro component is structured the way it is, it is necessary to bring together several strands of thought. These have already been mentioned in the previous chapter as:

▶ Trygve Reenskaug's MVC concept

▶ SAP's requirement that the data presentation and data processing layers should be completely decoupled from each other

▶ Karen Holtzblatt's concept of Focus Groups

It is assumed that the user has a continuity of knowledge concerning the business processes with which they work. In other words, the user can mentally "see" from one end of the business process to the other. Within this mental picture, discrete stages or steps will exist that are considered indivisible or atomic.[2]

One of the challenges of not just Web Dynpro design but all software design is to identify these "mental stepping stones" and translate them (as far as possible) into discrete units of software.

To achieve this, SAP found it necessary to alter Reenskaug's defined relationship between a model and its editor. It was recognized that an atomic unit of business processing may require the use of more than one model; therefore:

▶ The revised editor would have to behave as more than simply the visualization layer for a single model.

▶ A model would not necessarily have a one-to-one relationship with an editor.

---

2  The atom was split over 60 years ago, yet we still consider things that are indivisible to be "atomic." Strange, really …

The Web Dynpro component sits at a similar position in the design structure to Reenskaug's editor, but performs an expanded role. The editor formerly provided a user interface for a single model, whereas a Web Dynpro component implements the user interface for an atomic unit of business processing that may interact with zero[3] or more models (see Figure 2.3).

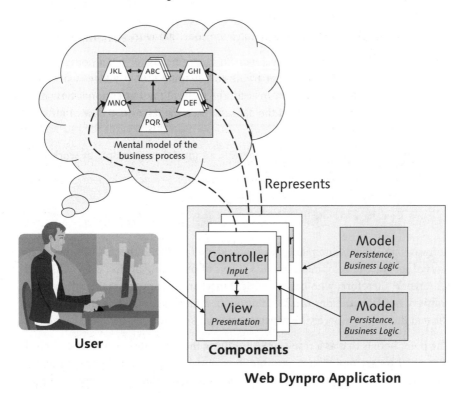

**Web Dynpro Application**

**Figure 2.3** Simplistic View of SAP's MVC Structure

Any time you write a Web Dynpro application, you must write at least one Web Dynpro component. These components can be reused as many times as required across many different applications, but the principle remains that the Web Dynpro component is both your unit of development and your unit of reuse.

### 2.2.2 Why Bother with Components?

It could be argued that views, controllers, and models could all be reused as independent units. This is true, but as stated above, this is not the type of reuse SAP required. If the only units of code that could be reused were low-level ones such as

---

3 Typically, a Web Dynpro component will interact with at least one model, but having a component that interacts with zero models is a perfectly legitimate use case.

views and controllers, then SAP would be writing a development toolset that did not advance user interface design software, but merely repeated the reusability limitations found in other toolsets.

Since the whole thrust of Web Dynpro is aimed at modeling and then solving business problems, the technical details of *how* the problem should be solved are of less importance. The Web Dynpro modeling process focuses on and defines *what* needs to be done, and the NWDS then generates the code that works out *how* to do it.

Consequently, a Web Dynpro developer no longer needs to spend hours fiddling around with HTML and JavaScript trying to get some screen widget working in three different flavors of browser. Instead, the focus of their attention is now modeling the user's mental picture of the data and then managing the flow of information through the business process.

When it comes to code reusability, there is an unspoken principle at work here, namely:

> Coding is bad ...
>
> if you have to write the same piece of code twice.

Software implementation managers are regularly faced with the task of squeezing $x$ days of software development into the $y$ days of remaining project time (where $x > y$). Anyone, therefore, who has an efficient mechanism for code reuse will find that software implementations can be achieved in a much shorter time frame, because the end product can largely be constructed from known, reusable building blocks.

The point here is that as a result of SAP shifting the focus away from the technicalities of UI programming and onto the flow of data through the business process, there has been a fundamental change in the way units of program code are aggregated for reuse. The emphasis for reuse is now is on the business process itself, and is not limited simply to the technical units of code written when the business process is implemented.

## 2.3 Inside the Web Dynpro Component

A Web Dynpro component is an aggregation of views and controllers that exist to perform a specific business task. Each controller within the component is implemented as an independent program; however, these programs cannot function independently from each other.

When we talk about reusability of Web Dynpro components, we are talking about two things:

▶ The reuse of a self-contained unit of *business* processing, not a low-level unit of *technical* processing.

▶ The reuse of the entire component. You can't reuse a part of a component — it's all or nothing.

In addition to a Web Dynpro component representing a discrete unit of business processing, one of SAP's stated design criteria was that it should be both backend and client neutral. Consequently, Reenskaug's distinction between views and controllers had to be modified.

As has been stated in the previous chapter, the controllers found within a Web Dynpro component come in two distinct varieties — visual and non-visual:

▶ Controllers that have no visual interface are referred to generically as *Custom Controllers*. These correspond to the controllers in Reenskaug's original design.

▶ Controllers that have a visual interface are referred to as *View Controllers*. SAP created these controllers to fulfill the design requirement of client independence. This design is an implementation of Karen Holtzblatt's concept of Focus Groups.

**Caveat Confector[4]**

The component is the basic building block of a Web Dynpro application — not the Web page (or view, in Web Dynpro terminology).

Do not attempt to place all your business functionality into a single component!

The overall architecture of a Web Dynpro component is described in Figure 2.4.

Notice that the diagram in Figure 2.4 has been divided vertically through the middle and horizontally across the top.

Those parts of the component that project above the horizontal line are public and therefore visible outside the scope of the component. Those parts that are below this line are private and therefore internal to the component.

The vertical line separates those parts of the component that are simply programmatic from those parts that are visual. The visual entities on the left represent those with which the end user can directly interact, whereas those on the right represent entities that can only be accessed programmatically.

---

4   Latin, meaning "Developer Beware!"

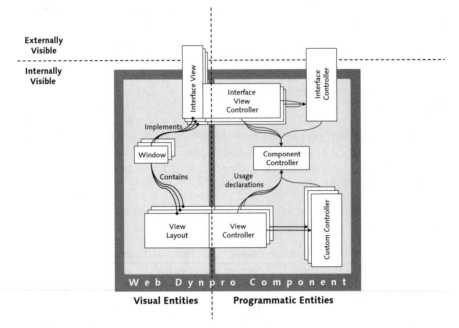

**Figure 2.4** Basic Component Structure

## 2.4 What Do the Different Parts of the Component Do?

As you can see from diagram in Figure 2.4, five boxes are labeled as being some type of controller, and there is also a box labeled Window. These different parts of the component are related to each other by various types of declarative relationship. Also notice that a view is made up of two parts: the view controller and the view layout, with each part living on either side of the visual–programmatic boundary. The interface view is similarly split, having both a visual and a programmatic part.

### 2.4.1 The Programmatic Parts of a Component

All of the controllers described below have been implemented as distinct Java classes. The component controller and the interface controller are created automatically when you declare the component. The other controllers are only created when you decide that such a controller is required.

**The Component Controller**

The component controller is the central controller within a component. Essentially, this controller *is* the Web Dynpro component. For any given instance of a component, there will only ever be one instance of the component controller. When the Web Dynpro Framework creates an instance of your component, the first controller to be instantiated is always the component controller. Likewise, when the component comes to the end of its lifecycle, the component controller is the last of the component's classes to be released.

You should consider this controller to be hierarchically superior to all other controller instances in the component. Consequently, when designing a Web Dynpro component, you should always place functionality that is central or common to the whole component in the component controller.

With respect to the other controllers in the component, the component controller should be considered both the generator and central repository of all data required by the component. This is particularly true when describing the relationship between the component controller and the view controllers.

### The Interface Controller

The interface controller is a developer's only point of communication with other Web Dynpro components. If you want one Web Dynpro component to be able to access the functionality found in another Web Dynpro component, it can only be done via the methods and events defined in the interface controller.

The interface controller will only ever be instantiated if the current component is used as the child of some other component. Even then, this controller will only ever be instantiated when one of its methods is called.

The Web Dynpro Framework will *never* call a method in an interface controller directly. The methods of this controller are only ever called by explicit application coding.

As with the component controller, for any given instance of a component, there can only ever be one instance of the interface controller.

When a Web Dynpro component is instantiated, the interface controller will not be instantiated unless a method or data within it is specifically referenced. This is an example of a basic concept in Web Dynpro architecture known as *lazy data access*. This principle states that data should not be generated and classes should not be instantiated unless they are actually needed.

### The Custom Controller

A custom controller is a developer-defined controller that may contain any functionality you feel is necessary to have encapsulated within a separate controller. By default, a Web Dynpro component will have zero custom controllers.

Custom controllers are typically required in situations in which you would need to use an inner class. An example of this is when implementing an Object Value Selector to provide search help values.

All custom controller instances are singletons with respect to the component controller and are managed by the Web Dynpro Framework. A custom controller instance will only be created when (or if) you call one of its methods.

### 2.4.2    The Visual Parts of a Component

Within a Web Dynpro component, two types of controller possess a visual interface: the view controller and the interface view controller. Although their names sound similar, they perform very different roles.

#### The View Controller

The view controller is the type of controller that must be created *if* you want to present any information on the client device. It is perfectly possible to create a Web Dynpro component that has zero view controllers. In this case, such a component is known as a *Faceless component*.

Faceless components are a very useful design option for encapsulating functionality into a reusable unit that needs no direct visual interface. For instance, if you are calling an ABAP function module that has a large or complex interface, you could use a Faceless component to simplify the use of that function module.

As discussed in the previous chapter, SAP has modified Reenskaug's concept of a view by creating a special type of controller that allows data to be visualized without the business application needing to know any specific details of the client implementation. Therefore, the manner in which UI elements are specified within a view's layout must be abstracted away from the HTML, JavaScript, and CSS that Web developers are accustomed to using.

Some developers see this as a negative point against Web Dynpro because they are unable to exert the same degree of control over the UI to which they have become accustomed. However, they forget that the solution to which they are accustomed prolongs the very problem SAP is trying to solve: namely, the presentation of data in a client- and device-specific manner. In addition to this, strictly speaking, Web Dynpro is not a "Web" development toolset. It has a different set of design goals than simply providing browser-based access to a short-lived business process (take another look at Section 1.4).

The part of a view controller on the programmatic side of the component (i.e., to the right of the vertical dotted line) is where the actual functionality is implemented. This is where the coding lives.

However, across the visual–programmatic boundary, the view controller has an associated view layout. This is where the UI elements are defined.

There are several important things to understand about a Web Dynpro view:

▶ The view controller and the view layout are *inseparable*. You cannot define UI elements outside the scope of a view controller. Similarly, if you create a view controller, you will always have a view layout — even if you choose not to do anything with it (which would be pretty weird).

▶ The UI elements in a view layout always act as consumers of data.

▶ With respect to the UI elements, the context of the view controller always acts as the supplier of data.

▶ The UI elements in a view layout can only obtain their data from fields in the context of the associated view controller. It is not possible to bind the property of a UI element found in view A, to a field in the context of view B.

▶ With respect to the component controller or the custom controllers in a Web Dynpro component, a view (as a whole) *always* acts as a consumer of data.

---

**Caveat Confector**

A view controller is *never* responsible for generating the data it displays.

This is the #1 error made by developers who do not understand the role of a view controller. They put the actual business logic into the view controller and think that because the program doesn't crash, their design is acceptable ... NO!

This point will be expanded in much more detail in later chapters.

---

**The Interface View Controller**

The interface view controller is the controller that actually implements a component's visual interface.

The number of views seen on the user's screen at any one time is often only a selection taken from the total number of views used by the whole Web Dynpro application. As the user interacts with the application, certain views will be removed from the screen and replaced with others in response to the user's actions. After each round trip from the client to the server, it is likely that the combination of views used to construct the next screen will be different from those used on the previous screen.

Therefore, the role of the interface view controller is to act as a container for the continually changing combination of views that make up a particular screen of the business application. In addition, since the visual interface of one Web Dynpro component can be nested within the visual interface of another component,[5] a

---

5  This creates a parent–child relationship between the embedding component and the embedded component.

component's interface view controller should not care whether the visual interface it is currently processing is derived from a single view or is the entire visual interface of some child component.

In reality, the interface view controller and its associated layout definition[6] do not fall entirely within the control of the Web Dynpro developer. A developer does not have the same level of control over this controller as they do over other controllers. This is because the interface view controller belongs to the abstraction layer within the Web Dynpro Framework that implements your application.

### Window

Notice in Figure 2.4 that in between a view and the interface view controller is an object called a *Window*.

A Window is a design time entity into which you embed all the views that will be used to construct the component's entire visual interface. You can think of a window and an interface view as two sides of the same coin.

At design time, you create a window and embed into it all the views that will take part in the component's visual interface. In addition to acting as a container for all views used in the component's visual interface, the window holds the navigation links that exist between the various views.[7] When users interact with a view, their interaction will cause a round trip to the server, and in response, it is entirely likely that one or more views making up the current screen will need to be replaced with other views. This is achieved by traversing the navigation links defined between the various views in the window.

As soon as a window is declared, the NWDS automatically creates a corresponding interface view controller, and this controller implements the visual interface seen by the user.

Thus, the window is the design time object that holds the sum total of all possible views used by the component's visual interface, and the interface view controller is the runtime object that presents only those views required to display the current screen.

Usually, the interface view controller shows only a subset of the views embedded into the window. Therefore, you can think of the window as the superset of all views that could possibly be used by the component's visual interface, and at any-

---

6  The layout of an Interface View Controller is the separate entity known as a *Window*, and the dynamic subset of views used to create any particular screen is known as the *View Assembly*.

7  Each end of a navigation link is terminated with a *plug*. When you want to replace one view with another, the typical situation is that the departing view fires an outbound plug. By means of a navigation link, the outbound plug is associated with a corresponding inbound plug in another view.

one one time, the interface view controller presents a subset of those views to the user.

This dynamically changing subset of views shown to the user after each round trip is known as the *View Assembly*.

## 2.5 Inside a Web Dynpro Controller

It is now necessary to take an initial look inside a Web Dynpro controller. This section will deal with the main architectural parts of a controller and will leave the lower-level technical details for the later chapters.

Broadly speaking, SAP has implemented two types of controller within a component. These component types are simply:

▶ Non-visual controllers

▶ Visual controllers

### 2.5.1 Architecture of Non-Visual Controllers

First, let's take a look at the non-visual controllers.

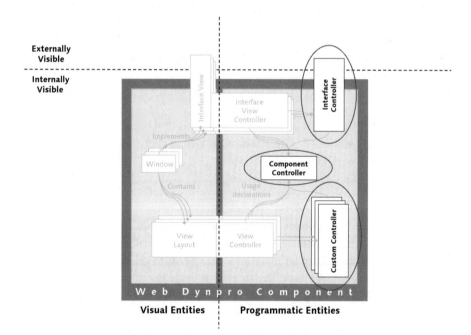

**Figure 2.5** The Non-Visual Controllers Within a Web Dynpro Component

In Figure 2.5, the non-visual controllers are circled. These controllers do not place information directly on the screen. Instead they are responsible for the generation of information that will be displayed by the visual controllers.

All non-visual controllers have the structure shown in Figure 2.6. This consists of a set of declarations seen on the left side of the diagram ("Required Controllers" and "Model Usage") and the actual implementation seen on the right.

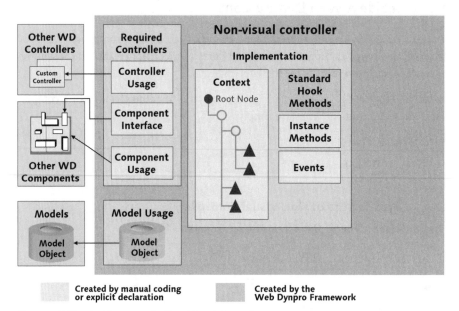

**Figure 2.6** The Architecture of a Non-Visual Controller

### Required Controllers

The configuration performed in this section of a controller is entirely declarative (see Figure 2.7).

### Controller Usage

Since a Web Dynpro component is not a single program, but a collection of inter-related programs, the individual controllers will not normally share information with each other. If one controller in a component needs to gain access to the methods or data within another controller, an explicit usage declaration must be made. Once made, the NWDS will generate the necessary coding API to make the interaction possible. This type of declaration allows one controller to gain access to the methods and data within another controller *in the same component*.

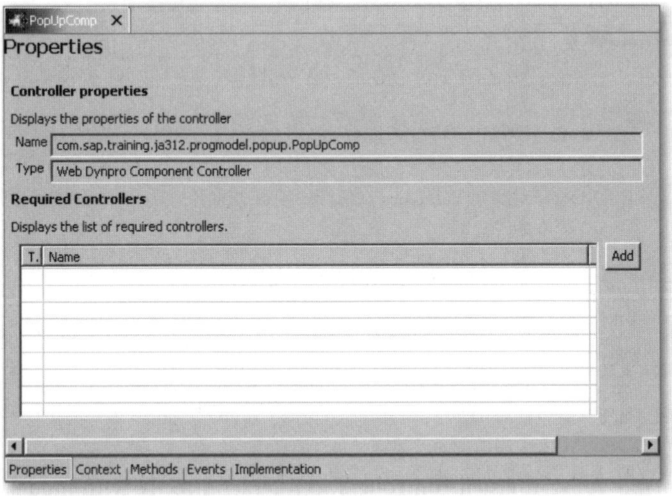

**Figure 2.7** The List of Required Controllers in a Controller's Properties Tab

**Component Usage and Component Interface**

If, however, you want to gain access to the methods and data found within a completely separate Web Dynpro component, then you must make a two-step declaration. First, the component that acts as the parent must declare a usage of the component that will act as the child. This declaration establishes a parent–child relationship between the two components and is made at the component level (i.e., outside the scope of an individual controller; see Figure 2.8).

Once done, a usage instance of the child component is created, the access to which is then inherited by all the controllers within the component.

The second declaration is then made within each individual controller. Since a Web Dynpro component has two interfaces (a programmatic one and a visual one), simply declaring the usage of the entire component is not sufficient to define exactly what functionality needs to be accessed. Now, using the inherited component usage, each controller must declare to which of the two interfaces it needs to gain access.

This is why you see both **Component Usage** and **Component Interface** boxes inside the **Required Controllers** box in Figure 2.6.

**Model Usage**

In a manner similar to child component usage, usage of models is performed at the component level, and then all controllers within the component have the ability to access the model objects within the model (see Figure 2.9).

**Figure 2.8** Component Usage

It is perfectly acceptable for non-visual controllers to interact directly with model objects, but it is always a sign of bad design if a visual controller interacts with a model object. Remember, visual controllers are not responsible for generating the data they display, so if you were to code direct access to a model object within a view controller, you would be violating this principle.

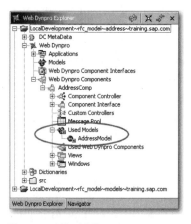

**Figure 2.9** Model Usage

### Implementation

The implementation is where the programmatic development of a Web Dynpro controller takes place.

### Context

The context is a hierarchical data storage area in which the controller holds its runtime data. Generally speaking, if the structure of the context is known at design time, it should be declared then. However, it is quite possible to create the context structure dynamically at runtime.

For non-visual controllers, the data in its context can be shared with other controllers. In other words, the context of a non-visual controller is permitted to act as a data generator (or data source). Therefore, the context of a non-visual controller is part of its public interface.

There are two types of entity in any context: nodes and attributes. The difference between them is simply that a node is permitted to have children and an attribute is not.

In the context diagram in Figure 2.6, the circles represent nodes and the triangles, attributes. A node is regarded as a type-safe collection of zero or more attributes and zero or more nodes. Although it makes no practical sense to do so, it is possible to create a node that has zero child attributes and zero child nodes.

At design time, the structure of the context could look something like Figure 2.10.

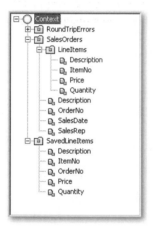

**Figure 2.10** The Context

#### Standard Hook Methods

As stated earlier, SAP has constructed a runtime environment known as the Web Dynpro Framework. Not only does the Framework provide the entire screen rendering functionality required to make your application accessible from multiple client devices, but it also handles all the session management and frontend and backend communication for you.

This means the Web Dynpro Framework must be able to run your application irrespective of the functionality it performs. Therefore, there must be a static interface between the Framework and your application. The standard hook methods provide this interface.

You cannot change the signature of a standard hook method, because if you could, you would break the interface between the Web Dynpro Framework and your application, thus rendering it useless!

At no time during the coding of a business application will you ever need (or be able) to call a standard hook method. However, you will need to have a good understanding of how round-trip processing works inside the Web Dynpro Framework to get the best results from both the Framework and your application.

There are two categories of standard hook method:

▶ **Lifecycle hook methods**
These hook methods are called once, and only once at the start and end of a controller's lifecycle. You can think of these methods as providing every controller with a constructor and a destructor method.

▶ **Round-trip hook methods**
These hook methods will be called no more than once per controller during every round trip.

Each type of controller contains its own specialized round-trip hook methods, so it is not possible to provide a generalized description of the purpose they serve at this time. This topic will be dealt with in much more detail in Chapter 4 on the Phase Model.

Figure 2.11 shows an example of the coding that could be placed into the lifecycle hook method wdDoInit().

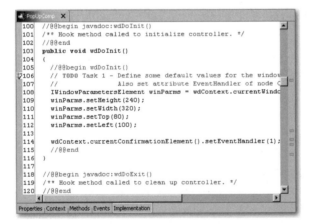

```
PopUpComp  X
100  //@@begin javadoc:wdDoInit()
101  /** Hook method called to initialize controller. */
102  //@@end
103  public void wdDoInit()
104  {
105    //@@begin wdDoInit()
106    // TODO Task 1 - Define some default values for the window
107    //            Also set attribute EventHandler of node C
108    IWindowParametersElement winParms = wdContext.currentWindc
109    winParms.setHeight(240);
110    winParms.setWidth(320);
111    winParms.setTop(80);
112    winParms.setLeft(100);
113
114    wdContext.currentConfirmationElement().setEventHandler(1);
115    //@@end
116  }
117
118  //@@begin javadoc:wdDoExit()
119  /** Hook method called to clean up controller. */
120  //@@end
Properties  Context  Methods  Events  Implementation
```

**Figure 2.11** Coding

**Instance Methods**

You may declare the existence of instance methods in your controller. These methods are declared using the NWDS (see Figure 2.12), and then the appropriate coding is generated for you. If you want to change the method's signature, you must edit the declaration; don't try to edit the generated Java code because the next time the code is regenerated, the signature will be recreated according to the declaration you first made.

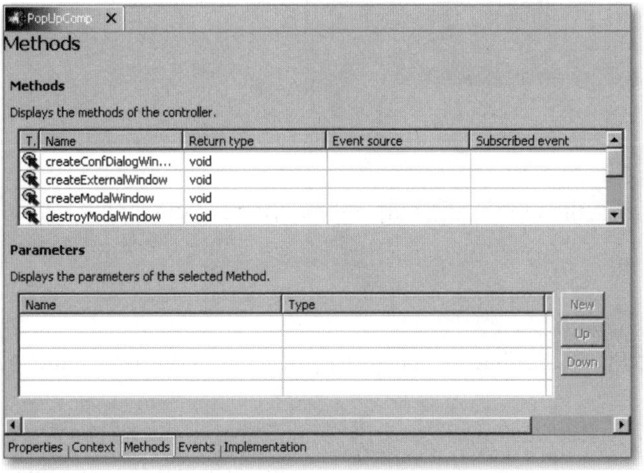

**Figure 2.12** Instance Methods

### What Do I Do if I Want To Create a Static Method?

Any method created using the declarative technique mentioned above will be an instance method. However, in certain situations it will be necessary for you to create static methods.[8] In these situations, you should open the source code of the controller and scroll down to the bottom of the file. Here you will see a pair of comment lines:

```
//@@begin others
```

```
//@@end
```

**Listing 2.1** Comment markers to delimit code outside the control of the Web Dynpro Framework

Between these comment lines you may add any coding you need.

### Events

Events are declared in the same way that methods are declared. Once an event has been declared, any method in any controller within the same component can subscribe to that event.

---

8  For instance, you may need to create a UI element structure dynamically at runtime. This is a situation in which a static method may be needed.

Figure 2.13 is a screenshot showing that an event called `ProcessConfirmation` has been declared and that it has an integer parameter called `idNo`.

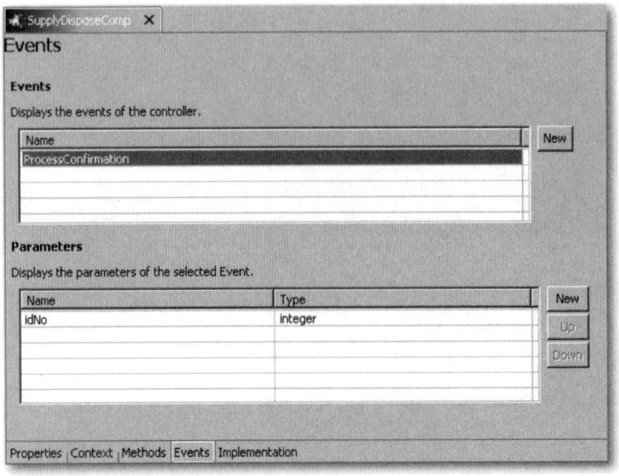

**Figure 2.13** Events

### 2.5.2 Architecture of Visual Controllers

There are two types of visual controller in a Web Dynpro component: the view controller and the interface view controller. These are shown in Figure 2.14. While their names are similar, their roles are different.

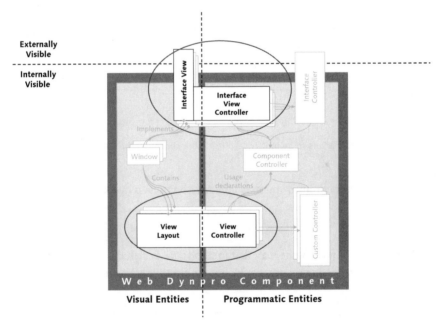

**Figure 2.14** The Visual Controllers Within a Web Dynpro Component

**View Controller**

A view controller is where you bring together individual UI elements to form what Karen Holtzblatt calls a Focus Group: a logical grouping of UI elements designed to present a collection of values that is treated as a single unit of data (e.g., an address).

The fundamental concepts of a view controller are as follows:

▶ The only mechanism for user interaction within a Web Dynpro application is through a view controller.

▶ A view controller is *always* a consumer of data, either from the user via the keyboard and mouse, or by receiving data from a non-visual controller.

▶ A view controller is *not* responsible for generating the data it displays.

▶ A view has exactly one visual interface (layout) associated with it.

▶ A view controller is subordinate to, and cannot exist without, the component controller.

▶ A view controller is reusable *only* within the scope of the component to which it belongs.

The view controller is split into a programmatic part and a visual part, and the two parts are coupled together using the concept of *data binding*. This means the various properties of the UI elements on the layout will obtain their information from some attribute of the view controller's context. A UI element property *can* operate with hard-coded values (stored in the UI element object itself); however, as soon as you wish to exert programmatic control over that particular property value, you should create an appropriate context attribute and bind the UI element property to it. This technique is called data binding and will be dealt with in greater detail in Chapter 5.

Typically, you will define a view layout at design time; however, it is possible to construct a view's UI layout dynamically at runtime.

A Web Dynpro screen may be composed from any number of view layouts, arranged in a wide variety of ways. As the user interacts with the application, various combinations of views will be presented to the user. Views will be added to the screen and removed as the user navigates around the application. This dynamically changing set of views is known as the view assembly, and its contents are managed by an entity called the window.

**Interface View Controller**

The interface view controller plays a role similar to that of a view controller, but the main difference is that the interface view controller does not manage an aggregation of individual UI elements; instead, it manages an aggregation of view layouts.

To see any information on the screen, you must embed at least one view within the window (whose location is shown in Figure 2.4 above).[9] In Figure 2.15, two views have been embedded into the window; on the left is the view called Customer, and on the right is the view called CaseDetail. These views themselves have other views nested within them by means of a special UI element known as a *View Container*.

Not only have views been embedded into the window, but navigation paths have also been defined between the various windows. Navigation takes place between special exit and entry points on a view called plugs. An outbound plug defines an exit point, and these are linked to inbound plugs via navigation links.

The purpose of the interface view controller is first to calculate which views are currently required on the screen (i.e., it calculates how the next view assembly is to be constructed) and then after navigation has been requested, it manages the removal of old views from the view assembly and the insertion of new views.

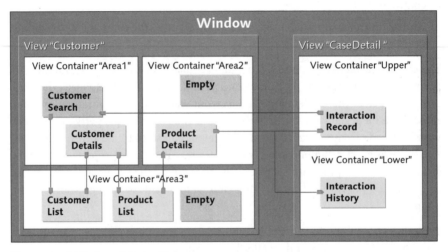

**Figure 2.15** A Window at Design Time

At runtime, you will not see all the views embedded into the window at design time (unless of course the window layout is extremely simple). When the Web Dynpro Framework renders the very first screen of the application, the user has obviously never seen the screen before, so there cannot have been any prior navigation requests. In this case, the interface view controller renders only those views that have their Default flag set to true. For the window shown above, this will yield the screen shown in Figure 2.16.

---

9  Otherwise, the component would have an empty visual interface, and when the user ran the Web Dynpro application, he would see an empty screen.

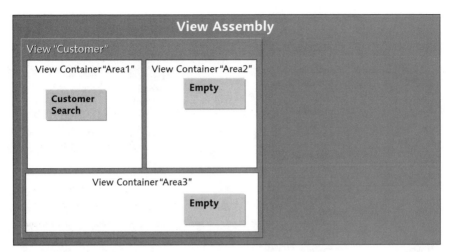

**Figure 2.16** A Window at Runtime

Notice that the title of the main area has changed from window to view assembly. The view assembly is the subset of views required on the current screen either as a result of rendering the screen for the first time or as a result of navigation processing.

The views labeled Empty are special null views that can be used specifically to blank out an area of the screen. You do not need to create an empty view yourself; it will be available to you automatically when you come to embed a view into a window.

**Architecture of a View Controller**

Figure 2.17 shows the layout of a view controller. As you can see, there are very few differences between it and a non-visual controller.

As an aside, in the SAP NetWeaver 7.0 (formerly SAP NetWeaver 2004s) release of Web Dynpro, the interface view controller is something of a special case insomuch as it is not under the control of the developer. You have no access to its context, its layout is the separate entity called the window, you cannot create your own methods in its implementation, and it has no actions.[10]

Instead, it has navigation links that join the inbound and outbound plugs defined in the individual views. Therefore, since this controller is a special case, we will focus on the view controller, since this is a very important controller — at least if you want your component to put any data on the screen.

---

10  In the SAP NetWeaver 7.1 and higher releases, this architecture is altered so that there is now a controller called the Window Controller. This controller can be modified by the developer and makes window and navigation management easier.

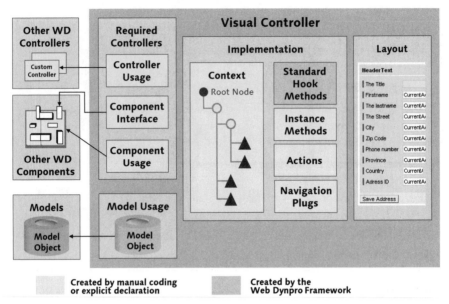

**Figure 2.17** The Architecture of a Visual Controller

The only things view controllers have that non-visual controllers don't are:

▶ **Navigation Plugs**

A navigation plug is an entry or exit point into or out of the view controller. Navigation plugs are used when views have been embedded into windows. Navigation links can then be created that join an outbound plug to an inbound plug.

The result of this is that when the outbound plug method is fired in the first view, that view is removed from the screen and replaced with the view on the other end of the navigation link.

▶ **A UI Layout**

This is the most important part of the view controller. The layout is where you define which UI elements will be present on the screen. In addition to defining the existence of the UI elements, you must also define from where the UI element properties will be supplied with data. Any node or attribute in the view controller's context can act as a supplier of data to a UI element property. When the property of a UI element is associated with a context node or attribute, this is known as *data binding*.

Notice the terminology being used here? It's the same data supplier–data consumer idea. This is how SAP has been able to decouple the definition of the user interface from any specific client device. The view controller's coding and the view controller's UI layout are decoupled from each other by means of the context. Your coding writes data to attributes in the context. These attributes are then bound to UI element properties, and the Web Dynpro Framework handles the screen rendering and data transport for you.

Conversely, when the user enters some data on the screen and then starts a round trip, the Web Dynpro Framework unloads the data from the UI elements and updates the corresponding attributes in the context.

Most of the time, therefore, your program need only concern itself with reading from and writing to the context. You do not need to access a UI element object itself to find out what data the user entered.

▶ **Instead of Events, Visual Controllers Have Actions**
Since a visual controller is not a generator of data, it does not raise events; instead, it is concerned with presenting information to the user and then responding to events that take place on the client. Therefore, there needs to be a mechanism for responding to a client-side event. This is the purpose of an Action.

Certain UI elements are capable of raising client-side events, such as a button or a checkbox. This event, however, is raised in the client and not in the server, so there needs to be a way of triggering a server-side response when a client-side event is raised.

When an action is declared in a view controller, by default, an action handler method will be created. This method contains the functionality that should be invoked when a round trip from the client is processed.

The next part is to associate the action with the appropriate event in the UI layout. As soon as this has been done, the Web Dynpro Framework knows two things:

▶ Since an action has now been associated with the client-side event, a round trip can now successfully be made when the event is raised.[11]

▶ The action handler method defined in the action will receive control when the round trip is processed.

**Context Differences**

There is also a difference between the contexts of visual and non-visual controllers. The difference lies not in the structure or behavior, but in its visibility.

Do you remember the principle described above that says a non-visual controller acts as a generator of data and a visual controller acts only as a consumer? Well, here is where that principle is put into practice.

---

11  If you fail to associate a client-side event with an action, a round trip from the client to the server will never take place because you have not defined to which server-side method control should be handed.

The context of visual controller is *never* part of the controller's public interface, for if it were, the visual controller could expose its context data to other controllers, and thus it would be able to behave as a data source (i.e., a generator of data). This is not permitted.

It is very important that this concept is thoroughly understood, because it will help keep the business logic in your applications simpler and much easier to maintain. This principle is ignored in many Web Dynpro implementations, and developers think that because the application doesn't crash and is functional, their architecture is sound.

Well, actually, no.

These same developers (6 months later) then arrive at the illogical conclusion that Web Dynpro can't be any good because the business application *they* wrote is really difficult to maintain. They find that because the business logic (which they wrote) is scattered around in various places in each component, they must perform an exhaustive search of all the controllers in all the components to find those parts in the code that need to be changed. Sometimes they call a BAPI or a Web service from the component controller, and sometimes from this view controller or that view controller, and sometimes from the interface controller...

The bottom line is that because the boundaries between data suppliers and data consumers were never understood, the resulting business logic was structured inconsistently. This results in a muddled architecture that frequently turns code maintenance into a real headache.

### 2.5.3 Controller Interaction

Several points must be clearly understood about the way controllers interact with each other:

▶ All controllers have a public and private interface.

▶ The interface controller defines the public interface of the entire Web Dynpro component.

▶ The declared methods and context of a non-visual controller are always part of its public interface and (after a suitable usage declaration) are therefore accessible to other controllers.

▶ The declared methods and context of a visual controller belong only to its private interface. Therefore, a view controller cannot act as a data generator. Remember, view controllers are *always* considered to be consumers of data.

▶ A non-visual controller can declare the use of any other non-visual controller within the current Web Dynpro component, but it cannot declare the use of a visual controller.

▶ A visual controller can declare the use of any other non-visual controller within the current Web Dynpro component, but it cannot declare the use of another visual controller.

▶ If the same data is to be displayed on different views, it should be held in the context of a non-visual controller. This will typically be the component controller. The context of the non-visual controller then acts as the data supplier for the contexts of the visual controllers through a technique called context mapping (see next section).

## 2.6 Communication Between Controllers

By now, you should be familiar with the concept that a Web Dynpro component is an aggregation of independent, but interrelated, controllers. No one controller in a component can function in isolation from any other controller, yet they are all independent programs.

Since the controllers in a component are all independent programs, they will not normally share any information with each other. Therefore, a mechanism has been built into a component that allows one controller to call the methods and share the data belonging to another controller.

### 2.6.1 Usage Declarations

If you look back at the section Required Controllers in Section 2.5.1, you can see that within certain limitations, one controller can declare the use of another controller. Each controller maintains a list of required controllers, and such a declaration must always be made as the first step.

As soon as a controller's name has been added to the list of required controllers, the NWDS will generate the necessary coding API for the declaring controller to call any method in the declared controller.

This is the first step toward the controllers sharing data.

Before looking at how two controllers can share information, it is worth expanding on the limitations of controller usage. Look back at Section 2.5.3. Both visual and non-visual controllers can declare the use of any other non-visual controller, but a visual controller can *never* be declared for use by another controller.

This is because of the separation made in Web Dynpro architecture between those parts of the program that generate (or supply) data and those parts that consume data.

### 2.6.2    Context Mapping

Once a usage declaration has been made (in other words, once you have added the name of a non-visual controller to the list of required controllers), you can now take the next step of declaring a context mapping. This is the technique that allows the data in the context of one controller to be accessed and manipulated as if it were part of the local controller's context.

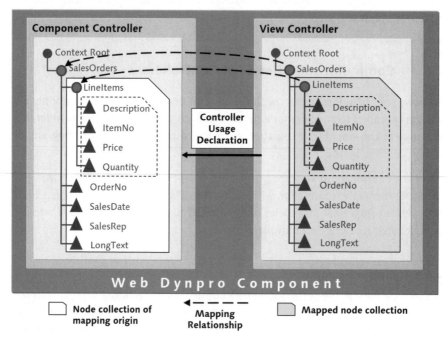

**Figure 2.18** Context Mapping

The dotted line in Figure 2.18 shows that the nodes on the right called SalesOrders and LineItems are mapped nodes. This means that the view controller thinks that the data it finds in these nodes are actually part of its own context. The reality, however, is that the mapped nodes in the view controller are simply references to the real data held in the component controller's context.

Context mapping is a very useful tool for allowing one controller to gain access to the data held in the context of another controller.

Context mapping does not cause the duplication of data. The nodes in the context of the component controller (on the left of Figure 2.18) are where the business data actually resides, and these nodes are therefore known as the *mapping origin* nodes. The nodes in the view controller are known as *mapped nodes* and simply hold a reference to their respective mapping origin nodes.

The type of mapping relationship described here is known as *internal mapping* because the origin node and the mapped node lie within the scope of the same component. An internal mapping relationship can be defined between any pair of controllers within a single component[12] or between the component controller of a parent controller and the interface controller of a child component instance. In the latter case, the child component usage is internal to the scope of the parent component.

However, there is another situation in which an *external mapping* relationship can be created. This special type of mapping relationship will be dealt with in Section 5.13.

### 2.6.3 Data Binding

Making the data in the component controller available to the view controller is fine, but how do we get the data onto the screen? This is where data binding comes in. As has already been described, the properties of any UI element can either contain a hard-coded value or can be bound to a suitable attribute in the context. This technique is the means by which the programmatic part of a view controller can transfer data to the visual part (i.e., the view layout).

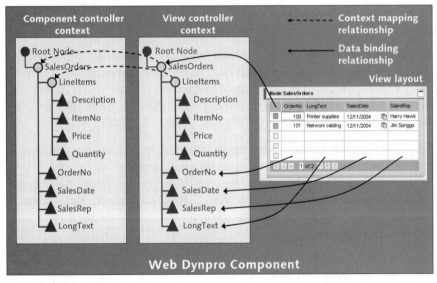

**Figure 2.19** Data Binding

As you can see in Figure 2.19, the diagram has now been extended to include the view layout within the view controller. There is an important architectural feature to understand here. The same type of decoupling that exists between the compo-

12  As long as the controller containing the mapping origin node is a non-visual controller.

nent controller and the view controller also exists between the coding in a view controller and its UI elements. The reason for this decoupling is to allow the UI layout to be specified in a client-independent manner.

So, if you want to put data on the screen, you should first put it into the context and then use that context node or attribute as a data source for the property of a UI element. The same principle is at work here that I've seen in other areas of Web Dynpro architecture — the separation of those parts of the program that generate (or supply) data, from those parts that consume data.

This principle is at work not only between different controllers in a component, but within the view controller itself. The context of the view controller is considered to be the data supplier, and the UI element properties are considered to be the consumers.

### 2.6.4 Summary of the Roles Played by the Different Controllers

Each Web Dynpro controller has been designed to fulfill a specific role within the architecture of the component. It is important that these roles are understood and that the functional boundaries are maintained.

The reason I stress (and will continue to stress) this point is that if these principles are not understood and adhered to, the total cost of ownership of a Web Dynpro implementation will be increased — sometimes significantly.

There are no tools or code checking wizards to police the application of these development principles. Instead, developers must take it upon themselves to write their Web Dynpro applications in a disciplined and orderly manner — not cutting corners or thinking that if the program doesn't crash, then the architecture must be OK.

Failure to follow this advice will not necessarily result in performance problems at runtime, but it will definitely result in increased difficulty, time, and cost during the maintenance phase because the business logic has not been implemented within the expected locations of your Web Dynpro components. Consequently, developers attempting to maintain the application will have to spend extra time understanding the excessively complex architecture.

Below are some tables that describe the role (either a supplier or consumer) played by the different controllers within a component and how the exchange of data is performed.

| Entity | Supplies data to | By means of |
|---|---|---|
| Non-visual controller | Visual controllers | Context mapping and eventing |
| | Non-visual controllers | Context mapping, method parameters, and eventing |
| Visual controller | Its own UI elements | Data binding |

**Table 2.1** Controllers Acting as Suppliers Within a Component

| Entity | Consumes data from | By means of |
|---|---|---|
| Non-visual controller | Non-visual controllers | Context mapping, method parameters, and event subscription |
| Visual controller | Non-visual controllers | Context mapping and event subscription |

**Table 2.2** Controllers Acting as Consumers Within a Component

## 2.7 Web Dynpro Applications or "Where Does My Component Sit in the Big Scheme of Things?"

Once those new to Web Dynpro have written their first component(s), it often the case that they loose sight of how the functionality provided by the individual components can be accessed by the end user. So let's look at how this is achieved.

### 2.7.1 Accessing Web Dynpro Functionality from a Browser

Once you have written a Web Dynpro component, you need to provide the users with access to its functionality. This is done by creating something called an Application.

To define an application, you need to nominate a Web Dynpro component to act as the entry point for your business functionality. Here, you must select not just the name of the component, but you must also select which of the component's visual interfaces will be seen by the user. This is necessary because it is possible for a component to have multiple visual interfaces.

The last piece of information that is required is the name of the start-up plug. This is simply an inbound navigation plug of the type StartUp. This is the only type of navigation plug that will be called by the Web Dynpro Framework without first requiring a navigation request from the user.

Once these values have been defined, the NWDS creates a URL from which a user can invoke the component's functionality.

### 2.7.2 Simple Application Structure

In Figure 2.20, you can see the structure of a very simple Web Dynpro application. Notice that the URL points to the component's visual interface.

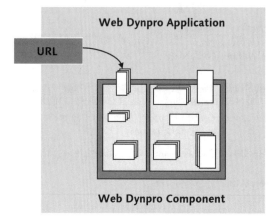

**Figure 2.20** The Architecture of a Simplistic Web Dynpro Application

### 2.7.3 More Realistic Application Structure

In the real world, however, it is very unlikely that you will be using Web Dynpro applications built from a single component. A more realistic scenario is the one in which you have multiple components that function together as a single unit and that interact with a backend system. In this case, your application could look like Figure 2.21.

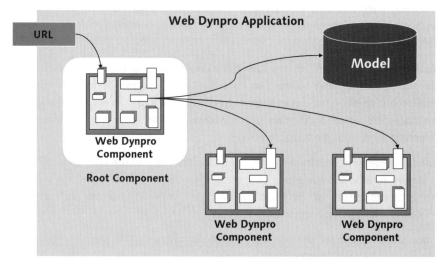

**Figure 2.21** The Architecture of a More Realistic Web Dynpro Application

Here, the component pointed to by the URL has a box around it labeled Root component. This means that since this component is the starting point for the functionality of the entire application, it will have special responsibility for managing the lifecycle and behavior of the other components.

Since all components are reusable, you cannot always know at design time whether the component will function as a child in, or the root of, a component hierarchy. If the component functions as the root, it may need to perform special functionality. Therefore, in view of this special role, a couple of standard hook methods[13] found in a component controller receive a Boolean parameter called `isCurrentRoot`. The purpose of this parameter is to allow the component to determine whether it is functioning as a Root component or not.

### 2.7.4  Application Properties

Each application can be assigned one or more properties. An application property is a hard-coded value that acts as a control constant to modify the behavior of the application.

SAP supplies five predefined property names. These are optional but if used will control some aspect of the application's runtime behavior:

▶ Expiration time: `sap.expirationTime`

▶ Default locale: `sap.locale`

▶ Is user authentication required? `sap.authentication`

▶ Logoff URL: `sap.logoffURL`

▶ Can the application be suspended? `sap.suspensibility`

The prefix `sap.` is reserved for SAP-specific values and should not be used for your own properties.

Custom properties are known as *self-defined* properties and can be used to control specific features of your application. For instance, if you have written an application to manage a certain type of business document, you would probably want to run this application in either display mode or edit mode. The switch between these two modes can be controlled by creating two applications, each pointing to exactly the same component, interface view, and start-up plug, but with different values for a self-defined property called, say, `editMode`.[14]

This property would then have a value of `false` for the display-only application and `true` for the application that provides edit capability. The coding in the Root component would then examine the value of this property and take appropriate action.

---

13  The standard hook methods that receive this parameter are `wdDoBeforeNavigation()` and `wdDoPostProcessing()`.

14  The choice of the property name `editMode` is completely arbitrary.

### 2.7.5 Application Parameters

In contrast to the constant values supplied by application properties, application parameters are variables received from the HTTP request that invokes the Web Dynpro application. This can be an HTTP GET or POST request.

The start-up plug in the component interface view defines the entry point into your Web Dynpro application and is a reference to the event handler that will receive control at the start of your application.

Assuming default names are used, the associated event handler method for this inbound plug will be called `onPlugDefault()`. To receive parameters automatically into this event handler method, all you need to do is declare that the event handler method has parameters of the same name as those expected in the HTTP request.

Please bear in mind that parameter names are case sensitive, and all must be of type `String`.

The following situations will *not* cause errors:

▶ Passing a query string parameter that has not been declared as an inbound plug parameter. The value will still be available programmatically.

▶ Omitting a query string parameter that has been declared as an inbound plug parameter. The inbound plug parameter will be null.

For instance, let's say your application has an interface view controller with a start-up plug called `StartWithUserName`. As the inbound plug name implies, you want to start your application with a user name obtained from the query string, for example, something like:

```
http://<WebDynpro_URL>?userName=Harry%20Hawk
```

Because the start up plug is called `StartWithUserName`, the interface view controller will have an event handler method called `onPlugStartWithUserName`. For the `userName` parameter to be passed automatically through to the event handler, you must first create a parameter called `userName` of type `String` in the start-up plug and then again in the event handler method's signature. Then as long as the HTTP request contains this parameter, its value will automatically arrive in this event handler.

### 2.7.6 Start Up and Shut Down

**Start Up**

When a user specifies the URL of a Web Dynpro application, the Web Dynpro Framework creates and initializes an instance of the root component. Then the inbound plug of type `Startup` in the component interface view is fired. Control now passes to the application coding in the Root component.

**Shut Down**

Several situations will cause the Web Dynpro Framework to shut down an application:

1. The Root component calls an outbound plug in its interface view controller of type `Exit`.

   This is a formal request from within the Web Dynpro application to terminate functionality and then redirect the browser to the address passed as a parameter to the `Exit` plug.

2. The Root component calls an outbound plug in its interface view controller of type `Suspend`. This causes the Web Dynpro application to be suspended while control is handed over to an external website. The handover of control is accompanied by a return URL parameter that the external website must use when handing control back to Web Dynpro.

   The user then performs some business task on the external website (e.g., adding items to a shopping basket), and then control is passed back to Web Dynpro using the previously received return URL.

3. No user interaction is received within the application's time-out period. The exact value of the time-out period will either be inherited from a global setting in the Java Server or defined in the application property `sap.expirationTime`. Both values are specified in seconds, and the global default is 3,600 seconds (1 hour).

4. The user either issues a different URL or shuts down his browser. Either of these actions will cause a round trip to the Web Dynpro server, and the application will be formally terminated.

Once the Web Dynpro application has been shut down, the browser must be redirected to a URL. This can be defined either through the `url` parameter of the `Exit` plug, or in the application property `sap.logoffURL`.

## 2.8    Managing Web Dynpro Components

Once a component has been written, it will be completely nonfunctional unless it is either used as the starting point for an application or is used as the child of another component. Either way, the component will have a distinct lifespan that is managed either by the Web Dynpro Framework or the component acting as its parent.

Since all components are ultimately under the control of an application, the lifespan of any one component cannot exceed the lifespan of the application that invoked it. The lifespan of the application is effectively the lifespan of the Root Component instance.

Component instantiation occurs either when the component functions as:

1. The Root Component of an application. In this case, the Web Dynpro Framework will manage the component's lifecycle.
2. A child of some other parent component.

In this case, there are two possible techniques for creating a child component instance:

▶ If the component's Lifespan parameter in the component usage declaration is set to createOnDemand, then the Web Dynpro Framework will create the child instance as soon as it is required. In other words, the child component instance will only be created when it is actually required, i.e., when you call a method in its interface controller, or you embed its interface view into the visual interface of the parent component, and the screen is now being rendered.

▶ If the component's Lifespan parameter in the component usage declaration is set to manual, then you are responsible for writing the coding that creates the child component instance.

Component instance disposal happens either when the user terminates the application or when the parent component decides that it no longer requires the current instance of the child component and disposes of it manually.

# 3    Designing a Web Dynpro Application

As mentioned in the previous chapter, one of the challenges of software design is to identify the discrete steps of the business process — as conceived in the mind of the user — and then translate these steps into recognizable units of software. In the Web Dynpro world, these units of software will be implemented as Web Dynpro components. In a very simple case, a single Web Dynpro component will be sufficient, but in a typical real-world scenario, you will be dealing with complex business scenarios that require multiple components to implement. In this situation, code reusability is a key design factor because with careful design, you can greatly speed up the development process by establishing a library of components. These components can then be reused — either individually or as complete component hierarchies — and will provide units of known or standardized functionality.

At this point in the discussion, it is necessary to take a brief step away from Web Dynpro and talk about two different, but related, topics:

▶ The SAP Component Model
▶ The SAP NetWeaver Development Infrastructure (NWDI)

The reason for the digression is to explain how these topics critically affect Web Dynpro development: first, in terms of how your units of software are aggregated together and, second, how Web Dynpro software is handled by the change management tool.

If you are going to develop software using the NWDI, then it is mandatory that you make use of the SAP Component Model

## 3.1    The SAP Component Model

Before explaining how the NWDI operates, we must first explain what it operates on.

When Sun Microsystems released the Java language, they left it up to each developer to manage the versions of their own source code and build archives. Many products have been released to fill this functional gap, but none satisfied SAP's requirement that:

▶ There should be a defined transport path through a system landscape.

▶ The unit of software being transported should represent a unit of business processing, as opposed to some low-level, technical unit such as an individual .java file.

▶ The unit of software being transported should carry within itself instructions for how it should be built.

▶ Only those units of software that are directly affected by a code modification should be rebuilt.

In order to implement these requirements, SAP developed the concept of a *Development Component* (DC). This is a wrapper around the actual business software that exists only for the purposes of building and transportation. To achieve this, a DC contains a variety of metadata that describe:

▶ The build process to be used

▶ Those units of functionality within the DC that are to be exposed publicly (known as Public Parts)

▶ The usage dependencies that exist between this and other development components (Used DCs)

Since all DCs contain metadata describing the functionality consumed from other DCs, it can be guaranteed that the minimum amount of coding is recompiled every time there is change. This avoids the need for the brute force approach to recompilation (the nightly build scenario).

A DC can have zero or more public interfaces (Public Parts). Each Public Part corresponds to a Java .jar file that is built explicitly to expose a certain unit of functionality. Here is an area in which developers new to Web Dynpro often make a mistake: they forget (or don't know) that a separate build process is required to build the Public Parts of a DC. This is not the same as simply selecting **Rebuild project**. So the best option here is always to perform a DC Build[1] when developing within the SAP component model.

DCs come in many varieties, for instance, Dictionary, J2EE, or Web Dynpro (to name but a few). The screenshot in Figure 3.1 is from the NWDS and shows the different categories of DC that can be created.

---

1  Strictly speaking, a DC build is not necessary if the modified coding is completely internal to the DC; however, for DCs with many Public Parts, it is always safer to opt for a DC rebuild.

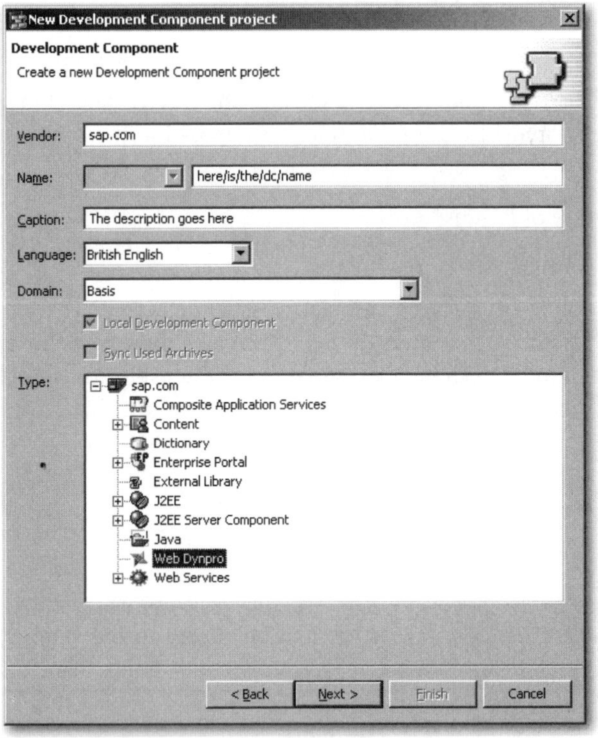

**Figure 3.1** Development Component Types[2]

### 3.1.1 Development Component Naming Conventions

SAP has not defined a naming convention for DCs, since it is not possible to define a generic convention that will be suitable in all cases; however, the following recommendation will make life easier when relating DC names with Java package names.

Notice that the name given to a DC can include forward slash characters as separators. This allows you to construct a name similar to that found in a Java package. Whilst there is no technical requirement to do so (nor are there any wizards to do it for you), it is a good idea to try to maintain a correlation between Web Dynpro DC names and Web Dynpro Java package names. For instance, you could create a Web Dynpro DC called:

▶ Vendor: mycorp.com

▶ DC name: foo/bar

▶ In NWDI track: BigProject_D

---

2  The *Domain* to which a DC is assigned is only of significance for internal SAP developers, as it is used for translation purposes.

This would result in a DC being created that has the name:

```
BigProject_D~foo~bar~mycorp.com
```

The `BigProject_D` part of the name comes from a track in the NWDI called `Big-Project`, and this is the development part of that track (as opposed to the consolidation part).

In general, the name structure of a DC is:

```
<track_name>~<DC_Name>~<vendor_name>
```

The slashes within the DC name are replaced automatically by the tilde (~) character. You may also use the following characters within a DC name; however, these characters are not considered to be separators and are therefore not substituted for tildes:

- "!" exclamation mark
- "$" dollar sign
- "-" hyphen
- "_" underscore

In this example, a DC called `foo/bar` has been created belonging to the vendor `mycorp.com`. Therefore, when you create Web Dynpro components within that DC, it is recommended that you use the Java package prefix `com.mycorp.foo.bar` followed by whatever class name you require, for example,

```
com.mycorp.foo.bar.guns_n_roses
com.mycorp.foo.bar.bells_n_whistles
```

### 3.1.2 Child Development Components

It should be noted that it is possible to create a type of DC known as a *Child Component*. This type of DC should only be used when an existing DC contains a lot of functionality and you want to make an internal subdivision of the code.

The concept of a Child Component is exactly the same as that of an Inner Class in regular Java programming. In reality, you will not require the use of a Child DC very often, but they can be created if required. Please be aware of the following limitations of Child DCs:

- A Child DC (like an Inner Class) is completely encapsulated within the parent DC.
- Functionality contained within a Child DC can be added to the Child DC's Public Part as per any normal DC, but these Public Parts can only be consumed directly by the Parent DC.
- Child DC functionality can only be exposed to the outside world indirectly through a Public Part belonging to the parent component.

Since the whole concept of a DC is to provide a compilation and delivery mechanism for diverse types of software development, there are not too many situations in which you will need to create a delivery wrapper around a unit of code wholly contained within a larger DC. To put that in simpler language, you'll hardly ever need to use a Child DC!

### 3.1.3 Software Components

Whenever a DC of any type is created, it must always be defined within the scope of a larger aggregation of code known as a Software Component (SC). An SC represents the unit of code delivered to the customer. In other words, this is the unit of code that is installed and upgraded as a single unit and the only unit of granularity that SAP's update and upgrade tools can handle.

Working with the NWDI, software development must be aggregated within SCs and DCs, but from a deployment perspective, a DC can also act as a unit of deployment. In this case it is delivered within an archive file known as a Software Delivery Archive (such files use an extension of .sda).

In a typical software implementation, all the software written for a particular project can be contained within a single SC, since this will represent the deliverable unit of code that, from an installation perspective, is treated as a single unit.

However, for large implementations, you may find it better to structure the software into multiple SCs, each of which forms an independent unit of deliverable functionality. I will not attempt to enter into a discussion of how best to structure SCs; suffice it to say that there are many ways to perform this task, and it is necessary have the correct NWDI training before embarking upon the design phase of the project. Without this training, you may well end up defining a poor NWDI architecture that becomes a liability in the future.

> **Important**
>
> A DC cannot be shared between two SCs. Therefore, consider carefully what SC structure you require, since you want to avoid having to implement the same functionality in two different DCs simply because you did not structure your SCs carefully enough.

### 3.1.4 Full Component Hierarchy

The overall component hierarchy is as shown in Figure 3.2.

We started at the bottom of the component hierarchy because the DC is the unit of code you will first encounter during Web Dynpro development. The individual files shown at the very bottom of the hierarchy are generated and managed by the NWDS — called Development Objects.

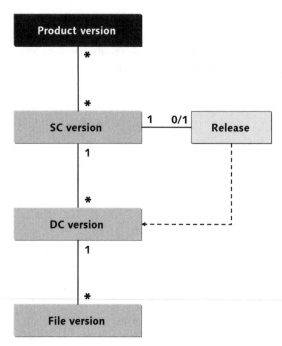

**Figure 3.2** Component Hierarchy

When you have finished your development, these files are transferred[3] to the source code repository (the Design Time Repository [DTR]) used by the NWDI.

At the top of the hierarchy is the entity called a Product. A Product is a *very* large unit of coding that SAP uses to deliver a complete functional system. A Product can contain any number of SCs, and the same SC can be shipped in multiple Products. The combination of SC versions aggregated together into a Product determines the specific version of the Product.

### 3.1.5 Developing Without the NWDI

In the event that you are developing applications outside the scope of the NWDI, you must be aware of the following limitations:

▶ Since all DCs *must* belong to an SC, when creating your DC, you must specify the dummy SC MyComponents.

▶ All such DCs will appear in the dummy track LocalDevelopment (see Figure 3.3).

▶ The NWDI cannot transport such developments to any other server in your system landscape; neither can your software be migrated into the DTR at a later time.

---

3 The correct terminology is *checked in*.

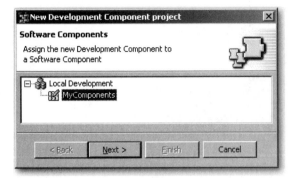

**Figure 3.3** Default Software Component

## 3.2    Architectural Concepts of the NWDI

When SAP first moved into the Java development area, it became clear that a source code version management, build tool, and transport system were required — not simply a system that performed these functions, but one that did so in a manner that met all of SAP's internal development requirements. After various experiments with both commercially available and open source products, it was decided that if *all* of SAP's requirements were to be met, then a custom written product was required.

One of the main criteria SAP required of such a system was that it could solve the problems associated with "nightly builds." Since Java provides no internal mechanism to say which class is consumed by which,[4] it has always been impossible to determine which classes should be rebuilt if some other class is modified — hence the brute force approach of rebuilding everything every night and then picking up the pieces in the morning. In addition to this, there were the aspects of modification support, maintenance, and transport to consider. These factors all provided the motivation for SAP to create the NWDI.

The aim of this section is not to provide a detailed explanation of how the NWDI works, but to provide a conceptual overview in order for you to understand what the NWDI is, why it exists, and the impact it has on Web Dynpro development.

The NWDI consists of several functional areas, each of which performs a distinct task (see Figure 3.4). These functional areas are implemented as services on the AS Java and can be installed on different physical hosts if necessary.

---

4  What SAP required here was the Java equivalent of the feature found in the ABAP Development Workbench called the "Where used list."

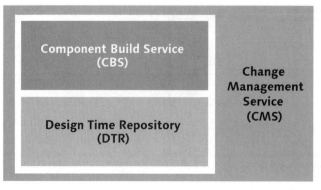

**Figure 3.4** Overview of the NWDI Architecture

### 3.2.1 The Design Time Repository (DTR)

The DTR is a file version management system, primarily designed for Java source code. It is a repository based on flat files and directories and can be accessed using the WebDAV or DeltaV protocols.

The DTR is divided into workspaces, each of which belongs to a specific development track. Within the NWDS there is a DTR perspective (see Figure 3.5) that allows you to view both the content within the DTR database and the files on your local file system that have been synchronized from the DTR.

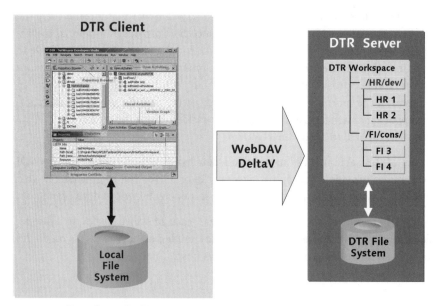

**Figure 3.5** DTR Overview

During ongoing development you can store your source code in the DTR using the "update" feature. Here the changes are only visible to you. This feature stands in contrast to a "Check in," which means you update the DTR workspace in its inactive space, and every developer can then see the updates.

### 3.2.2 The Component Build Service (CBS)

Once you have finished your developments, the next step is to inform the NWDI that your development is complete. After you have checked-in your source code and tested it locally, you can trigger the activation, which initiates the central build process on the NWDI development system.

The process of activation is where the CBS analyzes all the dependencies that exist in the checked-in code and then recompiles only the new, modified, and dependent coding. After a successful central build, the sources of the "active" workspace are updated. Furthermore, the CBS database is updated with the new compiled archives (see Figure 3.6).

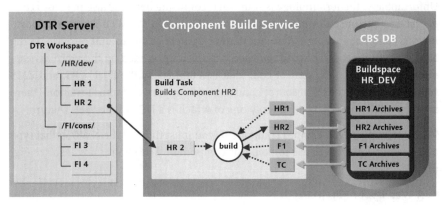

**Figure 3.6** CBS Overview

After the activation has completed, the software is also often deployed to the central development runtime system. Here the developer can perform the first real integration test.

After the test is successful, the developer releases the new development and hands it over to the NWDI administrator for transportation to other systems in the landscape.

### 3.2.3 The Change Management Service (CMS)

Finally, the last part of the process is to ensure that all the newly compiled code is deployed to the correct server(s). This is the role of the Change Management Service (CMS). You can nominate how the CMS deploys your coding: either automatically after activation or manually by an administrator. Refer back to Figure 3.4 to see how the CMS interacts with the DTR and the CBS.

The CMS is also responsible for (amongst other things):

▶ The configuration of development tracks (transportation paths through the system landscape for changes made to a known set of software components)

▶ Supplying development configuration information[5] to the NWDS

## 3.3 Building Web Dynpro Applications Using the NWDI

As has already been stated, when you build a Web Dynpro application, you must write at least one Web Dynpro component. However, we must now further qualify this statement and say that the one Web Dynpro component you write must always be packaged within a DC of type "Web Dynpro." The only reason for wrapping your Web Dynpro component in a DC is for transportation and compilation.

Unfortunately, the terminology is somewhat confusing here because the word *component* has been used to mean two different things. In the Web Dynpro environment, a component is both your unit of development and your unit of reuse. In the NWDI environment, the word *component* is always preceded by the word *development* and describes any unit of code that is managed by the DTR, CBS, and CMS services for the purposes of source control, build support, and transportation. There are many different types of DC, only one of which is a DC of type Web Dynpro.

When building a Web Dynpro component, you must first tell the NWDS what type of container you wish to use to hold this component. The choices are (also see Figure 3.7):

▶ A Web Dynpro Project

▶ A DC Project

You could be forgiven for thinking that you should use a Web Dynpro Project; however, this is *not* the correct project type![6]

You might be asking, "Why on earth does the *Web Dynpro Project* exist if we're not supposed to use it?"

Good question ...

---

5  Development Configuration (or Dev Config) is the information needed by the NWDS for it to interact with the NWDI. Before you can start an NWDI-based development, the NWDS must first have uploaded the Dev Config information so that it knows which development tracks are available for use.

6  If you have created a Web Dynpro Project, all is not lost! These projects can be migrated to DC-based projects.

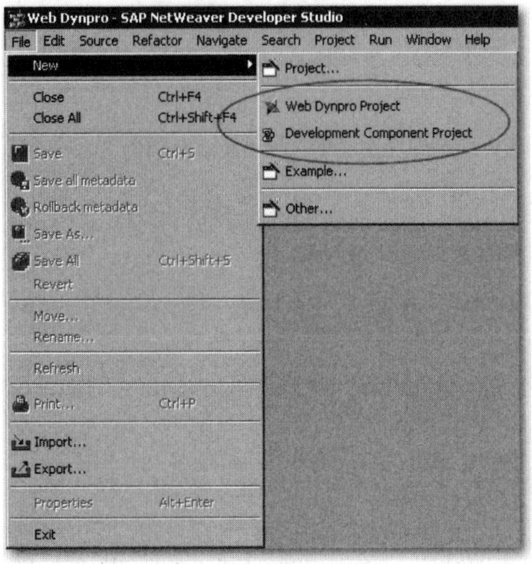

**Figure 3.7** Two Possible Project Types — Only One Is Correct

When Web Dynpro was first released in late 2003, the NWDI was still under development and therefore not publicly available. Consequently the NWDS had to use the only project type available at the time: the Web Dynpro Project. When the NWDI was released, customers had to transfer their developments manually from the older Web Dynpro Projects into the new DC of type Web Dynpro.

**Caveat Confector**

The Web Dynpro Project exists only as a legacy of former development practice and remains available as a means of creating small applications that are not intended to act as anything more than experimental developments.

For all productive Web Dynpro developments, you should *always* use DCs of type Web Dynpro.

The main limitation of the older Web Dynpro Project was that it behaved as a sealed container. Once you placed Web Dynpro components inside it, they could not easily be accessed from outside the scope of that project. Thus, one of SAP's main design criteria for Web Dynpro was not being met — namely code reusability.

### 3.3.1 A Frequently Asked Question

As soon as Web Dynpro developers understand that they need to build DCs of type Web Dynpro, the next question that needs to be answered is this: "How many Web Dynpro components should a DC contain?"[7]

---

7  From this point on in the book, instead of repeating the phrase "DC of type Web Dynpro," it should be assumed that all mention of DCs refers to DCs of type Web Dynpro unless explicitly stated otherwise.

The simple answer is "as many as are required," but this is like asking "How long is a piece of string?" and being given the reply "Half as long as there and back again." The answer is just as ambiguous as the question!

A more helpful answer can be derived by evaluating the following facts:

▶ A Web Dynpro component is both your unit of development and reuse.

▶ A DC can contain multiple Web Dynpro components.

▶ A DC is a compilation and transportation wrapper placed around your software, and provides an interface for exposing the functionality it contains.

▶ Each Web Dynpro component can be exposed (if required) by adding it to one of the DC's Public Parts.

Therefore, it makes sense to gather together those Web Dynpro components into a single DC that should be treated as a single unit *for the purposes of transportation.* Let's take a simplistic example. If, for instance, a single business process can be divided into three discrete steps, then each step of the process could be implemented as a single Web Dynpro component. In addition to this, you want to provide a framework component that can bring together the functionality found in these three business components, such that they function as a coherent unit.

Therefore, these four Web Dynpro components can be logically grouped together into a single DC because you will always want to transport the coding for the entire business process as a single unit.

As previously stated, this is a simplistic example, but it illustrates the principle that a DC should contain only those Web Dynpro components that are to be logically grouped together for the purposes of transportation and deployment. This principle also includes grouping components together to form a library of utilities.

Another common type of DC is one that contains *only* Web Dynpro model objects — and no actual Web Dynpro components. Each model object is added to a Public Part and can be consumed by any other DC as required. The reason for structuring DCs in this way is that the compilation process for model objects is both expensive and infrequent. Therefore, there is no reason to have the model objects in the same DC as your business functionality, since this will greatly slow down the recompilation process and thereby slow down the overall development process.

### 3.3.2   Sharing Web Dynpro Functionality Between Multiple DCs

If you have multiple Web Dynpro components within multiple DCs, you will need some mechanism whereby the Web Dynpro components in DC A can reuse the functionality of the Web Dynpro components in DC B. This is where the Public Parts mentioned earlier are so vital.

In this example, we have a component hierarchy in which component A is the parent component with respect to components B, C, and D.

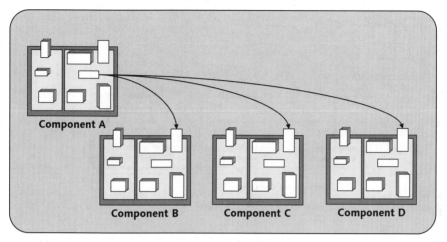

**Development Component "DC_1"**

**Figure 3.8** Example of a Component Hierarchy Within One DC

As can be seen from the diagram in Figure 3.8, we have a single DC called DC_1 within which are four Web Dynpro components. Taken together, these components implement a discrete, reusable unit of functionality required by a larger unit of business processing. Even though component A is shown as the parent component, the other components (B, C, and D) are still reusable units of functionality in their own right.

In this situation, component A acts simply as a container to bring together the functionality of components B, C, and D into a coherent unit. Therefore, we have four possibilities for reuse:

▶ Each of the three components B, C, and D could be reused individually.

▶ Component A is a reusable unit that combines the functionality of the three child components.

Therefore, we can define at least two different Public Parts to expose these different units of reuse: one Public Part can expose component A (which by implication exposes components B, C, and D), and another Public Part can be used to expose components B, C, and D individually.

As you can see from Figure 3.9, the DC has two Public Parts: pp1 and pp2 of type compilation. pp1 exposes only component A, and pp2 exposes components B, C, and D.

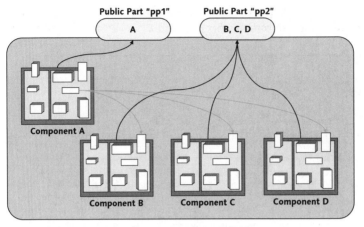

**Figure 3.9** Use of Public Parts to Expose Functionality

Let's now further say that we have a second DC called DC_2 (see Figure 3.10), which needs to use the functionality found in DC_1. To do this, the "DC Metadata" of DC_2 must be configured to include the name of the required Public Part within DC_1 (at build time). Once this configuration has been performed, component E within DC_2 is able to reference component A found in DC_1.

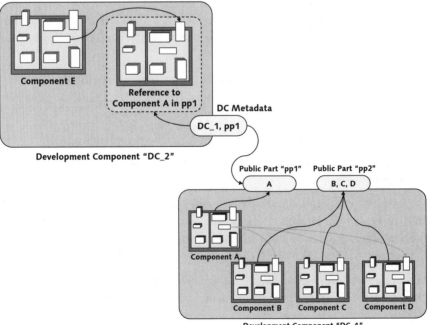

**Figure 3.10** One DC Can Use the Functionality Found in Another DC via a Public Part

> **Caveat Confector**
>
> In the examples shown in Figure 3.9 and Figure 3.10, what would happen if you forgot to perform a DC Build of DC_1?
>
> Quite simply, when you came to configure DC_2's DC metadata, you would find that you could not consume any functionality from DC_1 because it has no Public Parts (yet)!
>
> Always remember that each Public Part exists as its own .jar file, and these are constructed by a build process that is separate from the normal Web Dynpro compilation process. Therefore, you must always perform a DC Build in order:
>
> ▶ For each Public Part .jar file to be created in the first place.
>
> ▶ To allow the functionality in the Public Parts to be consumed by other DCs.

If you modify a Web Dynpro component in such a way that your change has no impact on the functionality exposed through a Public Part, then a normal Web Dynpro compilation can be performed without needing to perform a DC Build. In addition to this, if the Public Parts of a DC have not changed, then the dependent DCs will not be rebuilt (this is one of the main advantages of the CBS over the nightly build approach).

Figure 3.11 summarizes the relationship between the NWDS and the NWDI.

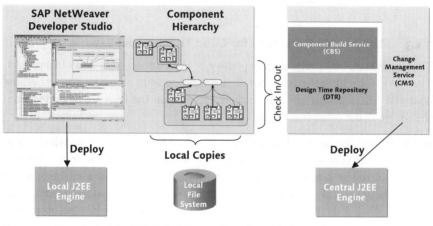

**Figure 3.11** Overview of the NWDI Architecture Together with the NWDS

## 3.4    Preparation and Planning

As stated in the opening chapter, it is far better to understand the principles by which problems can be solved than to apply a rigid, dogmatic set of rules. Now we will start to put these principles to work. The following section will deal not only with what you should do when designing a Web Dynpro application, but also what you should not do.

### 3.4.1 The Rule of the Seven P's

If you have never heard of the rule of the seven P's before, it is this: **P**roper **P**reparation and **P**lanning **P**revents **P**redictably **P**oor **P**erformance!

It is a truism to say that good planning and design always yields a better finished result. Furthermore, it doesn't take long for people to work out that without such planning and preparation, the result will be a predictably poor implementation.

Yet the increasing pressure for software implementations to be delivered against ever tightening budgets and time scales has led to situations in which, as long as a *result* is obtained by the required deadline and that result can be presented in a positive light, then the implementation is considered a success.

### 3.4.2 You Get What You Pay For

If an implementation is staffed by contract personnel, they are often chosen based on their cost rate, not their experience. Consequently, the quality of the coding is often low, which leads to problems that do not become apparent until much later on in the implementation process (e.g., during performance or user acceptance testing). In extreme situations, the code quality can be so bad that the whole implementation must be thrown away and rewritten.[8]

### 3.4.3 There Is No Substitute for Good Training and Experience

Training is sometimes seen as an expensive or even unnecessary delay to a project. Therefore, it is either bypassed or only a select few team members are sent on the course(s). These people are then expected to pass on the knowledge gained from the course to the other team members.

Unfortunately, this logic is deeply flawed. Would you expect someone who has just passed their driving test to be immediately promoted the status of driving instructor? No, of course not. You would wait until they have built up some experience before allowing them to train others, the simple reason being that knowledge without experience is dangerous. This may sound like a truism, but in a business environment in which success is often measured solely in financial terms such common-sense reasoning is often overlooked.

In my experience, the *number one* reason for poor-quality Web Dynpro implementations has been a lack of developer training. There are a variety of reasons for why the implementation staff members were not trained, but at the end of the day, the result has always been an implementation of very poor quality that can turn into a support nightmare.

---

8  Yes, I've seen one implementation that was this bad!

### 3.4.4   Oh and by the Way, Can You Just Add this Functionality?

If the scope defined during the initial design stage is allowed to expand without a corresponding adjustment of the delivery timeframe or resources, then the quality of the finished product must necessarily drop.

Remember that all projects (not just software projects) are governed by four fundamental factors:

► *Resources*: How much material and how many bodies can we throw at this?

► *Scope*: What is the sum total of tasks that need to be achieved?

► *Quality*: What standards must be attained for the delivered product to be considered acceptable?

► *Time*: How long have we got to do all this?

It does not matter how good a manager you are: It is a well-known fact that you can only exert a direct influence on three of these factors. Like it or not, the fourth one (no matter which one it is) will be controlled by the forces of nature.

For instance, if a project is working to an aggressive delivery date (making the time factor fixed), but for financial reasons there are insufficient developers available to deliver the required scope (also making the resources fixed), then either the scope or the quality will suffer. Either the required scope will be met with lowered quality or the required quality will be met, but at the cost of reduced scope.

Typically, the management of a project will decide that at least one of these factors is fixed (usually time — the delivery date), and then they try to juggle the resources and scope to maintain the quality and meet the fixed deadline. The big mistake here is that by fixing one of these factors (in this case time), you have chosen simply not to modify it. In other words, you've chosen *not* to control one of your three controllable factors. So now your level of control is down to only two factors, and the remaining fourth factor will still manage itself.

Even the most skilful manager can only ever have a direct influence on three of these factors; the fourth one will be a law unto itself. The skill of project management comes from recognizing that you can exert direct control over only three of these factors and then managing them in such a way that the fourth factor comes out the way you want.

### 3.4.5   The Partner Over-Sells Themselves

This is a common problem. An overzealous sales pitch from an implementation partner informs the customer's management that they can deliver the working solution in less time and at less cost than any other partner. Since such partners are often very persuasive in their sales abilities, the customer gets taken in — either because they do not know enough to challenge the claims or because they are being told what they want to hear. Whatever the reasons, this situation can sting the customer twice!

Firstly, it lulls the customer's management into a false sense of security by making them believe the required scope and quality can be delivered in a reduced time scale and at reduced cost. The hidden dangers of the project overrunning are not perceived at first. Then, when the project does start to overrun, the implementation partner has all manner of excuses for why it's not their fault that the deadlines could not be met.

Secondly, in order for the implementation partner to maintain a profit margin, they must reduce their costs. The easiest way to do this is to increase the ratio of low- to high-cost staff on the project (i.e., put in lots of junior consultants). Again we're back in the "knowledge without experience" situation.

Sometimes it is even worse than this. There have been cases in which the implementation partner's consultants were billed as "SAP Solution Architects," but they had *zero* experience with SAP software! By zero experience, I mean they had never even logged on to an SAP system before arriving at the customer site.

They could talk the talk, but they could not walk the walk. However, they covered up the situation by continually presenting the customer with a positive perception of progress and by producing mountains of meaningless documentation.[9]

I mention these things because, in my experience, these are some of the main hindrances to *proper* preparation and planning. Preparations *are* made, and plans *are* drawn up, but they are not done *properly*; consequently, the projects frequently run over budget or are delivered late.

There are many other (often legitimate) reasons for why projects overrun their budgets and deadlines. However, the problems mentioned above are ones I have often encountered during reviews of Web Dynpro implementation projects.

### 3.4.6 Functional Scope

When analyzing functional scope, it is important to determine whether the implementation of this software product will cause a fundamental change in the company's business processes or whether it will simply exist as a new UI layer for an existing business process. In many cases, there will be a combination of both factors. The company's business process(es) will often be modified somewhat to accommodate the requirements of the new UI software.

---

9 This is a frequently used stratagem in which activity is presented as productivity.

### 3.4.7 Realistic Deadlines and Trained Project Staff

There have been various examples of Web Dynpro implementations in which both the customer and the implementation partner operated in such a manner as to create a set of problems that turned into a vicious circle. The vicious circle works like this:

Let's say a consulting partner has won the business to perform a Web Dynpro implementation. However, in their enthusiasm to convince the customer that they should act as their "trusted SAP advisor," they omitted to tell the customer the "tiny detail" that none of their staff have much experience with this new thing called "Web Dingpro."[10]

"No matter," they think. "How hard can it be? After all, its just Java and web pages!"

Consequently, the consultants now have to implement the customer's business requirements whilst at the same time, learning Web Dynpro on the job. This means that if results are achieved, it is either by accident or through a process of trial and error.

Due to the self-taught nature of the consultants' knowledge, problems are often encountered in which it appears that Web Dynpro cannot perform a particular task. This situation can lead to one of the two following outcomes. Either:

1. The consultant implements an elaborate coding workaround — which is needed not because there is any deficiency in Web Dynpro, but rather to work around their own lack of understanding. The direct consequence of this is that large quantities of excessively complex and largely redundant code are written.

   Immediately, the maintenance of the software has become more complex, making enhancements and bug fixes more difficult, costly, and error-prone.

2. Alternatively, if the consultants cannot think of how to provide the required functionality, then rather than admitting their own ignorance, they state in categorical terms that SAP software is incapable of providing the required feature.

   As a consultant myself, I find this way of working particularly objectionable, since it is always better to be honest with the customer and say "I don't know how to do this, but I'll find out." This creates a win–win situation. The customer wins because they get the feature they require, and the consultant wins because they have expanded their capability to include this new solution. In addition, a sense of trust will develop between the customer and the consultant because the customer knows they are being treated with integrity.

   It is always wrong to confuse what you don't know how to do with what cannot be done.

---

10 Yes, that's really what they called it!

Now let's turn our attention to the customer's side of the project. The partner company has given such a wonderful sales pitch that the customer thinks they will achieve the required results in a shortened time-frame. Therefore, they decide to set implementation deadlines that are both aggressive and inflexible.

The consultants are now stuck. They must implement the business functionality in time to hit an ever-nearing date, but they don't have a clear understanding of how to get the best results from the development toolset. So, they develop a form of tunnel vision in which they focus simply on getting a result — not getting an *efficient* result.

This problem then compounds itself because the next time some functionality is required, or a fix is needed, the difficulty of implementing the new requirements will be greatly increased by the complexity created when the previous requirements were implemented.

These factors all contribute to the creation of a vicious circle, the result of which is a software product that will become a real maintenance nightmare. The vicious circle is illustrated in Figure 3.12.

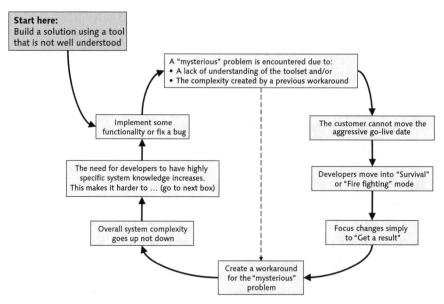

**Figure 3.12** The Vicious Circle

### 3.4.8    What's the Value of Not Making a Mistake?

This is really the million dollar question, because the value is often far higher than realized. To my knowledge,[11] there is no reliable way to quantify how much money

---

11  I'm not an accountant, so I could be wrong here.

has *not* been spent on a project due to traps and pitfalls having been successfully predicted and then avoided.

As an experienced Web Dynpro developer, here is where experience will pay dividends. Your knowledge and experience can be used to advise the customer not only on what they should do, but, more importantly, on how to avoid situations that you know will cause problems further on down the road. There is no substitute for this kind of experience and knowledge, and it can't be gained simply by attending a training course or reading a book. You've got to go out there into the real world and get knocked around by the situations of life to develop this skill.

Let's take a real-life example in which an experienced consultant or developer could have prevented the customer from making a very basic mistake. I was called to a customer site to examine what was reported as a "serious Web Dynpro performance problem." The problem was that during load testing, a couple of Web Dynpro applications were failing to meet their performance targets because their initial screen was taking between 6 and 16 seconds to arrive at the browser. So, naturally enough, I asked what processing was being performed *before* the first screen was displayed.

"Oh not much really," they responded. "Just calling a couple of ABAP function modules in the backend system."[12]

Rather that looking directly at the Web Dynpro Java coding, the first thing I did was examine the ABAP coding in the backend SAP system. Sure enough, I found that both of the function modules were selecting rows from some *very* large database tables. The ABAP statement to read one of the tables had been constructed in a way that did not make use of the table's primary key fields, and neither had a secondary index been defined for the fields that were being used. The SQL statement in the ABAP program looked something like this:

```
select * from <a_very_big_table>
       where <first non_key_field>  = 'a_value' and
             <second non_key_field> = 'another_value' and
             <third non_key_field>  = 'some_other_value'.
```
**Listing 3.1** The offending ABAP select statement

The above code sample would not have been at all inefficient if the database table had had a secondary index built from the non-key fields used in the SQL statement. However, since no secondary index existed, the net result was that every time this SQL statement was executed, the database had to perform a sequential scan of the table. This would not have been too bad had the table only had a few hundred rows in it, but the real killer was that the table contained approximately 8.4 million rows!

---

12  In my mind, the alarm bells now started to ring.

Under these circumstances, I thought a response time of 6 seconds was quite good. It took about 15 minutes to fix this problem...

In this example, an experienced consultant or developer could have prevented the problem from occurring in the first place. This in turn would have prevented a large amount of stress and emotion associated with a project that is threatening to go into escalation and would have avoided the need to alter coding that had already passed through user acceptance testing.

### 3.4.9    Access to Business Functionality

At first, the question of how you gain access to functionality in a backend system may seem to be a small technical detail, but the answer can create a significant impact on the performance of the implemented software if the consequences are not known and accounted for.

Irrespective of the communication technology used to access the backend business functionality,[13] the following areas need to be considered:

▶ Does the backend functionality already exist?

  ▶ If yes, has the interface to the backend system been stress tested to the maximum level expected by the predicted user population?

  ▶ Has the interface to the backend system been tested to the point of collapse? This type of testing is often omitted but is necessary because it will establish your absolute upper processing limit. Then, when the system is running under normal or peak workload, you can know with certainty what processing headroom your system has left.

  ▶ If no, are the developers experienced with transactional programming? If not, it must be ensured that the developers receive the correct training, or they will write coding that functions correctly when tested within the confines of the backend system but could behave erroneously when used over a remote connection.[14]

▶ Does the backend functionality need to be modified?

  ▶ If yes, are the modifications required to accommodate new business practices or to accommodate the new frontend or a mixture of both?

▶ Is the backend functionality being used "as is?"

  ▶ If so, is there a correlation between the screen changes planned for the new user interface and calls to the backend system? If not, what should be adjusted: the interface to the backend system or the UI layer design?

---

13  Web Dynpro can interface to functionality found in backend systems using Web Services (SOAP) or Remote Function Call (ABAP function modules) or by calling Java Beans.

14  This is a particularly important point when writing custom ABAP function modules to be called over the RFC interface.

- Given that your backend system already has a user population that create their own workload:

  - Is it going to be placed under more or less workload by the presence of a Web Dynpro UI layer?

  - Has the processing overhead created by the communication protocol been factored into the system performance analysis?

  - Are you aware of the limitations inherent within each communication protocol? For instance with RFC calls, the ABAP function module's interface should never contain nested or "deep" structures, as this greatly increases the time required for XML marshalling and unmarshalling. Technically, nested structures will function over the RFC interface, but their presence in the interface will degrade response times.

### 3.4.10 Planning the User Interface: Creating a Story Board

For a new development, I have always found it useful to start the UI design phase by creating a story board. This is nothing more than a mock-up of what information is required on each screen. The purpose of the story board is to plot the flow of business information through the business transaction. The screen mock-ups do not need to be concerned with the final appearance of the Web Dynpro screens; instead, the most important factor is to ensure that all fields present on each frame of the story board represent the business data that is required at that point in the business process.

### 3.4.11 Analysis of the Business Process from Various Perspectives

It is always useful to analyze a business process from not only the perspective of the people who work with it, but from the perspective of those who manage its results. To illustrate this, I'll use an analogy set in a period of time about 200 years ago: a time in which most people did not have their own watch, but rather relied for their time keeping on the clocks on various buildings in the town.

In this particular town, there is a clock on the front of the town hall, one on the church, one on the library, and one on the theater. In addition to this, there are three people in this town who are concerned that these clocks function correctly — but all for very different reasons.

#### The Clock Maker

Firstly, there is the clock maker. He built the clocks and is responsible for their day-to-day running. No two clocks are exactly the same; some are powered by main springs that must be wound up, some by falling weights that must be reset, and one is even powered by water pressure from a reservoir. The clock maker knows every inch of their design; he calculated the number of teeth required on each cog, he worked out how to build the mechanism so that it was virtually friction free, and he even designed a metal pendulum that would remain the same length whatever the temperature. In short, he knows his clocks from the inside out.

### The Director of Public Services

Then there is the town's director of public services. Amongst his many responsibilities, he must ensure that all the clocks across the town tell the correct time. He knows certain clocks need to be wound up once every week and others once every two weeks. He even knows that the water level in the reservoir behind the Town Hall must be kept at the correct height, or the pressure will not be maintained and the town hall's water-powered clock will run slow. However, the director of public services has far too many other things to concern himself with than to worry about the internal workings of each clock. He knows enough to ensure that each clock keeps running, but beyond that, the internal details are not his concern.

### The Mayor

Finally, there is the town's mayor. He does not know that the town hall's clock is powered by water pressure fed from a reservoir behind the building; neither does he know that the church clock must be wound every two weeks or the theater clock every week. All he is concerned with is that all the clocks *tell the same time*. This is very important for him since he is the chairman of the town's Guild of Commerce, and the merchants of the town all regulate their business lives around the information provided by the town's clocks. Shops in the town are required to open for business at 9 a.m., close at 12:30 p.m for a one-hour lunch break, and close for the day at 5 p.m.

However, if the library clock says it's 9:00 a.m., the theater clock says 9:06 a.m., the church clock says 8:52 a.m., and the town hall clock says 8:31 a.m. (because the water level dropped), then there will be many disgruntled shopkeepers raising complaints at the next meeting of the Guild of Commerce because they are unable to coordinate their business activities correctly. This will make them dissatisfied with the town's business climate, and if the problem were allowed to continue, they would sell up and leave, thus impacting the town's economic welfare.

### The Moral of the Story

The town is like a large company. Each of the people mentioned here is connected in some way to the functioning of the town's clocks (one of the company's business processes), but each has a different concern for different reasons.

The clock maker is the business process expert. This person is intimately connected with all the day-to-day operational details of this particular business process and can be consulted when detailed information of that process' functionality is required.

The director of public services is the senior manager responsible for making sure that all the business processes of the company are running smoothly. He knows what goes into each business process and what should come out, but the details of how the raw materials are transformed into the finished goods are not something with which he need concern himself.

Finally the mayor is the chairman of the board. He is responsible for ensuring that the shareholders (the merchants who trade in the town) are satisfied with the town's business climate and continue to trade there.

When a business process is being implemented in Web Dynpro, always try to obtain as wide a number of perspectives as possible on the role of that business process in the company. This will help you see the big picture.

Like the clock maker, use the planning phase to try to remove as much friction as possible from the inner workings of the business process. Then, see the role this one business process plays together with the other business processes of the company. Finally (and this may not always be possible), see if the impact of the business process on the functioning of the entire company can be assessed.

Admittedly, not all Web Dynpro implementations are large enough to be felt at a corporate level, but for those that are, it is important to try to assess the impact at this level.

## 3.5    Design

Strictly speaking, the planning phase and the design phase cannot be isolated from each other. As the plans are being made, you will naturally begin to think of suitable designs that will allow the plans to be implemented. Similarly, your knowledge of Web Dynpro design will guide the planning in such a way that features will not be planned that cannot be implemented.

As there is significant overlap between the planning and design phases, you should always think of the planning phase as the point in time where you start to think in terms of Web Dynpro components. As has been said previously, the Web Dynpro component is your fundamental unit both of development and reuse; therefore, you should see your application functioning in terms of the interaction between different components. Typically, components are arranged hierarchically, and it is this topic that will be examined next.

### 3.5.1 Avoid Monolithic Coding Structures

This type of application is easy to build if you do not put sufficient effort into the planning and design phases. Often, developers who migrate to Java from procedural programming languages[15] such as C, PL/1, or COBOL like to just start coding and allow the overall design to grow organically. Unfortunately, the typical result of this approach is the creation of a large, amorphous lump of un-reusable code.

Even if you used a design technique such as Jackson Structured Programming, the object of the exercise there was to map input data structures to output data structures — not to create a unit of reusable coding.

The problems of low code reusability can also happen in Web Dynpro if you find yourself adding more and more functionality to a single component. This will result in the functionality going way beyond the scope of a single business task. This type of architecture generally results from ad hoc enhancements made by inexperienced developers — often having to perform to aggressive deadlines.

If you find you have arrived at this point, then you've got a fundamental design problem!

A component should not be allowed to grow to contain functionality beyond that which is required in a single business task.

### 3.5.2 Avoid Excessive Fragmentation

It is also possible to go to the opposite extreme and implement a component structure that is too granular or fragmented to be of any practical use. It has even been suggested that each Label/Input field pair of UI elements on the screen should be implemented as a distinct Web Dynpro component. This is nothing short of lunacy, because the complexity of intercomponent relationships rises exponentially as the number of components increases. In addition to this, the application's runtime performance would be very poor due to the system overheads required to instantiate so many tiny components.

The degree to which your application architecture is broken down into individual components should be controlled by the level of reuse required from each component. If you find that a single Web Dynpro component does not contain sufficient functionality to encapsulate a specific task,[16] then your component architecture has become too fragmented.

Remember that a Web Dynpro component should be designed to encapsulate an atomic unit of business processing.

---

15 Such as myself: Prior to learning Java, I spent 10 years writing PL/1, System 370 Assembler, CLIST, and R/2 ABAP programs.

16 Or in the case of a utility component, it is possible that it could encapsulate several distinct tasks.

### 3.5.3    Getting the Balance Right

When a Web Dynpro component has been built correctly, your granularity will be midway between two extremes (see Figure 3.13).

1. Too many small components:

   ▶ Result in a sea of components, which reduces maintainability.

   ▶ Maintenance becomes difficult due to complex interrelationships between components.

   ▶ Application performance will be reduced due to system overheads incurred by component instance management.

2. Right component granularity:

   ▶ Results in the best reusability, extensibility and maintainability.

   ▶ Results in the lowest maintenance costs.

   ▶ Allows distribution of work between several developers.

3. Oversized components:

   ▶ Result in poor reusability, extensibility, and maintainability.

   ▶ Result in increased cost of maintenance.

   ▶ Distribution of work between several developers is difficult, if not impossible.

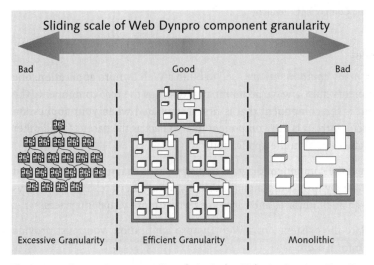

**Figure 3.13**  Correct Component Granularity Is the Midpoint Between Two Extremes

### 3.5.4    Component Hierarchy

As soon as we start to consider a component hierarchy, it becomes clear that the lowest-level components must have a high degree of reusability. In other words, the bottom of the hierarchy is populated by components that act as common utilities or simplify the interface to a backend system; as we move up the hierarchy, the degree of reusability drops as the specificity of functionality rises.

Often, a three-tier hierarchy is sufficient for meeting most business requirements. This is not a concrete rule and should not be taken as the only way a Web Dynpro application should be structured. However, this architecture will be suitable in many cases.

A three-tier architecture can be represented as shown in Figure 3.14.

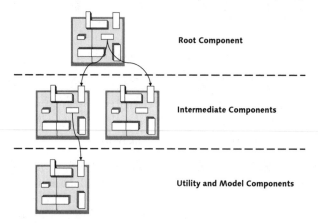

**Figure 3.14** A Basic Component Hierarchy

### Root Component

No matter how many components are used to build a Web Dynpro application, one of these components must always be nominated to act as the *root* component. The root component is the component that is first instantiated when your application starts, and consequently, it is this component that will act as the parent for all other component instances used in the application.

If you look back at the component diagram in the previous chapter (Figure 2.4), you can see that a Web Dynpro component has two types of interface. There is always a single programmatic interface, and there are zero or more visual interfaces.

When you declare the existence of a Web Dynpro application, you must provide three pieces of information:

▶ The name of the component that will act as the root component

▶ The name of the interface view controller that will provide the component's visual interface

▶ The name of the inbound navigation plug that will act as the entry point into the nominated interface view controller

Once you have done this, the NWDS will create a URL that can be issued from a client device to start the application (see Figure 3.15).

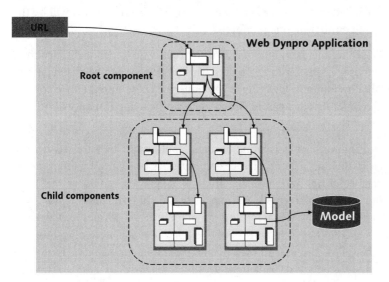

**Figure 3.15** The URL to Start an Application Always Points to the Root Component

Generally speaking, the root component will be designed to act as the UI container or *layout manager* for the intermediate components. Often this means the root component will not place its own UI elements on the screen, but rather, it will act as a manager controlling the presentation of the visual interfaces supplied by its various child components.

Another task performed by the root component is that of managing the lifecycle of the child component instances. In a large Web Dynpro application, you will have a higher degree of control over the child component instances if they are created manually. This means you must write some explicit coding that creates the instance of the child component and then destroys it when it is no longer required.

The principle here for component lifecycle management is this: instantiate late, destroy early. In other words, only create an instance of the child component when you actually need it, and then throw it away as soon as you know the application has no further use for it.

As far as reuse of the root component is concerned, you will probably never have a situation in which the root component can be reused as an individual component. This is because it is designed to act as a container and manager for the functionality found in other components. However, it is perfectly possible to reuse the entire component hierarchy starting from the root component. In this case you would be reusing the entire business process as delivered by the Web Dynpro application, rather than reusing any individual component used within the application.

**Intermediate Components**

The components shown immediately under the root component in Figure 3.15 can generally be referred to as *intermediate components*. These components will be the focus of most of your development effort.

The main role of intermediate components is to provide the functionality required for each atomic step of the business process. This will often involve making use of utility functionality found in lower-level components. These intermediate components form the building blocks from which your business application will be constructed.

Another area of importance is creating business applications that are sensitive to and can adapt to the user's locale. If your application is being run by users spread across different countries and speaking different languages, it is here that such adaptation should be implemented. This means that the intermediate components will adjust their visual interfaces according to a predefined set of rules for the user's particular locale. This factor is particularly important when designing business applications that allow the user to manipulate human resources–related information such as personal details or bank details.

For instance, human resource systems in the United Kingdom are required by law to record a person's ethnic origin as part of their personal details; however, in the United States such information must not be held. There is no reason to create two applications for each country; instead, you just write a single application that is sensitive to each country's requirements and switches the various fields on or off as appropriate. In this manner, each user only sees the fields relevant to their requirements, yet they are all served by a single Web Dynpro application.

Intermediate components would typically have a medium degree of reuse. This means that although reuse is not the primary focus of your attention, it should always be considered possible. An intermediate component will typically implement an atomic step in a business process; therefore, as long as this entire step (including the usage of all the child components) is reusable, then reuse will be feasible. However, it is unlikely that the intermediate component will be reusable outside of its location in the application's component hierarchy.

**Utility Components**

The lowest level of the hierarchy is where the utility coding is found. These components should all be designed with the highest possible degree of reuse, since the functionality they provide will be required across a large range of applications.

The purpose of a utility component is to encapsulate a specifically reusable unit of coding. A utility component can perform a wide variety of possible tasks, and consequently, you may encounter different names for this type of component. The following names have been used in various Web Dynpro blogs, documentation, and literature:

▶ Utility component

▶ Model component

▶ Data component

▶ Faceless component

These names all describe very similar types of Web Dynpro component.

A *utility component* performs routine tasks such as sorting the rows of a table. Typically, this task requires no interaction with the end user, and therefore the component can be "faceless" (see the paragraphs on the faceless component below).

A *Model* or *Data component* is very useful in situations in which the interface to a backend business process is complex. In a normal Web Dynpro application, a model is used to encapsulate the interface to a backend business process, and in doing so, hides the interface between the Web Dynpro application and the communication layer needed to access the backend system.[17]

However, the API into the business process itself may also be very complex. Should this be the case, it makes no sense to implement the same complex interface logic in each Web Dynpro component that uses the model. Instead, it is far better to wrap the interface to the model object in a Web Dynpro component that then provides a simplified interface. Such a component would be referred to as a model component.

Now, you could ask, "Is a model component a special type of Web Dynpro component?" No, it is just a regular Web Dynpro component that has been written to fulfill a specific purpose.

In an application setting, a model component would not only provide a simplified point of entry to the backend business process, but it would also provide a *single* point of entry. There is a technique within Web Dynpro coding known as *referencing mode* (see Section 3.6.2 for more information on this topic), which allows multiple parent components to share the same instance of a child component. Thus, if several components declare a usage of the same model component at design time, then by using referencing mode, at runtime they can all share the same *instance* of the child component. This guarantees that there will only ever be a single copy of the business data at runtime.

---

17  Currently supported communication layers are SOAP for Web Service calls, Remote Function Call (RFC) for ABAP function modules, and Remote Method Invocation (RMI) for Enterprise Java Beans.

> **Caveat Confector**
>
> Care must be exercised when using referencing mode because once multiple parent components share a reference to the same child component, it is technically possible for *any* one of those parents to destroy the instance of the child component. This can result in strange runtime errors if the lifecycle of the child component used in referencing mode is not managed very carefully.

A *faceless component* is any Web Dynpro component that makes no contribution to an application's visual interface. Any of the utility components mentioned above could be implemented in this manner; however, a word of clarification is needed here.

Notice I said that a faceless component makes no *contribution* to the application's visual interface. I did not say, however, that a faceless component has *no* visual interface. In reality, a faceless component will have no visual interface *that the end user would see*. This means your model component, for instance, would never present its visual interface when used as part of a business application, but this doesn't mean that it has zero visual interfaces.

If you have written a component that provides a simplified interface to a complex backend business process, then as part of the development process, you will need to perform unit testing. It is entirely possible, therefore, that you could give your faceless model component a visual interface that exists solely for the purposes of unit testing. The end users will never see this visual interface, because from a business perspective, it makes no sense to show it to them. However, its presence will mean you can test the model component as a stand-alone component.

In addition, an administrative interface may be required for the data manipulated by the model component. Therefore, you could create a second type of visual interface that provides a lower level of access to the business data. This interface would be used for administrative purposes only.

So a faceless component is simply a component that does not contribute to the application's overall visual interface but may have its own visual interface for testing or administrative purposes.

> **Caveat Confector**
>
> If you create a Web Dynpro component that genuinely has *no* visual interface, then it is impossible for it to be nominated as the root component in an application definition.

### 3.5.5 Using Model Components in the Component Hierarchy

If the interface to some backend functionality is particularly large or complex, then, as was stated in the previous section, that interface can be encapsulated within a model component. Furthermore, if your application uses multiple models, it is worth creating a DC in which you place *only* the model objects.

The benefit of having a DC that contains only models is that it will help speed up the development process. Models tend to be large and require a longer amount of time to compile. Also, models tend not to change very often; therefore, you do not want to have to compile them unless they have actually changed.

If you therefore place all your models into a single DC,[18] that DC need only be compiled once and then referenced by other DCs that contain the actual Web Dynpro components.

Alternatively, if you keep all the models inside the same DC that holds the Web Dynpro components, then every time a component needs to be recompiled, the models will also be unnecessarily recompiled. In some cases, this can cause a significant delay to the development process.

Within the model component DC shown in Figure 3.16, a Web Dynpro component has been created that acts as an interface to actual business functionality, so methods are present in its programmatic interface (the interface controller) that form the model component's API.

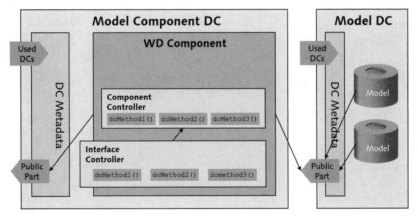

**Figure 3.16** A Model Component DC provides a Simplified API to a Large or Complex Backend Business Process

Look closely at the structure of the Web Dynpro model component in Figure 3.16. What is missing?

No visual interface has been defined. This is how a faceless component is structured. However, even if the component does not need to make any contribution to the application's visual interface, there is no reason for the model component not to have a visual interface defined for administrative or testing purposes (see Figure 3.17).

---

18  Of course, not forgetting to add the models to a Public Part.

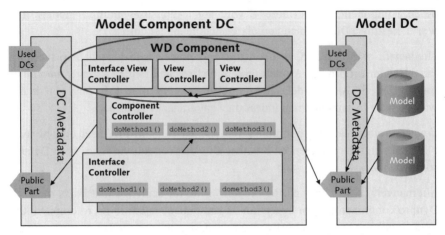

**Figure 3.17** A Model Component DC May Not Need to Contribute to the Application's Visual Interface, but It Can Still Have a Visual Interface for Testing and Administrative Purposes

Figure 3.18 shows the structure of three related DCs. The DC on the left contains the business logic, the DC in the middle contains the model component, and the DC on the right acts as a container for all the model objects used by the application.

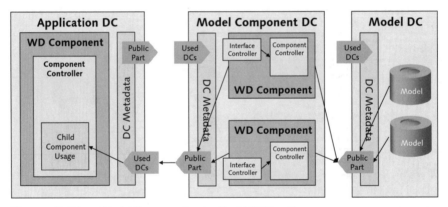

**Figure 3.18** Using a Model Component and a Model DC Together

### 3.5.6 Component Interface Definitions

The relationship between a parent component and its child components has been described as one of *tight coupling*. This means the parent component is tightly coupled to not only the child component's interface, but also to its particular implementation.

This can become a restriction if you want to swap out one child component implementation for another.

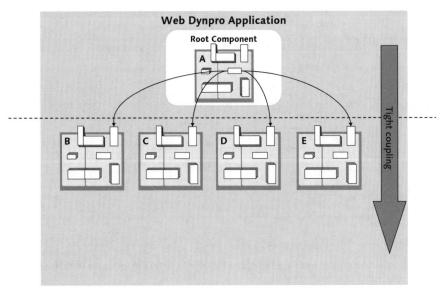

**Figure 3.19** Tight Coupling Between a Parent Component and the Specific Implementation Found in Each Child Component

In Figure 3.19, if we wanted to swap out component B and replace it with a different component, we would have to delete the root component's usage of component B and then create a usage declaration for the new component. In other words, you have to change the structure of the root component when nothing here actually needs to change. As long as the interfaces of component B and the new component are the same, why should we need to change anything in the parent component?

When one component declares a design time usage of another component, an instance of the child component will be declared to exist having a certain name. This instance name is then referred to in the coding. So you have actually created a reference to more than just the child component's interface; you have created a reference to the implementation within that child component.

What is needed here is a means of detaching a child component's interface from its implementation. Then you need only create a usage of the interface, without caring how the functionality behind the interface is implemented. This is exactly the purpose of a component interface definition.

In Figure 3.20, component B has been removed, and in its place is a component interface definition (CID). The purpose of a CID is to define a component interface. In a CID you may declare:

▶ The Programmatic Interface

  ▶ Interface controller methods

  ▶ Interface controller context structure

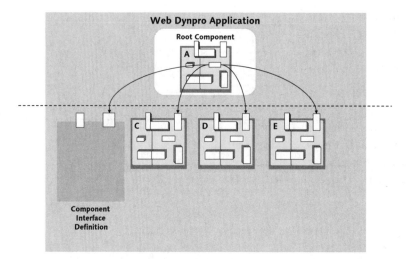

**Figure 3.20** A Component Interface Definition Detaches a Child Component's Interface from Any Specific Functional Implementation

- ▸ The Visual Interface
  - ▸ Windows
  - ▸ Interface view controller inbound and outbound navigation plugs
- ▸ Model Usages

The root component A then simply declares a usage of the CID and knows only about the interface. The actual implementation behind the interface is not known to the root component.

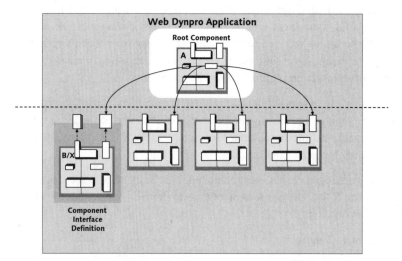

**Figure 3.21** A Component Interface Definition Detaches a Child Component's Interface from Any Specific Functional Implementation

Now component B (or X or any other component, for that matter) can be declared to implement the CID. Thus, it immediately takes on the interface definition found in the CID. Now when the root component calls a method in the CID, it is really calling the method in the component that implements the CID.

When the root component comes to create an instance of the child component, it is actually creating an instance of any component that implements the relevant CID. This concept can be extended so that the root component picks up the name of the child component to be instantiated from a configuration file. In this manner, the behavior of the overall application can be controlled by means of configuration, and child component instances swapped in and out as required at runtime.

> **Caveat Confector**
>
> In the current implementation of a Web Dynpro CID, the component that implements the CID does not *inherit* the interface in a true object-oriented manner. Instead, the interface definition in the CID is used as a template and copied into the various interface controllers found in the consuming component.
>
> Therefore, if you change the CID *after* it has been copied into some other component, those changes will not appear in the consuming component. They must be transferred manually.

### 3.5.7 Configuration Requirements

Often, it is worthwhile to create your Web Dynpro applications in such a way that their behavior can be modified by reading configuration values at start-up time. This configuration information could be stored in various places, including:

- Local .properties files on the AS Java
- Values held in a backend SAP system
- URL parameters

This type of configuration is particularly useful if you have implemented your business functionality through CIDs because you can swap in or out various specific components simply by getting the root component to read the name of the component it is to instantiate from the configuration settings.

Where you choose to locate the configuration information for your Web Dynpro applications depends entirely on how you choose to administer your applications. If the management of your system landscape has a strong Java focus, it would make sense to keep your Web Dynpro application configuration in .properties files. These files can then be administered through the SAP Java Visual Administrator tool.

If, on the other hand, the management of your system landscape is oriented toward SAP systems, it would probably be easier to hold your configuration information in tables in the SAP database and then have your Web Dynpro application call an ABAP function module to return the required values.

There is no particularly correct way of doing this; rather, you should implement a system that is easy to manage and fits your existing style of system management (assuming you already have such a thing).

### 3.5.8 Localization Requirements

If your Web Dynpro applications are going to be executed by different users in different countries, it will probably be necessary to build locale sensitivity into their functionality. This means that when a user starts the application, they will be presented with screens that are already configured according to their regional requirements. This means you should be sensitive to such things as:

▶ The current legislation in the user's country for the presentation of certain data fields.

For instance, if your application deals with the display of personnel information, in some countries you are legally required to hide the field holding an individual's ethnic origin, yet in other countries you are legally required to display it.

▶ The user's language requirements.

It is quite possible to create a Web Dynpro application that will operate in multiple languages. The only consideration here that makes the job easier is that you should plan for such functionality from the start of your development.

You should always decide upon a master development language for all your Web Dynpro development components. You should then perform unit testing and integration testing of your functionality in the chosen development language before ever considering starting the translation phase of development.

Generally speaking, you should try to delay the translation phase of a project to the last possible time. If you find you need to make functional changes (particularly to the user interface) to your application after you have performed the translation, you may find it a rather error-prone task of having to remember to include the change in all the translated versions of the application.

▶ For situations in which you need to support both Western languages with a left to right text direction, and Middle and Far Eastern languages with a right to left text direction, it is definitely beneficial to create specific UI components for each language type. These UI components would then implement a CID (see Section 3.5.5) to allow the parent component to swap the specific child component at runtime according to the user's locale setting.

▶ If you want to create a more advanced form of locale sensitivity, it is possible (again using the CID discussed above) to create interchangeable UI components that implement completely customized user interface layouts. This is necessary when users in different countries need to see not only their own set of fields, but also their own specific field layout.

▶ Don't forget that if you place text in an image, that image has immediately become language specific and will need to be translated.

### 3.5.9 Location of Business Processing

One of the most fundamental design considerations is that of planning and building an efficient communication interface between your UI application layer and your backend business processing layer.

One of Web Dynpro's key strengths is that it provides such a communication interface layer for you within its Framework. The Web Dynpro Framework allows you to communicate with any backend business system that implements either the SOAP (*Simple Object Access Protocol* or, more recently, *Service-Oriented Architecture Protocol*) or RFC protocols or for Java-to-Java-based communication, Remote Method Invocation.

The Web Dynpro Framework wraps these different communication protocols inside its own interface layer known as the Common Model Interface. Therefore, as far as a Web Dynpro application is concerned, all business objects look the same irrespective of the underlying communication technology required to access the particular back end business system.

#### Interfacing to an Existing Business API

If the Web Dynpro application you are writing is going to interface to an existing business API, it is important to establish how the different screens shown to the user will correlate with the existing API calls to the backend system.

▶ Does your screen arrangement map neatly onto calls to the backend system, or will you have to make use of model components to simplify the interface?

▶ Does the functionality in the backend system implement the concept of transactional processing, or is each call to the backend business API expected to perform a single, self-contained unit of processing? In other words, is your connection to the backend system stateful or stateless?

#### Interfacing with a Custom-Written Business API

Custom business APIs are most often seen when a Web Dynpro application is being written to interface with an SAP system. Often, the customer will want to write their own set of remote callable function modules in ABAP that are then called from the Web Dynpro UI layer.

There are several important points to watch out for here:

▶ Are the ABAP developers aware of the principles of RFC programming in ABAP? All too often, the answer here is unfortunately "no." In my experience, many ABAP developers have forgotten that certain coding techniques must be followed for ABAP-based transactional processing to be successful over an RFC connection.

These techniques are both well known and well documented in the ABAP literature.

▶ Is the ABAP development happening in parallel with the Web Dynpro development? If it is, this can cause a frustrating problem for the Web Dynpro developers.

When an ABAP function module needs to be called from Web Dynpro, the Web Dynpro developer should first create a model. This is a collection of different proxy objects, which taken together, represent the interface to one or more ABAP function modules. Models contain metadata. In other words, they contain information that describes how the Java world and the ABAP world can communicate with each other.

Let's says the Web Dynpro developer has created a model and has started working with the objects it contains. Now the ABAP developer decides that some extra piece of functionality is required or that some bug needs to be fixed and he then changes the structure of the function module's interface.

This will have an effect on the coding created by the Web Dynpro developer. If the change to the function module's interface is small — say a couple of new columns added to a table — then the impact will not be very large. However, if new table structures are added, or even worse, deleted, this will have a significant impact on the Web Dynpro application and the amount of rework needed to make the Web Dynpro program function with the new interface structure.

Therefore, if possible, try to write and test the ABAP function modules before building the Web Dynpro interface. Of course, real life has a bad habit here of messing up the ideal scenario, but if possible, aim for this sequence of events.

▶ Have the ABAP function modules been written with efficiency in mind?

As described earlier, some horrible performance problems can be introduced simply by not paying careful attention to the way database tables are being read in ABAP.

Since the distinction between ABAP coding being called from Java and regular Java-based Web Dynpro coding are completely invisible to the end user, they will perceive all performance problems to be directly related to the Web Dynpro application.

## 3.6    Implementation

Various topics need to be understood when implementing your business process using Web Dynpro components. Let's now take a look at some of the most important topics in this area.

### 3.6.1    Management of Child Component Instances

Parent components, and particularly the root component, are responsible for the management of the child component instances. There are two ways of doing this. Either the child component instance can be created automatically by the Web Dynpro Framework, or it can be created manually by writing explicit coding. The two options are:

▶ `onDemand`

This is the default setting and will probably be sufficient if your application's component architecture is simple. Here, the Web Dynpro Framework will create child component instances for you only when the child instance is actually referenced — either by a direct method call or by making use of its visual interface.

▶ `manual`

For most Web Dynpro applications of moderate or high complexity, it is recommended to use the "manual" lifecycle management setting. This is because you are then in control of exactly when a child component instance is created and destroyed.

The principle to follow here is "instantiate late, destroy early." In other words, the child component instance should persist only for as long as it actually required.

### 3.6.2    Intercomponent Communication

When you have a Web Dynpro application of any complexity, you will find that intercomponent communication becomes an essential part of the design. Several factors must be addressed here:

▶ In which hierarchical direction do you want to communicate?

  ▶ Parent to child (downward)

  ▶ Child to parent (upward)

▶ Do you need to give multiple components access to the same data?

▶ Is the shared data used only for data processing, or does it need to be displayed on the screen?

**Downward Communication**

In a normal object hierarchy, the type of relationship that exists between a parent and a child object is known as a tight coupling. This means the parent object (in this case a Web Dynpro component) has a detailed knowledge of its child's interface and functionality. Therefore, the relationship between the parent and its children is said to be tightly coupled.

If a parent component needs to access the data and methods held in one of its child components, then two main options are available: context mapping[19] and direct method calls.

Context mapping is a technique that allows data held within one Web Dynpro controller to be accessible to another controller. Context mapping can be set up in such a way that a chain of mapping references is created.

Figure 3.22 shows that as a result of context mapping, data originating in the component controller of component B is now directly available in the component controller of component A (the root component). Here, a chain of mapping relationships has been created from the child's component controller to the parent's component controller via the child's interface controller.

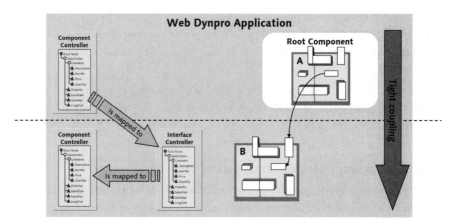

**Figure 3.22** Communication Down a Component Hierarchy Using Context Mapping

A direct method call is where functionality in the parent component can directly call a method in the interface controller of a child component as illustrated in Figure 3.23.

---

19  The details of context mapping are described in Section 5.12.

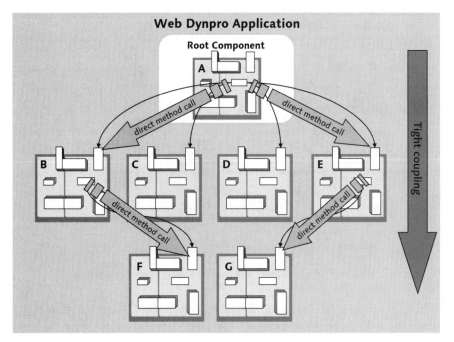

**Figure 3.23** Communication Down a Component Hierarchy Using Direct Method Calls

### Upwards Communication

In an object hierarchy, it is normal for a child component to have little or no knowledge about the functionality held within its parent. This is because when you write a child component, you have no idea of the identity of the parent component. Therefore, no assumptions can (or should) be made about what functionality will or will not be present.

Thus, if a child component needs to communicate with its parent, it must do so in a way that does not require the child to have any knowledge of the parent's identity. This is known as a loose coupling relationship.

Therefore, not knowing anything about the identity or functionality of its parent, the child component can only raise an event and leave it up to the parent component to respond to the event. This is shown in Figure 3.24.

### Giving Multiple Components Access to the Same Component Instance

Let's say you have a situation in which two components in your hierarchy both declare a usage of the same model component. It would be inefficient and risky to allow two instances of the same model component to exist at runtime. The risk comes from the fact that these two instances may end up holding different versions of your business data that ought only to exist as a single copy.

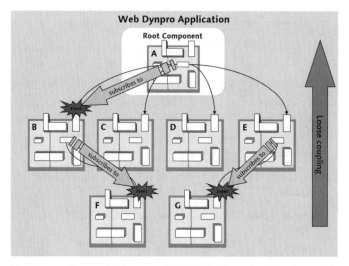

**Figure 3.24** Communication up a Component Hierarchy Using Event Subscription

Therefore, you can use a technique for child component instance creation called *referencing mode*. With this technique, two parent components can share the same instance of a child component at runtime.

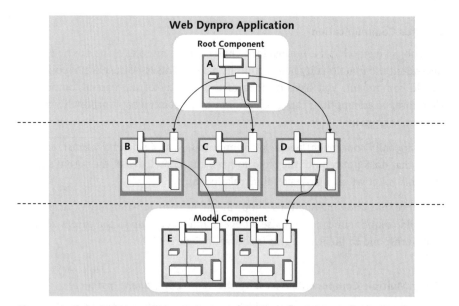

**Figure 3.25** Try to Avoid Having Two Instances of the Same Model Component at Runtime

In Figure 3.25, components B and D have both declared a usage of the model component E. Unless you code your application *very* carefully, you could end up with two versions of your business data in each of the instances of component E.

The way to avoid this problem is to alter the hierarchy somewhat. The reason for this is that components B and D are siblings; therefore, for a correct reuse strategy to be implemented, you would not want to write component B in such a way that it needs detailed knowledge of the functionality of one of its siblings.[20] For these two components to be properly reusable, they should not need to know anything about each other's need to use an instance of the model component E. Therefore, we will adjust the component hierarchy so that the root component also declares a usage of the model component E. The root component will now be responsible for managing the lifecycle of the model component.

In making this adjustment, we will not alter the fact that components B and D still maintain a design time declaration of model component E. All we are changing is how the instance of the model component is created and then referenced by components B and D.

Figure 3.26 shows the situation in which the root component creates an instance of the model component. The reference to the child instance will then be passed to the child components by calling a method in their respective interface controllers.

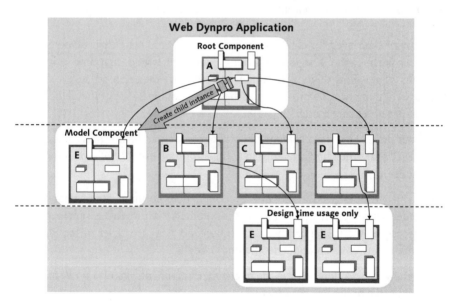

**Figure 3.26** Use the Root Component to Manage the Lifecycle of the Model Component

In the next step of the process, as shown in Figure 3.27, the root component calls a purpose built method in the interface controller of each child component and passes in a reference to the instance of the model component it has just created.

---

20  This is because there is no guarantee that two sibling components will be reused together in a different application scenario.

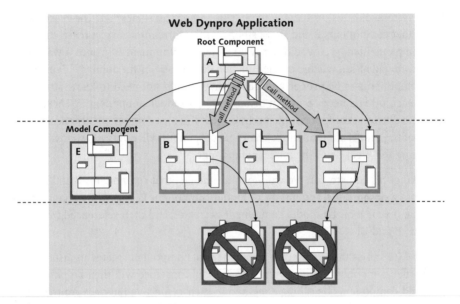

**Figure 3.27** Pass Reference to Child Components

Now, there is no need for child components B and D to create their own personal instances of the model component (even though their own design time usage declarations would allow them to do so). Instead, they use the reference received from the root component and with it, create their own child instance of the model component in referencing mode.

Once this process has been completed the root component A and child components B and D all share the same reference to a single runtime instance of the model component E.

From a business perspective, the root component does nothing with its reference to the model component instance. The root component is acting first as a manager for the lifecycle of the model component, and second as a dispatcher of the instance reference to any child components that may need it.

Figure 3.28 shows referencing mode in action. Components B and D now share the same reference to model component E.

---

**Caveat Confector**

You must write your coding carefully when using child component instances in referencing mode. Look back at the diagram in Figure 3.28. Components A, B, and D all share a common reference to the model component E. So, which component is able to destroy the shared instance of the model component? A, B, or D?

The answer is *any of them!*

---

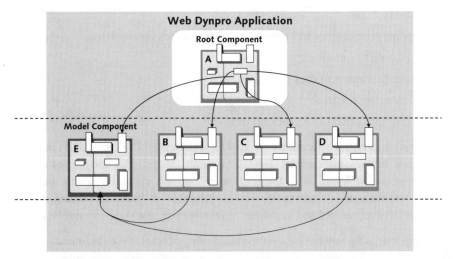

**Figure 3.28** Finished State of the Model Component Used in Referencing Mode

This is where you must be very careful not to write code in either components B or D that would destroy the instance of the model component E.

Technically, it is possible for any of the components acting as the parent of the model component to destroy the instance. However, you should write your coding so that the root component performs the lifecycle management of the model component and then notifies the child components (B and D) that it has either been instantiated or destroyed.

You can check to see if a child component instance is being used in referencing mode by calling the method `isReferencing()`.

### 3.6.3    Internal Data Storage Within Web Dynpro Components

In certain circumstances it is beneficial to take an alternative approach to data storage within a Web Dynpro controller. The typical situation is one in which you have a highly variable number of fields to display on the screen. At design time it is not possible to state which fields will, or will not, be present; therefore, you would want to avoid creating a massive context structure in which you declare the existence of every possible field, *just in case* it may be required at runtime.

**Use of the Context**

Normally, the hierarchical data storage area within each Web Dynpro controller (known as the context) is a perfectly acceptable location in which to store all the information required at runtime. There are many advantages to using the context because it provides:

▶ Developer convenience

▶ A type-safe collection for data

- A typed API into the type-safe collection[21]
- Mapping relationships to nodes in contexts of other controllers
- Typed access to model objects
- Automatic transfer of data from the:
  - Context to the UI during screen rendering
  - UI to the context after a round trip

However, in certain circumstances it may be more efficient to create and maintain your own business data object. Do not interpret this recommendation as saying that there are problems with the context or that it is somehow inefficient, but rather that there are circumstances in which the various features provided by the context are not required and as a point of efficiency should therefore not be used.

It is important that you have a clear understanding of what these circumstances are so you do not implement the following recommendations inappropriately. The main situations in which you should consider using a custom-written Java Bean as a light-weight alternative to the context are when:

- You have a large component hierarchy in which many components must share access to the same information.
- Binding a model object to a context node would result in a very large context structure being created, but due to the nature of the business data being processed, only a few fields would be needed, and the context structure would therefore be only sparsely populated.

In such situations, it is possible that if context mapping were used as the mechanism for transporting data created in a model component up to the root the component, then a long chain of mapping relationships[22] could be become awkward or complex to manage. In this situation, it may be simpler to create your model component in such a way that it generates a light-weight Java Bean. This is then passed up to the parent component(s).

The only time you are actually required to use the context is within a UI component, that is, within a component that is responsible for putting data on the screen. In this type of component you would need to unload the custom Java Bean into the context for the view controllers to supply data to their respective UI elements.

---

**Caveat Confector**

The recommendation to use your own Java Bean instead of the context will only be needed in the minority of design situations.

---

21  The generation of the typed context API can be switched off if required, but usually this is not necessary.

22  By "long chain of mapping relationships," we mean having to map context structures in such a way that the data passes through more than four components.

**Store or Calculate?**

Within each node in a Web Dynpro context, it is possible to decide that a particular attribute value be calculated rather than stored. This means that every time that attribute value is read from the context, the getter method will perform a small calculation to derive the value instead of returning a fixed, stored value.

These calculated attributes are very useful when a basic formatting process is required to prepare the data for display. For instance, if a salutation needs to be created from a form of address (Mr., Dr., Prof., etc.), a first name, and a last name, there is no need to duplicate these three values into a fourth formatted context attribute. Instead you can simply created a `Salutation` attribute and define that it is a calculated attribute. You then need to write some functionality into the getter method that formats the values into the required text string. This calculated value can then be presented on the screen to the user without any need to duplicate the information.

### 3.6.4 Centralized Functionality

In situations in which you will have a large user population, there will probably be cases in which the same data is required for all users of a particular Web Dynpro application. If you are implementing an application to be used by many users spread across multiple countries, it would be good to remove from the Web Dynpro application those areas of functionality that can be centralized. A good example is language-specific help and message text strings.

Let's say you have a user population of many thousands (e.g., >10,000), and each user will want to execute three or four key Web Dynpro applications, all of which provide the user with help text in their own language. Let's further assume that the help and message text will be stored in a backend SAP system.

In this situation, you would not want each individual Web Dynpro application to be responsible for retrieving and then storing such information, because at runtime, this would result in many copies of the same data being held across all the runtime instances of those Web Dynpro applications.

Therefore, you could consider writing a standard Java service that would act as a text engine. It would service incoming requests for text strings by first looking in its internal cache to see if the text has already been supplied, and if it is not found, retrieving it from the backend SAP system. Such a service has the key advantage of simplifying the Web Dynpro application's functionality because each component does not need to implement its own text retrieval logic.

It will also have the benefit that requests for text will only arrive at the backend system from a single Java application, rather than multiple requests for the same text from each individual application.

### 3.6.5    Correct Use of Standard Hook Methods

It is very important that you understand the purpose of each of the standard hook methods found in Web Dynpro controllers. These methods are the points of access from the Web Dynpro Framework into your coding, so no matter what business functionality you want to implement, the Web Dynpro Framework is able to execute your application.

You are not permitted to alter the signature of a standard hook method, for if you did, you would break the interface between the Web Dynpro Framework and your component.

There are two main categories of hook method:

▶ **Lifecycle hook methods**
These methods are only ever called once during the controller's existence.

▶ **Round-trip hook methods**
These methods are called every time there is a round trip from the client to the server.

What follows here is a basic description of the hook methods. A much fuller explanation will be given in the next chapter when the Phase Model is described.

**Lifecycle Hook Methods**

Three hook methods are involved in the lifecycle of a Web Dynpro controller. These are:

▶ `wdDoInit()`
This method behaves as a Web Dynpro controller's constructor. It is run once and only once at the start of the controller's lifecycle.

▶ `wdDoExit()`
This method behaves as a Web Dynpro controller's destructor. It is called once and only once at the end of a controller's lifecycle.

▶ `wdDoApplicationStateChange()`
This method is called when an entire Web Dynpro application is having its state changed. There are three different circumstances under which this method can be called:

 ▷ The application has issued a suspend request.
 The purpose of this state change is to allow part of your business processing to be performed by a non–Web Dynpro application. For instance, in a business-to-business purchasing scenario, you may want to fill your shopping basket with items from an external website and then have these brought back into your Web Dynpro application. This requires that your Web Dyn-

pro application be temporarily suspended whilst the external catalog website is being used.

When this state change is entered, you can elect either to do nothing and have the Web Dynpro Framework save the application's state for you or to write your own state persistence coding.

If you let the Web Dynpro Framework save the application's state, it will only remain suspended for a predefined time-out period, after which the suspended application will be terminated.

▶ The Web Dynpro Framework has received a resume request.
This request from an external website is received in the form of a URL and carries with it the identity of the suspended application. The Web Dynpro Framework will then resume the application for you.

▶ The application has exceeded its time-out limit and is about to be terminated.
If a Web Dynpro application remains inactive for longer than its time-out period permits, the Web Dynpro Framework will immediately call the wdDoApplicationStateChange() method with a state change reason of TIME-OUT. No round trip to the client will take place, and the user will receive an error message when he next attempts to perform a server round trip.
The purpose of this method is to allow you to implement some coding that can preserve the business data within the application before it is terminated. In this case, you would need to write coding that persists the application's context data to a backend database. The only difference here is that you cannot notify the user that the timeout has occurred until they next perform a round trip.

**Round-Trip Hook Methods**

A variety of round trip hook methods will be called every time there is a round trip from the client to the server. Different Web Dynpro controllers have different round-trip hook methods, so the list that follows is simply a list of all the round-trip hook methods that are used across all controllers.

▶ wdDoBeforeNavigation()
This method only exists in a component controller and is executed immediately before the requests on the navigation queue are processed. This method should be considered the final step of the input side of round-trip processing.

▶ wdDoModifyView()
This method only exists in a view controller and is called for each view in the

current view assembly.[23] Within this method is the only place at which you have direct access to the UI element objects themselves.

▶ `wdDoPostProcessing()`
This method only exists in a component controller and is called right at the end of round-trip processing. It is the last time at which application coding can execute.

It is essential that you have a good understanding of how your application is executed by the Web Dynpro Framework.

The standard hook methods act as the points of interface between the Framework and your application. Therefore, the next topic we will look at is the Web Dynpro Phase Model.

Once you understand this you will have a much better understanding of how your Web Dynpro application should be structured.

---

23  The view assembly is the name given to the set of views that make up the rendered screen for the current round trip.

# 4    Web Dynpro Phase Model

Every time a round trip occurs from the client to the Web Dynpro server, a hard-coded sequence of processing steps is executed. The Web Dynpro Framework is responsible for (amongst other things) managing this sequence of processing steps.

This sequence is known as the *Phase Model*, and the part of the Web Dynpro Framework that manages it is known as the *Phase Handler*.

No matter how many components are instantiated within your Web Dynpro application, the different steps of the Phase Model operate on all the components in the object hierarchy (if applicable) in a strict top-to-bottom order.

The processing steps within the Phase Model are arranged in a hard-coded sequence that cannot be modified by the application developer. Each step is processed no more than once, and after it has completed, it cannot be repeated during the same round trip. If an error situation is detected, certain Phase Model steps will be bypassed because their processing is inappropriate until the error has been corrected.

It may seem rather strange to be diving into such a technical, background topic at this early stage in the book, but as you will soon see, having a solid understanding of the Web Dynpro Phase Model is one of the key elements in understanding how to build high-quality Web Dynpro applications. Therefore, to get the best results from Web Dynpro, it is vitally important that you understand the processing performed in each step of the Phase Model, for these steps together form the processing engine that will drive your business application.

All through the subsequent chapters, frequent reference will be made back to this chapter to show you how the current topic fits into the big picture of Web Dynpro processing.

This chapter deals with the individual steps of Phase Model processing shown in Figure 4.1. Each step of the Phase Model is responsible for a distinct stage of round-trip processing. These steps include:

- Transporting the data from the client-specific request into the client-neutral format used by the Phase Handler
- Handling any high-priority requests such as logoff or abort
- Handling the processing request sent from the user
- Calculating which views should be included in the next screen

▶ Constructing and rendering the next screen

▶ Returning the response to the user

There are certain steps in this processing sequence that are outside the developer's control, and there are other steps where the Web Dynpro Framework hands control over to your application to perform its business processing.

Take another look at the section called Standard Hook Methods in Chapter 2. Remember we said the standard hook methods were the static interface between the Web Dynpro Framework and your application. Well, it's during the different stages of Phase Model processing that these hook methods will be called.

Essentially, Phase Model processing describes the interface between the Web Dynpro Framework and your business application. Understand this area, and you'll be able to write very efficient Web Dynpro applications. On the flip side, many poor-quality implementations are due to the developers having no clue about the function of the standard hook methods. Consequently, they implemented clever workarounds that serve no other purpose other than to add redundant complexity to the application.

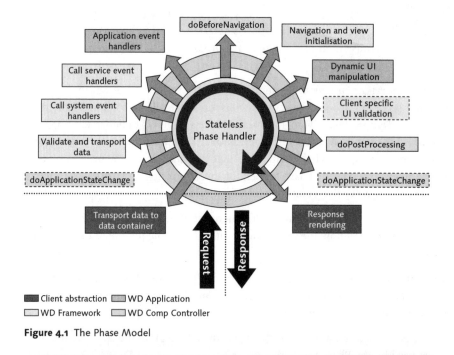

**Figure 4.1** The Phase Model

| Important |
| --- |
| The structure of the Phase Model shown above applies to releases of Web Dynpro from SAP NetWeaver 7.0 (formerly known as SAP NetWeaver 2004s) Service Pack 6 or higher. Prior to the release of SP6, the doApplicationStateChange step did not exist. |

## 4.1 Phase Model Processing and Component Instantiation

Is the Phase Model responsible for all aspects of Web Dynpro processing?
No.

When you call a Web Dynpro application for the first time, the component name specified in the application definition (known as the root component) must first be instantiated. The Web Dynpro Framework then examines the component hierarchy defined in the root component[1] and instantiates all child components using the following algorithm:

1. Is the lifecycle parameter is set to `createOnDemand`?
2. If yes, instantiate such components only when they are referenced:

   ▸ Explicitly via a method call to their interface controller

   ▸ Implicitly by having their visual interface embedded within the UI.

This logic is a continuation of the *lazy data access* principle seen throughout Web Dynpro architecture. If you don't need something, don't create it!

The component initialization step for the root component takes place outside the scope of the Phase Model. This means that any coding you place in either of the lifecycle methods `wdDoInit()` or `wdDoExit()` could be executed outside the Phase Model processing described below.

## 4.2 Web Dynpro Hook Methods

Within a Web Dynpro controller you will find various default methods known collectively as hook methods. These methods are created automatically and cannot be modified or deleted. All these methods start with `wd` and act as the interface between the Web Dynpro Framework and your application.

Different controllers within a Web Dynpro component have different hook methods, but two hook methods are common to all controllers. These are the lifecycle hook methods mentioned above: `wdDoInit()` and `wdDoExit()`.

These methods should be considered the controller's constructor and destructor, respectively. The following table shows which hook methods will be found in which controller and whether they are responsible for lifecycle or round-trip processing.

---

1  This hierarchy is defined by adding "Used Web Dynpro Component" references to the root component.

| | Controller Type | | | | Hook Method Type |
|---|---|---|---|---|---|
| **Hook Method Name** | **Comp** | **View** | **Custom** | **Interface** | |
| `wdDoInit()` | ✓ | ✓ | ✓ | ✓ | Lifecycle |
| `wdDoExit()` | ✓ | ✓ | ✓ | ✓ | Lifecycle |
| `wdDoBeforeNavigation()` | ✓ | | | | Round trip |
| `wdDoApplicationStateChange()` | ✓ | | | | Round trip |
| `wdDoPostProcessing()` | ✓ | | | | Round trip |
| `wdDoModifyView()` | | ✓ | | | Round trip |

**Table 4.1** Framework Hook Methods

The interface view controller is not listed in Table 4.1 because although it has the normal methods you would expect to find in a view controller (`wdDoInit()`, `wdDoExit()`, and `wdDoModifyView()`), they are not accessible to the application developer.

By the time the Phase Model processing described below has been entered, the `wdDoInit()` method of at least the root component will already have been processed.

## 4.3 The Relationship Between Phase Model Processing and Web Dynpro Windows

The visual interface of a Web Dynpro component is implemented through the interface view controller. This controller is responsible for the presentation of the root component's view assembly and therefore represents the rendered screen seen by the user.[2]

There is a one-to-one relationship between the rendered screen and an instance of the Phase Model. This means that no matter how many child components contribute their interface views toward the root component's visual interface, all processing required to handle one round trip from the client will be performed by a single instance of the Phase Model.

If, however, you create a modal pop-up window, then by definition, you have created a new window that will persist for multiple round trips before being closed.

---

2  Or if a Web Dynpro application is being run within an iView in the Enterprise Portal, the interface view of the root component represents only the contents of the HTML `<DIV>` within which the Web Dynpro iView is contained.

Therefore, for as long as the modal window remains opens, the round trips it initiates will be processed by a *separate* instance of the Phase Model.

## 4.4 Phase Model Processing

Referring to Figure 4.1, the incoming request from the client arrives at the bottom of the diagram along the arrow marked Request. Processing then proceeds in a clockwise direction, with each step being processed no more than once. If an error situation is detected, certain steps will be bypassed because the error situation will render their processing inappropriate.

### 4.4.1 Transport Data to Data Container

Since Web Dynpro is designed to be client independent, there needs to be an abstraction layer to convert the protocol-specific data received from the client into a neutral format that can be handled by the Web Dynpro Framework. This is the purpose of the `Transport Data to Data Container` step.

### 4.4.2 doApplicationStateChange: The Floating Step — Part 1

The `doApplicationStateChange` step is called a floating step because the point in time at which it is called can vary depending on the type of request that is received. From Service Pack 6 of SAP NetWeaver 7.0 onward, it has been possible to suspend and then resume a Web Dynpro application. This means that as a result of issuing a suspend request, you can place a Web Dynpro application in a dormant state and leave it there until a corresponding resume request is received.

An example of such a business scenario is a catalog-based purchasing application. The user is able to purchase items from various catalogues, some of which are local to the server running the Web Dynpro application and others of which are external. Any time the user wants to fill his shopping basket with items from an external catalog, the Web Dynpro application should be suspended because it is not known how long the user will take to complete this process.

**Resume Request**

To handle both normal round-trip requests and resume requests, it is necessary to check which type of request has been received. If it is a resume request, special coding may need to be executed to restore the application to its correct state before processing can continue.

After the data from the incoming request has been moved into the client-neutral data container, the next step is to determine which type of request initiated this round trip. As shown in Figure 4.2, if the incoming request is a normal round-trip from a client, the doApplicationStateChange step is not required and is bypassed; otherwise, this step will be entered.

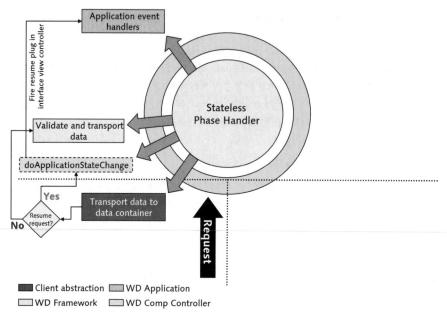

**Figure 4.2** doApplicationStateChange

The purpose of the doApplicationStateChange step is to give developers the opportunity to execute any special coding they might require when the application is resumed. For more details of how the suspend and resume functionality works, please see Section 11.2

Remember that if a resume request has been received, we are resuming an application that has previously been suspended. The resume processing works by first calling the method doApplicationStateChange. After this, the inbound plug of type resume belonging to the application's interface view controller is fired, and processing jumps immediately to the Application Event Handlers step.

**Timeout**

If an application has remained inactive for longer than its time-out period allows, the Web Dynpro Framework will immediately invoke the doApplicationState-Change method of the root component.

The state change reason will be set to WDApplicationStateChangeReason.TIMEOUT, and you then have the opportunity to preserve the data within your application by writing it to a backend database. After this, the Web Dynpro Framework forcibly shuts the application down.

---

**Important**

The type of processing you can perform here is limited for two main reasons:

1. **You have no any ability to interact with the user.**
   By the time the user next interacts with his browser, all he will see is the time-out error message. However, when he restarts the application, you can elect to build in functionality to the start-up process that checks the backend database for data belonging to timed-out sessions, and if applicable to your business process, this data can then be restored.

2. **You can only preserve context data.**
   It is not possible to preserve (or even identify) the current view assembly state. In other words, you cannot know which combination of views was used to display the screen last seen by the user. Therefore, if you attempt to restore timed-out data when the application restarts, it must be able to handle this data without knowing exactly which views were being displayed when the timeout occurred.

---

### 4.4.3 Validate and Transport Data

If we have received a normal round-trip request, the request originated from an existing Web Dynpro client screen as opposed to a resume request received from some external web page that is returning to Web Dynpro. All data received from the client is now copied back into the contexts of all view controllers within the current view assembly. All data modified by the user is transported in a type-safe manner.

All data derived from the UI layer is validated at this time. This validation is performed by the Java Dictionary layer that underlies the Web Dynpro Framework. If any errors are detected, a validation error will *always* be generated. Whether or not the Web Dynpro application reacts to the error depends on whether the round trip was invoked by a *validating* or *nonvalidating* action.

For a UI element to invoke a round trip, an action must be associated with at least one of the UI element's events.[3] If the action is defined to be a validating action (this is the default), by definition, we have stated that before any further processing can take place, all data received from the UI *must* be valid. If, therefore, an error is detected, the user is forced to correct the error before any subsequent processing can proceed. In Figure 4.3, you can see that if an error occurs during a validating round trip, all the steps of the Phase Model related to business processing are bypassed. In this case, processing jumps directly to the step in which the screen is rendered, the error messages are added to the screen, and the round trip finishes.

---

3 Certain UI elements such as Tables are capable of triggering a round trip without the direct association of an action with a UI element event.

However, if the action is defined to be nonvalidating, you've said that you really don't care whether the data received from the user is valid or not. The Java Dictionary will still report that an error has occurred, but the Web Dynpro Framework will ignore the error, and the associated application event handler method will be called as normal.

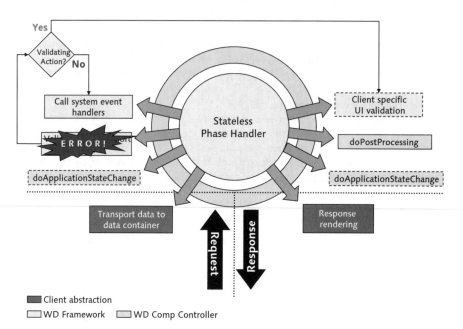

**Figure 4.3** Error Processing During the Validate and Transport Data Step

| Important |
| --- |

Care should be taken when you have a mixture of validating and nonvalidating UI elements associated with the UI elements on your view assembly. Consider the following situation in which we have three UI elements on the screen:

▶ **An input field**
This is bound to a context attribute that in turn is defined by a dictionary simple type. The dictionary simple type is of type `integer` and has maximum and minimum inclusive values of 999 and 0, respectively.

▶ **A table UI element that displays some data from a context node**
The table's `onLeadSelect` event has *not* been associated with an action. This means that clicking on a table row will still cause a round trip as long as the table UI element's `selectionMode` parameter has not been set to `none`.

▶ **A button**
This is associated with a validating action in the normal way.

Using only these UI elements, there are now two ways to initiate a server round trip:

1. The user clicks on the button. In this case the server-side action event handler associated with the button's `onAction` event is called.

2. The user selects a row of the table UI element. As long as the table UI element's `selectionMode` property has not been set to `none`, and even though the `onLeadSelect` event is not associated with an action, a server round trip will still take place.

Let's now say that a value of 1,000 is entered into the input field — clearly violating the maximum inclusive constraint defined by the dictionary simple type. The dictionary will always report that a validation error has occurred, but whether the `Validate and transport data` step of the Phase Model terminates with an error depends on how the round trip was triggered.

If the user clicked on the button (whose `onAction` event is associated with a validating action), the dictionary will report that the data is invalid, the Web Dynpro Framework will terminate the Phase Model step with an error condition, and the button's action event handler method will *not* be processed.

If, however, the table row selection is changed, a server round trip will be initiated, the validation check for the input field will still fail, but the Web Dynpro Framework will ignore the error because the action that caused the round trip (in this case, an empty server round trip) is a nonvalidating action.

Whenever you define an action to be nonvalidating, you're saying you don't care whether the data on the screen is junk or not — you're not interested in it anyway!

### 4.4.4 Call System Event Handlers

This step is reserved for future use. In the SAP NetWeaver '04 and SAP NetWeaver 7.0 versions of Web Dynpro, no processing is performed here.

### 4.4.5 Call Service Event Handlers

Before any application event handlers are called, certain service event handlers should be processed if required. Service event handlers are events raised by the Web Dynpro UI layer itself and are considered to have a higher processing priority than events raised by the business application displayed in the UI layer (see Figure 4.4).

| Important |
| --- |
| All Web Dynpro service events are considered to be nonvalidating because their functionality *must* be processed regardless of whether the data on the screen is valid or not. |

Service events are completely invisible to application developers. Nevertheless, if the service event invokes functionality that causes a supply function to be called, you will have a situation in which your application coding is being run without having been called via an action event handler. Consequently, the way you write the error handling part of a supply function becomes critical. In this case, if a supply function encounters any type of error, there is no application coding to which the error can be reported back.

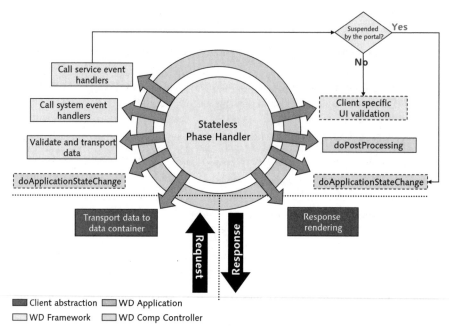

Client abstraction ▢ WD Application
WD Framework ▢ WD Comp Controller

**Figure 4.4** Call Service Event Handlers

Consequently, the supply function must handle and contain the error gracefully, since any unhandled exceptions raised by supply functions will cause the entire Web Dynpro application to terminate with a stack trace. See Chapter 11 for more information on error handling.

In the SAP NetWeaver '04 and SAP NetWeaver 7.0 versions of Web Dynpro, the following service event handlers are defined:

▶ `unload`
If the Web Dynpro application is running stand alone (i.e., outside the SAP NetWeaver Portal) and the user enters a new URL or closes the browser, an `unload` service event is raised. This is the trigger for the Web Dynpro Framework to terminate the active application. Consequently, the `wdDoExit()` hook methods will be called for all controllers in all active components in the current application. The Web Dynpro Framework always calls hook methods using a top-down traversal mechanism, starting with the root component.

▶ `logoff`
The `logoff` event is raised when a user logs off the SAP NetWeaver Portal. All Web Dynpro applications currently active on the user's screen receive this `logoff` event. The Web Dynpro Framework then handles the termination of all Web Dynpro applications in exactly the same way as for the `unload` event.

▶ `abort`

The `abort` event is much like the `logoff` event shown above, except that it is triggered by the user entering a different URL in the browser address line or by closing the browser. In this case, the user has not formally logged off the portal. The Web Dynpro Framework then handles the termination of all Web Dynpro applications in exactly the same way as for the `unload` event.

▶ `valueHelp`

A request is made for a `valueHelp` modal pop-up. This event causes the Web Dynpro Framework to invoke the functionality of an Object Value Selector.

▶ `suspend`

This is a special event raised only by the SAP NetWeaver Portal and must not be confused with a suspend request originating from within a Web Dynpro application!

Portal iViews can be defined as *suspendable*. If the SAP NetWeaver Portal raises a `suspend` event for a Web Dynpro iView, the Web Dynpro Framework treats it as a service event. It is very important to understand that under this circumstance, a Web Dynpro outbound plug of type `suspend` in the root component's interface view controller is *not* fired, and processing jumps directly to the `doApplicationStateChange` hook method with a state change reason of SUSPEND.

---

**Caveat Confector**

Do not confuse a `suspend` event received from the SAP NetWeaver Portal with the firing of a Web Dynpro outbound plug of type `suspend`. These are two different types of suspend events and are processed in slightly different ways.

Any attempt to call a Web Dynpro outbound plug of type `suspend` after receiving an SAP NetWeaver Portal event of type `suspend` will result in the Web Dynpro Framework throwing a runtime exception!

---

### 4.4.6    Application Event Handlers

By the time the Phase Model processing arrives at this step, we know that all the data in all controller contexts is valid and that no service events have been raised. This is when your business application processing can begin. The business application processing is initiated by the Web Dynpro Framework calling the event handler method associated with the event that triggered the round trip.

Once a user has raised a client-side event that causes a round trip, the associated `onAction${ui evt}()` method will be called (where `${ui evt}` is the name of the UI element event). Once you enter an `onAction${ui evt}()` method, you can call any number of other methods to achieve the required business processing.

Since an `onAction${ui evt}()` method belongs to a view controller, certain coding principles should be followed so that your application architecture does not violate the principles of good MVC design. The biggest mistake people make here is to embed business application processing directly into the action handler method itself. Technically, this will work, but it is very poor architecture. Remember, a view controller is not responsible for generating the data it displays. It simply receives the input from the user, checks that it is valid, and passes the request for business processing (i.e., the generation of data) over to a non-visual controller.

### 4.4.7 doBeforeNavigation

The doBeforeNavigation step of the Phase Model is the last time at which any application processing related to *user input* can be processed. This step marks the boundary between the input and output sides of the Phase Model processing. Everything that happens up to (and including) the doBeforeNavigation step relates to processing the user's input received from the client. Once this step has been passed, the Phase Model has entered the output half of its processing. The only processing that should take place after the doBeforeNavigation step has completed are those tasks necessary for construction of the new screen.

For large Web Dynpro applications, the consistency of user data often cannot be determined simply by examining the data in the context of a single controller, or even the data in all the controllers of a single component. The complexity of a Web Dynpro application could be such that to decide whether navigation should occur, it is necessary to check the validity of the data across multiple components.

The doBeforeNavigation step is the hook method (implemented by the root component) that provides you with the opportunity to perform these wide-ranging data validity checks. On the basis of these validity checks, you can then decide which navigation plugs should be fired.

This step of the Phase Model corresponds directly to the wdDoBeforeNavigation() method found in a component controller.

It is important to understand that when the Web Dynpro Framework calls any standard round trip hook method such as wdDoBeforeNavigation(), it does so by first calling the method in the root component. Once this method has completed its processing, the same hook methods are called in all subordinate components as the Web Dynpro Framework works its way down the component hierarchy.

**Caveat Confector**

The exact order in which the Web Dynpro Framework calls the hook methods in different child components cannot be predicted, and no assumptions should be made about any processing sequence other than to say that the root component's hook method will always be called first.

The above caveat has a very important consequence on the way you should write your error processing code. If you want to centralize all error processing within your application, it must be performed in the root component. Consequently, all child components must report any errors up to the root component *before* the doBeforeNavigation Phase Model step is entered. This has a knock-on effect for how navigation plugs should be fired in a large Web Dynpro application. See Chapter 11 for more details on how to manage cross-component error handling and navigation.

### 4.4.8 Navigation and View Initialization

Any time an outbound plug is fired, all you have done is place a request for navigation onto the navigation queue, and any further navigation processing is delayed until this step is reached. Each outbound plug in the navigation queue will have at least one corresponding inbound plug belonging to another view (unless, of course, the outbound plug is of type exit or suspend).

The Web Dynpro Framework now processes each request for navigation in the queue by calling the corresponding inbound plug(s).

The basic logic used to process the navigation queue is described by the flow chart in Figure 4.5.

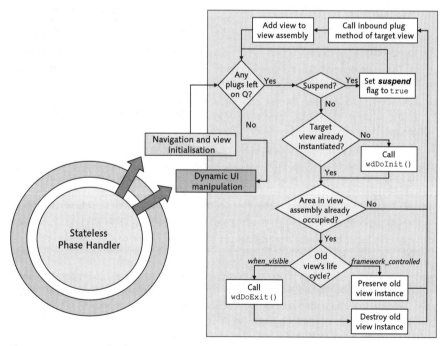

**Figure 4.5** Logic Involved in Basic Navigation Processing

153

**Caveat Confector**

The flow chart in Figure 4.5 shows only the basic logic used in view-to-view navigation processing because the page is not large enough show the entire flow of logic. In others words, it only covers situations in which you are navigating from one view to another within the scope of a single component. However, three processing situations are not illustrated:

1. If the view assembly is being rendered for the first time, the navigation queue will be empty. However, the Web Dynpro Framework will ensure that all views with their `default` flag set to `true` will be rendered. This is how the first screen of a Web Dynpro application can be constructed without the need for explicit navigation events.

2. If an inbound plug method immediately fires an outbound plug, then, as with calls to outbound plugs that occur during action event handler processing, calls to outbound plugs that occur as a result of inbound plug processing will sit on a nested or second generation navigation queue. The second generation navigation queue will be processed only after all the outbound plugs on the first generation queue have been completed. This means that not only will the Navigation and View Initialization step of the Phase Model handle inbound plug processing, but it will handle a nested level of navigation processing as follows:

   ▶ An outbound navigation plug is fired by an action event handler.

   ▶ The request for navigation is placed into the navigation queue.

   ▶ Once the Navigation and View Initialization step of the Phase Model is reached, the inbound plug methods associated with the outbound plugs in the navigation queue are called.

   ▶ If an inbound plug method immediately calls another outbound plug, this request is placed into a second generation navigation queue.

   ▶ All processing of inbound plug methods belonging to first generation navigation requests is completed.

   ▶ The second generation navigation queue now becomes the first generation navigation queue, and navigation processing is completed as normal.

   Whilst this style of coding is technically possible, it should be avoided because it will lead to the creation of very complex navigation paths that become difficult to debug and enhance.[4]

3. If an outbound plug is associated with an inbound plug belonging to the interface view of child component, it is possible that a whole set of subordinate view controllers will have to be processed to supply the visual interface of that child component. In other words, an outbound plug could point to a single view, or it could point to the entire visual interface of a child component — which, in turn, will contain its own navigation processing and references to views and possibly other child components ...

Now do you see why the flow chart only covers the basic view-to-view navigation scenario?

**Caveat Confector**

It is very important to understand that if an error occurs within an inbound plug method, navigation processing *cannot* be suppressed. Once processing of the navigation queue starts, it cannot be stopped half way due to some error condition.

---

4 Just because something is technically possible, does not make it a good idea.

Therefore, all inbound plug methods must run to completion, handling any errors that occur gracefully. Navigation must continue as well as possible, and you should build a facility into your destination views such that they can report any errors that might occur as a result of navigation processing.

### 4.4.9 Dynamic UI Manipulation

Referring back to the flow chart in Figure 4.5, you can see that once all the requests for navigation have been processed, the Web Dynpro Framework moves on to the Dynamic UI Manipulation step of the Phase Model. So we know that by the time we enter this step, all the views in the current view assembly have had both their wdDoInit() methods called (if necessary) and had their inbound plug processing completed. What remains now is for the view controller (if necessary) to manipulate the UI elements in its UI Tree so that the correct information is displayed on the screen. This is the purpose of this Phase Model step, and it corresponds directly to the wdDoModifyView() method found in all view controllers.

The type of processing performed in this method is typically concerned with the creation of UI elements (if the firstTime parameter is set to true).

Notice what type of processing should *not* be performed here. As already stated in Chapters 2 and 3, a view controller is not responsible for generating the data it displays. Consequently, a view controller's wdDoModifyView() method should *only* contain such coding as is necessary to manipulate the UI elements — *not* the coding needed to generate the data displayed by the UI elements!

You should not need to write any coding that alters the business data found in the view controller's context. Or at least if you do, there is a very good chance that you are not following the principles of good MVC design. Consequently, your application will be harder to maintain and enhance because the business logic has been placed within controllers in which it does not belong.

Certain types of processing should not be included in this Phase Model step:

▶ **Do not attempt to call an outbound plug.**
Why are you trying to perform navigation when navigation queue processing has already been completed?

▶ **Do not attempt to report error messages using the MessageManager.**
Normally, the only error messages that could be reported at this time are those related to the actual construction of the UI hierarchy. All the data from which the UI element hierarchy is being constructed should already be present in the context.

▶ **Do not attempt to alter the business data in the context.**
Are you still trying to perform business logic in a view controller? Why are you trying to write to the context at a point in the Phase Model when all business processing should have been completed?

All business processing should have been completed by the time the doBefore-Navigation step is finished. This is considered bad style because it leads to increased maintenance times due to the business logic being performed in places that violate the principles of good MVC design.

Its bad enough to perform business logic in a view controller, but then to put that business logic in the wdDoModifyView() method of a view controller is *really* bad style. Don't do it!

▶ **Do not create static references to UI element objects that you then attempt to reference outside the scope of wdDoModifyView().**
If you are trying to do this, it usually demonstrates that you have not understood the concept of data binding. Business information is not stored in the UI element object itself. Data always lives in the context, and UI element properties are then bound to the context.

Remember the data generator–consumer concept?

The context acts as the data generator (or supplier), and the UI element property acts as the consumer. These two are associated with each other using data binding. See Chapter 8 for more details on data binding.

It is possible that attempts to modify the context during execution of the wdDoModifyView() method could lead to unpredictable results. For instance, if accessing a context node causes a supply function to be called, this could generate data that earlier business processing steps were unaware of. This in turn could lead to unpredictable or even erroneous results.

### 4.4.10 Client Specific UI Validation

This step of the Phase Model is new for SAP NetWeaver 7.0 versions of Web Dynpro. It was added to avoid any supply functions being called during the last step of the Phase Model, called *Response Rendering* (see Figure 4.1). Notice that the Response Rendering step occurs below the horizontal dotted line. This indicates that the step belongs to the Client Abstraction Layer of the Web Dynpro Framework. If a supply function were to encounter an error at this time, it would be absolutely impossible for that error to be reported back to the application coding for some appropriate action to be taken. Prior to the addition of this Phase Model step, the Web Dynpro Framework used to terminate Web Dynpro applications with a stack trace if they encountered an error in a supply function that was called during screen rendering.

To avoid this problem, an extra step has been added that actually renders the output for the entire screen. In doing so, it forces all supply functions involved in providing data to the UI to execute. The rendered output is then cached for reuse in the Response Rendering step.

If an error should occur during the execution of a supply function, there are coding procedures you can follow so that the error can be reported back to the user. See Chapter 11 for more information on error handling.

If the incoming request to the Web Dynpro Framework came from an HTML-based client, then to reduce the volume of HTML sent to the client, only the data that is actually visible is rendered. You may see this step referred to in the documentation as "Validate by rendering"; internally, however, this step is known as `Retrieve-Data`.

For non-HTML clients, it is possible that the entire UI tree will be rendered and sent to the client — irrespective of whether the data is visible.

Each client device has its own rendering procedure, and it is not possible to generalize about exactly how the output will be rendered. Suffice it to say that this step forces all supply functions involved in providing data to the UI to be executed.

> **Important**
>
> This is the last point in the Phase Model at which a supply function should execute.

### 4.4.11 doPostProcessing

The `doPostProcessing` step corresponds directly to the method `wdDoPostProcessing()` found in a component controller and is the last time at which application coding can be executed.

The purpose of this step is to provide a time at which errors from supply functions can be handled. Since supply functions are called only when the data they provide is explicitly required, the exact step of the Phase Model in which they will execute cannot generally be predicted. However, we know that the previous Client Specific UI Validation step will have forced all supply functions involved in providing data to the UI to execute. Therefore, any supply functions errors can be reported at this point.

The typical manner in which supply function errors are handled is to write the error information to some dedicated context node, and then in `wdDoPostProcessing()`, the content of the error node is examined and messages issued to the UI as appropriate.

Since reporting error messages to the UI involves calling the `MessageManager`, this action modifies the screen that was rendered in the previous Client Specific UI Validation step. By calling the `MessageManager` in the `wdPostProcessing()` method, you cause the previously generated output to become invalid. In this situation, the Response Rendering phase will need to rerender the output. Therefore, SAP recommends that you only report serious or fatal errors during the execution of the `wdDoPostProcessing()` method.

As with the wdDoModifyView() method, if you find yourself coding functionality that writes business data to the context, there is a good chance that you are violating the principles of good MVC design!

### 4.4.12 doApplicationStateChange: The Floating Step – Part 2

This is the other time at which the doApplicationStateChange() method can be called. All that is required for this method to be entered at this time is that the Web Dynpro Framework's suspend flag has been set to true. This flag is switched on whenever an outbound plug of type suspend is fired.[5] Refer back to the flow chart in Figure 4.5 for more details.

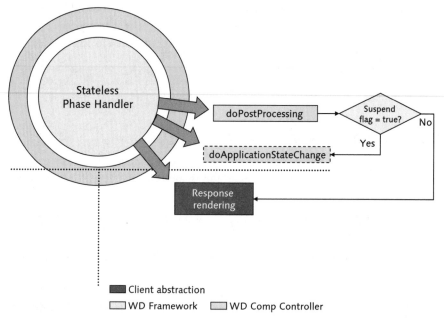

**Figure 4.6** doApplicationStateChange

When this method is entered due to a suspend request being issued, two courses of action are available to you:

1. **Do nothing and let the Web Dynpro Framework handle all the suspend processing for you.**
   The application will remain suspended until the time-out period has expired. The length of the time-out period is set either on a per-application basis or globally for all Web Dynpro applications running on that particular SAP NetWeaver AS Java node.

---

5 Remember that outbound plugs of type suspend are only found in interface view controllers. You will not find this plug type in a regular view controller.

The length of time that the application may remain suspended is limited by the configuration of the various time-out parameters. See Section 11.2 for more details on suspend and resume processing.

2. **Write your own suspend processing.**
   This is for the limited number of cases in which you can restart the application using only the data held in the context. Since you cannot preserve or even identify the state of the current view assembly, your application must be able to restart without knowing from which views the business data was derived. Whether this is possible in practice will depend entirely on both the nature of your business process and your applications's screen flow.

   Bear in mind that if you use this technique for suspending the Web Dynpro application, you are entirely responsible for writing your own coding to retrieve the application's state when the corresponding resume request is received.

### 4.4.13  Response Rendering

This is the client abstraction step that converts the internal, client-neutral data container back into the format appropriate for the specific client device that initiated the current round trip. As stated earlier, the output for the entire screen has already been rendered by the Client Specific UI Validation step of the Phase Model, and as long as the MessageManager has not been called, the output generated from this step is simply passed back to the client without requiring any additional processing.

If, however, the MessageManager was called during the doPostProcessing step, then the previously rendered output will be invalid (because it does not contain the error message[s]) and must therefore be rerendered.

Application developers have no access to the processing contained within this step of the Phase Model.

The final step is to return the output using whatever protocol is appropriate for the client device.

## 4.5  Summary

The steps of the Phase Model are processed by the Web Dynpro Framework during every round trip from the client to the server. No matter how many components exist in your component hierarchy, the Phase Model steps will be performed sequentially on all components in a top-to-bottom manner.

Now that you are familiar with the runtime environment provided by the Web Dynpro Framework, we can now look at how to build a Web Dynpro application that will functional efficiently inside this framework.

# PART III
## Basic Development

# 5   The Context at Design Time

Every controller has exactly one hierarchical data storage structure known as a context.[1] The data held in the context exists only for the lifespan of the controller. Once the controller has been terminated, all data held within its context is lost.

The structure (i.e., the metadata) of a context is typically defined at design time; however, at runtime, it is possible not only to modify the contents of the context, but also to modify its structure.

A context is a hierarchical arrangement of entities known as *nodes* and *attributes*. In simple terms, the difference between a node and an attribute is that a node may have children and an attribute may not.

All context hierarchies start with a special node known as the root node. The root node is created automatically when the controller is initialized, and its properties are immutable.

> **Important**
>
> Any attempt to modify the properties of the context root node will result in the context throwing an exception and the user being shown a Java stack trace.

## 5.1   Nodes

Context nodes are arranged hierarchically and are permitted to have children. The children of a node may be entities known as attributes or other nodes.

A context node is an object whose primary function is to hold a collection.

"A collection of what?" you might ask. A collection of whatever attributes and nodes have been declared as its children. This definition means that a node holds a type-safe collection, where the data type of each element in the collection is defined by its set of child nodes and attributes.

For readers with an ABAP background, a context node can be thought of as behaving very much like an internal table. Each attribute defined in the node becomes a column of the table, and each child node becomes another table nested within a single cell of the table. Each element in the node collection is then a row of the table.

---

1   Every controller, that is, except an interface view controller.

For the sake of brevity, context nodes will be generically identified with the variable ${cn}, and if this node has another node as one of its children, the child node will be referred to with the variable name ${chn}.

## 5.2 Attributes

An attribute is an entity in the context which can have any data type you care to define. An attribute is *always* the child of some other context node (be it the context root node or some other node), and it is *not* permitted to have children.[2]

We will refer to a generic context attribute using the variable name ${ca}.

## 5.3 Node and Attribute Data Types

In the SAP NetWeaver 7.0 (formerly SAP NetWeaver 2004s) version of Web Dynpro, a distinction is made between nodes that inherit their metadata from a model object and nodes that do not.[3]

Any context node that is bound to a model object immediately inherits the model object's metadata. Thus, the structure of the model object is reflected in the structure of the node. Such a node is known as a model node and has a blue icon in the NWDS. This is shown in Figure 5.1. The node is called MaintainAddress and has 11 attributes. Since this is a model node, each of the attributes has been derived from the model object's metadata to which the node has been bound.

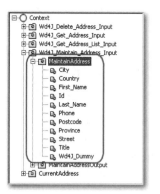

**Figure 5.1** A Context Model Node

---

2  This means that a context attribute may not have dependent objects that Web Dynpro Framework recognizes as subordinate. However, it is possible to have some Java Bean class defining an attribute's data type. Just don't expect the context to be able to interpret its internal structure.

3  From SAP NetWeaver 7.1 and onward, this distinction is removed.

In Figure 5.2, you can see the Properties View of the model node selected in Figure 5.1. There is a set of properties under the heading **Model**, one of which is the property `modelClass`. This is the class from which the selected model node will obtain its structure. The `structure` property shown Figure 5.2 holds the model class's package name.

| Properties | | |
|---|---|---|
| **Property** | **Value** | |
| **⊟ Misc** | | |
| cardinality | 0..1 | |
| collectionType | list | |
| initializeLeadSelection | true | |
| name | MaintainAddress | |
| selection | 0..1 | |
| singleton | true | |
| supplyFunction | | |
| technicalDocumentation | | |
| typedAccessRequired | true | |
| **⊟ Model** | | |
| modelClass | AddressModel.Wd4J_Address | |
| structure | com.sap.training.ja312.rfcmodels.models.address.types.Wd4J_Address | |
| supplyingRelationRole | Address | |

Tasks | Properties | DTR Console | J2EE Engine | General User Output

**Figure 5.2** Properties of a Model Node

Alternatively, if you want to define the data structure of the node yourself, you can create your own attributes and child nodes. Such a node is known as a *value node* (see Figure 5.3) and is identified in the NWDS with a red icon.

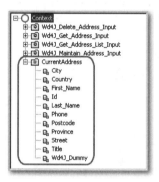

**Figure 5.3** A Context Value Node

It is important that you understand what each of the value node's properties control, because if you don't, the node will behave in an unexpected manner at runtime.

In the example shown in Figure 5.4, you can see that there is an entry in this node's structure property. The value of this property is a class name found in the Java Dictionary. So rather than creating each node attribute individually, it is possible to define a structure in the dictionary and then use this as the data type for the node. This is known as structure binding.

| Properties | | |
|---|---|---|
| Property | Value | |
| cardinality | 1..1 | |
| collectionType | list | |
| initializeLeadSelection | true | |
| name | CurrentAddress | |
| selection | 0..1 | |
| singleton | true | |
| structure | com.sap.training.ja312.rfcmodels.models.address.types.Wd4J_Address | |
| supplyFunction | | |
| technicalDocumentation | | |
| typedAccessRequired | true | |

Tasks | Properties | DTR Console | J2EE Engine | General User Output

**Figure 5.4** Properties of a Value Node

> **Important**
>
> If you use structure binding to define a node, you are not permitted to extend the node's structure. If you wish to add a new field to a context node bound to a Java Dictionary structure, you must modify the dictionary structure.

If, however, you do not want to create a dictionary structure to define the node, you can simply add the attributes manually (in which case, the node's structure property will remain blank). An example of a manually created node is shown in Figure 5.5.

**Figure 5.5** A Manually Created Value Node

The properties of the SalesOrders node are shown in Figure 5.6. Notice that the **structure** field is empty.

| Properties | | |
|---|---|---|
| Property | Value | |
| cardinality | 0..n | |
| collectionType | list | |
| initializeLeadSelection | true | |
| name | SalesOrders | |
| selection | 0..1 | |
| singleton | true | |
| structure | | |
| supplyFunction | | |
| technicalDocumentation | | |
| typedAccessRequired | true | |

Tasks | Properties | DTR Console | J2EE Engine | General User Output

**Figure 5.6** Properties of a Manually Created Value Node

Although it makes little sense to do so, it is possible to define a node that has zero children; however, in reality, you will always create a node to have some combination of attributes or other nodes as children. The set of children declared for any node defines the data type of the node's type-safe collection mentioned above.

## 5.4 Context Attribute Data Types that Can Supply Data to UI Elements

Table 5.1 lists the data types that must be used if the attribute is going to supply data to a UI element. These data types are built into the Web Dynpro Dictionary and are all defined in the package `com.sap.dictionary`.

| Built-In Type | Is a Primitive? | Java Class Equivalent |
|---|---|---|
| Binary | Yes | byte[ ] |
| Boolean | Yes | Boolean |
| Date | | java.sql.Date[4] |
| Decimal | | java.math.BigDecimal |
| Double | Yes | Double |
| Float | Yes | Float |
| Integer | Yes | Int |
| Long | Yes | Long |
| Short | Yes | Short |
| String | | java.lang.String |
| Time | | java.sql.Time |
| Timestamp | | java.sql.Timestamp |

**Table 5.1** Built-In Web Dynpro Dictionary Data Types

**Important**

Only a few UI elements can be bound to binary context attributes; these include Office-Control, FileDownload, and FileUpload. Other UI elements, such as TextField and InputField, cannot be bound to binary context attributes because there is no general way to parse or format binary data.

---

4  Notice that this is not the java.util.Date class. The default data format used by Web Dynpro is derived from the format used by ABAP within an SAP system. This is based on the YYYY/MM/DD format. In Java, this translates to a java.sql.Date.

It is perfectly acceptable to create a context attribute of type `java.lang.String`; however, you will not be able to use this attribute as a data source for a UI element. This is because, although the classes `java.lang.String` and `com.sap.diction-ary.string` are functionally equivalent, they are not compatible when it comes to screen rendering.

The Server-Side Rendering part of the Client Abstraction Layer within the Web Dynpro Framework (see Figure 2.2) does not know how to render any string data types other than the ones defined in `com.sap.dictionary`. You are welcome to create an attribute of type `java.lang.String`, but don't expect to be able to bind it to a UI element.

Context attributes that will not be used to supply data to a UI element may be of any available Java class.

## 5.5 Terminology Concerning Nodes and Attributes

At this point, it is worth mentioning a point of terminology to do with the general way in which nodes are named.

All nodes and attributes that have the root node as their immediate parent are referred to as being *independent,* and all nodes and attributes that have some other node as their immediate parent are referred to as being *dependent* (see Figure 5.7).

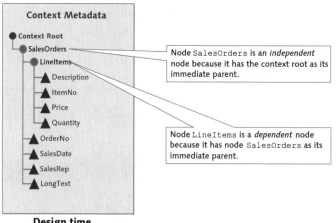

**Figure 5.7** Independent and Dependent Context Nodes

These names may seem rather arbitrary and academic, but there is good reason for making the distinction: Because the properties of the context root node are immutable, the nodes and attributes immediately underneath it have certain restrictions placed upon them.

This naming convention can be best understood to describe the node's existence at runtime. A node described as "independent" is called this because its existence is independent of any action your code performs at runtime. In other words, for nodes that have the root node as their immediate parent, it is always safe to assume that such a node instance will exist without any programmatic action being required.

As you might expect, therefore, a dependent node is one whose existence is dependent upon programmatic actions taken at runtime. So an instance of such a node may or may not exist. It all depends and what coding you have written.

Independent attributes are attributes that belong to the collection maintained in the root node. Since the root node's properties are immutable, it immediately means you will have one and only one instance of an independent attribute at runtime. This is because the root node's collection is limited to contain a single element (more about this later).

From a coding style point of view, it is considered better to place all attributes within a node of your own definition, rather than creating attributes with the context root as their immediate parent.

## 5.6 What's the Difference Between Value Nodes and Model Nodes?

As described in Section 5.3, there are two types of node in a Web Dynpro context. The basic differences between these two node types relate to the location of the node's metadata and the nature of the information held in the node at runtime.

### 5.6.1 Value Nodes

**Metadata Location**

A value node is a node in which all the metadata is stored within the node itself or is obtained from a local Java Dictionary object. The attributes of value nodes can be added manually as required and do not have to be present in any predefined data structure.

If you know that a certain combination of fields will be used frequently across the different contexts in your application, then rather than repeating the structure declaration for each value node in each controller context, it is more efficient first to create a dictionary structure and then use structure binding to define the node's metadata. A value node that uses structure binding may not have any further child *attributes* added to it, but you may add further child *nodes* (which may use structure binding if desired).

> **Important**
>
> An unmapped value node maintains its own element collection, with each element in the collection holding the actual runtime data.

### The Nature of the Data in a Value Node

Very simply, the data held in a value node is just that — data. There is no additional functionality associated with that information: it's just plain data.

## 5.6.2 Model Nodes

### Metadata Location

A model node is designed to give a model object the same API as a value node. Therefore, the metadata used to define a model node's structure is not defined by the developer or derived from a Java Dictionary structure; rather, it is obtained from a model object.

Model objects, in turn, are created by the Model Import Wizard and act as proxy objects for functionality held in a backend system.

### The Nature of the Data in a Model Node

The most important difference to understand between a value node and a model node is that the model node's collection is designed to hold references to model objects. In turn, model objects are proxies for accessing functionality in some backend system. Therefore, in addition to the business data held in a model object, there is also the functionality to access the backend system.

Thus, when creating elements in a model node, do not simply create element objects and populate them with data as you would a value node, because whilst the model node will store that information, it will be completely unrelated to the functionality in the backend system required to process it.

See Chapter 6 for the coding needed to operate with model nodes.

> **Important**
>
> A model object holds business data *plus the ability to invoke functionality in a backend system*. Value nodes, on the other hand, simply hold data that can only be processed when your coding performs some operation on it.
>
> In other words, don't use model nodes as if they were value nodes.

### Binding Context Model Nodes to Model Objects

*Model binding* is the name given to the association between a model node and a model object. Once a model node has been bound to a model object, the data in the model can be accessed through the standard context API. This effectively makes a model object look exactly like the element of a context value node.

When you define the structure of a model node using the Model Binding Wizard, you can elect to replicate some or all of the model object's structure into the context. If certain branches of the model object's hierarchy are not required, there is no need to bind these to the model node.

It is also possible to extend the structure of a model node by adding further child nodes and attributes that are not part of the model object. These additional children can be either model or value nodes. The only condition here is that if you add a model node or attribute, it must have an explicit binding to a corresponding model object.

> **Important**
>
> The structure of a model node can be extended by the addition of child value nodes and attributes. Thus, the children of a model node can be a mixture of nodes and attributes supplied by the model object's metadata *and* any required additional value nodes and value attributes.
>
> The children of a value node, on the other hand, may *only* be other value nodes or value attributes.
>
> You cannot mix value and model nodes or attributes together if the parent is a value node.

## 5.7    The Most Important Node Properties to Understand

In a typical design situation, you would define the context metadata at design time. This metadata must match the expected structure of the data you will work worth with at runtime. However, when you do not know what the structure of your data will be until runtime, it is possible to build the context according to metadata received at runtime.

Either way, you must have a good working knowledge of how the context functions in order to build it correctly. Whether built at design time or runtime, there are two particular node properties that play a critical role in the behavior of your context. These properties are `cardinality` and `singleton`.

These properties will be given special attention in the next couple of sections.

> **Caveat Confector**
>
> If you do not fully understand the function of the `cardinality` and `singleton` properties, then at runtime, you can arrive at the false impression that data is missing from your context.

### 5.7.1 Node Cardinality

As with any type-safe collection, a node's element collection can be accessed using a zero-based index value. However, SAP has given a context node an additional property called `cardinality`. This property controls the number of elements that can exist in the collection at runtime. All nodes contain an element collection, even if the maximum number of elements within that collection is limited to one.

The `cardinality` property is actually a pair of values: one for controlling the minimum number of permitted elements and the other for controlling the maximum number of permitted elements.

The minimum number of permitted elements in a node collection is either 1 or 0. Internally this property is represented as the Boolean value called `mandatory`. In other words, is it mandatory for the element collection to contain an element?

The maximum number of permitted elements is either 1 or "more than 1." Internally, this property is represented by the Boolean value called `multiple`. In other words, is it permitted for the context node to have multiple elements in its collection?

A node's cardinality is therefore one of the four possible values shown in Table 5.2.

| Minimum (isMandatory) | Maximum (isMultiple) | Result |
|---|---|---|
| 0 (false) | 1 (false) | Zero or one elements permitted |
| 1 (true) | 1 (false) | One and only one element permitted |
| 0 (false) | n (true) | Zero or more elements permitted |
| 1 (true) | n (true) | One or more elements permitted |

**Table 5.2** Node Cardinality Values

The node's `cardinality` property value is then displayed as one of 0..1, 1..1, 0..n, or 1..n.

As you can see from Figure 5.8, the nodes whose cardinality is "one to something" have an element within them called the default element. This is because the minimum number of elements permitted in the node collection is one. Therefore, when the node object is instantiated, the Web Dynpro Framework automatically creates an empty element. You can then do any manipulation you like to the node collection as long as you leave at least one element behind. After you have deleted elements, it doesn't matter which element is left behind as long as there is at least one left.

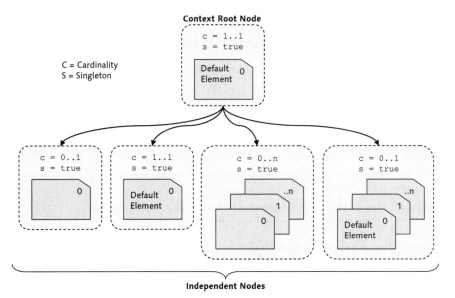

**Figure 5.8** How the Cardinality Affects the Number of Elements Permitted in a Context Node

Any attempt to execute coding that would violate a node's cardinality will result in the context throwing an exception. So, if the node has a cardinality of 1..1 or 1..n, do not attempt to delete the last element. Similarly, if a node has a cardinality of 0..1 or 1..1, do not attempt to add a second element.

From a coding perspective, the base class used to define all context nodes is IWDNode. This is an abstract interface that is implemented by every Web Dynpro controller when its context is defined.

A regular Java Collection is simply an interface that acts as the parent to a set of subinterfaces such as a List or a Set or a Map. If you want, you can build an element collection outside the scope of the context node to which it will be bound. This is done by first creating a Vector object (make sure its elements are all of the same data type as defined for the node) and then binding it to the node. This will cause the current contents of the node collection to be discarded and replaced with the contents of the Vector.

If you want to determine a node's cardinality programmatically, the IWDNode class is not the place to look. The correct place to look is in the node's metadata. This can done by calling the method IWDNode.getNodeInfo(), which returns an instance of the node metadata class IWDNodeInfo. From this metadata object, you can then determine the node's cardinality; however, because the cardinality is a pair of values, you must call two different methods depending on which part of the cardinality you're after.

Using the context structure shown in Figure 5.5, the following code will return the cardinality values of the node called `SalesOrders`:

```
// Get a reference to the SalesOrders node
IWDNode soNode = wdContext.nodeSalesOrders();

// Get a reference to the node's metadata
IWDNodeInfo soNodeInfo = soNode.getNodeInfo();

// Determine the node's cardinality
boolean minCardinality = soNodeInfo.isMandatory();
boolean maxCardinality = soNodeInfo.isMultiple();
```

**Listing 5.1** Coding to obtain the cardinality of a value node called SalesOrders

### 5.7.2 Node Selection Cardinality

In addition to there being a cardinality value to control the number of elements in a node collection, a second cardinality value controls the number of elements that may be selected at any one time. This property is called the `Selection Cardinality`. Its values are exactly the same as those shown in the table above, but in this case they are used to control the number of elements that may be flagged as `selected`.

```
// Get a reference to the SalesOrders node
IWDNode      soNode      = wdContext.nodeSalesOrders();

// Get a reference to the node's metadata
IWDNodeInfo soNodeInfo = soNode.getNodeInfo();

// Determine the node's selection cardinality
boolean minSelCardinality = soNodeInfo.isMandatorySelection();
boolean maxSelCardinality = soNodeInfo.isMultipleSelection();
```

**Listing 5.2** Coding to obtain the selection cardinality of a value node called SalesOrders

The selection cardinality controls the number of elements that may be concurrently selected. This value may be any one of the four standard cardinality values, so long as it does not contradict the node's collection cardinality. Therefore, if the node's cardinality limits the collection to a maximum of one element (i.e., `0..1` or `1..1`), then it would be invalid to specify a selection cardinality of `0..n` or `1..n`, because you would be saying that the user can select more elements than are permitted to exist in the node collection.

The coding to determine whether a particular collection element is part of a multiple selection is not in the place most people expect. The method `isMultiSelected()` belongs to the context node itself, and not to the individual elements. Therefore, to determine how many elements are members of a multiple selection, you simply call

`IWDNode.isMultiSelected()` and pass as a parameter the index number of the element in question.

To continue the coding seen in the previous listing:

```
int numSalesOrders = soNode.size();

for (int i=0; i< numSalesOrders; i++) {
  if (soNode.isMultiSelected(i)) {
    // Do something with the selected element
  }
}
```

**Listing 5.3** Coding to process each multiselected element in a value node

Even though it is possible to flag multiple elements as being selected, only one of the selected elements can be processed at any one time. The element currently being processed is referred to as the element at the *lead selection*. The method `IWDNode.getLeadSelection()` returns the index of the currently selected element. If this method returns a value of $-1$, it indicates that no element is currently selected.

---

**Important**

It is very important to understand the significance of which element is at the lead selection because this critically affects the data within singleton child nodes.

---

### 5.7.3 The Singleton Property

The `singleton` property critically affects the number of instances of child node `${chn}` that will be created for a given parent node `${cn}`.

If child node `${chn}` is declared at design time, the generated interface for this node will vary depending on whether it is a singleton or non-singleton node.

The use of the term *singleton* here is not the normal Java usage of this term. When a context node is referred to as being a singleton, it means there is a single instance of that object *with respect to its parent node*, not with respect to the Java Virtual Machine.

---

**Important**

▶ If a child node is declared to be a non-singleton child node, the number of child node instances that can exist at runtime is determined by the number of elements in the parent node's collection.

Therefore, you should think of non-singleton child nodes as being associated with a specific element in the parent node's collection. There is a one-to-one relationship between each element in the parent node's collection and the corresponding non-singleton child node.

---

> If ${cn} has *n* elements in its element collection, you will have at most *n* distinct instances of the non-singleton child node ${chn}.
>
> The relationship between a non-singleton child node and its parent node exists on a *per element* basis. Therefore, the element in the parent node is able to create its own specific instance of the child node. This method will not be found in elements having singleton child nodes.
>
> ▶ Singleton child nodes, however, are associated with their parent node on a *per-node* basis. Therefore, irrespective of the number of elements in the parent node's element collection, *there will only ever be one instance of the singleton child node* ${chn}.
>
> This immediately means the data in the singleton child node can only be relevant for one particular element in the parent collection. This element is always the element *at the lead selection in the parent node's collection*. The logical conclusion from this is that as soon as the element at the lead selection in the parent node changes, the data in the singleton child node becomes invalid and needs to be replaced. This situation is handled automatically by the Web Dynpro Framework but requires you to write something called a Supply Function. This topic will be dealt with in Section 5.14.
>
> The relationship between a singleton child node and parent node exists on a per-node basis. Since there is only ever going to be single instance of the child node, the method to create the child node belongs to the parent node and not to each element in the parent node's collection.

Figure 5.9 shows how the singleton flag affects the number of instances of ${chn} that may exist at runtime. Since the context root node always has exactly one element, all nodes that have the context root node as their immediate parent must, by definition, be singleton nodes.

It is important to notice how the relationships between the independent nodes and their child nodes are represented. For the dependent singleton node on the left, the arrow pointing from the parent node to the child node starts at the *node* boundary. However, the arrows pointing from the parent node to the dependent non-singleton child nodes on the right start from the element boundaries. This is to illustrate the type of relationship that exists.

Singleton child nodes are related to their parent *node*, whereas non-singleton child nodes are related to their parent *elements*.

### Why do Singleton Nodes Exist?

The reason singleton nodes have been implemented is primarily for efficiency, but also to follow another one of Web Dynpro's fundamental design principles, namely: lazy data access. In other words, if the user hasn't asked to see some data, don't bother fetching it!

These principles are implemented in the context through singleton nodes. Imagine you have a real-life situation involving the context structure shown in Figure 5.5. Let's say there are over 100 elements in the SalesOrders node.

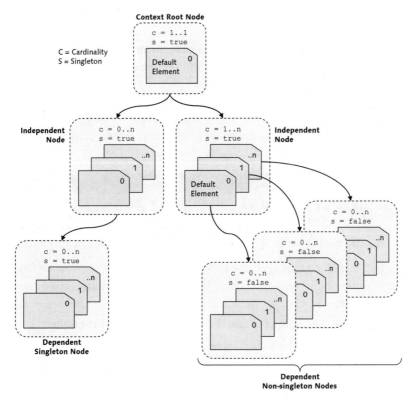

**Figure 5.9** The Relationship Between a Child Node and its Parent Depends on the Value of the Singleton Property

It would not be at all efficient to populate all 100 instances of node LineItems in the hope that the user *might* want to look at that information. Instead, the LineItems child node is declared to be a singleton node. Then the single instance holds only the data the user is currently interested in. In addition, we have ensured that memory consumption is limited to only that required by the user's actual requirements.

## 5.8 Should Node Names Be Singular or Plural?

The name chosen for context node ${cn} should reflect the potential number of elements it will contain at runtime. The upper limit is either 1 or many and is determined by the second part of the node's cardinality property.

If a node has a cardinality of ?..1, there will be, at most, one element in that node collection. Therefore, the node name should be singular.

If, however, the node has a cardinality of ?..n, the node collection could contain multiple elements. Therefore, the node name should be plural.

## 5.9    General Naming Conventions

When choosing a name for a context node or attribute, you do not need to include the words *node*, *element*, or *attribute* within the entity name. If at design time, node $\{cn\}$ is created with the typedAccessRequired property set to true, then the NWDS will generate various methods and classes whose names are formed from the above words and the supplied name $\{cn\}$. If you want to identify that a certain entity is part of the context, it is unnecessary to add these words, as they will be added automatically when a typed interface is generated.[5]

| Important |
| --- |
| For any given Web Dynpro controller, all node names within the context must be unique. |

The following principles should apply when naming context nodes and attributes:

▶ All node and attribute names should start with an upper case letter. You are free to select any meaningful name that obeys the Web Dynpro naming convention for context names.

▶ All node names must be unique within the scope of the current controller.

▶ All attribute names must be unique within the scope of their parent node.

▶ For any value node $\{vn\}$, if the node property typedAccessRequired is left at the default value of true, then the NWDS will generate a set of classes and methods to give you a typed API to these context entities

▶ A model node name $\{mn\}$ generally has the same name as the model object to which it is bound. If your executable model object represents an ABAP RFC module, this function module can have a name that is up to 28 characters long. When various suffixes such as _Input or _Output are appended to the name, this can create class names that are awkward to work with. Therefore, model node names are usually the same as the model object, as long as the name does not become too long to work with.

You should pay particular attention to the context node names generated by the Adaptive Web Service Model Wizard. Sometimes these names can become very long and will probably need to be shortened simply for the sake of convenience. We leave it to your discretion to decide exactly how long is too long.

▶ Generally speaking, the names of model attributes are inherited from the model object to which the parent model node is bound. You are free to rename model attribute names if you want, but this is a manual process and is usually only done

---

5  The exception to this rule is when the name of the business data being held by the context contains the word *node*, *element*, or *attribute*. An example of this might be a context node that holds SAP Work Breakdown Structure (WBS) Elements. Here the word element is part of the business name and does not have any reference to the Web Dynpro context.

when a name clash occurs or the generated class name is considered too long for convenient use.

See Tables 6.1 to 6.4 for a complete list of classes and methods that are generated when `typedAccessRequired` is set to `true`.

## 5.10    Identifying a Specific Node Attribute

The structure of a context node is much like a table, that is, it has rows and columns. Don't push this analogy too far, however, because a context node has no concept of key fields; therefore, unless you implement some kind of sort order yourself, the data held within a context node is not held in a normalized form.

The point here is that if you want to identify a specific cell in a table, you must identify both the row and the column. Together, both of these values identify a specific cell.

In terms of a context node, identifying a specific attribute value amounts to the same process, only this time the row corresponds to the element in the node's collection, and the column corresponds to the metadata of the particular attribute. These two values together exactly identify a context attribute. The following code fragment shows how to do this:

```
// Get a reference to the context node
I${cn}Node thisNode = wdContext.node${cn};

// Get a reference to the specific node element
int i = <some index value>
I${cn}Element thisEl = thisNode.get${cn}elementAt(i);

// Get the metadata of the attribute
IWDAttributeInfo attrInfo =
  thisNode.nodeInfo().getAttribute("${ca}");
```
**Listing 5.4** Taken together, the objects thisEl and attrInfo exactly identify a context attribute

However, there is a specific context object that will hold both of these values. This is known as an attribute pointer. The coding shown above in Listing 5.4 can be simplified as follows:

```
// Get a reference to the context node
I${cn}Node thisNode = wdContext.node${cn};

// Get a reference to the specific node element
int i = <some index value>
I${cn}Element thisEl = thisNode.get${cn}elementAt(i);
```

```
IWDAttributePointer attrPtr =
   thisEl.getAttributePointer("${ca}");
```
**Listing 5.5** An attribute pointer object exactly identifies a context attribute

Now instead of needing two objects to exactly identify the attribute, there is a sin-gle IWDAttributePointer object.

## 5.11 Calculated Attributes

To make certain simple but repetitive data formatting tasks easier, a special type of context attribute is available known as a calculated attribute. This is typically used when data needs to be formatted ready for display on the screen.

This type of attribute differs significantly from a normal attribute in that the data it contains is *never stored* within the element to which it belongs. Instead, the value is calculated on demand whenever the attribute's getter method is called.

An example of where a calculated attribute would be useful is assembling a saluta-tion from a title, a first name, and a last name (see Figure 5.10).

**Figure 5.10** The Result of a Calculated Attribute

For example, the salutation "Mr. Harry Hawk" is composed of the title "Mr.," the first name "Harry," and the last name "Hawk." If these values have already been stored in three individual context attributes, there is no need to duplicate the data as the assembled full name in a fourth attribute. This is where a calculated attribute can be used to assemble the information — but only when the salutation is actually required.

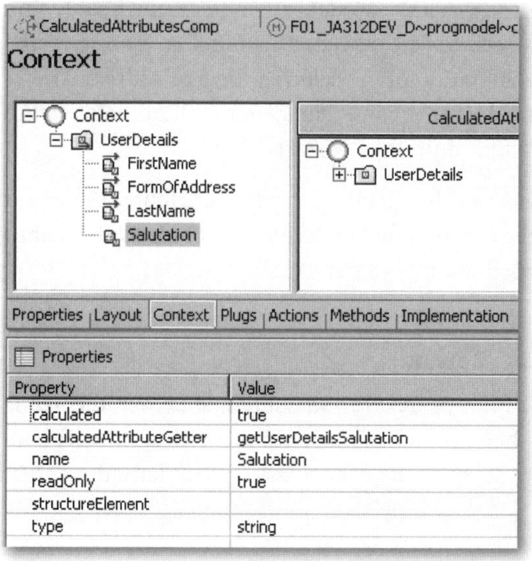

**Figure 5.11** The Context Definition for a Calculated Attribute

The screen shot in Figure 5.11 shows the context of a view controller that will display the salutation described above. There are several things to notice here:

1. The context node UserDetails and the attributes FirstName, LastName, and FormOfAddress all have small blue arrows in the icons. This means this node and these three attributes are mapped. In other words, they do not hold any data themselves; they simply point to a corresponding node and attributes in another controller. However, there is no arrow on the Salutation attribute.

   This means the Salutation attribute is local to the current controller's context (in this case, we are looking at a view controller's context).

   There is no problem in defining a context node that contains a mixture of mapped and unmapped attributes.

2. Look at the Properties of the Salutation attribute shown at the bottom of Figure 5.11. Both the calculated and readOnly properties are set to true. This means that:

   ▸ A getter method called get${cn}${ca} will be generated. In this case the method name will be getUserDetailsSalutation().

   ▸ No setter method will be generated because the readOnly flag is set to true.

3. The form of address field is a drop-down list. This typically means that the context attribute holding this value has been defined in the Java dictionary. As part of the dictionary definition, an enumeration has been declared to hold the various values seen in the drop-down list (e.g., Mr., Mrs., Dr., Prof., etc.). This will have an impact on the coding in the Salutation getter method because if you

simply access the value of the FormOfAddress context attribute, you will only find an index number, not the text seen on the screen. This number represents the index within the dictionary enumeration of the selected form of address. Therefore, to translate this index back to a text value, the getter method will need to look in the dictionary enumeration to find the correct value.

Now when a UI element is bound to this calculated context attribute, the getter method will be called as soon as the Server-Side Rendering part of the Web Dynpro Framework reads the value to place it on the screen.

### 5.11.1 Implementing a Getter Method

The coding to generate the value of the Salutation attribute is shown in the listing below. Each step of the logic has been coded explicitly to make clear what is happening. In reality, you would want to write the code in a more condensed manner.

```
public String getUserDetailsSalutation(
             IPrivate${nv}.IUserDetailsElement element) {
//@@begin
    // First, get the metadata of the node in which the
    // parameter "element" lives
    IWDNodeInfo nodeInfo = element.node ().getNodeInfo();

    // Next, get the metadata of the attribute that
    // contains the enumeration
    IWDAttributeInfo attrInfo =
                nodeInfo().getAttribute("FormOfAddress");

    // The title text descriptions are held in the value
    // set that is part of the dictionary simple type
    ISimpleValueSet vs = attrInfo.getSimpleType().
                            getSVServices().getValues();

    // Get the form of address from the value set using
    // the index value stored in the context attribute
    String foa = vs.getText(element.getFormOfAddress());

    // Get the first name and last name
    String fn  = element.getFirstName();
    String ln  = element.getLastName();

    // Concatenate the different parts together omitting
    // those parts that are blank
    foa = (foa == null) ? "" : foa + " ";
    fn  = (fn == null)  ? ""
                        : ((ln == null) ? fn : fn + " ");
    ln  = (ln == null)  ? "" : ln;
```

```
    return foa + fn + ln;
//@@end
}
```

**Listing 5.6** Coding for the Salutation calculated attribute

Several very important principles must be followed when writing a calculated attribute's getter method:

1. The getter method is always passed a parameter called `element`. This is *always* the current element of the context node to which the calculated attribute belongs.

2. The functionality of the getter method should never need to look beyond the data available from the `element` parameter to generate the required result.

3. Do not write any coding in the getter method that attempts to change the lead selection of the node to which the calculated attribute belongs.

---

**Caveat Confector**

When coding a getter method, all the data you need to calculate the required value must be available from the `element` parameter. If you need to look beyond the scope of the `element` parameter, there is something wrong with the design of your context node.

Also, whilst it is technically possible, do not perform any expensive tasks in a getter method, such as calling some kind of business functionality in a backend system. If you need to do this within a getter method, then you have a real problem with the architecture of the data flow within your application.

---

### 5.11.2 Implementing a Setter Method

Figure 5.12 shows a simplistic example in which a calculated attribute's getter method implements a non-reversible process.

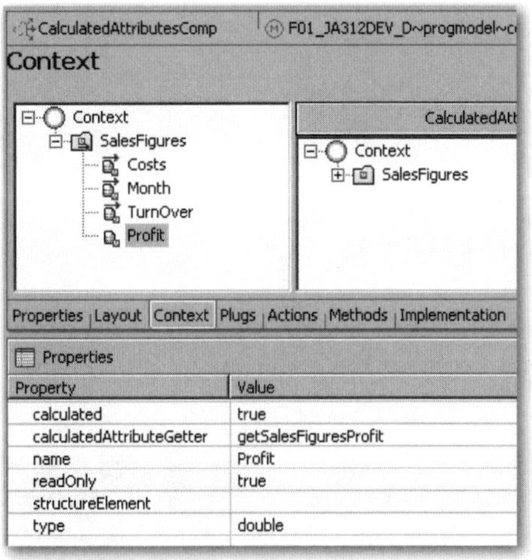

**Figure 5.12** The Context Definition for a Calculated Attribute

In this case, we will take the simplistic approach of saying that profit can be calculated by subtracting costs from turnover.

```
public Double getSalesFiguresProfit(
        IPrivate${nv}.ISalesFiguresElement element) {
  //@@begin
  // If only it were this simple!
  return element.getTurnOver() - element.getCosts();
  //@@end
}
```

**Listing 5.7** Simplistic coding for deriving the value of the Profit calculated attribute

This will give the results on the screen shown in Figure 5.13.

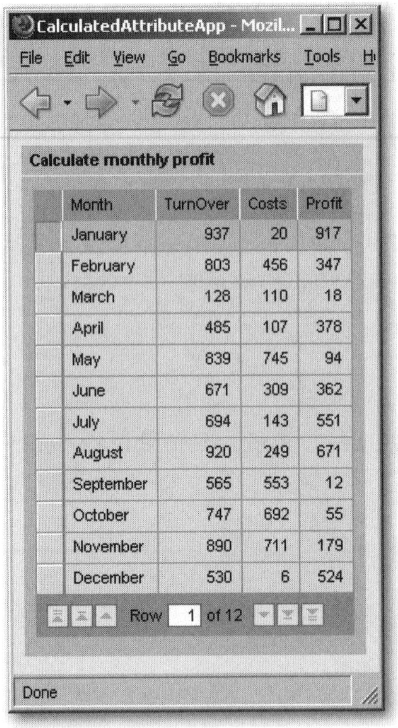

**Figure 5.13** The On-Screen Result of the Calculated Attribute

As you can see, it will be impossible to implement a setter method for this particular calculated attribute because the functionality of the getter method is irreversible.

| Important |
| --- |
| Implementing a setter method for a calculated attribute is a potentially complex and, in certain cases, impossible task. |

In reality, the majority of calculated attributes will be read-only for the following reasons:

▶ The setter method must parse and then validate the user's input.

▶ Since you are expecting the user to enter a value composed of several parts, the parsing and validation algorithms could easily become very complex. Therefore, the development effort required to implement a setter method could exceed the benefit obtained from having such a method.

▶ The functionality implemented in the calculated attribute's getter method may not be reversible. This would make it impossible for the calculated attribute to have a setter method.

### 5.11.3 Coding Principles for Getter and Setter Methods

When writing getter and setter methods for calculated attributes, there are some coding principles that must be clearly understood:

▶ The point during a server round trip (see Chapter 4 on the Phase Model) at which the calculated attribute's getter method will run is not predictable. Consequently, all errors must be handled gracefully.

▶ If your getter or setter method raises an unhandled exception, the Web Dynpro Framework will terminate your entire application.

▶ If you have designed your context structure correctly, you should never need to look beyond the values supplied in the getter method's `element` parameter to calculate the required result.

▶ Do not attempt to access data in other nodes or change the lead selection of the current node. This could have unpredictable results if calls to supply functions are involved.

▶ Do not implement model object interaction in a getter or setter method. If you do, then besides causing a potential performance bottleneck, something is probably wrong with your architecture.

▶ Make the coding in your getter method as efficient as possible, because it will be called every time the context attribute is read.

If it really becomes necessary to implement a UI element that *supplies* data to a calculated attribute, then for the purposes of error handling, the setter method should write to a specific context node with suitable attributes to record any error messages produced during the validation process.

## 5.12    Internal Context Mapping

As mentioned before, the primary mechanism for sharing data between different controllers is known as context mapping. From a technical perspective, when a node is defined to be a mapped node, it ceases to maintain it own collection. Instead, it references the collection found in the mapping origin node. In this manner, it is possible for the coding in the controller containing the mapped to node, to access the data held in another controller.

As described in Section 2.6.2, internal mapping is the name given to any mapping relationship where the mapping origin node and the mapped node are within the scope of the same component. This includes mapping origin nodes found in the interface controller of a child component instance.

Figure 5.14 shows the contexts of two controllers. On the left is a component controller, and on the right, a view controller. Before the mapping relationship can be established, the view controller must declare that the component controller is a "required" controller. In other words, the view controller declares that it will act as a data consumer and that it will obtain its data from the component controller (acting as the data generator).

Once the roles of data consumer and data generator are sorted out, the mapping relationship can be defined. The dotted arrows indicate that a mapping relationship exists. The nodes in the view controller are the mapped nodes, and the nodes in the component controller are the mapping origin nodes.

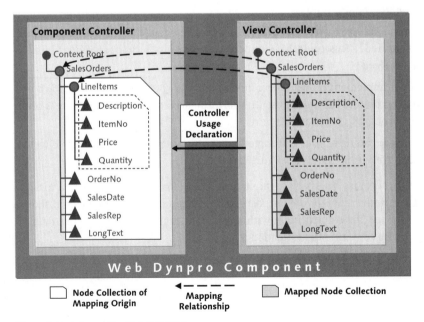

**Figure 5.14** Internal Context Mapping

## 5.13    External Context Mapping

As the name implies, an external mapping relationship is one in which the mapping origin node lies outside the scope of the current component. Such a relationship cannot be formed from the context of any controller, because only one controller is publicly visible beyond the scope of a component, and this is the Interface controller.

If you examine the properties of nodes found in an interface controller, you will see that there is an extra Boolean property called `isInputElement`. You will not find this property on a node in any other controller, and if it is set to `true`, you are declaring that that particular node in the interface controller's context will be a mapped node.

Well, that's nice, but you can't have a mapped node without saying which node will act as the mapping origin. So where is the mapping origin node?

That's exactly why Figure 5.15 shows a question mark for the mapping origin node. When you write the component containing this externally mapped node, you have no idea *which* node will act as the mapping origin. All you know is that the mapping origin node lies outside the scope of the current component. This means that until this component is used as the child of some other component, the mapping relationship will remain incomplete, and the component will therefore be unusable.

As a slight aside, can you see a familiar concept at work here? Any context node that acts as a mapping origin node is fulfilling the role of a data generator (or supplier), and any mapped node is fulfilling the role of data consumer. Anyway, back in Gotham City …

Notice that in Figure 5.15, the component containing the externally mapped node is called a child component. This is a very important point, because as soon as you decide to use an external mapping relationship, you immediately relegate that component to functioning as a child component. Said the other way around, without there being some other component present to act as a parent, the external mapping relationship will always remain incomplete.

> **Caveat Confector**
>
> A component containing an externally mapped node in its interface controller can only ever function as a child component.

The external mapping relationship can only be completed when the parent component declares the use of the child component. At this point, the parent component must nominate one of the nodes in its component controller to act as the mapping origin node. Only then will the interface to the child component be functional. Figure 5.16 shows the completed external mapping relationship. The important point to understand here is that the mapping origin node can only live in a parent component.

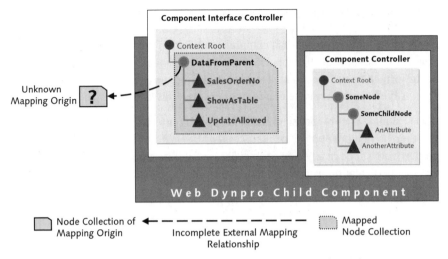

Node Collection of    ◄ – – – – – – – – – –    Mapped
Mapping Origin      Incomplete External Mapping    Node Collection
                                 Relationship

**Figure 5.15** The First Step in Defining an External Context Mapping Relationship

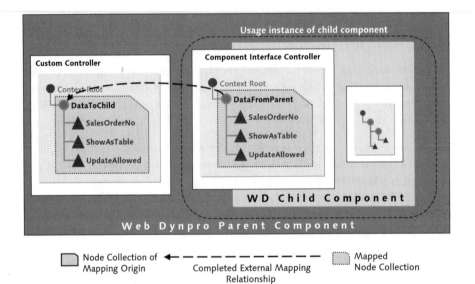

Node Collection of    ◄ – – – – – – – – – –    Mapped
Mapping Origin      Completed External Mapping    Node Collection
                                 Relationship

**Figure 5.16** Completing an External Context Mapping Relationship

---

**Caveat Confector**

External mapping should only be used in a very specific set of circumstances:

▶ External mapping is appropriate for components that will *only* be reused as child components because it creates a tight coupling from the child up to its parent. Normally, tight coupling should only be used for parent → child relationships, not child → parent.

▶ Legitimate use cases are limited to components that perform utility tasks. These tasks could include sorting the elements in a node or a faceless model component supplying information to a UI component.

▶ When you write the child component with the externally mapped node, it is not possible to identify the node that will act as the mapping origin. Therefore, extra restrictions are placed upon the node in the parent component that can act as the mapping origin:

- The mapping origin node may have a different name from the externally mapped node.

- All the attributes in the mapping origin node *must* have the same names as the attributes in the externally mapped node. This is because the mapping relationship is calculated by the Web Dynpro Framework dynamically at runtime on a per-name basis. Therefore, if the attribute names do not match, the Web Dynpro Framework will be unable to establish the mapping relationship at runtime, and the application will be terminated.

- The attributes in the mapping origin node must be of the same data type as those in the externally mapped node in the child component.

## 5.14 Supply Functions

As stated earlier, if you have a singleton child node, then no matter how many elements there are in the parent collection, there will only ever be one instance of the child node. This type of context structure is shown in Figure 5.17.

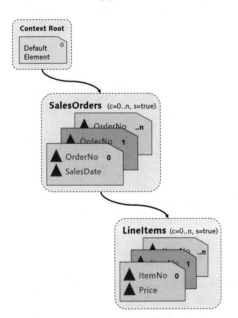

**Figure 5.17** The LineItems Node Is a Singleton, so It Must Have a Supply Function

In this situation, you must create a supply function for the LineItems node; otherwise, when the lead selection in the parent node changes (i.e., the user selects a different sales order), the data in the LineItems node would cease to be valid.

In other words, every time the lead selection in a parent node changes, all singleton child nodes must be rebuilt. This is why supply functions exist.

---

**Important**

The following points must be clearly understood about supply functions:

1. A supply function is used to populate an *entire* context node.

2. *Any* context node may have a supply function defined for it.

3. All singleton nodes *must* have a supply function defined.

4. The existence of a supply function is defined declaratively.

5. A supply function is called automatically by the Web Dynpro Framework when an attempt is made to read a dirty node collection.

6. A node collection could be dirty for any one of the following three reasons:
   - It has never been populated before.
   - The lead selection in the parent node collection has changed.
   - Application coding has explicitly invalidated the element collection.

7. The functionality in the supply function must leave the node in a state that obeys the node's cardinality.

---

Figure 5.18 shows the properties of a context node that has a supply function defined for it. Notice that the default name for a supply function is supply$`{cn}`. This name can be changed, but the default name is usually quite satisfactory.

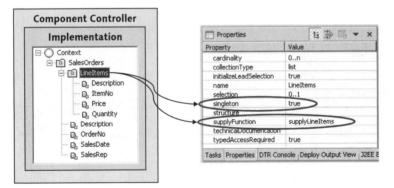

**Figure 5.18** Declaration of a Supply Function

The demo scenario illustrated in Figure 5.19 shows how the SalesOrders node seen in Figure 5.18 is initially populated. As the user selects different sales orders from the table on screen, this causes round trips to the server, which causes the supply function to be called automatically.

In Figure 5.19, you can see that the wdDoInit() method in the component controller first reads some data from a backend system (step ❶), and, second, uses it to populate the SalesOrders node (step ❷).

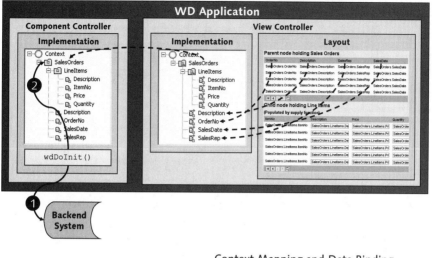

Context Mapping and Data Binding relationships

**Figure 5.19** Populating the SalesOrders Node

The view controller then contains exactly the same context structure as the component controller, and a mapping relationship exists. Thus, the view controller has access to the data held in the component controller's context. Also, there are two table UI elements in the view controller's layout. These are bound to the SalesOrders and LineItems nodes, respectively.

After the SalesOrders node has been populated, no further processing takes places, and the screen is rendered.

Using the chain of mapping and data binding relationships seen above, it is possible to take the data held in the context of the component controller and present it on the screen without having to write any coding to transfer the data between controllers or populate UI element objects.

One technical point about this example: When the SalesOrders node is populated, the node's lead selection is deliberately left set to –1,[6] meaning that no element is selected. Then when the data in node SalesOrders is rendered as a table, no rows from the table will be highlighted. This is done to prevent the supply function for the LineItems node from running when the screen is rendered for the first time.

Notice in Figure 5.20 that the table to display the LineItems data is empty. This is because the supply function has not run yet, so the LineItems node has an empty collection.

---

6   Refer back to Section 5.7.2.

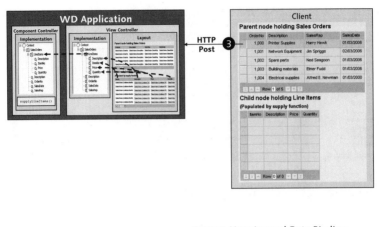

- - - - - - - - Context Mapping and Data Binding
relationships

**Figure 5.20** The User Selects a Row from the Table

When the user selects a row from the table (step ❸ in Figure 5.20), the action of clicking on a table row (by default) causes an automatic round trip to the server. What happens next is entirely automated by the Web Dynpro Framework. As long as you have written the supply function, it will be called for you automatically.

Remember that the lead selection of the SalesOrders node was deliberately left set to –1 (i.e., no selection)? Well, now that the user has clicked on a row in the Sales-Orders table, a specific element has been selected from the context node. In other words, the lead selection of the context node visualized by that table UI element has been changed.

Now when the Web Dynpro Framework processes the round trip, it sees that an element has been selected from node SalesOrders. This would have no effect at all if it were not for the fact that on the screen, we have a table UI element bound to the LineItems node. Now when the screen is rendered, the following sequence of events take place:

▶ The table UI element must be populated using data obtained from the context node specified in the UI element's dataSource property.

▶ The UI element's dataSource property points to the LineItems node, so a read request is made on this node.

▶ The node is currently empty. What to do … ?

▶ The Web Dynpro Framework checks for the existence of a supply function, and finding that one exists, calls it, passing as a parameter the newly selected element from the parent node (SalesOrders).

▶ The supply function populates the LineItems node with information relevant for the newly selected sales order.

In Figure 5.21, the supply function calls the backend system to read the line items for the newly selected sales order (step ❹). This data is then written back into node LineItems (step ❺).

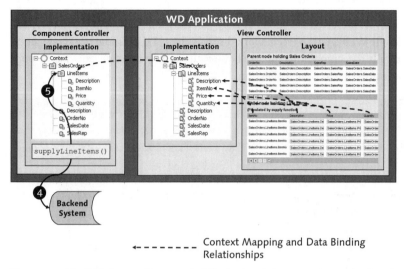

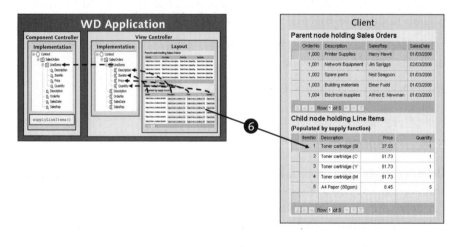

**Figure 5.21** The Web Dynpro Framework Calls the Supply Function Automatically When the Lead Selection in the Parent Node Changes

Finally, the screen is rendered using the data written into the LineItems node by the supply function (step ❻ in Figure 5.22).

**Figure 5.22** Now that the LineItems Node Has Been Populated by the Supply Function, the Table UI Element Is Able to Display the Data

193

Now, let's say the user selects a different sales order. The same sequence of events will take place, but with one important difference. The first time the screen was rendered, the LineItems node was empty, so the supply function simply populated the node and that was that.

Now, however, the LineItems node already contains some data and must be repopulated. So the Web Dynpro Framework discards the old data in the LineItems node and then calls the supply function. As before, the supply function only has to populate an empty context node collection.

> **Caveat Confector**
>
> A supply function must leave the node in a state that does not violate its cardinality. The Web Dynpro Framework will only check the cardinality of the node *after* the supply function has finished execution.
>
> This means it is possible to do crazy things in a supply function such as:
>
> ▶ Adding more than one element to a node of cardinality 0..1 or 1..1.
> ▶ Leaving a node of cardinality 1..1 or 1..n empty.
>
> Should your coding leave the context node in such a state, it will cause an exception when the supply function hands control back to the Web Dynpro Framework, because it is only then that the node's cardinality constraints are checked.

At this point, you might be asking, "What happens to the old data that is thrown away?" That's a good question, and it raises the problem of potential data loss.

If the user has selected a particular sales order, and the supply function then populates the LineItems node, this data has been presented to the user, and it is entirely possible that the user could then modify it.

What happens to the modified data? If we were to leave things as they stand now, the modified data would be lost.

So let's take a look at dispose functions.

## 5.15 Dispose Functions

Unless you have been trawling around in the Web Dynpro Javadoc, you will probably have never heard of dispose functions before. The reason is that unlike supply functions, dispose functions cannot be created declaratively. Since they do not appear as properties of a context node, many people are unaware of their existence.

The purpose of a dispose function is to process the data in a context node that is about to be thrown away. In our example, if the user needs to modify line item information for multiple sales orders, we need a mechanism to preserve the modified line item data once a new sales order has been selected. This is where a dispose function will be required.

A dispose function can only be defined programmatically, and then only for nodes that are either unmapped or act as mapping origin nodes. If you create a dispose function for a mapped node (in a view controller, for instance), this will not cause an error, but neither will it do anything.

Let's extend the above supply function example to incorporate a dispose function. To do this, we must edit the source code of the component controller where the LineItems node is defined.

The source code required for this task will look something like this:

```
public void wdDoInit(){
  //@@begin wdDoInit()
  // Create a new dispose function instance
  DisposeLineItems liDisposer = new DisposeLineItems();

  // Associate the dispose function instance with the
  // metadata of the LineItems context node
  wdContext.nodeLineItems().
    getNodeInfo().setCollectionDisposer(liDisposer);
  //@@end
}


...


//@@begin others
private class DisposeLineItems
        implements IWDNodeCollectionDisposer {
  public void disposeElements(IWDNode node) {
    // Implement the dispose functionality here
  }
}
//@@end
```

**Listing 5.8** Stub coding used to define a dispose function for the context node LineItems

In Listing 5.8 above, you can see that an instance of the dispose function class is created and associated with the LineItem context node's metadata. This task is performed in the standard hook method wdDoInit() belonging to the component controller. This is because this task only needs to happen once per lifecycle of the component. For more information on the standard hook methods, see Chapter 4 on the Phase Model.

The dispose function itself has been created as an inner class of the component controller. Notice the //@@begin others and //@@end comment lines? These comments always occur at the end of every source file for a Web Dynpro controller. Between these comment lines you can add any coding you require.

The naming convention for supply functions has been extended now to include dispose functions; hence, the name of the dispose function class is Dispose${cn}. Irrespective of the name of this class, the important thing is that it implements the interface IWDNodeCollectionDisposer and, specifically, the method disposeElements().

The parameter node passed to the disposeElements() method is the context node that is about to have its contents destroyed. You do not need to empty this node yourself; you just need to implement the coding that will preserve the modified data.

The data type of the node parameter is the generic base class (IWDNode) implemented by all context nodes. Since you know that this dispose function is specific to the node called LineItems, you can make use of the typed context interface by casting the node parameter as a LineItems node class.

The next question is, "What to do with the modified data?" In this simple example we will just write the modified line item data to a separate context node.[7] So the context structure seen in Figure 5.5 can be extended to include a SavedLineItems node (see Figure 5.23).

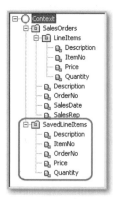

**Figure 5.23** New Context Node Used to Hold Modified Line Item Data

---

7   In a more realistic situation, the dispose function would probably write the modified data back to the backend system as an update.

The purpose of this node is to act as a holding area for line item information that has been modified.

The first step is that the user modifies the line item information and then simply selects a new row from the sales order table. This is shown in Figure 5.24 (step ❶). The act of selecting a new table row (step ❷) causes a round trip to the server, and this is where the dispose function and supply function will be invoked.

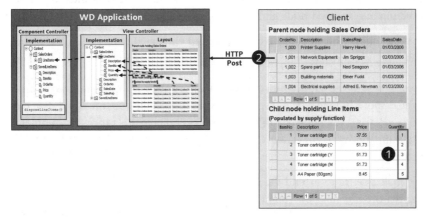

**Figure 5.24** User Modifies the Line Item Information

Since the data has been modified by the user via the UI, the changed data is copied back into the LineItems node (step ❸ in Figure 5.25). The Web Dynpro Framework recognizes that the context node in the view controller is a mapped node, so it updates the information in the mapping origin node. In this case, this is the Line-Items node in the component controller.

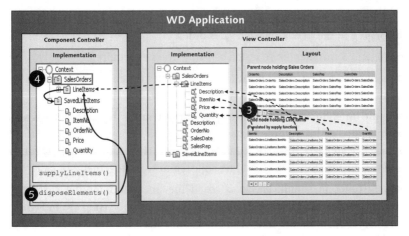

**Figure 5.25** The Modified Data is Copied Back to the Context and the Dispose Function Is Called

Now that our modified data has been safely stored back in the LineItems node, the change of lead selection for node SalesOrders is processed (step ❹ in Figure 5.25). This immediately flags the data we have just saved in the LineItems node as "dirty." Since the LineItems node is part of the rendered screen, this node will be reread to create the new screen that is about to be sent to the user. The act of rereading the LineItems node forces its supply function to be called.

Before the supply function is called, however, the Web Dynpro Framework looks at the data in the LineItems node and realizes two things:

▶ The contents of this node have been modified via the UI.

▶ This node has a dispose function defined for it.

Therefore, before the supply function is called, the Web Dynpro Framework first calls the dispose function. The dispose function then copies the modified data out to the SavedLineItems node (step ❺ in Figure 5.25). Once this process is complete, it is safe for the node collection to be destroyed and repopulated by the supply function.

It now makes sense to extend the functionality of the supply function for the following reason. Consider the following sequence of events:

1. The user selects his first sales order.

2. The supply function for node LineItems executes and retrieves the associated data.

3. The user modifies the line item information and then selects another sales order.

4. The Web Dynpro Framework sees that the line item data has been changed through the UI, so it calls the dispose function, which stores the data in the SavedLineItems node.

5. The supply function repopulates the LineItems node with the line item information belonging to the newly selected sales order.

6. Steps 3, 4, and 5 can then be repeated as many times as required.

7. It is possible that the user will want to look at a sales order that he has already modified.

8. If the supply function now looks in the backend system for this data, we will not be showing the user his modified data stored in the SavedLineItems node. Effectively, we have allowed the modified data to be lost. Therefore, the supply function and the dispose function should be adjusted to work together as a pair.

9. The supply function should check to see if the line items for the currently selected sales order already exist in the SavedLineItems node (step ❻a in Figure 5.26). If they do, move the data from there into the LineItems node; if they don't, only then should the backend system be accessed (step ❻b).

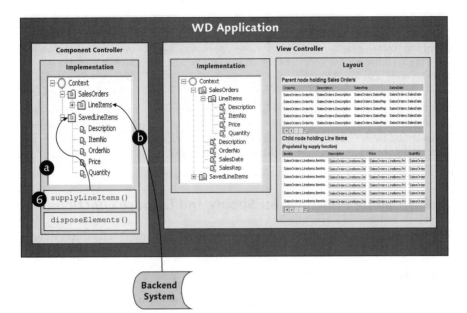

**Figure 5.26** The Supply Function Now Checks the SavedLineItems Node Before Accessing the Backend System

The situation documented here is only valid if you are implementing a business transaction that will modify a *set* of sales orders as a transactional unit. To make this scenario a more realistic business case, you should decide how updates to the back-end database are to be handled: either add a button to the screen that causes all the modified sales order line items to be saved as a single update or alter the functionality of the dispose function to save each set of changes as soon as they take place back to the backend system — in which case there would be no need for the SavedLineItems node.

The situation with supply and dispose functions has been illustrated in this manner to show that they need to work together as a pair of functions that operate on an internal cache (in this case, the SavedLineItems node). How you choose to implement this functionality depends on the transactional nature of your business application.

---

**Caveat Confector**

Remember that the Web Dynpro Framework will only call a dispose function when the following set of conditions has been met:

▶ The lead selection in the parent node has changed.

▶ The data in the child node has been modified via the UI.

▶ A dispose function exists for the child node.

There is one situation in which a dispose function must be very careful to prevent the loss of data. Let's say you decide the dispose function should write each set of changed line items directly back to the backend system through some BAPI call (Business Application Programming Interface). If the BAPI call fails, or if some type of error prevents the dispose function from storing the modified data, then there is no way for the dispose function to tell the Web Dynpro Framework to veto the change of lead selection that occurred in the parent node. Consequently, the supply function will *always* run, causing the data that led to an error to be overwritten.

Therefore, it is wise to create an alternative storage area in which the modified data can be stored if the dispose function is unable to complete its normal processing. The modified data should be moved to the alternative storage area (say, some dynamically created context node) and then notify the user that the update failed.

## 5.16 Coding Principles for Supply and Dispose Functions

The following principles must be followed when writing supply and dispose functions:

▶ Handle all errors gracefully.

▶ Use a dedicated context node located in the component controller into which supply and dispose function error information can be written.

▶ Avoid calling the message manager directly. Whilst this is not always going to create problems, in larger applications with more complex component hierarchies, it is a good principle to follow.

▶ Never call a method of the message manager whose name starts with raise...(), as this will immediately and forcibly terminate your application logic.

## 5.17 Recursive Context Nodes

A recursive context node is generally required under the following circumstances:

▶ The depth of child nodes under a given node will not be known until runtime.

▶ The structure of each successive child node down the hierarchy is the same as the structure of the parent node.

For instance, when parsing a file system structure such as that shown in Figure 5.27, you will not know how many levels of subdirectory exist until the entire tree has been traversed. Consequently, to build a context that reflects a file system structure will require the use of recursive nodes.

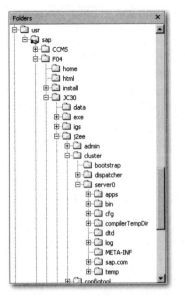

**Figure 5.27** A File System Is an Example of a Hierarchical Structure of Unknown Depth

### 5.17.1  Creating Recursive Context Nodes

A recursive node can be defined in any controller and will always be a dependent node. It is not possible to create an independent, recursive node; that is, a recursive node may not have the context root node as its immediate parent.

Before creating a recursive node, you must first create a node that will act as the node to be repeated. In the example of parsing a file system, we will create a node structure to represent a basic directory. We start with a node called Directory and add to it a few attributes to describe files.

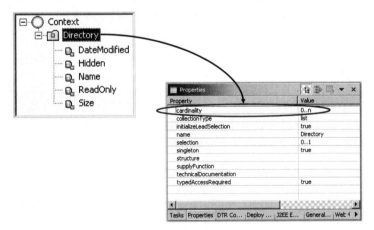

**Figure 5.28** The Node Called Directory Will Act as the Repeated Node

Notice in Figure 5.28 that the node to be repeated must have multiple cardinality, that is, a cardinality of ?..n.

The next step is to add the recursive context node. Notice in Figure 5.29 that this type of context node only has two properties: its name[8] and the property called `repeatedNode`. The `repeatedNode` property must be configured to point to one of the recursive node's parents. Usually, this property will point to the recursive node's immediate parent, but if you want to create a more complex recursive structure, it is possible for the `repeatedNode` property to point to any parent node along the path back up to (but *not* including) the root node.

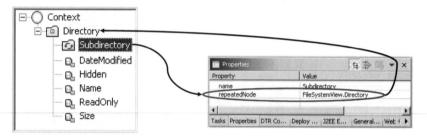

**Figure 5.29** Now the Recursive Node Can Be Added to the Context Structure

**Caveat Confector**

A recursive node's `repeatedNode` property may not point to the context root node.

Normally, all context node names must be unique within the scope of any particular Web Dynpro controller. However, the Web Dynpro Framework makes an exception with recursive nodes. The reason for this is that when you create a recursive node at design time, you are simply adding a placeholder into the context structure and telling the Web Dynpro Framework that at runtime, an instance of the node named in the `repeatedNode` property will occupy that location in the context structure.

So using the example shown above, at runtime, the location in the context shown by the recursive node `Subdirectory` will be occupied by an instance of the `Directory` node. However, once a new instance of the node `Directory` has been created, it will have its own child node called `Subdirectory`, which is a recursive node that allows a new instance of node `Directory` to exist at that point in the hierarchy, which has a child node called … you get the picture?

Every time a new instance of the node `Subdirectory` is created, the structure of the node `Directory` is used (because this is the `repeatedNode`), and the new instance is called `Subdirectory`. The runtime structure will then look something like Figure 5.30.

---

8  Incidentally, the name of a context node is the only parameter for which data binding makes no sense.

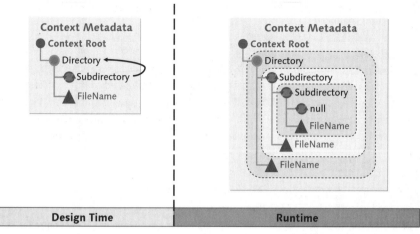

**Figure 5.30** The Design Time Structure of a Recursive Node Compared to the Runtime Structure

### 5.17.2 Mapping Recursive Context Nodes

There is a popularly held misconception that recursive node structures cannot be mapped to different controllers. Why people arrive at this conclusion can be illustrated as follows.

If the context structure shown in Figure 5.29 exists in a component controller, you may perform the following steps in an attempt to create a corresponding mapped node structure in a view controller:

1. Define the context structure in the component controller.
2. Open the Data Modeler tool by double-clicking on the component name.
3. Create a data link between the view controller and the component controller.
4. The Context Mapping Wizard opens and you drag the `Directory` node from the component controller across to the view controller.
5. You find that you can select all the nodes and attributes *except* for the recursive node.

After completing this sequence of events, many people conclude that recursive context nodes cannot be mapped. Fortunately, this conclusion is not correct!

To map recursive context nodes successfully, you need to make a slight rearrangement to your sequence of declarations. These steps are shown in Figure 5.31.

First, manually create the context node called `Directory` in the view controller (step ❶). Don't forget to add the component controller's name as one of the view controller's required controllers.

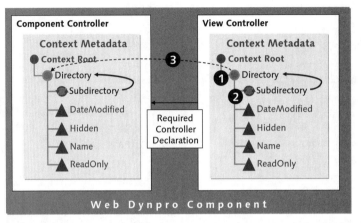

**Figure 5.31** The Steps Required to Create a Mapped Recursive Node in a View Controller

Next, in the view controller, manually create the recursive node Subdirectory (step ❷). You must configure the repeatedNode property to point to the parent node Directory — even though the Directory node in the view controller has no attributes yet. The important point is that context structure in the view controller now has the same *node* structure as the component controller. The Mapping Wizard can now be used to add the missing attributes and define the mapping relationships.

As long as you create the recursive context node manually and configure its local repeatedNode, any context structure that includes a recursive node can be successfully mapped using the Mapping Wizard (Step ❸).

### 5.17.3    Restrictions on the Use of Recursive Nodes

The following restrictions exist when using recursive nodes:

▶ The metadata for recursive context nodes is typically declared at design time but can also be defined dynamically at runtime.

▶ Actual recursive node instances can only be created programmatically.

▶ You cannot declare a recursive node to act as a mapping origin node.

▶ You cannot create an independent recursive node.

▶ The context root node may not be nominated as the repeatedNode.

From a technical point of view, all recursive nodes are implemented internally as non-singleton nodes and should be built on demand. This topic will be expanded in the next chapter.

## 5.18    Fundamental Principles of the Context

The behavior of the context is based on the following fundamental principles:

1. All attributes `${ca}` and child nodes `${chn}` of node `${cn}` are aggregated into a unit known as an element.

2. All context nodes contain a collection of elements.

3. An unmapped node[9] maintains its own element collection, but a mapped node does not. Instead, a mapped node maintains a reference to the element collection of its mapping origin node.

4. The cardinality property controls the maximum and minimum number of elements that `${cn}` may contain at runtime:

   ▶ If `${cn}` has a cardinality of `1..?`, the collection must always contain at least one element. This mandatory element is known as the default element, and whilst it is not important *which* element remains in the collection, at least one must be there, and it *may not* be removed.

   ▶ If `${cn}` has a cardinality of `0..?`, element 0 must be created explicitly at runtime.

   ▶ Do not perform any action on a context node that would violate the constraints of its cardinality. For example, don't try to delete the default element from a node of cardinality `1..?` or add a second element to a node of cardinality `?..1`.

5. The singleton flag describes the relationship between a child node `${chn}` and its parent `${cn}`. By default, all dependent nodes will have their singleton flag set to `true`.

   ▶ If `${chn}` is a singleton with respect to its parent node `${cn}`, then no matter how many elements `${cn}` contains, there will only ever be one instance of the child node `${chn}`.

   ▶ If `${chn}` is a non-singleton with respect to its parent node `${cn}`, then for each of the *n* elements in `${cn}`, there will be at most *n* instances of `${chn}`.

   ▶ The data within a singleton child node is specific to the element at the lead selection in its parent node. Therefore, the lead selection of parent node `${cn}` must first be correctly positioned before the singleton child node `${chn}` can be accessed. Now when a read request is made on the data in `${chn}`, its supply function will be called automatically.

   ▶ The contents of a non-singleton child node can be referenced directly without needing to reposition the lead selection of the parent node.

---

9  This includes the context root node whose element collection always contains exactly one element.

6. When iterating around the elements of node `${cn}`, there are two ways to obtain a reference to each element. The method you choose will largely depend on whether or not the node has singleton child nodes.

   ▶ If `${cn}` contains non-singleton child nodes, it is sufficient simply to call method `node${cn}.getElementAt(int index)` (which will not alter the value of the node's lead selection). The returned element instance then has direct access to its non-singleton child node instances.

   ▶ If `${cn}` contains singleton child nodes, you must first position the node's lead selection by calling method `node${cn}.setLeadSelection(int index)`. Then you may call `node${cn}.current${cn}Element()` if a typed interface has been created or `IWDNode.currentElement()` if the generic context API is being used.

# 6 Context Structure at Runtime

Now that you understand how context nodes and attributes are declared at design time, we will take a look at how those declared objects behave at runtime. It is here that you will see why it is very important to make accurate design time decisions, since these decision critically affect runtime behavior.

## 6.1 Generated Classes

Unless you explicitly choose not to do so, whenever you make a design time declaration to create a node or attribute, the NWDS will generate a set of classes and methods to give you a typed API into those context entities. This behavior can be switched off if you want by setting the node's **typedAccessRequired** property to **false**. Either way, any nodes declared at design time are known as *static nodes*, and nodes created at runtime are known as *dynamic nodes*.[1]

> **Caveat Confector**
>
> The context of a non-visual controller is publicly accessible, but the context of a visual controller is always private. This is to ensure that the data generator–data consumer concepts of MVC design are enforced. In other words, a visual controller is not permitted to provide its context for other controllers to map to, for in doing so, it would become a data generator. Therefore, the following differences exist concerning the scope of the declared classes.
>
> The context of a non-visual controller belongs both to its IPublic${n_c} interface and its IPrivate${n_c} interface.
>
> The context of a visual controller belongs only to its IPrivate${n_v} interface.

### 6.1.1 The Typed Context API

Assuming that typed access is required, the generated node and element classes will implement different methods depending on whether ${cn} has any child nodes and, if it does, whether the child node ${chn} is a singleton node.

Table 6.1 shows the methods that are created for all nodes. This set of methods will be found in the private interface of all controllers and the public interface of all non-visual controllers.

---

1 For any controller, it is quite possible to work only with the controller's IPrivate${n_{ctl}} interface.

| Generated Class for All Nodes | Method |
|---|---|
| I${cn}Node | I${cn}Element create${cn}Element() |
| | I${cn}Element current${cn}Element() |
| | I${cn}Element get${cn}ElementAt(int) |
| | void bind(I${cn}Element) |

**Table 6.1** Typed API Methods Generated for a Node Without a Non-Singleton Child Node

The methods shown in Table 6.1 will always be generated for a node, irrespective of the type of child nodes it has.

If ${cn} has a child node ${chn} that is a non-singleton, some additional methods will be created. These methods are shown in Table 6.2.

| Generated Class for a Node | Method |
|---|---|
| IPublic${n_c}.I${cn}Node | I${chn}Node node${chn}() |
| | I${chn}Node node${chn}(int) |

**Table 6.2** Typed API Methods Generated for a Node with a Non-Singleton Child Node

Along with the node interface I${cn}Node that is created, is another interface for the elements that live within the node's element collection. As with the node interface, the element interface will always be present in the controller's private interface and in the public interface if the controller is non-visual.

${ca} is any context attribute whose data type is represented by ${dt_{ca}}.

Table 6.3 and Table 6.4 show the classes and methods generated for a context element.

| Generated Class for a Context Element | Method |
|---|---|
| I${cn}Element | ${dt_{ca}} get${ca}() |
| | void set${ca}(${dt_{ca}}) |

**Table 6.3** Typed API Methods Generated for a Context Element

| Generated Class for a Context Element | Method |
|---|---|
| I${cn}Element | I${chn}Element current${chn}Element() |
| | I${chn}Element get${chn}ElementAt(int) |
| | I${chn}Node node${chn}() |

**Table 6.4** Typed API Methods Generated for a Context Element with a Non-Singleton Child Node

Under certain circumstances you might elect not to use the typed context API. This would be for one of two reasons:

1. The node or attribute was created at runtime, and therefore the typed API classes and methods simply do not exist.

2. You deliberately switch off the **typedAccessRequired** flag at design time. This property flag is shown in Figure 6.1.

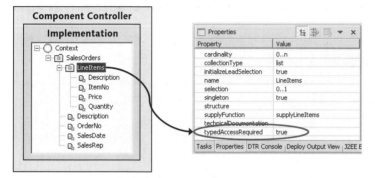

**Figure 6.1** The typedAccessRequired Node Property

Normally, the `typedAccessRequired` flag should be left set to its default value for two reasons:

1. The generated typed API makes coding with the context much easier and less error prone.

2. There is another performance enhancement feature within the NWDS that will reduce the size of the compiled Java code.

If it really becomes necessary to limit the amount of source code generated as a result of your context structure, this flag can be switched off, but normally this is only required for extremely large context structures.

### 6.1.2 Background to the typedAccessRequired Flag

The `typedAccessRequired` flag was added as a performance enhancement feature in an early version of the SAP NetWeaver '04 release of Web Dynpro. The reasoning behind it was to give the developer the ability to reduce the size of the generated source code for controllers containing very large context structures.

Once this flag has been switched off, the only way to access the nodes and attributes in the context is via the generic API. When using this API, you must know the names and data types of the nodes and attributes you want to access.

Whilst this was effective at reducing the size of the final application, it was not so convenient to work with, and so a better performance option was developed.

### 6.1.3 The Byte Code Minimizer

Since that time, a better performance enhancement feature has been added that still allows you to work with all the convenient features provided by the typed context API but reduces the size of the generated code by operating on the compiled Java byte code rather than the source code. This feature is called the Byte Code Minimizer. To check the setting of this performance-enhancement feature, you should select the properties of your entire Web Dynpro DC, by right-clicking on the DC name and selecting **Properties**. Then select **Web Dynpro Generation** as shown in Figure 6.2.

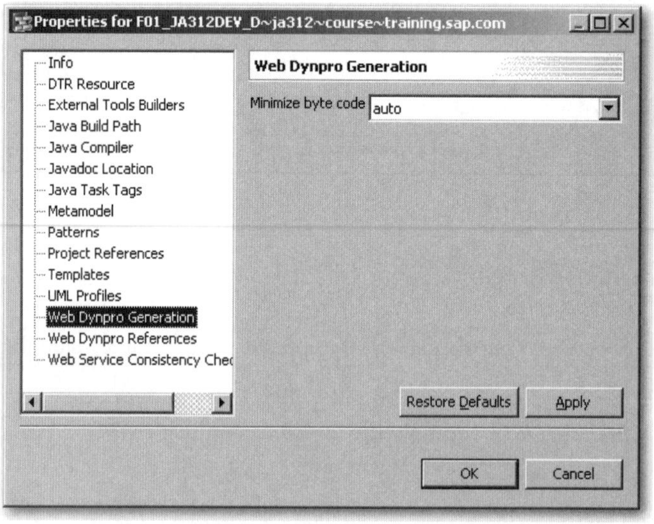

**Figure 6.2** The Byte Code Minimizer Setting in the Development Component Properties

| Important |
| --- |
| This performance-enhancement feature is only available for DCs of type Web Dynpro. You will not see this feature if you create one of the older (and obsolete) Web Dynpro Projects. |

The default setting for this feature is **auto**, but there are four options:

▶ **no**
Do not minimize byte code

▶ **auto**
The same as **wd-only**

▶ **wd-only**
Minimize only generated Web Dynpro classes

▶ **max**
Minimize *all* application classes in the DC

The Byte Code Minimizer works by parsing the Java byte code and removing all coding related to unreferenced methods. The **auto** and **wd-only** options are the same and operate only on the coding generated by the NWDS for the context. It is possible, however, to set the Byte Code Minimizer to the **max** option, in which case it will operate on all classes in your component — not just the classes related to the context.

> **Caveat Confector**
>
> Do not use the **max** setting unless you are *absolutely* sure your coding does not use Java reflection. The Byte Code Minimizer cannot know about any methods called via reflection, so this setting could result in runtime errors if not used carefully!

The best option is simply to leave this feature set to its default value, in which case it will provide the same (or slightly better) code reduction as setting the typedAccessRequired flag to false for each node in your context. The added advantage of this feature is that you still have the convenience of the typed context API.

### 6.1.4 Generated Classes and Context Mapping

Consider the following situation:

▶ We have a simple Web Dynpro component called DemoComp.

▶ The context of the component controller contains a single node called UserPreferences.

▶ The component contains a single view controller called DemoView.

▶ The context of the view controller also contains a single node called UserPreferences.

▶ The UserPreferences node in view controller is mapped to the UserPreferences node in the component controller.

So let's think about how many Java classes will be created as a result of these declarations. For the component controller we have:

▶ IPublicDemoComp
  A public interface to the component controller, which exposes …

▶ IUserPreferencesNode
  An interface to the UserPreferences node in the component controller's context, which contains …

▶ IUserPreferencesElement
  An interface to the element of the UserPreferences node in the component controller.

For the view controller we have:

- ▶ IPrivateDemoView

  A private interface to the view controller,[2] which contains …

- ▶ IUserPreferencesNode

  An interface to the UserPreferences node in the view controller's context, which contains …

- ▶ IUserPreferencesElement

  An interface to the element of the UserPreferences node in the view controller.

Notice that the interface names for the UserPreferences node and element are the same in *both controllers*. This is perfectly legal, but you must be careful in the following situation.

Let's say you want to add an element to node UserPreferences in the *component controller*. You would use code something like the following:

```
IUserPreferencesElement userPrefEl =
                      wdContext.nodeUserPreferences().
                         createUserPreferencesElement();
wdContext.nodeUserPreferences().addElement(userPrefEl);
```
**Listing 6.1** Adding an element to a value node called UserPreferences

When you first enter this coding, the class name IUserPreferencesElement will appear with a wavy red line under it. This indicates that the NWDS cannot resolve the class name from any of the currently imported packages, so you need to organize your import statements. This is done either by right-clicking within the NWDS Java editor and selecting **Source • Organize Imports** from the side menu or simply pressing ⌨Ctrl + ⌨⇧ + ⌨O (for organize).

Since two classes answer to the name of IUserPreferencesElement, the NWDS will not know which one to import. One class belongs to the view controller, and the other, to the component controller. Consequently, you will see the pop-up window shown in Figure 6.3.

---

**Caveat Confector**

It is very important that you select the class name for the controller you are currently editing. In the above example, do not select the view controller class containing IUserPreferencesElement because it will be considered incompatible with the UserPreferences node in the component controller even though they are semantically identical.

---

2  Notice that this interface name contains the word *private*. You are not permitted to expose a view controller's methods or context.

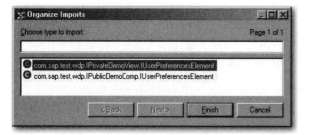

**Figure 6.3** Class Name Ambiguities Must Be Resolved when the Import Statements Are Organized

## 6.2    Working with Value Nodes

Value nodes are context nodes that maintain their own collection. This is the node type you will use most frequently.

### 6.2.1    Accessing the Context Through the Typed API

When creating a new element for a value node's element collection, the node object can create the element object using the metadata stored within it. In a generalized form, the coding looks like this (where `${cn}` is the name of any value node):

```
I${cn}Element newValueEl =
                wdContext.node${cn}.create${cn}Element();
```

**Listing 6.2** Generalized coding for using the typed context API to create a new node collection element

The following discussion assumes you have not switched the `typedAccessRequired` flag to `false`.

In general, any node `${cn}` (irrespective of its position in the hierarchy) can be accessed by calling the method `wdContext.node${cn}`. From this node instance, you can obtain the node's metadata by calling the method `getNodeInfo()`. This will return an object of class `IWDNodeInfo`. A node info object contains all the metadata for the specific node and is not type specific.

Let's say, for example, that in your component controller's context you have an independent value node called `SalesOrders` with four value attributes called `Long-Text`, `OrderNo`, `SalesDate`, and `SalesRep`. Since this node is independent (i.e., it has the context root node as its immediate parent), it is forced to be a singleton node. Also, because we have not changed the default cardinality of `0..n`, you know immediately that the node will start out containing zero elements (an empty collection) and may grow to contain as many elements as required.

The value attributes have their data types set as follows: `LongText` and `SalesRep` are of type `string`, `SalesDate` is of type `Date`, and `OrderNo` is of type `integer`. Remember, these data types all belong to the package `com.sap.dictionary` and are the only types suitable for supplying data to UI elements.

These declarations will cause the following classes and methods to be created:

▶ `wdContext.nodeSalesOrders`
  To access the node

▶ `wdContext.createSalesOrdersElement`
  To create a new typed element for node `SalesOrders`

▶ `wdContext.currentSalesOrdersElement`
  To access the collection element at the lead selection

Within the `ISalesOrdersElement` class will be a set of typed getter and setter methods to manipulate the runtime data stored in each element of the collection.

These methods are generically listed in Table 6.1 to Table 6.4 in Section 6.1.1.

### 6.2.2    Accessing a Node Element

Using the context shown in Figure 6.4, the elements in the node `SalesOrders` can be accessed as follows:

```
// Get the element at the lead selection of node SalesOrders
ISalesOrdersElement thisSoEl =
                    wdContext.currentSalesOrdersElement();

// Access the element's attribute values
String          longText  = thisSoEl.getLongText();
java.sql.Date   salesDate = thisSoEl.getSalesDate();
String          salesRep  = thisSoEl.getSalesRep();
int             orderNo   = thisSoEl.getOrderNo();
```

**Listing 6.3**  Accessing the attributes of a value node element

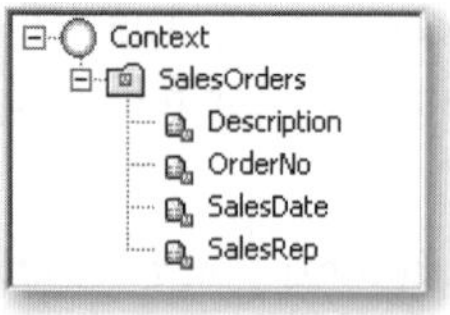

**Figure 6.4**  Example Context Structure

Be careful when reading the coding in Listing 6.3, it has taken a shortcut! Since the node `SalesOrders` is independent, it will be a singleton with respect to its parent node (the context root node); therefore, there can only ever be one instance of this node. Knowing this, we can call the method `currentSalesOrdersElement()` directly from the context root (wdContext) knowing that there is no ambiguity over which instance of node SalesOrders is to be accessed.

---

**Caveat Confector**

If you want to access elements belonging to non-singleton nodes that do not lie on the current selection path, then the coding shortcut shown in Listing 6.3 cannot be taken. Instead, you should first make an explicit reference to the required node instance, and only then can you select an element from the node collection.

---

### 6.2.3   Accessing all Elements in a Node

It is often necessary to process all the elements in a node collection. This is particularly true if the user is permitted to select multiple rows of a table. Since each table row is represented by a node element, selecting multiple rows will cause the node's isMultiSelected() flag to be switched on for that element.[3] The following code sample shows how such elements can be identified:

```
// Access all the elements of node SalesOrders
ISalesOrdersElement thisSoEl;
ISalesOrdersNode soNode = wdContext.nodeSalesOrders();
int noSalesOrders      = soNode.size();

// Loop around all the elements in the node
for (i=0; i<noSalesOrders; i++) {
  // Is the current element selected?
  if (soNode.isMultiSelected(i)) {
    thisSoEl = soNode.getSalesOrdersElementAt(i);

    // Do something useful with the selected element
  }
}
```

**Listing 6.4** Accessing all the selected elements of a value node

Remember that the flag to indicate whether a particular element is multi-selected is not held within the element object; it is held within the node object. This is a separate set of flags than the single lead selection flag. Only one element can be at the lead selection in a node collection, but multiple elements can have their multiSelected flag switched on (as long, of course, as the node's selection cardinality permits this).

Once we have decided that the particular element has been multi-selected, the way in which we access the element must be altered slightly. This is because the act of iterating around the elements in the node collection does not update which element is at the lead selection. Therefore, once we have determined that the *i*th ele-

---

3   This assumes that the node has a selection cardinality of ?..n.

ment is multi-selected, we must ask the node itself to return it. This is done by calling the method get$`{cn}`ElementAt().

### 6.2.4 Creating a New Node Element

Creating a new element in a node collection is a three-stage process:

1. Create a new element object using the method create$`{cn}`Element(), available either directly from `wdContext` or from `wdContext.node${cn}`. The element object returned by this method call is not yet the member of any node collection.

2. Call the various setter methods to populate the element's attributes with appropriate values.

3. Add the element to the node's element collection. This can be achieved by calling either of `${cn}`'s addElement() methods. Alternatively, if you want to replace the entire node collection, use one of its bind() methods.

---

**Caveat Confector**

You must ensure that whenever you manipulate an element collection, you do not violate the node's cardinality!

You will get runtime exceptions in the context if you attempt either of the following:

▶ Delete the last element from a node of cardinality 1..?

▶ Add a second element to a node of cardinality ?..1

---

**Important**

The creation of a new node element does not cause that element to be added to the node's element collection. You must add the node yourself. This is because you may want to maintain your own sort order for the elements in the node collection.

---

Whether you need to maintain a sorted element collection or not, each new element must be added manually. In generic terms, the coding to add the element created above is as follows:

▶ `wdContext.node${cn}.addElement(newNodeElement);`
   Append the new element to the end of the node collection.

▶ `wdContext.node${cn}.addElement(idx, newNodeElement);`
   Insert the new element at index position `idx` of the collection.

The following code sample will add two elements to the node `SalesOrder` described above.

```
public void wdDoInit() {
  //@@begin wdDoInit()
  // Create two new element objects for node SalesOrders
```

```
ISalesOrdersElement soEl1 =
  wdContext.createSalesOrdersElement();
ISalesOrdersElement soEl2 =
  wdContext.createSalesOrdersElement();

// Populate the first element
soEl1.setLongText("Printer supplies");
soEl1.setSalesDate(new Date(System.currentTimeMillis()));
soEl1.setSalesRep("Harry Hawk");
soEl1.setOrderNo(100);

// Populate the second element
soEl2.setLongText("Network cabling");
soEl2.setSalesDate(new Date(System.currentTimeMillis()));
soEl2.setSalesRep("Ned Seagoon");
soEl2.setOrderNo(101);

// Append elements to node collection
wdContext.nodeSalesOrders().addElement(soEl1);
wdContext.nodeSalesOrders().addElement(soEl2);
//@@end
}
```

**Listing 6.5** Create two value node elements and append them to the end of the node collection

This coding example is simplistic in the sense that hard-coded values are being added to the context attributes. A more typical situation is one in which the data to be added to the context is obtained from a model object, which has derived it from some backend system.

To make this situation more realistic, the context should be extended to show how a child node under SalesOrders would behave.

The node SalesOrders has now had a child value node added of cardinality 0..n, called LineItems. This node has four child attributes: ItemNo, Description, Quantity, and Price.

ItemNo is an integer, Description is a string, and Quantity and Price are both decimal.

Do you remember how the node property singleton changes the node's runtime behavior? (Look back at Section 5.7.3 if you don't.) If we just accept the default value of true, this will critically affect how the data in the node is managed.

Figure 6.5 shows the structure of the context that we will build. In the following examples, we will deal with LineItems first as a singleton node and then as a non-singleton node.

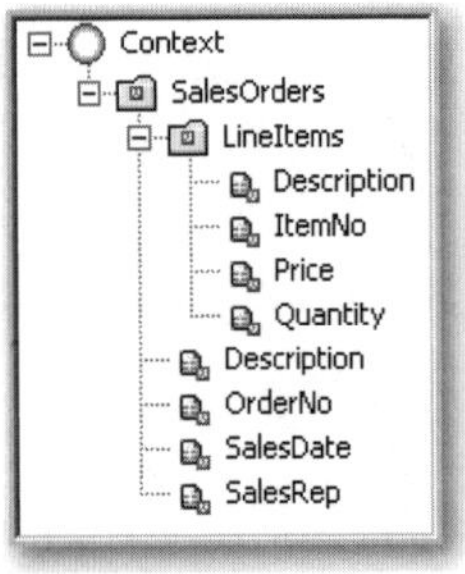

**Figure 6.5** Context Value Node with a Child Node

### 6.2.5 Treating the Node LineItems as a Singleton Node

Declaring the LineItems child node to be a singleton means there will only ever be one instance of this node with respect to its parent node SalesOrders. This has two immediate consequences:

▶ The node LineItems *must* have a supply function (see Section 5.13).

▶ The SalesOrders node *cannot* be displayed using a tree UI element (see Section 10.1).

The coding example given below shows the processing required to add two elements to the SalesOrders node and then four elements to the LineItems node that vary depending on which element in SalesOrders is selected. Coding is required in four different methods:

▶ wdDoInit(): Called once at controller initialization time

▶ supplyLineItems(): A supply function called automatically by the Web Dynpro Framework

▶ doNewSalesOrder(): A utility method

▶ doNewLineItem(): A utility method

Again, the example is simplistic because, in reality, you would probably not hard-code the attribute values into the program. Also observe that the class and package names of the input parameters to the supplyLineItems() method and the two utility methods have been generalized.

```
public void wdDoInit() {
  //@@begin wdDoInit()
  // Create two new SalesOrders elements
  ISalesOrdersElement soEl1 =
    wdContext.createSalesOrdersElement();
  ISalesOrdersElement soEl2 =
    wdContext.createSalesOrdersElement();
```

```
// Populate SalesOrders elements
  java.sql.Date today =
    new Date(System.currentTimeMillis());
  ISalesOrdersNode soNode = wdContext.nodeSalesOrders();

  soNode.addElement(
    doNewSalesOrder(soEl1, 100, "Printer supplies",
                    today, "Harry Hawk"));
  soNode.addElement(
    doNewSalesOrder(soEl2, 101, "Network Cabling",
                    today, "Ned Seagoon"));
  //@@end
}

public void supplyLineItems(
  IPrivate${nc}.ILineItemsNode node,
  IPrivate${nc}.ISalesOrdersElement parentElement) {
  //@@begin supplyLineItems(IWDNode,IWDNodeElement)
  // Create four new LineItems elements
  ILineItemsElement el1 = node.createLineItemsElement();
  ILineItemsElement el2 = node.createLineItemsElement();
  ILineItemsElement el3 = node.createLineItemsElement();
  ILineItemsElement el4 = node.createLineItemsElement();

  // Populate the new line item elements based on the order
  // number found in the parent element
  switch(parentElement.getOrderNo()) {
    case 100:
      node.addElement(doNewLineItem(el1, 10,
                                    "Cyan cartridge",
                                    new BigDecimal(90.12),
                                    new BigDecimal(10)));
      node.addElement(doNewLineItem(el2, 20,
                                    "Magenta cartridge",
                                    new BigDecimal(90.12),
                                    new BigDecimal(10)));
      node.addElement(doNewLineItem(el3, 30,
                                    "Yellow cartridge",
                                    new BigDecimal(90.12),
                                    new BigDecimal(10)));
      node.addElement(doNewLineItem(el4, 40,
                                    "Black cartridge",
                                    new BigDecimal(35.89),
                                    new BigDecimal(10)));
      break;
    case 101:
      node.addElement(doNewLineItem(el1, 10,
                                    "100m reel CAT 6",
                                    new BigDecimal(35.03),
```

```
                                           new BigDecimal(4)));
        node.addElement(doNewLineItem(el2, 20,
                                      "RJ45 connectors (50)",
                                      new BigDecimal(15.25),
                                      new BigDecimal(5)));
        node.addElement(doNewLineItem(el3, 30,
                                      "Crimp tool",
                                      new BigDecimal(85.37),
                                      new BigDecimal(1)));
        node.addElement(doNewLineItem(el4, 40,
                                      "40 bay patch panel",
                                      new BigDecimal(130.45),
                                      new BigDecimal(2)));
      break;
    default:
    }
    //@@end
}


public ${pkg1}..${pkgn}.wdp.IPublic${nc}.ISalesOrdersElement
       doNewSalesOrder(${pkg1}..${pkgn}.wdp.IPublic${nc}.
                       ISalesOrdersElement salesOrder,
                       int orderNo,
                       String description,
                       java.sql.Date date,
                       String salesRep ) {
    //@@begin doNewSalesOrder()
    salesOrder.setOrderNo(orderNo);
    salesOrder.setLongText(description);
    salesOrder.setSalesDate(date);
    salesOrder.setSalesRep(salesRep);

    return salesOrder;
    //@@end
}


public ${pkg1}..${pkgn}.wdp.IPublic${nc}.ILineItemsElement
       doNewLineItem(${pkg1}..${pkgn}.wdp.IPublic${nc}.
                     ILineItemsElement lineItem,
                     int itemNo,
                     String Description,
                     java.math.BigDecimal Price,
                     java.math.BigDecimal Qty) {
    //@@begin doNewLineItem()
    lineItem.setItemNo(itemNo);
    lineItem.setDescription(Description);
    lineItem.setPrice(Price);
    lineItem.setQuantity(Qty);
```

```
  return lineItem;
  //@@end
}
```

**Listing 6.6** Populating the singleton node LineItems using a supply function

Now that the node `LineItems` has a supply function defined (method `supplyLineI-tems()`), the Web Dynpro Framework will call it automatically every time the lead selection in the parent node collection changes, or after the node has been explicitly invalidated by calling `nodeLineItems.invalidate()`.

### 6.2.6 Treating the Node LineItems as a Non-Singleton Node

If we now modify the `singleton` property of the node `LineItems` and change it from `true` to `false`, a distinct instance of this node can now exist for every element in the `SalesOrders` node collection. This has two general consequences:

▸ The memory requirements can grow rapidly if there are multiple levels of non-singleton nodes in a hierarchy.

▸ A tree UI element can now be used to display the sales order and line item data.

Now that `LineItems` is a non-singleton node, it does not *require* a supply function. However, it is still a good idea to provide it with one because then you can implement the principle of lazy data access. This means the data for a particular instance of the node `LineItems` will only be retrieved when the user wants to look at it. Up until that point, the various instances of child node `LineItems` won't even exist.

Alternatively, if the process of populating all the instances of `LineItems` is not expensive, you could opt for this processing to take place once at the start of the controller's lifecycle. In the following example, the coding has been amended based on the assumption that all the `LineItems` node instances need to be populated at the start of the controller's lifecycle.

> **Important**
>
> In reality, you will find that writing a supply function for a node is the more efficient approach. Remember that *any* context node (value node or model node, singleton or non-singleton) can have a supply function defined for it. Generally speaking, you should not spend the time populating nodes with data if the user has no need to see that data on the screen.

Notice in the coding that follows that all the work to populate the context now takes place in the `wdDoInit()` method. This method is called once and only once at the start of the controller's lifecycle. In this case, the node `LineItems` has had its supply function removed. The methods `doNewSalesOrder()` and `doNewLineItem()` are unchanged.

```java
public void wdDoInit() {
  //@@begin wdDoInit()
  // Create new element objects for node SalesOrders
  ISalesOrdersElement soEl1 =
    wdContext.createSalesOrdersElement();
  ISalesOrdersElement soEl2 =
    wdContext.createSalesOrdersElement();

  // Processing must be performed in the following order:
  // 1) Create and populate a SalesOrders element. This is
  //      done by calling method doNewSalesOrder()
  // 2) Add it to the SalesOrders node
  // 3) Using each SalesOrders element object, create a
  //      LineItems child node
  // 4) Populate the LineItems element
  // 5) Add the LineItems element to the LineItems node

  // Populate SalesOrders elements
  java.sql.Date today =
    new Date(System.currentTimeMillis());
  ISalesOrdersNode soNode = wdContext.nodeSalesOrders();

  soNode.addElement(
    doNewSalesOrder(soEl1,100,"Printer supplies",
                    today, "Harry Hawk"));

  // Create non-singleton instance of child node LineItems
  ILineItemsNode     liNode1  = soEl1.nodeLineItems();
  ILineItemsElement so1LiEl1 =
    liNode1.createLineItemsElement();
  ILineItemsElement so1LiEl2 =
    liNode1.createLineItemsElement();
  ILineItemsElement so1LiEl3 =
    liNode1.createLineItemsElement();
  ILineItemsElement so1LiEl4 =
    liNode1.createLineItemsElement();

  liNode1.addElement(doNewLineItem(so1LiEl1, 10,
                                   "Cyan cartridge",
                                   new BigDecimal(90.12),
                                   new BigDecimal(10)));
  liNode1.addElement(doNewLineItem(so1LiEl2, 20,
                                   "Magenta cartridge",
                                   new BigDecimal(90.12),
                                   new BigDecimal(10)));
  liNode1.addElement(doNewLineItem(so1LiEl3, 30,
                                   "Yellow cartridge",
                                   new BigDecimal(90.12),
                                   new BigDecimal(10)));
```

```
liNode1.addElement(doNewLineItem(so1LiE14, 40,
                               "Black cartridge",
                               new BigDecimal(35.89),
                               new BigDecimal(10)));

// Populate second SalesOrders element and add it to the
// SalesOrders node
soNode.addElement(
  doNewSalesOrder(soE12,101,"Network Cabling",
                  today, "Ned Seagoon")));

// Create non-singleton instance of child node LineItems
ILineItemsNode      liNode2  = soE12.nodeLineItems();
ILineItemsElement so2LiE11 =
  liNode2.createLineItemsElement();
ILineItemsElement so2LiE12 =
  liNode2.createLineItemsElement();
ILineItemsElement so2LiE13 =
  liNode2.createLineItemsElement();
ILineItemsElement so2LiE14 =
  liNode2.createLineItemsElement();

liNode2.addElement(doNewLineItem(so2LiE11, 10,
                               "100m reel CAT 6",
                               new BigDecimal(35.03),
                               new BigDecimal(4)));
liNode2.addElement(doNewLineItem(so2LiE12, 20,
                               "RJ45 connectors (50)",
                               new BigDecimal(5.25),
                               new BigDecimal(5)));
liNode2.addElement(doNewLineItem(so2LiE13, 30,
                               "Crimp tool",
                               new BigDecimal(85.37),
                               new BigDecimal(1)));
liNode2.addElement(doNewLineItem(so2LiE14, 40,
                               "40 bay patch panel",
                               new BigDecimal(130.45),
                             new BigDecimal(2)));
 //@@end
}
```

**Listing 6.7** Populating the non-singleton node LineItems

There are several things to notice about the above code sample:

▶ The coding to create the SalesOrders elements is unchanged.

▶ The elements soE11 and soE12 *must* be added to the SalesOrders node collection before any attempt is made to create the respective LineItems child node instance. If you try to create a non-singleton child node before the parent element has been added to its node collection, you will get a runtime exception in the context.

▶ The method call to `nodeLineItems()` belongs to the parent *element*, not the parent *node*. This is possible only for non-singleton nodes.

---

**Important**

A singleton child node has a one-to-one relationship with its parent *node*, irrespective of the number of elements contained in the parent node. When the lead selection of the parent node changes, all child nodes are flagged as dirty. If supply functions exist, they will be called automatically at the first attempt to access the child nodes.

The only methods available to create a new instance of a singleton child node belong to the classes `wdContext` and the `node${cn}`.

A non-singleton child node has a one-to-one relationship with its parent *element*. Therefore, if the node `${cn}` contains *n* elements and has a non-singleton child node `${chn}`, then there will be up to *n* separate instances of `${chn}`.

A non-singleton child node can also be created directly from the parent *element* by calling `wdContext.current${cn} Element.node${chn}()`.

---

**Caveat Confector**

Regardless of its position in the hierarchy, every node in the context can be accessed directly by calling the method `wdContext.node${cn}()`. What must be clearly understood is that when the getter method of an arbitrary node is called, the node instance returned is always the one that corresponds to the element at the lead selection of each successive parent node up to the root node.

If, however, you want to access a child node that does not lie on the lead selection path, two approaches can be taken:

1. For a hierarchy of singleton nodes, start at the root node and perform a step-wise parent-to-child traversal down the hierarchy, setting the lead selection of each node before traversing to the next child.

2. For a hierarchy of non-singleton nodes, the specific child node can be accessed by first obtaining the parent element of the non-singleton node and then via the instance of the parent *element*, calling the `node${chn}()` method.

---

### 6.2.7 Accessing the Context Through the Generic API

If a node is created at design time with the `typedAccessRequired` property set to `false` or is created dynamically at runtime, no typed interface will be available. In such cases, the generic context API must be used. This amounts to nothing more than learning to handle context nodes through the base class `IWDNode`.

To access a node generically, you need to know the following:

▶ The name of the node

▶ The index of the element in the parent node's collection to which this child node instance pertains

As Figure 6.6 shows, all singleton child nodes belong to the element at the lead selection in the parent node. Nodes with the context root as their immediate parent belong to only one possible element: element zero of the root node. Consequently, all nodes with the context root as their immediate parent are forced to be singleton nodes.

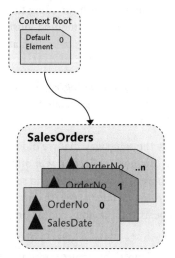

**Figure 6.6** Independent Nodes Can Only Be Related to Element 0 of the Root Node

Since the generic context API knows nothing about the node's data type, we cannot expect to be able to use the method wdContext.node**${cn}**() (if you need to use the generic context API, it will be because this method doesn't exist). Using the context shown in Figure 6.6, you can access the SalesOrder node using the following code:

```
// Get child node SalesOrders via the generic context API
IWDNode salesOrderNode =
  wdContext.getChildNode("SalesOrders",0);
```

**Listing 6.8** Accessing the independent node SalesOrders using the generic context API

There are several things to notice about this coding:

▶ We must use the general-purpose context method wdContext.getChildNode(). This node can be used to access any node instance anywhere in the context.

▶ The method getChildNode() requires two parameters:

  ▶ The name of the node to be retrieved

  ▶ The element index in the parent node collection to which this child node pertains: set to zero in this case

▶ The node object returned by method getChildNode() is of the generic class IWD-Node.

Since we know that the `SalesOrders` node is an independent node, it must therefore have the context root node as its immediate parent. Furthermore, we know that the root node's cardinality is hard-coded to `1..1`, so it contains only a single element, which means there can only ever be single instances of the child nodes immediately below it (hence, all independent nodes are singletons).

Therefore, we know that if we are going to access an independent node using the generic context interface, the index parameter to the `getChildNode()` method must be set to zero — because the root node only has a single element in its collection at index position 0.

If we needed to access a dependent node further down the context hierarchy, we would first have to ensure that the parent node has been correctly populated; only then would we be able to access the correct child node instance.

We can access the node's element collection in exactly the same way that we did in Listing 6.4. However, the elements contained within this node collection will only ever be of the generic class `IWDNodeElement`; that is, there will be no getter and setter methods for any of the element's attributes. Therefore, we must access the node attributes generically. (The next coding fragment repeats the previous coding and then adds some new statements.)

To access a node attribute held in an `IWDNodeElement` object, you must know the attributes name and data type.

```
// Get a reference to the independent node SalesOrders via
// the generic context API
IWDNode soNode = wdContext.getChildNode("SalesOrders",0);

// Get the current element of  SalesOrders
IWDNodeElement thisSoEl = soNode.getCurrentElement();

// Get the value of the SalesRep attribute
// Since we know the SalesRep attribute is of type String,
// we can use method getAttributeAsText(), instead of the
// more generic getAttributeValue() which just returns an
// Object
String salesRep = thisSoEl.getAttributeAsText("SalesRep");
```
**Listing 6.9** Accessing a context attribute using the generic context API

If you don't know the data type of a particular attribute, you can interrogate the node info object associated with the node. This holds all the metadata for the node and can supply you with the names and data types of all attributes in the node. This technique is used when context nodes need to be dynamically replicated from one context to another. See Section 9.2.3 for more details.

The following example shows the coding needed to access the LineItems node shown in Figure 6.5. Since the child node LineItems could be either a singleton or a non-singleton with respect to its parent node SalesOrders, there are two possible approaches to accessing this child node.

### Accessing the Singleton Node LineItems with the Generic Context API

If the child node LineItems is a singleton with respect to its parent node SalesOrders, the coding to access LineItems is as follows:

```
import java.sql.Date;
// Get the independent node SalesOrders via the generic context API
IWDNode soNode = wdContext.getChildNode("SalesOrders",0);

// Set the lead selection of node SalesOrders
soNode.setLeadSelection(<some_integer>);
IWDNodeElement thisSoEl = soNode.getCurrentElement();

// Get the attribute values for the current SalesOrders
String longText  = thisSoEl.getAttributeAsText("LongText");
int OrderNo =
  ((Integer)thisSoEl.getAttributeValue("OrderNo")).
                      intValue();
String salesRep = thisSoEl.getAttributeAsText("SalesRep");
Date salesDate = (Date)thisSoEl.
                  getAttributeValue("SalesDate");

// Get the instance of node LineItems that belongs to this
// SalesOrders element
// The following call to getChildNode() will automatically
// trigger the execution of the node's supply function
IWDNode liNode =
  soNode.getChildNode("LineItems", soNode.getLeadSelection());

int liNodeSize = liNode.size();
// Loop around all the elements in node LineItems
for (int i=0; i<liNodeSize; i++) {
  // Get the current LineItems element
  IWDNodeElement liEl = liNode.getElementAt(i);

  // Do something useful with the current LineItems element
}
```

**Listing 6.10** Accessing a singleton node via the generic context API

Notice the following points:

▶ Because the node `LineItems` is a singleton with respect to its parent node `Sale-sOrders`, we must position the lead selection within the node `SalesOrders` before we can obtain the correct element. Hence, the call to the method `so-Node.setLeadSelection()` is followed by the call to the method `soNode.getCur-rentElement()`.

> **Caveat Confector**
>
> Don't think you can sidestep these two statements by simply calling `soNode.getElementAt(i)`, because this method does not alter a node's lead selection. Therefore, if you were then to call the method `soNode.getChildNode("LineItems", soNode.getLeadSelection)`, the child node you get back will be the one related to the element at the lead selection of the node `soNode`, which is not necessarily the element returned by `soNode.getElementAt(i)`.

▶ As soon as the lead selection of the node `SalesOrders` is changed, the Web Dynpro Framework flags any of its singleton child nodes as being dirty. This flag will later trigger the automatic execution of the child node supply functions. In this case, the call to `soNode.getChildNode()` will automatically trigger the Web Dynpro Framework to run the supply function.

▶ All attributes that can usefully be cast as `strings` can be retrieved from the current element using the method `getAttributeAsText()`. Attributes of other data types should be retrieved with `getAttributeValue()` and then cast to the appropriate type.

▶ Now that the lead selection of the node `SalesOrders` has been positioned, the correct instance of the node `LineItems` can be obtained by calling `soNode.getChildNode()`.

> **Important**
>
> If the second parameter to this method is not set to the same value as the node's lead selection, a runtime exception will occur — hence, the use of `soNode.getLeadSelection()` to ensure that this value is always correct.

**Accessing the Non-Singleton Node LineItems with the Generic Context API**

If the child node `LineItems` is now changed to be a non-singleton with respect to its parent node `SalesOrders`, the coding to access `LineItems` is slightly different from that shown in Listing 6.10 above. The differences are shown in bold in Listing 6.11.

```
import java.sql.Date;

// Get child node SalesOrders via the generic context API
IWDNode soNode = wdContext.getChildNode("SalesOrders",0);
```

```
// Set which element we want to access in node SalesOrders
int i = <some_element_number>;

// Get the correct parent element of node SalesOrders
// Since the child node LineItems is now a non-singleton,
// we do not need to worry about repositioning the lead
// selection of node SalesOrders
IWDNodeElement thisSoEl = soNode.getElementAt(i);

// Get the attribute values of the current SalesOrders
String longText  = thisSoEl.getAttributeAsText("LongText");
int OrderNo =
  ((Integer)thisSoEl.getAttributeValue("OrderNo")).
    intValue();
String salesRep  = thisSoEl.getAttributeAsText("SalesRep");
Date salesDate =
  (Date)thisSoEl.getAttributeValue("SalesDate");

// Get the instance of node LineItems that belongs to
// the SalesOrders element at index i
IWDNode liNode = soNode.getChildNode("LineItems",i);

int liNodeSize = liNode.size();

// Loop around all the elements in node LineItems
for (int j=0; j<liNodeSize; j++) {
  // Get the current LineItems element
  IWDNodeElement liEl = liNode.getElementAt(j);

  // Do something useful with the current element
}
```

**Listing 6.11** Accessing a non-singleton node via the generic context API

Notice the differences between accessing a singleton and a non-singleton node:

▸ Since the node LineItems is now a non-singleton with respect to its parent node SalesOrders, there will be multiple distinct instances of the node LineItems for each element within the node SalesOrders. Therefore, it is unnecessary to reposition the lead selection of the node SalesOrders before attempting to access the child node. In this situation, we can access the element directly by calling getElementAt().

▸ The method getChildNode() can now be called with any index value we like because the node instance being returned is a non-singleton.

Apart from the two statements in bold, the remaining code is identical.

## 6.3 Working with Model Nodes

It is an easy mistake to make to think that model nodes behave like value nodes. Unfortunately, this misunderstanding can lead to some odd runtime problems in which you appear to have the correct data in your model node, but then you cannot invoke the related processing in the backend system. So the first point to tackle here is to ensure that you do not make this mistake.

### 6.3.1 Adding Elements to a Model Node Collection

Simply creating an element for a model node and adding it to the node collection is not the correct way to use this type of context node. For instance, the following code sample (where ${mn} is any model node) will not cause any errors — but it won't work properly either.

```
// Get reference to the model node, then create an element
I${mn}Node    modelNode = wdContext.node${mn};
I${mn}Element newModelEl = modelNode.create${mn}Element();
```

```
// Add the model element to the node collection
modelNode.addElement(newModelEl);
```

**Listing 6.12** A code sample that looks plausible but will not work as required

This coding would be perfectly good if it weren't that we are dealing with a model node, not a value node. In Listing 6.12, the element instance newModelEl will happily store all the information belonging to the model object, but that is just the point — it's only the information *belonging to* the model object's functionality. The data has been detached from the model object's functionality and is consequently not executable.

Node elements are not executable; only model objects are.[4]

To use a model node correctly, you must perform the following steps:

1. Create a model object instance of the same type as the model node. This is your executable object that has access to the functionality found in the backend system.

2. Store your business data in the model object instance.

3. Add (or bind) the model object instance to the model node's collection.

The correct coding for using model objects will be shown using a somewhat more realistic coding scenario. We will assume that the Model Import Wizard has already

---

4 This statement needs to be qualified by saying that it is possible to have a non-executable model object. However, in the sequence of processing we are dealing with here, we must always start with an executable model object, and then as a result of the model object's execution, non-executable model objects are created.

been used to create a model for calling the ABAP function module BAPI_FLIGHT_
GETLIST. The result of creating such a model is that two model objects are now
available:

▶ **BAPI_FLIGHT_GETLIST_INPUT**
This is the executable model object.

▶ **BAPI_FLIGHT_GETLIST_OUTPUT**
This model object is created as a result of BAPI_FLIGHT_GETLIST_INPUT's execution and is non-executable.

You can see that both the generated model object names start with the name of the
ABAP function module and are then suffixed with _INPUT and _OUTPUT, respectively.

The next preparatory step is that a model node must be created in the context and
bound to the model object BAPI_FLIGHT_GETLIST_INPUT. Typically, the model node
and the model object have the same name. The action of binding the model node to
the model object causes the node to take on the structure of the model object.

When creating the elements of a model node's collection, you should not think of
a model node as being the same as a value node. Instead, if you use the createEle-
ment() method belonging to a model node, it must be passed an instance of a relevant model object. Only then will a node element be created that correctly references a model object instance.

For instance, a new element can be added to the collection of model node BAPI_
FLIGHT_GETLIST_INPUT as follows:[5]

```
// Create a new model object instance
Bapi_Flight_Getlist_Input bapiIn =
                        new Bapi_Flight_Getlist_Input();

// Get a reference to the model node
IBapi_Flight_Getlist_InputNode modelNode =
                wdContext.nodeBapi_Flight_Getlist_Input();

// Create a new model node element by referencing the model
// object instance
IBapi_Flight_Getlist_InputElement newModelEl =
    modelNode.createBapi_Flight_Getlist_InputElement(bapiIn);

// Append the new element to the model node's collection
modelNode.addElement(newModelEl);
```

**Listing 6.13** Adding an element to a model node by referencing a model object instance

---

5  This is not the only way of adding an element to a model node. The bind() method can
also be used.

Notice that the create${mn}Element() method of a model node cannot create a new element object on its own; its needs to be passed a reference to an existing model object. The model object is the actual repository for the runtime data, and the attributes and child nodes in the model node are simply references to data held in the model object.

Here is the same coding in generalized form:

```
// Create a new model object instance
${mo} bapiIn = new ${mo}();

// Get a reference to the model node
I${mn}Node modelNode = wdContext.node${mn}();

// Create a new model node element by referencing the model
// object instance
I${mn}Element newModelEl = modelNode.create${mn}Element(bapiIn);

// Append the new element to the model node's element collection
modelNode.addElement(newModelEl);
```

**Listing 6.14** Generalized coding for adding an element to a model node by referencing a model object instance

This technique of creating model object instances and then using them to create new model node elements is useful if you want to maintain a model node that has multiple elements (i.e., references to multiple model objects) in its collection.

### 6.3.2 Binding Elements to a Model Node Collection

An alternative approach for working with model nodes is to use the IWDNode.bind() method. This method is preferable when you need to maintain only a single model object reference in the node.

The IWDNode.bind() method takes the parameter you pass it (either a single element or a collection of elements) and uses it to replace the entire node collection. If, therefore, you only need the model node to reference a single model object instance, the following coding is simpler.

```
// Create a new model object instance
Bapi_Flight_Getlist_Input bapiIn = new Bapi_Flight_Getlist_Input();

// Bind the model object instance to the node collection
wdContext.nodeBapi_Flight_Getlist_Input().bind(bapiIn);
```

**Listing 6.15** Adding an element to a model node by referencing a model object instance

In effect, the `bind()` method takes the model object and uses it to create a corresponding element without you needing to handle the element object directly. However, since `bind()` throws away the old node collection and replaces it with the parameter value, it should only be used when the previous contents of the element collection are no longer needed.

## 6.4 Working with Recursive Nodes

If you want to represent a recursive data structure within the context, a recursive node is the correct node to use. The simplest example of recursive data within a hierarchical structure is a file system. A directory can contain either files or subdirectories. This definition is then repeated for each subdirectory level down the hierarchy.

Within the context, a recursive node is a special node that has only two properties: `name` and `repeatedNode`. As with any context node, a recursive node must have a name, but the `repeatedNode` property is where the recursion is defined. This property holds a reference to some parent node and indicates that, at runtime, the location of the recursive node will be occupied by a node instance of the type indicated in the `repeatedNode` property.

Think of a recursive node as a design time placeholder used to indicate that a node will be created at this location at runtime and will be of the type named in the `repeatedNode` property. The node name identified by `repeatedNode` must lie on the direct path back to the context root node.

When a recursive node is created at runtime, it is always created as a non-singleton node. This is a hard-coded feature and cannot be changed.

> **Important**
>
> The depth to which recursion will occur is determined at runtime, not design time. At design time, you simply indicate that recursion is possible and leave it to the runtime code to establish exactly how deep that recursion will be.

Please see Appendix C for a detailed description of how to build a Web Dynpro application that displays a file system structure using a recursive context structure and a Tree UI element.

## 6.5 Using the WDCopyService

The `WDCopyService` is one of the utility services provided to make manipulation of context information easier. This service class has three methods:

▶ copyCorresponding(Object source, Object target)
This method inspects each attribute of the source element and searches for a compatible attribute in a target element. If a compatibility is found, the attribute value is copied.

For attributes to be considered compatible, their names and data types must match. The following classes and primitives are considered compatible:

▶ Numerics:
Classes Byte, Short, Integer, Long, Float, Double, BigInteger, and BigDecimal and the primitives byte, short, int, long, float, and double

▶ Character class and the primitive char

▶ Boolean class and the primitive boolean

Failing any generic, data-type compatibility, the source and target classes must be identical.

▶ copyElements(IWDNode source, IWDNode target)
Copies all the elements from the source node to the target node using repeated calls to copyCorresponding(). If the source and target nodes are both model nodes bound to the same model object, then after the copy, each element in the target node will share a reference to the model instances found in the source node.

The lead selection value will also be copied.

Copying data from a node that holds a mixture of model and value attributes will only copy the model instance reference, but copying from a model node to value node will function correctly.

Attempting to copy from a source model node bound to one model object, to a target node bound to a different model object will result in a WDRuntimeException being thrown.

▶ copySubtree(IWDNode source, IWDNode target)
Copies both the elements and child nodes of the source node to the target node. This is done by first calling copyElements() to copy the elements, followed by a search for equally named child nodes and recursive calls to copySubtree().

To copy the attributes from one element to another, the following code fragment can be used:

```
// Copy current source element to destination element
ISourceElement       srcEl =
                            wdContext.currentSourceElement();
IDestinationElement destEl =
                        wdContext.currentDestinationElement();

WDCopyService.copyCorresponding(srcEl, destEl);
```

**Listing 6.16** Copying attributes from one context element to another

Figure 6.7 illustrates how the contents of one node can be copied into another compatible node. To do this, the following code fragment can be used:

```
// Copy current source element to destination element
ISourceNode      srcNode = wdContext.nodeSource();
IDestinationNode destNode = wdContext.nodeDestination();

WDCopyService.copyElements(srcNode, destNode);
```

**Listing 6.17** Copying all the elements from one node to another

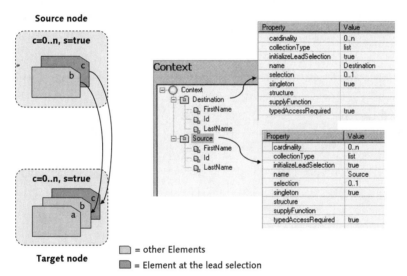

**Figure 6.7** The WDCopyService Will Copy Elements from the Source Node into the Target Node

# 7 UI Elements

The abbreviation UI stands for user interface, and a UI element is any object that is used in the construction of the screen seen by the end user.

UI elements are usually objects with which the user interacts, such as drop-down lists, checkboxes, input fields, or radio buttons. However, many non-interactive UI elements are available in Web Dynpro such as captions, horizontal gutters, and legends. It is also possible for a UI element to be completely invisible. Examples include the iFrame or a transparent container. Figure 7.1 shows how a table UI element would look in the view layout editor at design time.

---

**Important**

A UI element is not necessarily going to be visible. Certain UI elements are designed to act simply as containers that hold other (visible) UI elements. UI containers can hold anything from individual elements to a view controller to the entire visual interface of another component.

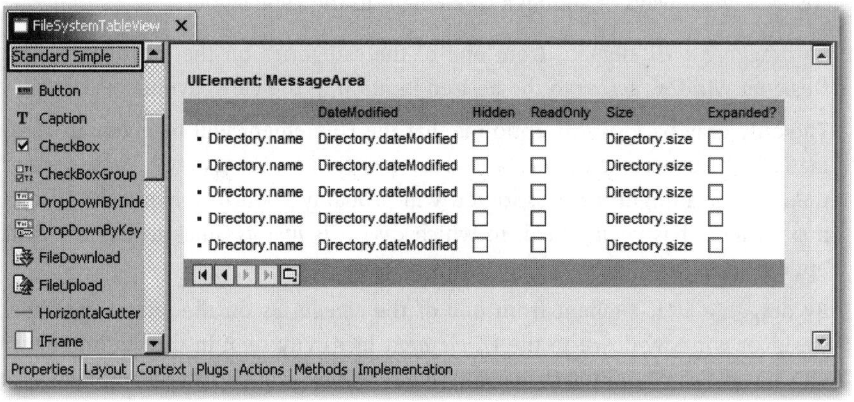

---

**Figure 7.1** An Example of a Table UI Element Seen in the NWDS at Design Time

## 7.1 How are UI Elements Stored Within a View Controller?

All UI elements are represented as a hierarchy within a view controller's layout. At the top of the hierarchy, there is always a UI element called `RootUIElementContainer`. It is beneath this UI element that all other UI elements will be defined (see Figure 7.2).

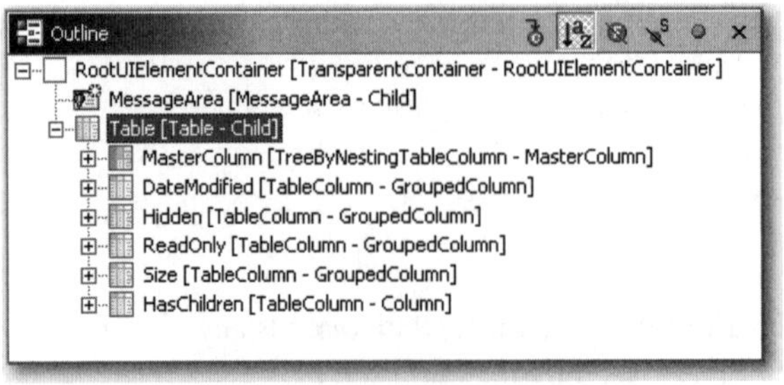

**Figure 7.2** The UI Element Hierarchy for Figure 7.1

The `RootUIElementContainer` is always of type `TransparentContainer`. This means this UI element is not visible.

## 7.2    Editing a View Layout

In this section we will look at the design time process of editing a view controller's layout.

### 7.2.1    Adding UI Elements to the View Layout

There are several ways of adding a UI element to the view layout:

1. By dragging a UI element from one of the categories on the left of the View Designer window across to the desired location in the view layout.

   The only drawback of this option is that the UI element will be given an automatically generated name such as `InputField4` or `DropDownByKey2`. These are not the most meaningful names, so you will probably want to rename the UI element after it has been added, in which case it is just as quick to use the next option.

2. By dragging a UI element from one of the categories on the left of the View Designer window down to the UI element hierarchy seen in the Outline view. This has the same drawback in that the UI element will be named automatically and may therefore need to be renamed manually.

3. By right-clicking on the container UI element in the Outline view (shown in Figure 7.2) and then selecting **Add Child**. A pop-up window is then displayed from which you can select the required UI element. At this point you can specify the name of the UI element that is about to be added.

4. This UI element is then added at the last position within the parent UI container's list of children.

5. By right-clicking on the container UI element in the Outline view (shown in Figure 7.2) and then selecting **Apply Template**. A wizard then opens and asks you what type of template you would like to apply. It will create either a table or a set of label–input field pairs of UI elements based on the attributes that have already been defined in the context.

### 7.2.2 Editing Existing UI Elements on the View Layout

Once a UI element object has been added to the view layout, it always becomes a child of some container UI element. The view layout therefore has a hard-coded container UI element called `RootUIElementContainer` (of type `TransparentContainer`), and all UI element objects are ultimately the children of this parent object.

The UI element hierarchy is traversed in the normal top-to-bottom, left-to-right manner. If you want to move a UI element within this hierarchical structure, you can do so in one of two ways. In the Outline view of the view layout:

1. Right-click on the UI element and from the pop-up menu select **Move Up** or **Move Down**.
2. Or click on the UI element and drag it up or down in the hierarchy.

> **Important**
>
> Be careful when using the drag and drop method of repositioning a UI element within the hierarchy! Sometimes the UI elements do not want to be dragged. Furthermore, sometimes they won't drop into the place you require.
>
> In these situations, it's always more reliable to use the **Move Up**, **Move Down** options from the pop-up menu.

## 7.3 Putting Data on the Screen

Two things must happen before data can be put on the screen. First, you must have defined the view controller's context. Second, you must decide which UI elements will be used to display the data held in the context.

### 7.3.1 Data Binding

Once these two decisions have been made, you must connect the UI element properties with the nodes and attributes in the context that contain the data. This is a process known as *data binding*, and is where you define which node or attribute in the context will act as a data source for that particular UI element property.

Can you see a familiar principle in operation here? It's the same data generator–data consumer principle at work, except this time, it is happening within the scope of a single controller. The view controller's context is behaving as the data source (or data generator), and the UI element properties are the data consumers (see Figure 7.3).

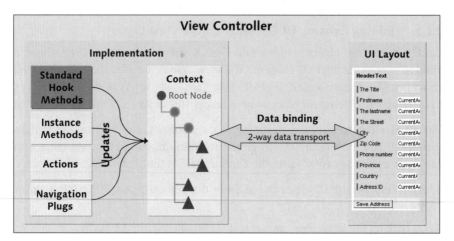

**Figure 7.3** The Context Acts as a Supplier of Data to the UI Element Properties via Data Binding

The separation between the UI element properties and the context has been implemented to achieve client independence (see Section 2.5.3).

### 7.3.2    Binding UI Properties to the Context

Which UI element properties can be bound to the context? The answer is, almost all of them. The only UI element properties that can never be bound to the context (i.e., the only UI element properties that cannot have variable values) are the id property and the properties related to the UI element's layout manager. Other than this, almost all UI element properties can obtain their value from the context (once a suitable data binding has been made).

In the following example, some name and address details are displayed on the screen. However, as you can see in Figure 7.4, the readOnly property of the First_Name input field contains the hard-coded value of false (❶). This means this UI element will *always* be open for input (❷).

By creating a dedicated context attribute (❸) of the correct data type (❹), you can programmatically control whether or not the First_Name field is open for input. This shown in Figure 7.5.

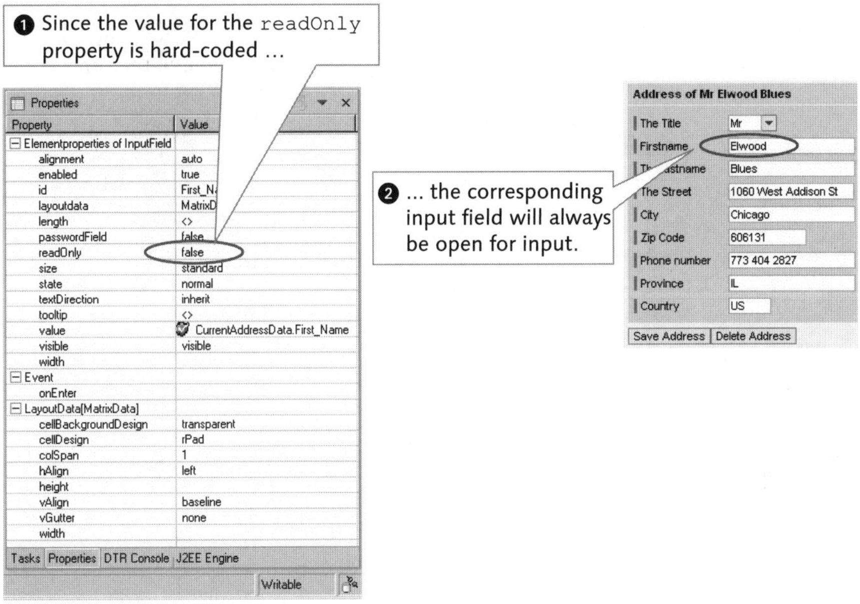

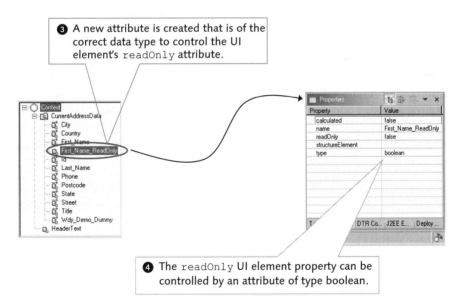

**Figure 7.4** A Hard-Coded Property Value Gives the UI Element a Fixed Behavior

**Figure 7.5** A Dedicated Context Attribute Can Be Used To Alter the Behavior of a UI Element

Now that a dedicated context attribute exists, the UI element's readOnly property can be bound to this attribute (Figure 7.6, step ❺). Now at runtime, the input field will only be open for input (❻) if the corresponding context Boolean attribute is set to false.

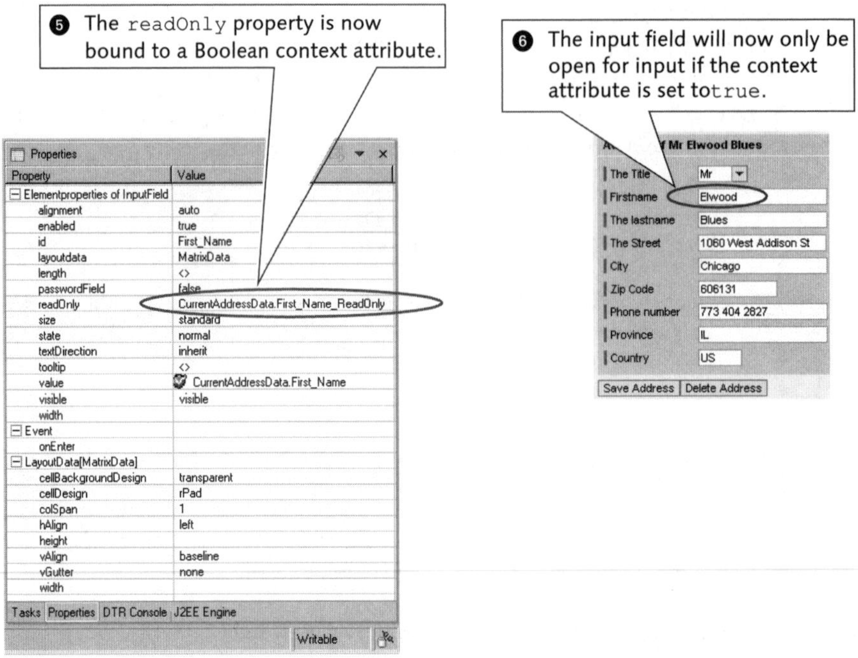

**Figure 7.6** The readOnly Property of the First_Name Field Can Now Be Controlled Programmatically

There is a very important detail to notice about this new context attribute. The context node to which this attribute has been added (CurrentAddressData) is a mapped node, and all its attributes are mapped. However, the attribute First_Name_ReadOnly that has just been added is not mapped; it is local to the view controller's context. This means the data in the First_Name_ReadOnly attribute will be local to the view controller's context, but the rest of the data in the context will be derived from the mapping origin node living in a different controller.

It is perfectly permissible to create a context node that contains a mixture of mapped and unmapped attributes. In fact, this is a good design because even though data appears to belong to a single node, the attributes that hold the business data are mapped (i.e., they function as consumers of data from a non-visual controller), and the attributes holding data only concerned with the display of the business data are not mapped.

### 7.3.3 Controlling UI Element Behavior from the Context

Most of the properties of a UI element can be bound either to a node or an attribute of the context. The behavior of the UI element can then be controlled by manipulation of the context. Properties such as visible, enabled, and readOnly are the ones you will typically use for dynamic alteration of a user interface.

Many UI elements have an `enabled` property, and those capable of receiving input from the user will probably have a `readOnly` property. Both of these properties are Boolean and don't affect whether a UI element is visible; they simply control whether the user can interact with it. However, if you want a UI element to be completely removed from the rendered screen, you need to manipulate the `visible` property. This property takes three possible values that are held in the constant `WDVisibility`.

▶ **VISIBLE**
Present on the screen and visible, but the user cannot necessarily interact with it

▶ **BLANK**
Present on the screen but invisible

▶ **NONE**
Completely absent from the screen

The `visible` property of a UI element must be bound to a context attribute of type `Visibility`. A context attribute can be assigned this data type as follows:

▶ Create a context attribute called, say, `InputVisibility`.[1]

▶ The default data type for any context attribute is `string`. Change this by clicking on the ellipsis button that appears to the right of the data type field.

▶ In the pop-up window, the radio button should be set to **Dictionary Simple Type**. Expand the tree node **Local Dictionary**.

▶ Expand the tree node `com.sap.ide.webdynpro.uielementdefinitions`, scroll down the list, and select **Visibility**.

▶ Create your UI element in the view layout and bind the `visible` property to this context attribute.

From the coding in your view controller, you will now be able to control the value of this context attribute using the values found in the `WDVisibility` class.

### 7.3.4 Impact of Data Binding on the Coding

The consequences of data binding mean that when you want to write some code that gets or sets the value of a UI element property, there is no need to access the UI element object itself. As long as you have bound the particular property of the UI element to a suitable attribute of the context, your coding need only manipulate the context attribute value.

Because the UI element property has been bound to the context, the Web Dynpro Framework will automatically transport the data from the context to the UI element

---

1 This name is completely arbitrary. You could call it `ChickenSoup` if you want, but that would probably not be very helpful.

when the screen is rendered and then automatically transport the user's input from the UI element back to the context when a round trip is initiated.

---

**Caveat Confector**

One of the tell-tale signs that an untrained developer has been using Web Dynpro is that when they want to put data on the screen, they write coding that obtains a direct reference to the UI element, and then they hard-code the values from the context directly into the UI element properties.

This style of coding is completely redundant 99 % of the time!

Do not write coding this way, as it will greatly increase the complexity of your application *without providing any benefits*. This will unnecessarily increase the maintenance effort required to modify and support the application.

In other words, you've just raised the application's total cost of ownership.

Bad news. Don't do it.

---

Certain UI element properties do not correspond to the simple data types such as `integer` or `string` or `boolean`. Such properties are ones such as `visibility` or `design`.

If you want to create a context attribute for controlling, say, the visibility of a UI element, you should set the context attribute's data type to a class found in one of the following packages:

1. `com.sap.dictionary.predefined.*`
2. `com.sap.ide.webdynpro.uielementdefintions`
3. `com.sap.ide.webdynpro.uielementlibraries.*`

These classes are available when you define a context attribute's data type by clicking on the ellipsis button that appears to the far right of the field when the data type is selected. Once you click on this button, you will see a pop-up window that gives you access to all the data types available from the local dictionaries (see Figure 7.7).

For instance, if you create a context attribute to control the visibility of one or more UI elements, this attribute must be of type `com.sap.ide.webdynpro.uielementdefinitions.Visibility`.

## 7.4 Avoiding a Possible Source of Confusion

As already stated, the Web Dynpro design paradigm is based on the separation of those parts of the program that *generate* data from those parts that *consume* data. This is the fundamental concept that underlies the more well-known principle of separating data *processing* from data *presentation*. The latter concept is just one use case of the former concept.

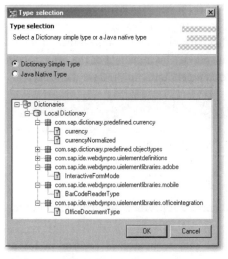

**Figure 7.7** UI Element Data Types Are All Available from the Local Dictionary

Every Web Dynpro UI element has a set of properties, most of which can be bound to different context nodes or attributes. Once a UI element property has been bound to a context node or attribute, you can directly control its behavior and appearance without ever needing to reference the UI element object itself. In other words, by means of data binding, you can manipulate one or more UI elements via the data held in the context.

However, developers who are experienced in Web development will have become accustomed to ambiguities that exist within HTML. These ambiguities concern the function performed by certain HTML tag parameters.

A good example is the difference between the `size` and `maxlength` properties of the HTML `<input>` tag. The `size` parameter controls the visible appearance of the UI element itself, but the `maxlength` parameter controls the maximum number of characters you can type into that input field.

"Well, so what?" you may say. And that's exactly my point: you're so used to the ambiguity that you probably don't even recognize it as a problem. Web Dynpro is more rigorous than this, though. In Web Dynpro you are not permitted to have UI element parameters that mix the control of data presentation (e.g., the `size` parameter) with the control of data processing (e.g., the `maxlength` parameter). In Web Dynpro UI element properties strictly control the presentation of data, not the processing.

The problem originates from the fact that when Tim Berners-Lee created the first version of HTML, he never envisaged that a metadata repository would ever be needed to define the data being displayed. Consequently, such a facility does not exist in HTML, and this makes the resulting ambiguities inevitable.

This blurred distinction in the use of UI element properties is not permitted in Web Dynpro, so when you look at the `length` parameter of an `InputField` UI element, for instance, you are looking at a property that controls only the appearance of the UI element — not the length of the data it displays. The metadata of the information being displayed by the UI element is held independently in the Java dictionary.

> **Important**
>
> UI element parameters control only the appearance of the UI element itself, not the data being displayed.

To recap on some UI element design principles:

1. The properties of a UI element control only its appearance and behavior, not the data being displayed.
2. The majority of UI element properties can be bound to context nodes or attributes.
3. The metadata of the information displayed through a UI element is determined by the context node or attribute to which it is bound, which can be controlled by a structure or simple type held in the Java Dictionary.

## 7.5    Layout Managers

The purpose of a layout manager is to manage the arrangement of UI elements within their parent container. All Web Dynpro UI element containers make use of a layout manager of some sort.

Every Web Dynpro view is represented as a hierarchy of UI elements. The root UI element of this hierarchy is created automatically whenever a view controller is declared and always has the following properties:

▶ It is always of type `TransparentContainer`.

▶ It is always called `RootUIElementContainer`.

▶ By default, the `RootUIElementContainer` always has the `FlowLayout` layout manager assigned to it.

▶ All UI elements subsequently added to the view become children of `RootUIElementContainer`.

When a layout manager is assigned to a UI element container, a set of property values must be specified for each child UI element within that container. It is within the layout data object that you specify how that child UI element should appear when rendered with the given layout manager.

### 7.5.1 Flow Layout

The FlowLayout is the simplest of the layout managers in that it renders its child UI elements in a simple left-to-right sequence. If more UI elements have been defined than will fit horizontally across the screen, the extra UI elements will flow onto a new row.

As you resize the window within which the FlowLayout container lives, you will see the UI elements wrap or flow automatically within the available screen space (see Figure 7.8 and Figure 7.9). It is not possible to define any form of vertical alignment within a FlowLayout container.

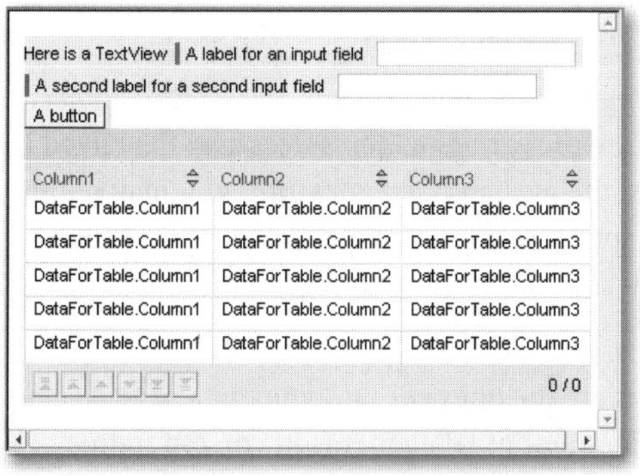

**Figure 7.8** UI Elements Arranged in a Container Using a Flow Layout Manager: Narrow Screen

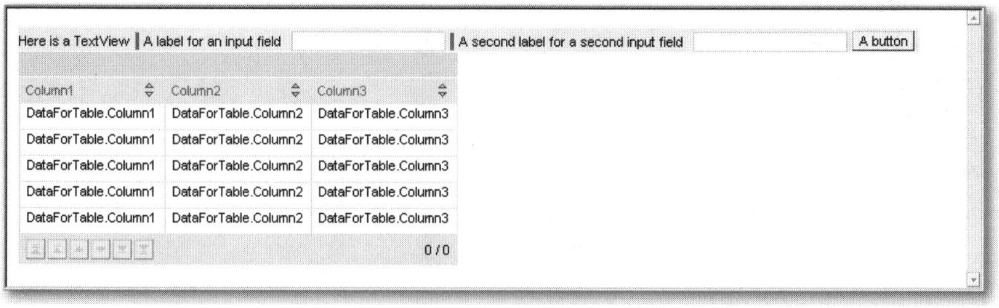

**Figure 7.9** UI Elements Arranged in a Container Using a Flow Layout Manager: Wide Screen

### 7.5.2 Row Layout

The RowLayout layout manager has been implemented primarily to overcome the performance overhead incurred by browsers having to render multiple levels of nested HTML <table> tags.

If you want to subdivide some area of the view into horizontal rows, but you do not require any vertical alignment between the resulting columns, you should use a RowLayout layout manager. This layout manager should be thought of as an enhanced form of FlowLayout.

Within a row of a RowLayout container, each child UI element will either contain a RowHeadData object or a RowData object. These objects are stored in the property aggregation called layoutdata and determine whether the UI element will be rendered at the start of a new row or just be a row member. The default is that all child UI elements contain RowData objects (i.e., they do not occur at the start of a row).

If you change a child element to contain a RowHeadData object, you are telling the RowLayout layout manager that this element must be rendered at the start of a new row. UI elements nominated to contain RowHeadData objects will always occupy the left-most position in a row.

A RowHeadData object has a set of general properties that apply to all UI elements in the row, that is, all UI elements up until the next RowHeadData object.

Once you have specified which UI elements will be that row's RowHeadData objects, the other UI elements in the row are free to rearrange themselves as if they lived in a FlowLayout container. Depending on the available screen width, you may see the contents of a RowLayout container wrapping around to form a new row. As with a FlowLayout container, the minimum width at which wrapping stops is imposed by the widest UI element on the screen.

In Figure 7.10 the outlined UI elements are the ones with a layout data of RowHeadData. Notice that there is no vertical alignment of UI elements in corresponding columns.

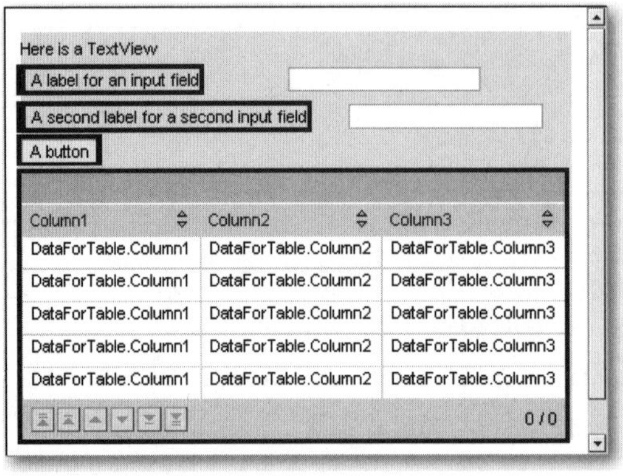

**Figure 7.10** UI Elements Arranged in a Container Using a Row Layout Manager

### 7.5.3 Matrix Layout

The MatrixLayout layout manager is a further enhancement of the capabilities of the RowLayout layout manager.[2] A RowLayout layout manager allows you to specify when

---

2 UI elements arranged in a MatrixLayout or GridLayout are implemented in a browser using an HTML <table>.

new rows should start but provides no facility for the vertical alignment of elements into columns. This capability is provided by the `MatrixLayout` layout manager.

The `MatrixLayout` layout manager creates a tabular grid on the screen in which the cells are aligned both horizontally and vertically. As with the `RowLayout` layout manager, you still have to specify which child UI elements will be at the start of a new row, but now all the row elements will be vertically aligned into columns.

Using a `MatrixLayout` layout manager, you can produce a grid with a variable number of columns per row.

In a manner similar to `RowLayout`-managed UI containers, each child UI element assigned to a `MatrixLayout`-managed container will contain either a `MatrixData` object or `MatrixHeadData` object. Again, these objects are stored in the `layoutdata` property aggregation. The default object type is `MatrixData`, but if you want to start a new row, you must change this to `MatrixHeadData`.

In Figure 7.11 the outlined UI elements are the ones with a layout data of `Matrix-HeadData`. Notice that there is now a tabular arrangement of the UI elements, and the two input fields have been pushed across to the right-hand side of the screen. This is because these two UI elements occupy the second column of the grid, with the width of the first column being defined by the widest UI element it contains — the table.

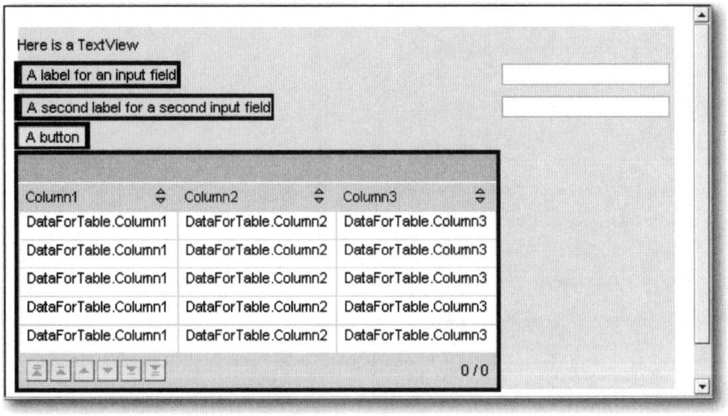

**Figure 7.11** UI Elements Arranged in a Container Using a Matrix Layout Manager

### 7.5.4 Grid Layout

The `GridLayout` layout manager divides the view area into a tabular grid with a fixed number of columns. As UI elements are added to a `GridLayout` container, they are positioned within the grid in a left-to-right, top-to-bottom manner. The number of columns in the grid is determined by the value of the `colCount` property, and the number of rows is dependent upon the number of UI elements added to the container.

To achieve a uniform look and feel across all of your Web Dynpro applications, SAP recommends that the MatrixLayout be used in preference to the GridLayout.

---

**Important**

The time taken for browsers to render a screen rises significantly if the HTML contains multiple levels of nested <table> tags. Since the GridLayout and MatrixLayout layout managers are implemented in a browser using an HTML <table>, if possible, you should try to avoid nesting these layout managers within each other.

---

A better approach when designing a screen layout is to divide the screen into horizontal areas as early as possible. The horizontal subdivisions can be implemented using a RowLayout layout manager, and each child added to the row could then be some sort of container such as a TransparentContainer. This will avoid the drop in browser rendering performance because you will not be using an HTML <table> to provide the major structural subdivisions of the screen.

The view shown in Figure 7.12 is the same layout as seen in the previous figures, but now that the view container is using the GridLayout layout manager with the colCount parameter set to 2, all the UI elements have been assigned an arbitrary position in the table, on a left-to-right, top-to-bottom basis. Also, the table UI element has had its colSpan parameter set to 2. 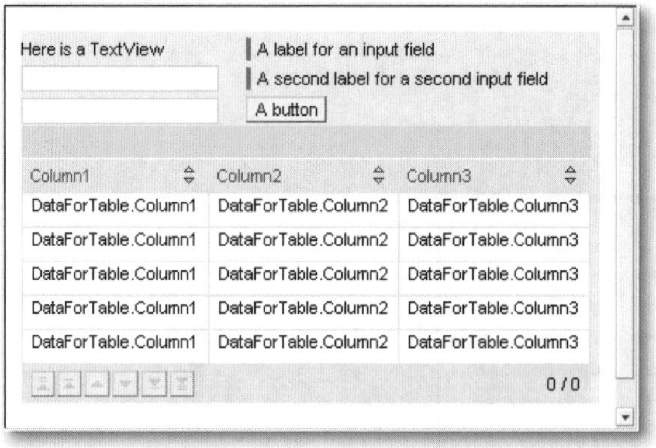

**Figure 7.12** UI Elements Arranged in a Container Using a Grid Layout Manager: colCount = 2

This layout is obviously not satisfactory because we want some rows to have only one UI element in them. If you are using the GridLayout layout manager, you will need to pad the empty grid cells with invisible UI elements. These are shown Figure 7.13.

If you require a tabular layout for your UI elements, SAP recommends that the MatrixLayout layout manager should be used in preference to the GridLayout layout manager.

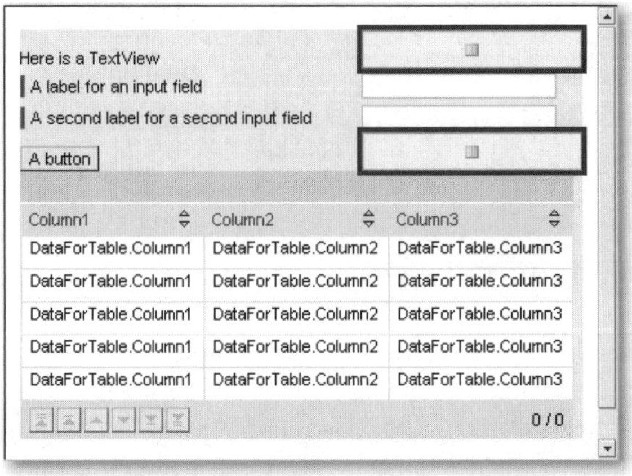

**Figure 7.13** UI Elements Arranged in a Container Using a Grid Layout Manager: Invisible Elements Used for Padding

### 7.5.5 Layout Manager Properties

Each of the layout managers has a set of associated properties (see Table 7.1 to Table 7.4). Many of these properties are then inherited by the UI elements within the container.

| FlowLayout | | |
|---|---|---|
| **Layout Manager Properties** | **Data Type** | **Default Value** |
| defaultPaddingBottom | String | " " |
| defaultPaddingLeft | String | " " |
| defaultPaddingRight | String | " " |
| defaultPaddingTop | String | " " |
| wrapping | Boolean | True |
| **Layout Data Properties** | **Data Type** | **Default Value** |
| paddingBottom | String | " " |
| paddingLeft | String | " " |
| paddingRight | String | " " |
| paddingTop | String | " " |

**Table 7.1** Properties of the FlowLayout Layout Manager

| RowLayout | | |
|---|---|---|
| **Layout Head Data Properties** | **Data Type** | **Default Value** |
| hAlign | WDCellHAlign | LEFT |
| rowBackgroundDesign | WDCellBackgroundDesign | TRANSPARENT |
| rowDesign | WDLayoutCellDesign | R_PAD |
| vGutter | WDLayoutCellSeparator | NONE |

**Table 7.2** Properties of the RowLayout Layout Manager

| MatrixLayout | | |
|---|---|---|
| **Layout Manager Properties** | **Data Type** | **Default Value** |
| stretchedHorizontally | Boolean | True |
| stretchedVertically | Boolean | True |
| **Layout Data Properties** | **Data Type** | **Default Value** |
| cellBackgroundDesign | WDCellBackgroundDesign | TRANSPARENT |
| cellDesign | WDLayoutCellDesign | R_PAD |
| colSpan | Integer | 1 |
| hAlign | WDCellHAlign | LEFT |
| height | String | "" |
| vAlign | WDCellVAlign | BASELINE |
| vGutter | WDLayoutCellSeparator | NONE |
| width | String | "" |

**Table 7.3** Properties of the MatrixLayout Layout Manager

| GridLayout | | |
|---|---|---|
| **Layout Manager Properties** | **Data Type** | **Default Value** |
| cellPadding | Integer | 0 |
| cellSpacing | Integer | 0 |
| colCount | Integer | 1 |
| stretchedHorizontally | Boolean | True |
| stretchedVertically | Boolean | True |

**Table 7.4** Properties of the GridLayout Layout Manager

| GridLayout | | |
|---|---|---|
| **Layout Data Properties** | **Data Type** | **Default Value** |
| colSpan | Integer | 1 |
| hAlign | WDCellHAlign | LEFT |
| height | String | " " |
| paddingBottom | String | " " |
| paddingLeft | String | " " |
| paddingRight | String | " " |
| paddingTop | String | " " |
| vAlign | WDCellVAlign | BASELINE |

**Table 7.4** Properties of the GridLayout Layout Manager (cont.)

### 7.5.6 Principles for the Efficient Use of Layout Managers

Please observe and implement the following principles when using layout managers.

1. Wherever possible, try to avoid complex layouts involving multiple levels of nesting.
   When you have the option of nesting UI containers within each other (each with its own layout manager), always opt for the design that results in the fewest levels of nesting. From a performance point of view, it is better to place multiple UI elements directly into one large UI container using a grid or matrix layout (with columns and rows that span where necessary) than to nest transparent containers within the individual cells of the parent container.

2. Only use a transparent container when it is genuinely required. Containers such as the Group control are composite UI elements based on a transparent container. Therefore, it makes no sense to embed a transparent container as the top-level child into a Group container, because it already implements one.

3. If vertical alignment is not required, the row layout should be chosen in preference to the grid or matrix layout.

4. If vertical alignment is required, the matrix layout should be chosen in preference to the grid layout. This is not a performance consideration (both layout managers are ultimately implemented using an HTML <table>), but it is an easier layout manager to work with. You don't have to specify a column count, and you can put as many UI elements into one row as you like.

5. The matrix layout allows some predefined values for cell padding. The property cellDesign can have the predefined values shown in Figure 7.14. The Standard option is also referred to as rPad.

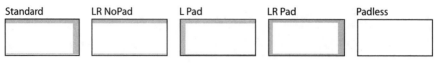

**Figure 7.14** The Different Padding Options for the cellDesign Property

## 7.6    Composite UI Elements

A composite UI element is any UI element that requires further child UI element objects to function correctly. The composite UI elements that you will use quite regularly are Group, Table, and Tree (among others).

### 7.6.1    A Simple Composite UI Element

A simple composite UI element is the Group. This UI element is a transparent container that has a Caption UI element defined within it to hold the text seen in the title bar (see Figure 7.15). Beyond that, you can add any other UI elements you choose. Remember that the Group UI element is an extended TransparentContainer, so there is no need to embed another transparent container before adding more UI elements.

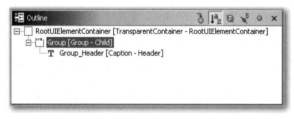

**Figure 7.15** The Group UI Element is the Simplest of the Composite UI Elements

### 7.6.2    Composite, Composite UI Elements

No, that's not a misprint in the heading; there are certain composite UI elements that contain other composite UI elements as children. The Table UI element is a frequently used example of such a UI element.

You will always start with a Table UI element under which must be at least one TableColumn UI element.[3] The TableColumn UI element is a composite UI element that contains a Caption and some other UI element that functions as the cell editor. Notice in Figure 7.16 that both CheckBox and TextView UI elements are used as cell editors.

---

3    The Table UI element must contain at least one TableColumn UI element, but there are many other UI elements that can be inserted into a Table. These include a MasterColumn (for embedding a tree into column 1), a GroupedColumn, a ToolBar, and a Popin.

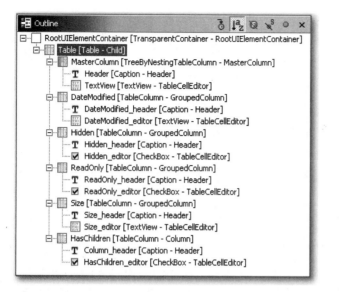

**Figure 7.16** The Table UI Element Uses a Hierarchy of Composite UI Elements

By default, whichever UI element you nominate to be the cell editor will appear in every cell down that table column. Therefore, if you select a TextView UI element to be a column's cell editor, every value in that column will be presented using this UI element.

It is possible to modify the cell editor on a per-row basis. Thus, rather than presenting a table with every cell in every row open for input, you can use a default cell editor that presents the data in a read-only manner, and then when the user selects a particular row, the cell editors can be switched to input fields.

### 7.6.3 Binding Table UI Elements to the Context

When a Table UI element is added to a view layout, you need to make multiple data bindings for both the table and all its child composite UI elements to function correctly.

To start with, the Table itself must be bound to the context node that is being visualized. You cannot take data from multiple context nodes and display them in a single table. The node to which the Table is bound must have multiple cardinality. That is, the cardinality must be set to 0..n or 1..n. This is shown in Figure 7.17.

Now that the Table knows which context node will act as its data supplier, each TableColumn UI element can be associated with a particular attribute. Each attribute in the context node now acts as a potential data supplier for a TableColumn UI element (see Figure 7.18).

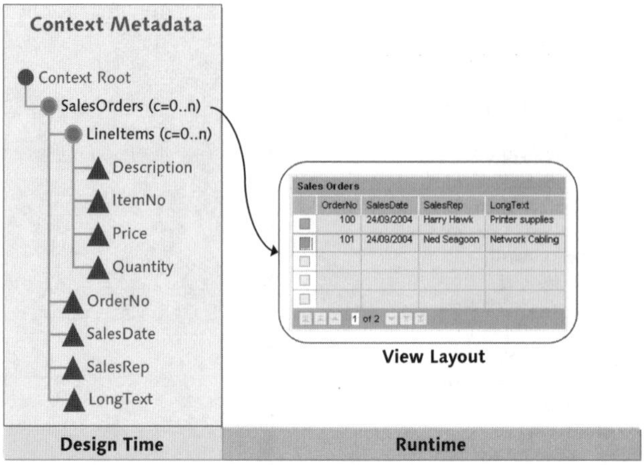

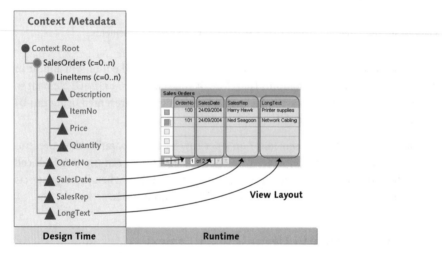

**Figure 7.17** The Table UI Element Must Be Bound to a Context Node with Multiple Cardinality

**Figure 7.18** Each Context Attribute Acts as a Potential Supplier of Data to a TableColumn UI Element

### 7.6.4    Runtime Behavior of a Table UI Element

Once a Table UI element is displayed on the screen, whichever node element is at the lead selection will be highlighted as the selected table row. If the context node does not have an element at the lead selection (i.e., lead selection = –1), the table will be displayed with no rows highlighted.

Certain UI elements raise events that cause round trips to the server, even if the UI element event has no action associated with it. The Table is such a UI element. Figure 7.19 shows that when a user selects a row from a Table UI element, this will cause a round trip to the server to take place.[4] If the Table's onLeadSelect event has not been associated with an action in the view controller, only the node's lead selection value will be updated, and control will return to the screen.[5]

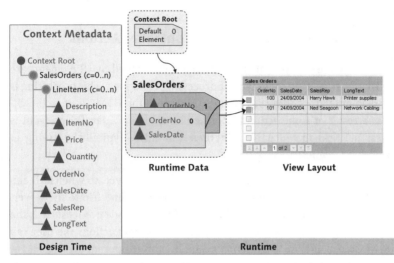

**Figure 7.19** Selecting a Row from a Table Causes a Round Trip to the Server

In certain circumstances the change of lead selection could result in the loss of data. Therefore, a `Table` UI element has a `selectionChangeBehaviour` parameter that controls the order in which processing takes place in the server. This property has three possible settings:

▶ **auto**
First, the Web Dynpro Framework updates the node's lead selection automatically. Then, if it exists, the associated action event handler is called. This is the default behavior.

▶ **manual**
The Web Dynpro Framework does not update the node's lead selection. If it exists, the associated action event handler method is called. It is then up to this method to change the node's lead selection manually.

▶ **ifNoLoss**
This behaves in the same manner as **auto**, but with the added condition that all data must first have been successfully copied to the context. If this condition is met, **ifNoLoss** behaves in the same way as **auto**.

All of the above situations *may* cause supply functions to be called if the node whose lead selection is being changed has child nodes. So even if no action handler

---

4  Row selection from a table causes a non-validating event to be raised.
5  If the node has child nodes with supply functions, the change of lead selection could trigger their execution.

is associated with the table's `onLeadSelect` event, it is still possible for supply function coding to be executed as a result of the change in lead selection.

## 7.7    UI Element Events and View Controller Actions

In any browser-based development situation, the events raised by UI elements are the mechanism for triggering some type of processing to happen. This processing is typically implemented by adding JavaScript coding into the HTML sent to the client. Then, as a result of some action performed by the user, a JavaScript event is raised (such as `onClick`), to which the client then responds — typically by issuing an HTTP GET or POST request.

In Web Dynpro, all business processing takes place on the server, so when a UI element raises a client-side event, this will typically trigger a round trip to the server. Many Web Dynpro UI elements are capable of raising client-side events such as the button shown in Figure 7.20. These events relate to different actions the user can perform. For instance, the `Table` UI element can raise three different events: `onFilter`, `onLeadSelect`, and `onSort`.

Whether a round trip takes place depends on two things:

▶ What type of event was raised?

▶ Does the Web Dynpro Framework know what to do in response to the event?

Some UI element events always cause round trips to the server (such as the `Table`'s `onLeadSelect` event). Other events, however, only cause a round trip to the server if you have told the Web Dynpro Framework what to do as a result of that event being fired.

### 7.7.1    Declaration and Association with a UI Element Event

The next question is, "How do you tell the Web Dynpro Framework what to do when a client-side event is fired?" This is the role of an *action*.

Actions are defined in the view controller and are the runtime objects that associate a client-side event with a server-side response. Since actions are runtime objects, they can be instantiated, enabled, and generally manipulated programmatically.

When you declare an action, you are creating an object that can be associated with any number of UI element events.[6] Figure 7.21 shows that as a result of the action's declaration, an action handler method will typically be created. The creation of an action handler method specific to the action is the default behavior; this can be overridden if you want.

---

6    It is quite legal to assign the same action to multiple UI elements.

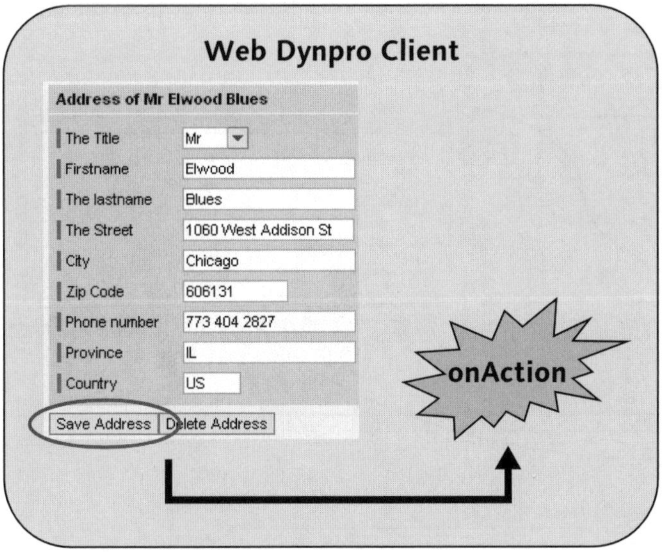

**Figure 7.20** An Event is Fired in the Client When the Button is Pushed

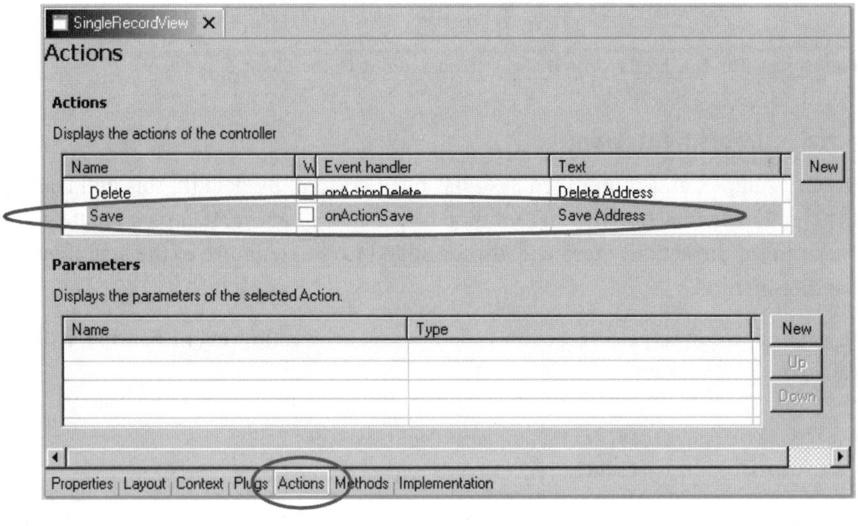

**Figure 7.21** By Default, Declaring an Action Causes an Action Handler Method To Be Created

Once the action has been declared, it can be associated with a UI element event. This association is shown in Figure 7.22.

Actions can be given parameters that will appear in the signature of the action event handler method. See Section 7.8 for the full discussion of the use of action parameters.

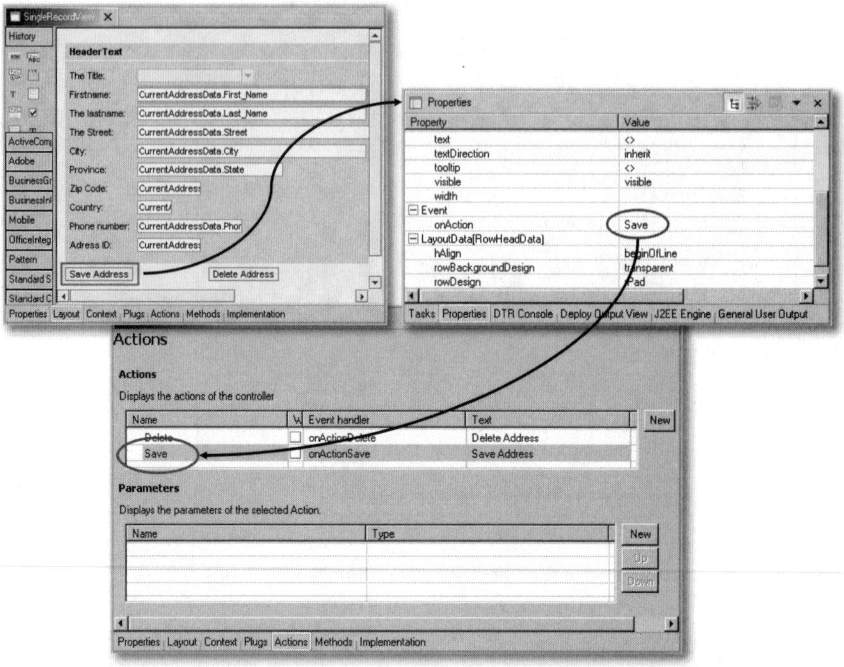

**Figure 7.22** The Declared Action Must Be Associated with the Client-Side Event

### 7.7.2    Implementation

In our example, an action called Save has been created. By default, this will lead to the creation of an action handler method called onActionSave. If any parameters are declared for the action, these will also be added to the signature of the action event handler method.

In general, if you create an action called ${act}, the action event handler will be called onAction${act}.

```
public void onAction${act}(IWDCustomEvent wdEvent) {
 //@@begin onAction${act}(ServerEvent)

 //@@end
}
```

**Listing 7.1** Stub coding created in a view controller for a default action handler method

The action event handler is the method in which you should implement the view controller's response to the client-side action. Figure 7.23 shows that an action associates a client-side event with a server-side event handler method.

> **Caveat Confector**
>
> Do not implement any business logic directly in a view controller. This is *very* bad design because it creates a Web Dynpro application that is difficult to maintain.
>
> Will this style of coding:
>
> ▶ Cause the application to crash? No.
>
> ▶ Cause runtime performance issues? Not normally.
>
> ▶ Cause the application to be non-functional? No.
>
> ▶ So therefore it's a good architecture? **NO!**
>
> The problems caused by this style of coding will not normally become visible until after the software has gone live. Then, several months later, the users start to ask for modifications. Now the design problems will jump up and bite you.
>
> The reason is that the business logic has been spread out (inconsistently) between visual and non-visual controllers, so it is difficult to know where backend interaction takes place. This makes the modification process more time-consuming and error-prone.
>
> These problems are completely avoidable if developers are disciplined enough to follow these design principles.
>
> If, in response to the client-side event, the program needs to call some business logic in a backend system, *do not* put the coding directly in the view controller's action event handler. Instead, the action event handler should simply call a method in a non-visual controller (say, the component controller), and this method then interacts with the backend system.
>
> Remember, view controllers are consumers of data, not generators. They are not responsible for generating the data they display; that's the role of a non-visual controller.

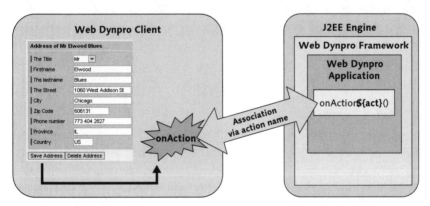

**Figure 7.23** Once a Client-Side Event Is Linked with an Action, the Web Dynpro Framework Knows What Method to Call when the Event is Raised

### 7.7.3 Action Types

There are two types of action: validating and non-validating. The difference between them defines how the Web Dynpro Framework reacts when validation errors occur. When you declare an action, you define it to be either with or without validation (*see* Figure 7.24).

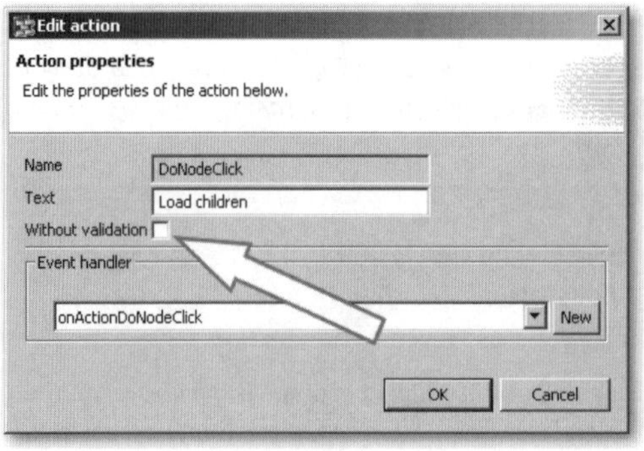

**Figure 7.24** Defining an Action With or Without Validation

When a user wants to perform the next step of a business process, they normally enter data on the screen and then press a button. The Web Dynpro Framework then copies the data the user has entered from the UI element properties back into the context attributes of all the view controllers involved in the current View Assembly. During the copy process, this data is validated by the Java Dictionary.

If the data fails the validation test, the Web Dynpro Framework will receive an error message from the underlying Java Dictionary. If the round trip was initiated by a validating action, the Web Dynpro Framework will abort any further processing and inform the user of the error.

If, however, the round trip was initiated by a non-validating action, you are saying to the Web Dynpro Framework that even if an error occurs, you don't care — carry on processing anyway.

Non-validating actions are essential to process events such as `logoff`.

### 7.7.4 Event Types

Web Dynpro UI elements can raise two different types of client-side event. These are known as primary and secondary events. As mentioned above, an action is a runtime object that can be enabled or disabled. If you disable an action object that is associated with a UI element, this will affect the behavior of the UI element. However, not all UI elements react in the same way when the actions associated with their events are enabled or disabled.

Enabling or disabling an action has different consequences depending on whether the action is linked to a primary or secondary event.

▶ A primary event is one whose enablement or disablement affects the entire UI element.

An example of a primary event is the `onSelect` event of a checkbox. If the action associated with this event is disabled, you have disabled the entire UI element.

Only primary events will be considered as evaluation candidates during a call to `IWDViewController.requestFocus()`.

▶ A secondary event is one whose enablement or disablement affects only part of the functionality of a UI element.

An example of a secondary UI element event is the `onLeadSelect` event of a table. If the action associated with this event is disabled, the table will be perfectly functional, except that selecting different rows of the table will not trigger a round trip.

### 7.7.5 Coding Generated by an Action Declaration

For each action declared in a view controller, a constant will be created that allows you programmatic access to the action object. In general, for any action `${act}`, the following constant will be created:

```
IPrivate${nv}.WDActionEventHandler.${act}
```

**Listing 7.2** Constant generated when an action is declared

Therefore, if two actions called `GenericAction` and `RowSelect` have been declared for a view controller called `ShowOrders`, the following constants will be available:

```
IPrivateShowOrders.WDActionEventHandler.GENERIC_ACTION
IPrivateShowOrders.WDActionEventHandler.ROW_SELECT
```

**Listing 7.3** Constant generated when an action is declared

---

**Important**

Action names should be declared using the standard Java naming convention for a class. That is, the words of the name are concatenated together with each word starting with an upper case letter. This mixture of upper and lower case letters in one identifier is commonly known as *camel case*.

As a result of your action name being in camel case, the resulting constant name will be converted to upper case with underscore characters inserted between the words, as shown in Table 7.5.

---

| Action Name | Generated Constant Name |
|-------------|-------------------------|
| DoNodeClick | DO_NODE_CLICK |
| SaveAddress | SAVE_ADDRESS |
| Action_Name | ACTION__NAME |

**Table 7.5** Conversion of Camel Case Action Names to Upper Case Constant Names

If you add underscore characters into the action name, the resulting constant name will contain two adjacent underscore characters as shown in the last row of Table 7.5.

## 7.8    Parameter Mapping

To ensure that server-side controllers can react intelligently to user actions on the client, it is often necessary to pass parameters back to the server with certain client-side events. For instance, when the user selects an item from a `DropDownByKey` UI element, the action event handler method in the view controller needs to know more than just the fact that *an* item has been selected; it needs to know exactly *which* item has been selected.

For instance, when an `onSelect` event is fired in the client, the key of the selected item is passed as a parameter back to the server (see Figure 7.25).

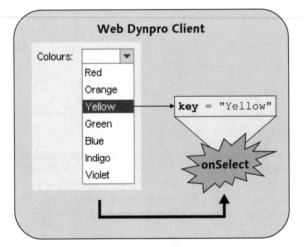

**Figure 7.25**  A DropDownByKey UI Element Passes a Parameter Called key to Indicate Which Item Has Been Selected

| Important |
| --- |
| Event parameter names are hard-coded within each UI element. |

If an event has an associated event parameter, the UI element will automatically place a value into the event parameter. The Web Dynpro Framework does this part of the coding for you automatically; however, you must ensure that this value is received by the server-side action handler.

The next step then is to find of the names the client-side event parameters. There are two ways to do this:

▶ Read the help file for the UI element in question. Look for the heading *Events*. It may first be necessary to open the documentation of an abstract base class before the details you require are shown.

▶ Look in the UI element's class definition. The name of the parameter will be found in the comment block above the mappingOf`${ui`evt`}`() method, where `${ui`evt`}` is the UI element event name such as `OnSelect` or `OnToggle`.

The help for any particular UI element can be accessed by right-clicking on the UI element icon in the View Designer toolbar (see Figure 7.26).

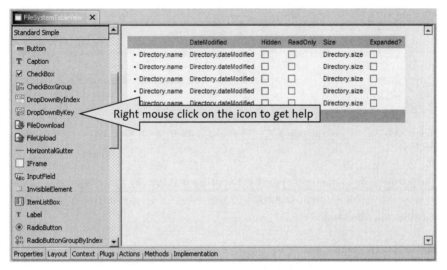

**Figure 7.26** Right-Click on an Icon To Get UI Element Help

Sometimes, the events are documented in the UI element's abstract base class rather than the UI element class itself. The event parameter for the `DropDownByKey` UI element is shown in Figure 7.27.

In the case of the `DropDownByIndex` UI element, the hard-coded parameter is called `index`. You must implement the coding to pass this parameter from the UI element event to your action handler. This process is known as parameter mapping.

In the following example, we have a `DropDownByKey` UI element in the view layout. When this UI element's `onSelect` event is fired in the client, a round trip to the server will take place and an action event handler method in the view controller will receive control. This method has a parameter called `selectedKey`. Although these parameter names are different, they refer to the same value; therefore, we must associate the two.

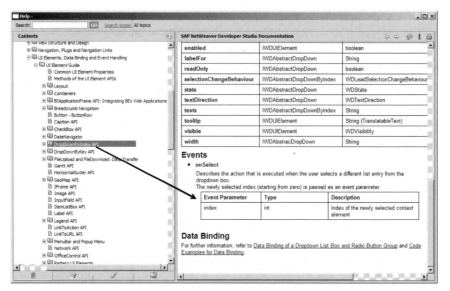

**Figure 7.27** Event Parameter Names Can Be Found in the Help File for the Associated UI Element

The purpose of parameter mapping is to ensure that the `key` parameter value of the DropDownByKey UI element is passed to the `selectedKey` parameter of the action event handler method.

```
public static void
 wdDoModifyView(IPrivate${nv} wdThis,
         IPrivate${nv}.IContextNode wdContext,
         IWDView view, boolean firstTime) {
 //@@begin wdDoModifyView
 if (firstTime) {
  IWDDropDownByKey ddByKey =
  (IWDDropDownByKey)view.getElement("DropDownByKey");
  ddByKey.mappingOfOnSelect().addSourceMapping("key",
                 "selectedKey");
 }
 //@@end
}
```

**Listing 7.4** Coding to associate the DropDownByKey UI element's key parameter with the action event handler's selectedKey parameter

In addition to the coding that actually associates the two parameter values, there are two more things to notice about the coding in Listing 7.4:

1. The coding is contained within the `wdDoModifyView()` method of the same view controller as the action event handler method.

2. The wdDoModifyView() method is passed a Boolean parameter called firstTime. This will be set to true if this is the first time this instance of the view controller has had its screen rendered. In other words, if the user has never seen this screen before, firstTime will be set to true.

These coding details are not optional! First, the coding must be performed inside the wdDoModifyView() method because this is where you have access to the UI element hierarchy; second, you only need to map the parameters once per lifecycle of the view controller.

### 7.8.1 Multiple UI Element Events Handled by One Action Event Handler

Since the event-to-action parameter assignment is specific to the UI element and not the action, it is perfectly acceptable to generalize the use of an action handler so that it can respond to events from multiple UI elements.

Let's say we have an action called HandleCheckBox. As the name implies, you would expect the associated action event handler to receive control when the onToggle event of a checkbox is raised. Let's further assume that we have multiple checkboxes on the screen. It would be far more efficient to have a single event handler processing *all* the checkbox events than to write a separate event handler method for each checkbox UI element.

So now when an onToggle event is raised in the client, control is passed to the onActionHandleCheckBox event handler. The only question to be answered now is, "On which checkbox did the user click?" (see Figure 7.28).

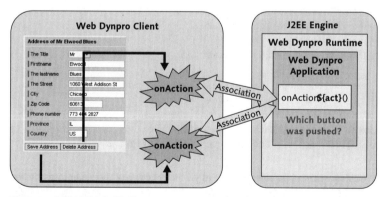

**Figure 7.28** If Multiple UI Elements Are Assigned to the Same Action Handler, How Do You Tell Who Raised the Event?

This question is answered by adding another parameter to the HandleCheckBox action. This extra parameter has nothing to do with the client-side event itself; therefore, it is completely independent from the client layer.

1. Select the action `HandleCheckBox` and define a new parameter called `checkBoxId` of type `integer`.[7]

2. The corresponding action event handler method `onActionHandleCheckBox()` will now have its signature automatically modified to include this new parameter.

3. Now that the action event handler method can receive a new parameter, these parameters must be assigned values. In effect, we have created an extra parameter that can be used for any purpose we like. In this case we will assign each checkbox UI element an arbitrary integer value.

4. The coding to do this will be found in the `wdDoModifyView()` method of the view controller in which the UI elements are defined.

   The coding is as follows:

```
if (firstTime) {
  // Get references to all three checkbox UI elements
  IWDCheckBox cb1 =
    (IWDCheckBox)view.getElement("checkBox1");
  IWDCheckBox cb2 =
    (IWDCheckBox)view.getElement("checkBox2");
  IWDCheckBox cb3 =
    (IWDCheckBox)view.getElement("checkBox3");

  // Link the client-side event parameter "checked" to
  // the server-side action parameter "state"
  // This parameter is UI-element specific, and therefore
  // identical for all three checkboxes.
  cb1.mappingOfOnToggle().
    addSourceMapping("checked", "state");
  cb2.mappingOfOnToggle().
    addSourceMapping("checked", "state");
  cb3.mappingOfOnToggle().
    addSourceMapping("checked", "state");

  // Now set the checkbox ids that enable the server-
  // side event to distinguish between each checkbox.
  cb1.mappingOfOnToggle().addParameter("checkBoxId", 0);
  cb2.mappingOfOnToggle().addParameter("checkBoxId", 1);
  cb3.mappingOfOnToggle().addParameter("checkBoxId", 2);
}
```

**Listing 7.5** Adding a custom parameter to identify which check box UI element was clicked

Notice that the `addSourceMapping()` method is used to associate a parameter from the event source with a parameter on the action event handler, but the `addParameter()` method is used to give a custom parameter a hard-coded value.

---

7  The data type of this parameter is deliberately chosen to be a primitive so that we can use a Java `switch` statement.

5. Now in the associated action event handler method, you can implement a finite state engine to process each UI element appropriately:

```
public void onActionHandleCheckBox(
                IWDCustomEvent wdEvent,
                int checkBoxId) {
  //@@begin onActionHandleCheckBox(ServerEvent)

  switch(checkBoxId) {
    case 0:
      // First check box
      break;
    case 1:
      // Second check box
      break;
    case 2:
      // Third check box
      break;
    default:
      // That's odd. Why are we here?
  }
  //@@end
}
```

**Listing 7.6** Coding in the action event handler to distinguish which UI element was clicked

### 7.8.2 Further Decoupling of the UI

The degree of abstraction between the event parameter and action parameter can be taken a degree further if desired. Consider the following set of requirements:

▶ A context node is to be displayed as a table.

▶ The number of columns to be displayed is unknown until runtime.

▶ You want to give the user the ability to sort the table simply by clicking on a column header.

Situations like this call for a generic action handler that can sort the table based, not on some arbitrary integer value, or even the name of the table column UI element, but on the name of the *context attribute* being visualized by that table column. In other words, the information provided to the sort algorithm needs to be the name of the context attribute that will act as the sort key, *not* the name of the table column UI element that is visualizing the information.[8]

---

8  Here is another example of how important a role the context plays in Web Dynpro processing. UI elements are simply the superficial layer through which the context data is visualized. Actual data processing always takes places using the objects in the context, not the UI element objects used for visualization.

This level of abstraction between the table UI element and the sort algorithm allows you to put any table on the screen, made up of any number of columns of any name, and the sort logic will still function.

In this scenario, the IWDTableColumn UI element provides a client-side event parameter called col, which is passed when the onAction event is raised. However, the col parameter value is not of much use to us because it contains the name of the *UI element* on which the user clicked. What we really need is the name of the context attribute to which the UI element is bound.

We will go back to our SalesOrders context node. In this situation, a table of sales orders is to be displayed, but the number of columns is configurable and therefore not known until runtime. The user can sort the table by clicking on the header of the column he wishes to use as the sort key. The name of the action handler that performs the sort is HandleSortRequest, and it receives a single string parameter called colAttrib. To implement this type of parameter mapping, the following steps need to be taken:

▶ The standard parameter col for the table column's onAction event is ignored. This is easy to achieve — do nothing.

▶ Create an action called HandleSortRequest and give it a parameter called colAttrib of type String.

▶ The attributes that will be displayed as table columns live in a context node called SalesOrders. As we have seen with earlier demos, the attributes of node SalesOrders are called LongText, OrderNo, SalesDate, and SalesRep.

▶ In the wdDoModifyView() method of the view controller, the following code should be added. In this example, the coding to create the table column UI elements has been omitted, but they are called tabCol1, tabCol2, tabCol3, and tabCol4.

You should associate the context attribute supplying data to the table column with the static parameter colAttrib.

```
// Obtain references to the table column UI elements
IWDTableColumn tc1 =
  (IWDTableColumn)view.getElement("tabCol1");
IWDTableColumn tc2 =
  (IWDTableColumn)view.getElement("tabCol2");
IWDTableColumn tc3 =
  (IWDTableColumn)view.getElement("tabCol3");
IWDTableColumn tc4 =
  (IWDTableColumn)view.getElement("tabCol4");

// Hard code the value of the "colAttrib" parameter to
// be the dot delimited name of the context attribute.
// Notice this is a string value, not an object reference!
```

```
tc1.mappingOfOnAction().
   addParameter("colAttrib", "SalesOrders.LongText");
tc2.mappingOfOnAction().
   addParameter("colAttrib", "SalesOrders.OrderNo");
tc3.mappingOfOnAction().
   addParameter("colAttrib", "SalesOrders.SalesDate");
tc4.mappingOfOnAction().
   addParameter("colAttrib", "SalesOrders.SalesRep");
```

**Listing 7.7** Action handler using a context attribute name

Now when the action event handler method `onActionHandleSortRequest()` is called, it will receive a `String` containing the name of the context attribute that is to be used as the sort key in the string parameter `colAttrib`.

The action handler must now use the value of the string parameter `colAttrib` to create a reference to the relevant context attribute. The sort algorithm should then be passed this context attribute reference as its sort key.

### 7.8.3 Advanced Parameter Mapping Example

When processing the events raised by tree nodes, it is vitally important that the action handler knows not only the name of the node on which the user clicked, but also the exact element within that node. This is particularly important because all context nodes displayed using trees must be non-singletons. Thus, there will very likely be multiple instances of the same node name at runtime.

Therefore, parameter mapping must be done in the following manner:

1. As with all previous examples, you need to know the name of the event parameter raised by the `IWDTreeNodeType` UI element.[9] The required event parameter is called `path` and is of type `String`.

2. Before creating the action parameter, you must identify the name of the generated node element class that the `TreeNodeType` UI element represents. For instance, an element of context node `WBSElements` in view controller `ShowProjectAsTreeView` will be called `IPrivateShowProjectAsTreeView.IWBSElementsElement`.

3. In general, for any element of context node $\{cn\}$ belonging to the view controller $\{n_V\}$, the generated class name will always be `IPrivate${n_V}.I${cn}Element`.

4. Assuming that the action is called `HandleNodeClick`, create a parameter called `selectedEl`. It is most important that the data type of this parameter is *not* `String`! It must be of the data type of the generated node element class identified in the previous step.

---

9  In the case of this UI element, the `onAction` event is not defined in the class `IWDTreeNodeType`, but in the base class `IWDAbstractTreeNodeType`.

5. As in the previous examples, the event parameter must be associated with the action parameter using the following code fragment:

```
// Get a reference to the tree node WBS_Els
IWDTreeNodeType tn =
  (IWDTreeNodeType)view.getElement("WBS_Els");
tn.mappingOfOnAction().addSourceMapping("path", "selectedEl");
```

**Listing 7.8** Action handler using a context node reference

6. Now when the user clicks on the displayed node, the client will pass the path name to the context element as a `String` value in the event parameter `path`.

7. Before the value of `path` is transferred to the server-side action parameter `selectedNodeElement`, the Web Dynpro Framework recognizes that the parameter to the action event handler is declared as a node element class and will automatically convert the `String` value held in the event parameter `path` into the object reference required by the action handler.

8. The action handler method now has an object reference to the exact node element on which the user clicked.

## 7.9    Generic UI Services

Any time a context attribute of a certain data type is bound to, say, an `InputField` UI element, if it is available, a UI service appropriate for that data type will be provided to help you enter data. For instance, if you have a context attribute of type `date` and you display this value through an `InputField`, Web Dynpro will immediately create a date picker UI service to help you enter a valid date.[10]

In addition to the date picker, three generic UI services are available for use. Which one you use depends first on whether the context attribute possesses an enumeration and, second, on the type of UI element being used.

The three types of generic UI service are:

▶ The Simple Value Selector
▶ The Extended Value Selector
▶ The Object Value Selector

The values displayed by a Simple or an Extended Value Selector can be obtained as a static list from the Java Dictionary, the values can be constructed dynamically at runtime, or you could have a combination of static and dynamic values.

---

10  As opposed to something like October 32nd.

### 7.9.1 Simple Value Selector

The Simple Value Selector is the name given to the values that appear in a drop-down list. The runtime part of Figure 7.29 shows an example.

To obtain this list, you must do the following:

1. Create a dictionary simple type containing an enumeration. (e.g., Color).

2. Create a context attribute based on this simple type.

3. Bind the `selectedKey` property of a `DropDownByKey` UI element to the context attribute.

This chain of connections is illustrated below in Figure 7.29.

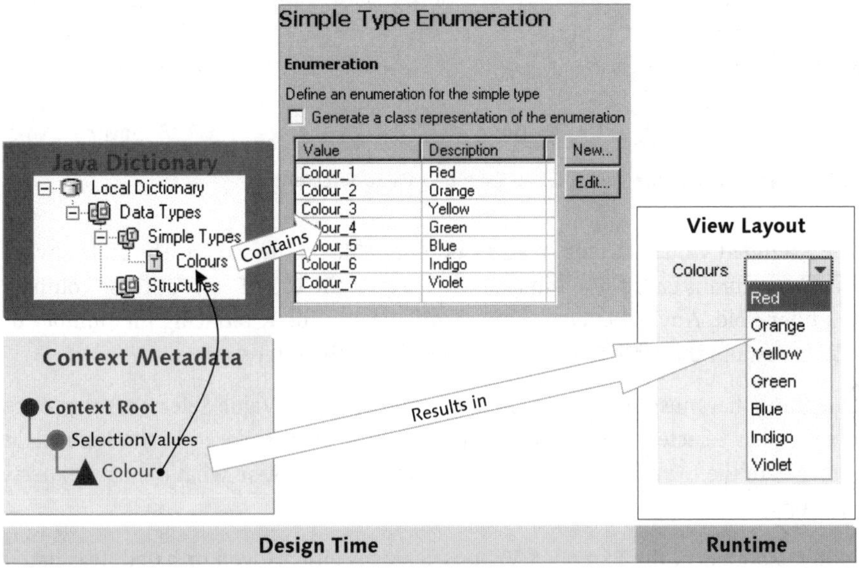

**Figure 7.29** Defining the Values for a Simple Value Selector

A Simple Value Selector should be used when the user is presented with no more than 30 or so options. Any more options than this and this method for presenting the user with a choice of inputs becomes increasingly user *unfriendly*.

### 7.9.2 Extended Value Selector

An Extended Value Selector is created in exactly the same way as a Simple Value Selector, the only difference being that an `InputField` UI element is used to display the data rather than a `DropDownByKey` UI element. Figure 7.30 shows an example of the Extended Value Selector including the process of defining its values.

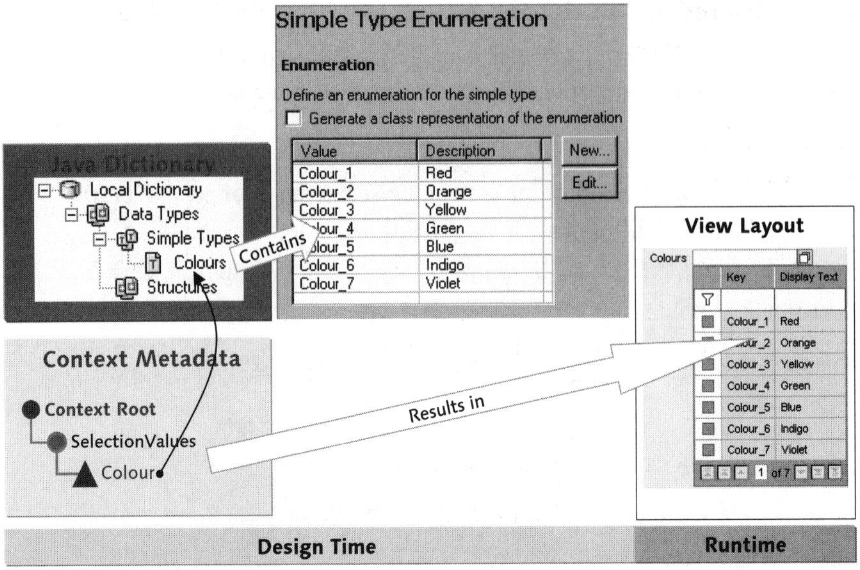

**Figure 7.30** Defining the Values for an Extended Value Selector

The Extended Value Selector creates a pop-up table on the screen. The table always has two columns called Key and Display Text. At the top of each of these columns is a filter field. Any value entered here will act as a filter, reducing the number of visible rows in the table to only those that match the filter value.

One thing that must be understood about the Extended Value Selector is that once the user has selected the required value, the Key value is placed in the input field rather than the Display Text value. This may or may not be what the user expects or wants.

In my experience, the Extended Value Selector is either loved or hated. It is hated by some users because the Key value placed back in the input field is a technical value that has no meaning to them. Other users love it because the text descriptions from which they are selecting contain duplicates. Therefore, to ensure that the correct value has been selected, the users need to see the Key value.

Since it is not possible to replace the Key value with the Display Text value in the input field once the user has selected the required value, you should carefully evaluate the user reaction to such a UI element before building it into your visual interface.

### 7.9.3 Extending the List of Values Shown in a Simple or Extended Value Selector

As mentioned earlier, a Simple or an Extended Value Selector obtains a list of values from either:

▶ An enumeration defined in the Java Dictionary

▶ A set of dynamic values defined at runtime

▶ A set of static values that have been supplemented with dynamic values at runtime

If a context attribute is defined on a Simple Type found in the Java Dictionary, and this Simple Type has an enumeration defined for it, then the values from the enumeration will *always* be presented to the user as a Simple or Extended Value Selector.

Any enumeration values held in the Java Dictionary are immutable.

However, it is quite possible to create an enumeration dynamically at runtime. The following coding shows how to extend the range of colors seen in the above example.

```
// Get the metadata for node SelectionValues
IWDNodeInfo selValsNodeInfo =
 wdContext.nodeSelectionValues().getNodeInfo();
// Get the metadata for the child attribute Colours
IWDAttributeInfo attrInfo =
  selValsNodeInfo.getAttribute("Colour");

// Get the modifiable simple type for this attribute
ISimpleTypeModifiable msType =
  attrInfo.getModifiableSimpleType();

// Set the column header caption seen in the EVS table
msType.setFieldLabel("Alt Colours");

// Get the modifiable simple type's value set
IModifiableSimpleValueSet valueSet =
  msType.getSVServices().getModifiableSimpleValueSet();

// Define a new value set
valueSet.put("Colour_10", "Pink");
valueSet.put("Colour_11", "Tan");
valueSet.put("Colour_12", "Saffron");
valueSet.put("Colour_13", "Lime");
valueSet.put("Colour_14", "Sky Blue Pink");
valueSet.put("Colour_15", "Turquoise");
valueSet.put("Colour_16", "Purple");
```

**Listing 7.9** Creating a dynamic set of values seen in a Simple or Extended Value Selector

Now, when the Colors context attribute is displayed, you will see not only the immutable set of values held in the Java Dictionary enumeration, but you will also see the additional values created by the above coding.

### 7.9.4 Object Value Selector

In many application scenarios a type of value help is needed in which the user searches for objects instead of values. In the example shown in Figure 7.31, the users are required to enter a customer id. If they do not know the correct value, the Object Value Selector will allow them to enter search criteria and then perform a search of a backend system. A table of results is then presented, from which the user can choose the item they require.

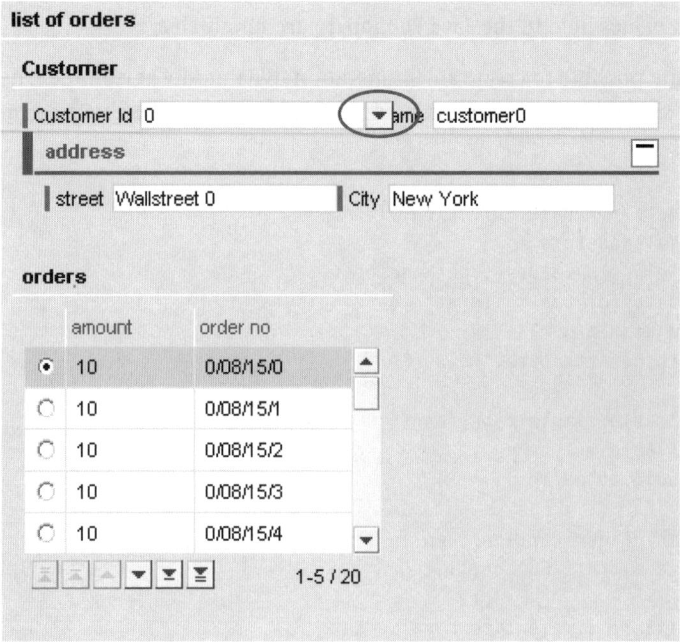

**Figure 7.31** The User Must Enter a Customer ID, but They Only Know the Customer's Name

In contrast to the Simple and Extended Value Selectors, the Object Value Selector is only partially based on a declarative approach. For embedding this type of value help into your Web Dynpro application you have to write a class that implements the IWDOVSContextNotificationListener interface. Once defined, the Web Dynpro Framework automatically renders a generic Object Value Selector pop-up window for you (see Figure 7.32).

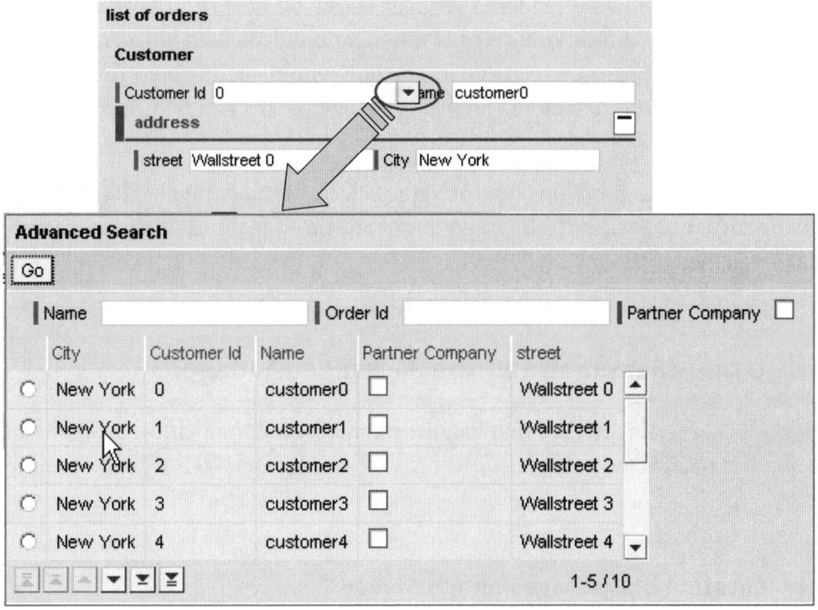

**Figure 7.32** The OVS Pop-Up, Created by the Web Dynpro Framework

### 7.9.5 Implementing an Object Value Selector

The following steps are needed to implement an Object Value Selector (OVS):

1. Create a custom controller that can supply an instance of your OVS object.

2. The custom controller must instantiate a subclass that implements `IWDOVSContextNotificationListener`. This requires an implementation of the following three methods:

   ▶ `applyInputValues(IWDNodeElement datafromApp,`
   `    IWDNodeElement inputToOvsQuery)`

   ▶ `onQuery(IWDNodeElement inputToOvsQuery,`
   `    IWDNode ovsQueryResults)`

   ▶ `applyResult(IWDNodeElement dataForApp,`
   `    IWDNodeElement selectedOvsResultElement)`

3. In the `wdDoInit()` method of the view controller, you must associate the relevant context attribute with the instance of the OVS object created by your custom controller. This is done by calling the following method:
   `WDValueServices.`
   `addOVSExtension(IWDAttributeInfo[] startupAttributes,`
   `    IWDNode queryInputNode,`
   `    IWDNode queryResultNode,`
   `    IWDOVSContextNotificationListener queryListener)`

The input field will now be rendered with an OVS icon next to it. When the user clicks on it, a Value Help service event is raised, and the Web Dynpro Framework will then handle the pop-up screen and interaction with the OVS object for you. See Section 4.4.5 for more details on how service events are handled during Phase Model processing.

Since the implementation of this type of Value Selector is more involved, the details will be discussed in Section 10.8, where more advanced features of the user interface are explained.

## 7.10    Using Messages and the Message Manager

The MessageManager is the class that handles all messages for an entire component. Only one instance of the MessageManager is ever needed per Web Dynpro component.

### 7.10.1    Location of Messages on the Screen

Every view layout in Web Dynpro contains an implicit location in which messages will be displayed. By default, all messages will be displayed at the bottom of the screen as shown in Figure 7.33. However, it is quite possible to move this location.

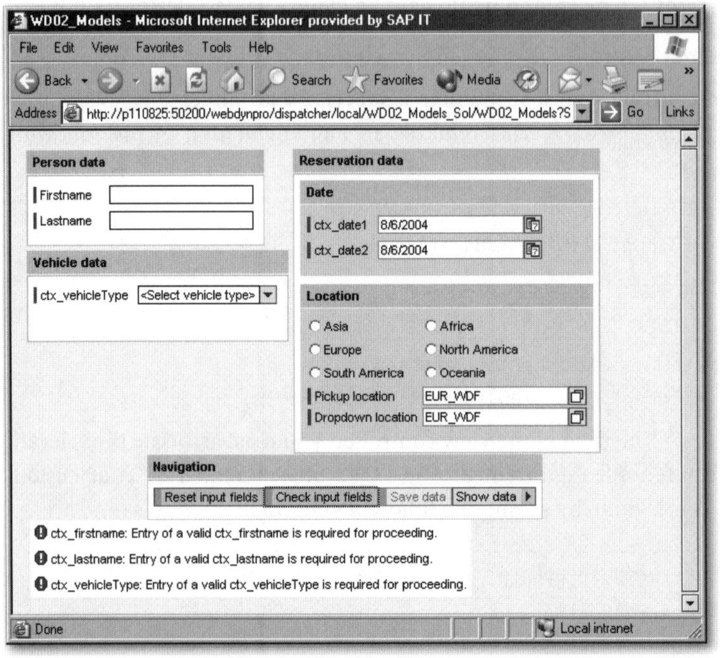

**Figure 7.33** The Default Location for Messages Is at the Bottom of the Screen

The message location can be moved by adding a MessageArea UI element to the view layout. Wherever this UI element is positioned, all messages for that View Assembly will be displayed at that location. It is often useful to insert a MessageArea UI element very near the top of your view layout. This means the user will not need to scroll the screen down to the bottom to see any messages that may be displayed.

**Important**

If defined, only one MessageArea UI element is required per View Assembly. If you have multiple MessageArea UI elements defined, the Web Dynpro Framework will use the first one it encounters for the message location, and the others will be ignored.

### 7.10.2 Accessing the Message Manager

From a programmatic point of view, there is only one instance of the IWDMessageM-anager class per component instance. It is therefore worth while to create a class-wide reference to the message manager in your component's component controller.

```
//@@begin others
 IWDMessageManager msgMgr;
//@@end
```
**Listing 7.10** Declare a class-wide reference to the message manager

The object reference can then be set by calling the following code in the wdDoInit() method of the component controller.

```
public void wdDoInit() {
  //@@begin wdDoInit()
  msgMgr = wdComponentAPI.getMessageManager();
 //@@end
}
```
**Listing 7.11** Defining the message manager object reference

Notice that the shortcut variable used to create this object reference is wdComponent-API, not wdThis.

### 7.10.3 Reporting a Simple Message

The simplest way to place a message on the screen is to call the message manager's reportSuccess() method. This method simply requires a string parameter as the message text.

```
  msgMgr.reportSuccess("Everything is fine");
```
**Listing 7.12** Using the message manager to display a simple message

When the screen is next rendered, the text string "Everything is fine" will appear in the message location for the current View Assembly.

### 7.10.4 Locale-Dependent Text at Runtime

It is not good practice, however, to hard-code text strings into your coding — especially if your application needs to support multiple languages. Therefore, Web Dynpro gives you the ability to create locale-dependent message objects within your component.

Each Web Dynpro component has something called a message pool, and within this pool you may create four types of message:

► Standard

► Warning

► Error

► Text

> **Important**
>
> For developers with ABAP programming experience, Web Dynpro messages are somewhat different from ABAP messages in that in Web Dynpro, the message type (i.e., Success, Warning, or Error) is part of the message object's definition. This stands in contrast to ABAP, in which a message is just a predefined text string that has a type assigned to it at runtime when the MESSAGE statement is used.

The first three message types are the ones used by the IWDMessageManager class and become runtime constants within a generated class IMessage${n_c}.java, each message being of type IWDMessage.

To extract the information from an object of type IWDMessage, it is first necessary to cast it as a WDMessage object; then you will have access to all the message properties. In the following example, a message called ErrorMsg has been created in the message pool of component ${n_c}. This leads to the creation of a constant in class IMessage${n_c} called ERROR_MSG.

```
WDMessage errMsg = (WDMessage)IMessage${n_c}.ERROR_MSG;

// Get the component name, the message key
// and the message text
String msgComp = errMsg.getCompName();
String msgKey = errMsg.getMessageKey();
String msgText = errMsg.getMessageText();

if (errMsg.getType().equals(WDMessageType.ERROR)) {
  // Its an error message
```

```
}
else if (errMsg.getType().
                equals(WDMessageType.WARNING)) {
 // Its a warning message
}
else if (errMsg.getType().
                equals(WDMessageType.STANDARD)) {
 // Its a standard message
}
```

**Listing 7.13** Obtaining the properties of a message object

---

**Important**

Only message pool messages of type Standard, Warning, and Error are addressable as constants in the generated class IMessage$\{n_c\}.java. Messages of type text *do not* appear in this generated class.

---

Messages of type Text are not accessible to the IWDMessageManager class; instead, you can access them through class IWDTextAccessor. Messages of type text are text strings that either have been created as language-specific texts or have been extracted from existing code using the NWDS Externalize Strings wizard.

### 7.10.5  Reporting a Message Held in the Message Pool

For applications in which multi-language support is needed, you should always make use of the message pool as a repository for message texts. This allows the text to be translated without you having to modify your coding in any way.

The following generalized code fragment shows how to call the message manager so that it displays a message derived from the message pool.

```
IWDMessageManager msgMgr =
                wdComponentAPI.getMessageManager();

msgMgr.reportMessage(IMessage$/nc}.{MessageKey},
                new Object[] {p1,…,pn} ,
                boolean);
```

**Listing 7.14** Display a message held in the component's message pool

In the above example, we can make direct reference to the message text by means of the message constant created for us in class IMessage$\{n_c\}.\{MessageKey\}$ (where $\{n_c\}$ is the name of the current Web Dynpro component).

The object array is a list of parameters to be passed to the message, and the Boolean parameter tells the Web Dynpro Framework whether the entire navigation queue should be aborted. See Chapter 11 for more details on navigation processing.

### 7.10.6 Relating Messages with UI Elements

Very often, when an error message is sent to the screen, it will be as a result of some kind of erroneous input made by the user. Therefore, to help the user identify which field (or fields) contain the erroneous value(s), the relevant UI elements can be highlighted when the message is displayed (see Figure 7.34).

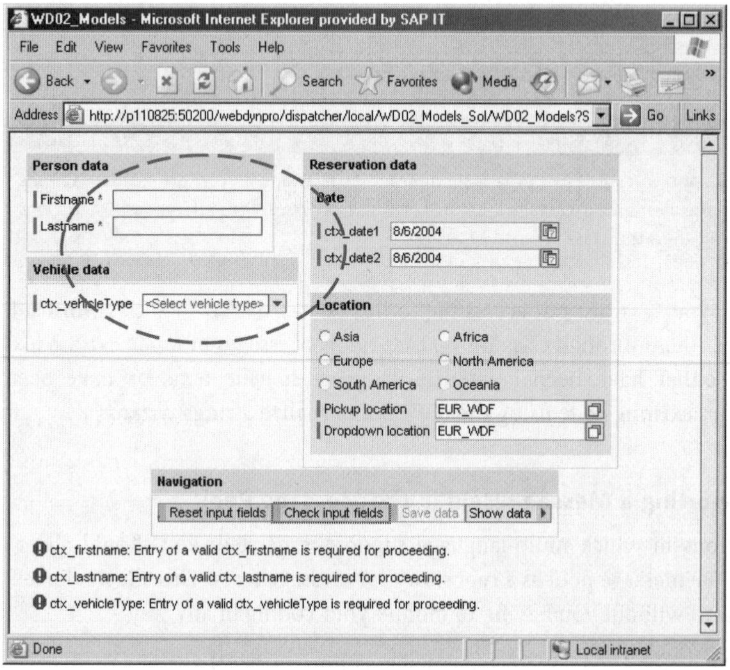

**Figure 7.34** The Associated UI Elements Are Highlighted in Red with the Message

Although this may seem counterintuitive, when you want a UI element to be highlighted with the display of an error a message, you don't need to know anything about the UI element — the Web Dynpro Framework works that out for you.

Remember that UI elements are simply the means by which context data is visualized. Ask yourself this question: "Where does the data live that is visualized on the screen? In the UI element object itself or in the context?"[11]

Therefore, to cause a UI element to be highlighted when an error message is displayed, you only need to know which attribute in the context holds the erroneous value. The Web Dynpro Framework then works out which UI element is bound to this attribute and highlights it for you. Remember, the UI element is only the superficial skin on top of the data held in the context.

---

11 If you said "In the UI element object," then you've haven't yet grasped a fundamental concept of Web Dynpro. Go back and reread Section 7.4.

The following code shows how to call the message manager so that in addition to the display of an error message, the UI element being used to visualize the context attribute holding the erroneous value is also highlighted. `${cn}` and `${ca}` are the respective names of the context node and attribute in question.

```
IWDMessageManager msgMgr =
                   wdComponentAPI.getMessageManager();

IWDNode          errNode = wdContext.node${cn}();
IWDNodeElement   errEl   = errNode.
                           current${cn}Element();
IWDAttributeInfo errAttr = errNode.
                           getNodeInfo().
                             getAttribute("${ca}");

msgMgr.reportContextAttributeMessage(errEl,
                 errAttr,
                 IMessage${nc}.{MessageKey},
                 new Object[] {p1,…,pn},
                 boolean);
```

**Listing 7.15** Highlighting a UI element when an error message is displayed is done by identifying the associated context attribute.

In this code fragment, the last three parameters are exactly the same as the parameters used in Listing 7.14. However, there are two new parameters. The first parameter is a reference to the element in the context node that holds the erroneous value, and the second parameter is the metadata of the context attribute in error.

If you think of a context node as being like a table with rows and columns, then the element reference identifies the table row, and the context attribute metadata reference identifies the table column. These two values taken together exactly identify the specific attribute holding the erroneous value.

### 7.10.7    Locale-Dependent Text Defined in the Java Dictionary

In addition to the four categories of message described above is a fifth category of locale-dependent text within a Web Dynpro application. These are texts that belong to dictionary simple types, and they can be accessed through the ISimpleType interface (see Figure 7.35).

Once the application is deployed, the locale-dependent texts are stored in standard resource bundle files.

The following example assumes that a message called Message1 of type text has been defined in a component's message pool. To access this message, you need to use the following code.

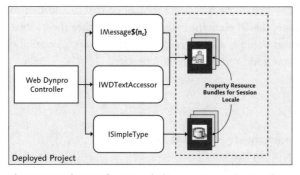

**Figure 7.35** The Interfaces Needed to Access Locale-Specific Text

```
// Get the text accessor from the current component
IWDTextAccessor textAccessor =
                     wdComponentAPI().getTextAccessor();

// Get the message by name from the message pool
String msgFromPool = textAccessor.getText("Message1");
```

**Listing 7.16** Code fragment for obtaining a message of type text from the message pool

Remember that the component's message manager has no access to messages of type text, so these types of messages should be used only to supply UI elements. The purpose of the IWDMessageManager interface is to supply the user with informative messages about the success or failure of the application's functionality.

The code fragment below assumes a message called Message2 of type error is in the message pool. This message will be reported to the user with no parameters (the null parameter value), and navigation will not be cancelled as a result of the error (the false parameter value).

```
// Get the message manager from the current component
IWDMessageManager
        msgMgr =  wdComponentAPI().getMessageManager();

// Issue a warning message using a text constant from
// the generated IMessage${nc} class
 msgMgr.reportMessage(IMessage${nc}.MESSAGE2,
                     null, false);
```

**Listing 7.17** Fragment for issuing a message of type "error" from the message pool

Within any component ${c}, any statically defined text, such as message pool texts or hard-coded text values for UI elements, will be placed into a generated resource bundle file called Resource${c}.properties.

This file can be viewed (but must not be edited) from the Package Explorer view in the NWDS. The general path name is:

```
${pr}.
  gen_wdp/packages.
    ${pkg1} … ${pkgn}.
      ${nctl}.
        wdp.
          Resource${c}.
            properties
```

### 7.10.8 Defining Placeholders Within a Message Text

There is often the need to be able to substitute a variable value into a static message string. This can be achieved with numbered placeholders within the text string. Messages containing such placeholders are known as message text patterns.

For instance, if you are writing an application that creates business documents, you probably want to inform the user what number the newly created document has. Therefore, you would enter the message text into the message pool as shown in Figure 7.36.

| Message Key | Message Type | Message Text |
|---|---|---|
| DocumentCreated | standard | Document {0} has been successfully created |

**Figure 7.36** A Placeholder in a Text Message

If you want to have more than one placeholder within the text message, simply increment the placeholder number as shown in Figure 7.37, where {0} is the document number, {1} is the time, and {2} is the date.

| Message Key | Message Type | Message Text |
|---|---|---|
| DocumentCreated | standard | Document {0} successfully created at {1} on {2} |

**Figure 7.37** Multiple Placeholders in a Text Message

---

**Caveat Confector**

All message placeholders must be sequentially numbered integers, and their values must be supplied as Java strings.

Message text patterns use `java.text.MessageFormat` without using element formats.

---

The code to issue the above `documentCreated` message must now supply a parameter value:

```
// Get the message manager from the current component
IWDMessageManager msgMgr =
                wdComponentAPI().getMessageManager();

// Get the document number from somewhere...
String docNo = getDocumentNo();
```

```
// Issue a warning message using a text constant from
// the generated IMessage${nc} class
msgMgr.reportMessage(IMessage${nc}.DOCUMENT_CREATED,
                     new Object[] {docNo},
                     false);
```

**Listing 7.18** Code fragment for issuing a standard message with placeholder parameters

Please be aware that in Listing 7.17 and Listing 7.18 that the class name for the IMessage${nc} class has been generalized.

### 7.10.9 Process Control Using the Message Manager

The message manager must be used carefully; otherwise you could find that subsequent processing logic becomes disrupted — especially if you are implementing centralized error and navigation processing (see Chapter 11). There are two reasons for this:

1. Many of the message manager methods have a Boolean parameter called cancel-Navigation. If this is set to true, no matter what other outbound navigation plugs are fired, processing of the entire navigation queue is aborted.

   If you are attempting to perform centralized error and navigation management and then you allow a view controller to issue a message with the cancelNavigation parameter set to true, you will find that your centralized processing logic will have been circumvented.

2. Any time you call a message manager method that starts with the word *raise*, you will immediately terminate all further application processing. These methods hand control to the Web Dynpro Framework, and it is never handed back again. Such methods should only be used in the event of very serious or fatal error situations.

   For non-fatal errors, always use a message manager method that starts with the word *report*.

There is one exception to the rule about methods starting with the word raise. The message manager has a method called raisePendingException() that can be used to act as a conditional exit point. This means that if method calls to the message manager have been made previously, then calling this method will conditionally terminate the round trip. If no pending messages are found in the message manager, this method exits silently.[12]

See Section 11.3 for more information on how error and navigation processing can be disrupted by careless use of the message manager.

---

[12] Call me old-fashioned, but I prefer not to use a method such as raisePendingException() because I believe a program should have only one entry point and one exit point. The use of this method creates an extra, conditional exit point.

# 8   Writing Multilanguage Applications

One of the continual problems with the distribution of software products within geographical regions such as Europe has been that of language support. The French don't want to speak German, the Italians don't want to speak Spanish, and the English and Americans can *only* speak English!

This problem has produced a variety of solutions; some vendors distribute entirely new versions of their products with the language-specific text embedded within the executable code, and other vendors have opted to separate the language-specific content from the executable code.

The requirement for multilingual operation has, from SAP's earliest days, been a fundamental design criterion of all its software products. In the R/2 and later the R/3 systems (and all of the derivative systems), the data stored in their relational database tables is organized in third normal form. This has the direct consequence that business data and the text that describes the business data are always stored in separate tables related by a foreign key.

## 8.1   Internationalization

The word *internationalization* is used to describe either the design process required to make a software product functional in all required languages or the modification process by which existing software is adapted from single language operation to multilingual operation. The result is a software product in which all language-specific text is external to the executable code that uses it.

Because the word *internationalization* is so long, it is abbreviated to *i18n* — that is, you write the first letter *i*, skip over the 18 letters in the middle, and then write the final *n*. From now on, we will talk about the i18n process or Web Dynpro i18n rather than using the full word.

## 8.2   Externalization

Externalization is the process by which hard-coded text strings are removed (i.e., externalized) from a source code file and placed into a .properties file. The original source code is then modified to access a generated resource bundle accessor class.

Within the NWDS, an Externalize Strings wizard automates the extraction and code modification process.

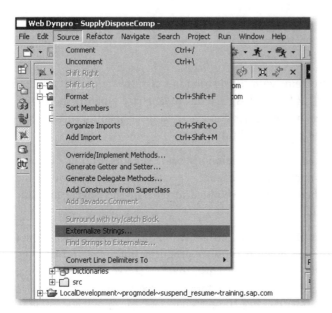

**Figure 8.1** Externalize Strings Wizard for Removing Text Strings from Java Source Code

For more information on this process, see the standard SAP documentation "Internationalization in the SAP NetWeaver Developer Studio."

## 8.3    Web Dynpro i18n Concept

In keeping with the R/3 tradition of separating data from the text that describes the data, the Web Dynpro i18n concept separates text strings from the programs that manipulate those strings. Therefore, Web Dynpro Java class files, metadata files, and dictionary simple types do not contain any hard-coded language-specific text. The standard Java class `java.util.ResourceBundle` is used for managing language-specific text at runtime. See the Javadoc for more information on the exact details of the operation of this class.

> **Important**
>
> When a Web Dynpro DC is created, a language is required such as `British_English` or `Spanish` or `Hebrew`. This language setting serves several purposes:
> ► To inform a translator of the language in which the Web Dynpro DC was originally written.
> ► To define the default language for all current and future metadata files.

This value is *not* read at runtime by the Web Dynpro Framework when determining the session locale of an application.

---

**Caveat Confector**

The project language cannot be changed after a project has been created, and you cannot copy metadata between projects of different languages without the loss of text strings.

Not all locales recognized by Java are permissible within a Web Dynpro DC. The permissible languages are *only* those found in the drop-down list seen when a DC is created. The reason for this is that internally, SAP uses an R/3 system to serve as a translation engine. This immediately reduces the set of permissible Web Dynpro languages to the subset of languages (or dialects) within which R/3 operates.

Languages not known to R/3 are not permissible in Web Dynpro.

---

## 8.4 S2X: SAP's Use of the XLIFF Standard

SAP has taken the XML Localization Interchange File Format (XLIFF)[1] and produced a reduced and somewhat modified variant known as the *SAP Supported XLIFF* or S2X.

SAP's S2X-compliant files all use the .XLF file extension and differ from standard XLIFF in the following ways:

▶ S2X imposes the following restrictions upon standard XLIFF:

  ▶ XLIFF's mechanism for handling alternate translations from different sources, such as a Translation Memory System or a Machine Translation System, has not been implemented.

  ▶ Certain textual content is encoded using only the lower half of the ASCII character set, that is, 7-bit ASCII.

▶ S2X extends standard XLIFF in the following areas:

  ▶ Certain XLIFF extensions have been implemented that can accommodate the classification of SAP's software according to software component, development component, and release.

  ▶ Certain XLIFF constraints have been made optional.

An S2X file contains two types of data: header data and content data.

▶ Header data describes the properties of all the contents stored in the file.

▶ Content data are the text items accompanied by supplementary information, such as unique identifiers, that may be used in reuse or update strategies.

This can be seen in the S2X editor as the tabs **Header** and **Resource Text** (see Figure 8.2 and Figure 8.3).

---

1  See *http://www.xliff.org* for more details of the original standard.

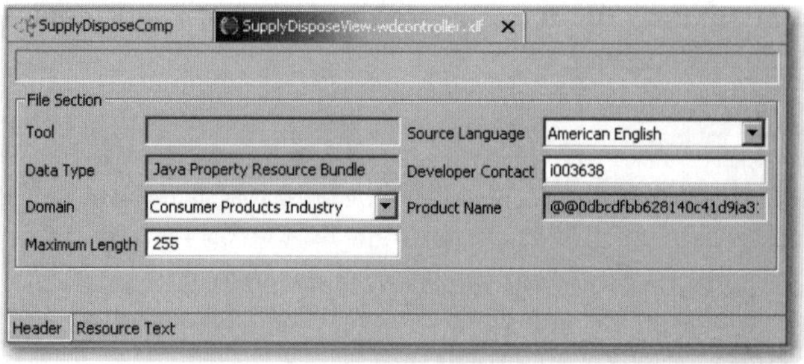

**Figure 8.2** S2X Editor Showing XLF Header Information

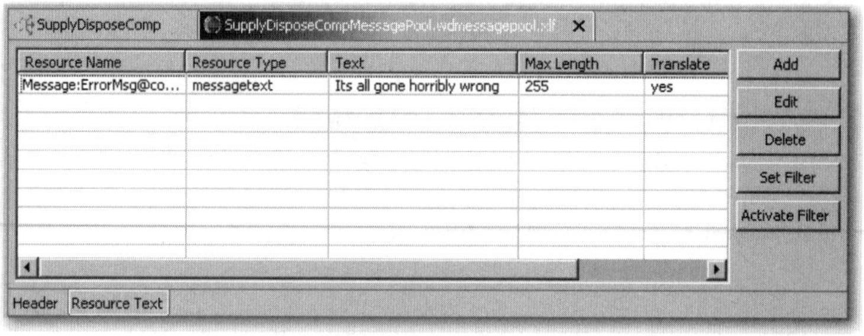

**Figure 8.3** S2X Editor Showing XLF Resource Text Information

## 8.5 Storing Language-Specific Text in XLF Files

For each type of entity that can hold language-specific content, a corresponding XLF file is created. These XLF files are only created if the developer adds some text, for example, hard-coding a value for the text property of a Label UI element.

In general, the following XLF files are created when language-specific content is added:

- ► `${nᵥ}.wdcontroller.xlf`
  Action texts in a view controller
- ► `${nᵥ}.wdview.xlf`
  UI element `text`, `tooltip`, and `imageAlt` values in a view layout
- ► `${w}.wdwindow.xlf`
  The value of the window's title property
- ► `${nᵨ}MessagePool.wdmessagepool.xlf`
  Component message pool content
- ► `${st}.dtsimpletype.xlf`
  Enumeration display texts, field labels, column headers, and tooltips for dictionary simple types

---

**Important**

Notice that none of the above file names contain a locale value. During the development of a Web Dynpro application, the developer only works in a *single* language — the one specified when the project was created.

Consequently, all XLF files generated during the development of the application are assumed to contain text belonging to this locale.

Be careful not to create your Web Dynpro DC in one language and then start entering text descriptions in another language — this will really confuse the translation process!

---

## 8.6 Translating XLF Files

There is not yet an integrated development environment (IDE)-based tool for translating XLF files. The creation of an XLF file for any language other than the project default needs to be performed manually. However, this amounts to nothing more than locating the original XLF file in your NWDS workspace directory and creating a copy of it in the same directory.

The most important thing to remember is to include the new locale value at the correct position in the file name.

For any new locale `${l}`, the original file should be copied and renamed as shown in Table 8.1.

| File Name in Original Language | File Name in New Language |
|---|---|
| `${nv}.wdcontroller.xlf` | `${nv}.wdcontroller_${l}.xlf` |
| `${nv}.wdview.xlf` | `${nv}.wdview_${l}.xlf` |
| `${w}.wdwindow.xlf` | `${w}.wdwindow_${l}.xlf` |
| `${nc}MessagePool.wdmessagepool.xlf` | `${nc}MessagePool.wdmessagepool_${l}.xlf` |
| `${st}.dtsimpletype.xlf` | `${st}.dtsimpletype_${l}.xlf` |

**Table 8.1** Where to Add the New Locale Value in the File Name

Once new locale-specific XLF files have been created, the project view in the Package Explorer should be refreshed, and then the S2X editor can be used to perform the translation.

## 8.7 Use of the S2X Editor Within NWDS

SAP has created an editing tool within the NWDS that allows you to edit XLF files in SAP's specific S2X format.

**Caveat Confector**

The S2X editor is *not* a Web Dynpro-specific tool. It has been provided only to fill a functional gap in Eclipse.

The S2X editor should *never* be used to edit language-specific content in the project's default language. If you have created your project in German, then all German text belonging to UI elements, dictionary simple types, and message pools should be edited using the standard Web Dynpro tools.

Using the S2X editor, it is possible to change the source language of an XLF file, but this change will not cause the filename to be updated (remember, all text belonging to languages other than the default project language must have the locale $\{1\}$ embedded in the file name); therefore, such changes create inconsistencies within your Web Dynpro DC.

If you use the S2X editor to change the XLF file associated with a Web Dynpro view (for instance) *and* you have already opened that view through the normal Web Dynpro editor, you will not see your text changes in the view layout until you reload the project.

## 8.8    Editing Message Pool XLF Files

If you double-click on the Message Pool belonging to a Web Dynpro project from the Web Dynpro Explorer menu, you will see a version of the S2X editor applicable to `MessagePools` (see Figure 8.4).

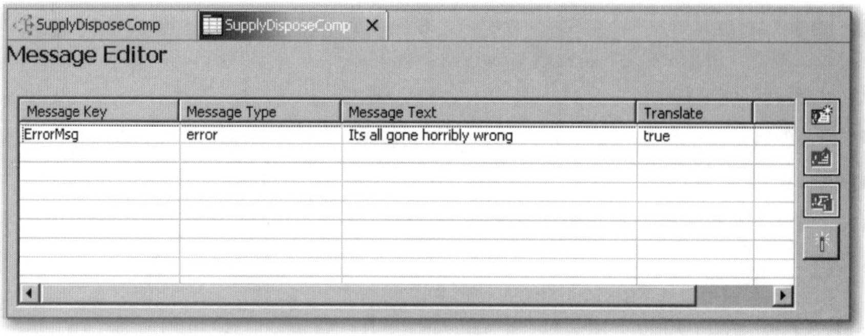

**Figure 8.4**  S2X Editor for a Component Message Pool

To edit the XLF files associated with view controllers, windows, and dictionary simple types, you should change from the Web Dynpro Explorer view of the project to either the Package Explorer or Navigator views. Here you can expand the `src` directory and locate the XLF files. These files are marked with a 🌰 icon.

The Package Explorer (shown in Figure 8.5) provides the most direct route to the XLF files.

By double-clicking on the view controller's XLF file (`I18NView.wdview.xlf`) shown above, you will see the editor screens in Figure 8.2 and Figure 8.3.

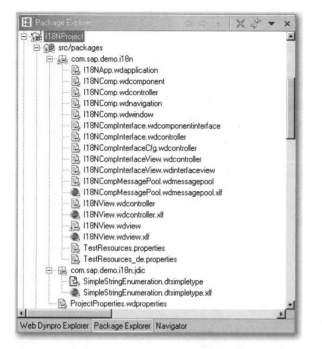

**Figure 8.5** Navigator View of the XLF Files in a Web Dynpro Project

The application developer can edit all the text resources for a project using the S2X editor. As stated earlier, these XLF files are assumed to contain text that belongs to the language specified when the project was created.

Notice that the view of the S2X editor shown in Figure 8.4 is slightly different from the view shown in Figure 8.3. There is a good reason for this. The view of the S2X editor seen when editing a message pool from Web Dynpro imposes two restrictions:

▶ The available message types are limited to Standard, Warning, Error, and Text because these are the only message types applicable to a Web Dynpro Message Pool.

▶ The S2X header information is not available for editing.

However, when the S2X editor is started from either the Navigator or Package Explorer views, you will see the full S2X editor, in which both the header information and the full range of message types are accessible.

---

**Caveat Confector**

Do not use the S2X editor to change any text belonging to your project's default language! These changes should only be made through the Web Dynpro tools in order to ensure the consistency of the underlying XLF files.

---

## 8.9    Runtime Locale Determination

Within the scope of a Web Dynpro DC, the locale of an application can be defined using the application property DefaultLocale. This hard-coded value acts as the application's default locale unless it is explicitly overridden.

Web Dynpro makes use of the standard fallback process within java.util.ResourceBundle to determine which locale value should be used for a particular application.

Table 8.2 shows how the fallback process works. The first column indicates the type of user accessing the system. The "Developer" user is the only user for which the sap.locale URL parameter is considered legitimate. Once a Web Dynpro application has been developed, the URL parameter sap.locale should not normally be used.

If a Web Dynpro application's authentication flag is set to true, valid user credentials must first be supplied to the Web Dynpro Framework before the application can be run. If the user credentials are obtained from the SAP NetWeaver Portal, the required locale value will be supplied.

| User | Locale Specified In | | | | | | |
| | URL | User Id | Browser | DefaultLocale property | WD system | VM default | Final locale |
| --- | --- | --- | --- | --- | --- | --- | --- |
| Developer | en | de | fr | it | ru | jp | en |
| Authenticated | | de | fr | it | ru | jp | de |
| Anonymous | | | fr | it | ru | jp | fr |
| Anonymous | | | | it | ru | jp | it |
| Anonymous | | | | | ru | jp | ru |
| Anonymous | | | | | | jp | jp |

**Table 8.2**  Fallback Process for Locale Determination

# PART IV
## Advanced Development

# 9 Dynamic Context Manipulation

Under certain circumstances you will need to create context nodes at runtime; such nodes are known as *dynamic nodes*, as opposed to the *static nodes*[1] declared at design time.

In Chapter 6, we looked at how the typed and generic context interfaces are used. Now when creating context nodes and attributes at runtime, we will only have the generic or untyped interface available. As you will appreciate by now, a significant coding convenience is provided by declaring your nodes and attributes at design time, since the node and attribute names are then built into the generated Java class and method names.

Nonetheless, you may find yourself in a situation in which the metadata of the information you are working with is unknown until runtime.

## 9.1 Dynamic Addition of an Unmapped Context Node

First, we look at how to create context value nodes and attributes at runtime and then how to access them. Since we are now dealing with dynamically defined nodes, the convenient typed getter and setter methods used in the previous examples are not available; instead, we must use the generic context interface.

The coding example that follows dynamically builds the context value node and attributes shown in Figure 9.1 and then adds exactly the same data as seen in the previous example.

**Figure 9.1** An Unmapped Context Node to Be Created Dynamically

---

1  The definition of a *statically defined* node assumes that you have left the `typedAccessRequired` node property set to its default value of `true`.

> **Caveat Confector**
>
> This code should *not* be put into a view controller!
>
> Why not?
>
> Well, let's say you implement the following coding in a view controller:
>
> ► Create an unmapped context node.
>
> ► Retrieve the data required to populate that node from some backend system.
>
> ► Display the generated node through some dynamically created UI elements.
>
> What role is your view controller now performing?
>
> Data generator or data consumer?
>
> What role should a view controller play?
>
> The answer is *not* a data generator. View controllers are not responsible for generating the data they display. If you think that because your application does not crash and is functional, your architecture is sound, then:
>
> *Go directly to jail, do not pass Go, do not collect £200!*
>
> By placing business logic into a view controller, not only are you blurring the distinction between the role of visual and non-visual controllers, but you are greatly increasing the effort required to maintain that application because you are not being consistent about the location of business logic.
>
> This is not good. Don't do it.

### 9.1.1 Before the Coding Details Are Discussed, Though ...

It's always simpler to work with context nodes and attributes that have had a typed interface created at design time. Therefore, always ask yourself this question: "Is the extra complexity of dynamic node creation really necessary?" Are you sure the node cannot be created at design time — even in a generic manner?

If the answer is that you simply cannot implement the required functionality any other way, then fine; go ahead and create your nodes dynamically. If, however, you're just copying the coding out of a book because you think it will make you look smart, then don't do it.

Every line of code you write should contribute to the overall simplicity of the application, not its complexity.

Notice that the coding to create a context node exists in the wdDoInit() method of a non-visual controller (typically the component controller). This is because the decision to create dynamic nodes is usually made at controller initialization time, and thereafter the controller works with the created context structure.[2]

---

2  This recommendation is not a hard and fast rule, but it will certainly make your coding simpler if you follow it.

### 9.1.2 Now for the Coding

```
public void wdDoInit() {
  //@@begin wdDoInit()
  // Create metadata for a new SalesOrders value node
  // Get metadata object for the context root node
  IWDNodeInfo rootNodeInfo = wdContext.getNodeInfo();

  // Create metadata object to describe a new
  // independent value node called "SalesOrders"
  IWDNodeInfo salesOrdersInfo =
    rootNodeInfo.
      addChild("SalesOrders",    // Name
               null,             // Structure reference
               true,             // Is singleton?
               false, true,      // Cardinality
               false, false,     // Sel cardinality
               true,             // Init lead selection?
               null,             // Datatype
               null,             // Supplier function
               null);            // Disposer function

  // Add attribute metadata to the new node info object
  salesOrdersInfo.
    addAttribute("OrderNo",
                 "ddic:com.sap.dictionary.integer");
  salesOrdersInfo.
    addAttribute("LongText",
                 "ddic:com.sap.dictionary.string");
  salesOrdersInfo.
    addAttribute("SalesDate",
                 "ddic:com.sap.dictionary.date");
  salesOrdersInfo.
    addAttribute("SalesRep",
                 "ddic:com.sap.dictionary.string");

  // Create a new context node using the metadata we
  // just created
  IWDNode soNode =
          wdContext.getChildNode("SalesOrders",0);

  // Create two new elements in node SalesOrders
  IWDNodeElement soEl1 = soNode.createElement();
  IWDNodeElement soEl2 = soNode.createElement();

  // Populate the two new elements
  soEl1.setAttributeValue("OrderNo",
                          new Integer(100));
```

```
soEl1.setAttributeValue("LongText",
                        "Printer supplies");
soEl1.setAttributeValue("SalesDate",
                new Date(System.currentTimeMillis()));
soEl1.setAttributeValue("SalesRep",
                        "Harry Hawk");

soEl2.setAttributeValue("OrderNo",
                        new Integer(101));
soEl2.setAttributeValue("LongText",
                        "Network cabling");
soEl2.setAttributeValue("SalesDate",
                new Date(System.currentTimeMillis()));
soEl2.setAttributeValue("SalesRep",
                        "Ned Seagoon");

// Add elements to the node collection
soNode.addElement(soEl1);
soNode.addElement(soEl2);
//@@end
}
```

**Listing 9.1** Creating and populating the unmapped node SalesOrders in the component controller

The coding performs the following processing steps:

1. Before a context node can be created, the metadata that describes the node must be created. This information is held in IWDNodeInfo objects. To create such an object, you must call the addChild() method belonging to the parent node info object. In this case, the context is completely empty; therefore, our new SalesOrders node will have the context root node as its immediate parent. This makes it an independent node.

   Get a reference to the context root node's metadata object using wdContext.get-NodeInfo().

2. Using the context root node as a parent, add metadata information to describe the new node SalesOrders. The parameters to the addChild() method are used as follows:

   ▶ The name of the new node.

   ▶ A reference to a Java Dictionary structure from which structural metadata information can be inherited if required.

   ▶ A Boolean flag that determines whether the new node is a singleton or not. In our case, we are creating an independent node; therefore, it *must* be a singleton.[3]

---

3  Try setting this parameter to false, and see what happens!

> A Boolean flag that determines the first part of the node's cardinality. This is the **Mandatory** flag.

> A Boolean flag that determines the second part of the node's cardinality. This is the **Multiple** flag.

> A Boolean flag that determines the first part of the node's selection cardinality. This is the **Mandatory Selection** flag.

> A Boolean flag that determines the second part of the node's selection cardinality. This is the **Multiple Selection** flag.

> A reference to a non-dictionary structured data type.

> The name of the supplier function.

> The name of the disposer function.

3. Once the metadata for the node has been created, it is now possible to add the metadata describing the node's attributes; this is done using the `addAttribute()` method.

---

**Important**

Notice the syntax used to define the data type of the new attributes. If you want to use data types defined in the Web Dynpro dictionary, you must start the class name with the namespace identifier `ddic:`. If, however, you want to use a standard Java class, you must start the class name with the namespace identifier `java:`. Failure to use a namespace identifier will cause a runtime error.

---

**Caveat Confector**

Creating a context attribute using the data type `java:java.lang.String` is perfectly acceptable, but don't expect to be able to bind a UI element to it. A UI element can be bound only to a context attribute whose data type comes from the Web Dynpro dictionary. For a string, you must use the functionally equivalent data type `ddic:com.sap.dictionary.string`.

---

4. Once the `addAttribute()` method has been called for each new attribute, we are ready to create an actual node object in which runtime data can be stored. We are now switching from the manipulation of metadata, to the manipulation of actual data.[4]

5. Since this node has been created dynamically, the method `wdContext.nodeSalesOrders()` used in the previous examples cannot be called — it doesn't even exist. Therefore, we must use the generic context API for node creation.

6. The method `${cn}.getChildNode(String, int)` returns an instance of the named child node belonging to the element index. In this case, the parent node is the context root, so `${cn}` == `wdContext`. Also, the context root node has one and only

---

4  Always maintain a clear distinction in your mind between the manipulation of context metadata and actual data.

one element. Therefore, the element number passed to the getChildNode() method must be zero (or if you want to avoid hard coding such values IWDNode.LEAD_SELECTION).

7. The act of calling ${cn}.getChildNode(String, int) causes the child node instance to be created. This method either returns an existing child node instance[5] or creates a new child node instance. Either way, it never returns null.

8. Now that we have a reference to the new node instance, we can create an element for it. However, we can operate only with the generic, untyped element class of IWDNodeElement, so we must call createElement().

9. A node element of type IWDNodeElement has no specific getter or setter methods for the declared attributes, so we must set the attribute values using the generic method setAttributeValue(), passing in the name of the attribute and the required value as an object.

10. Now the elements can be added to the node collection in exactly the same way as before.

As you can see, declaring nodes at design time (with the typedAccessRequired property set to true) makes the coding much easier because you don't have to use the generic context interface.

### 9.1.3 Dynamic Creation of a Hierarchy of Context Nodes

When creating a hierarchy of context nodes at runtime (such as that shown in Figure 9.2), the following sequence of steps must be followed.

1. Obtain a reference to the parent node instance. If the parent is the context root node, it can be referenced via the shortcut variable wdContext.

2. From the node instance obtained in step 1, call the getNodeInfo() method to get a reference to the parent node's metadata.

3. Call the addChild() method of the parent node's metadata object to define the new child node.

**Figure 9.2** An Unmapped Context Node Hierarchy to Be Created Dynamically

---

5  If the child node is a non-singleton.

When creating a hierarchy of context nodes dynamically, the above three steps need to be executed as a loop.

Each time you want to create the next child down the hierarchy, take the node name created in step 3 and use it as the value of ${cn} in step 1.

The coding principles used here to create an independent node can be extended to create the dependent child node LineItems. However, you must follow the steps listed above. If you call wdContext.addChild() again to create the node LineItems, don't expect the resulting metadata to have the node SalesOrders as its parent; instead, you will have created two sibling nodes that both have the context root as their immediate parent: one called SalesOrders and the other called LineItems.

You also need to pay close attention when setting the value of the singleton flag. If you create a singleton node dynamically, you *must* specify the name of a supply function. In this situation, you'll have to write a single, generic supply function that can populate all dynamically created context nodes. This means you must know *a priori* which nodes are likely to be created at runtime, or at least create context nodes in such a way that their content types can be generically identified via their names. This is a much more dynamic approach to context manipulation and, consequently, the situations in which it is required are more complex. Therefore, we not deal with in any greater detail in this book.

## 9.2    Dynamic Addition of a Mapped Context Node

As explained in Section 5.12, a mapped node does not maintain its own element collection; rather, it contains a reference to the element collection of the mapping origin node.

> **Caveat Confector**
>
> Do not allow the functional boundaries that exist between visual and non-visual controllers to become blurred. Non-visual controllers are always generators of data with respect to a visual controller. Visual controllers are *always* consumers of data.
>
> Maintaining this distinction is going to become even more important now that we're dealing with dynamic context node creation.
>
> I've said it before, and I'll say it again: do not put any functionality into a view controller that would cause it to perform the role of a data generator. The reason is simply that you will create for yourself a real maintenance headache.

In this coding example, we create a mapped node dynamically. The usual reason for this type of processing is that a component controller has dynamically created a context node and populated it. The data now needs to be displayed to the user. Therefore, before the view controller can create any UI elements, the context node in the view controller to hold the data must first be created.

Since there is no need to duplicate any data between the component controller and the view controller, we simply create a mapped node in the view controller and use the component controller node as the mapping origin node.

Since the mapping origin node has been created dynamically, it follows that any nodes that map to it must also be created dynamically.

To display this information, a chain of references must first be established. Starting from an individual UI element and working back to the mapping origin node, the following chain of references usually exists:

▶ A UI element in a view controller may only be bound to a context node or attribute in its own context.

▶ The nodes in a view controller's context that hold business data are mapped to a mapping origin node in the context of a non-visual controller.

▶ Business data is derived by a non-visual controller from a model object, and stored in its local context.

The coding that created the unmapped node in the previous example populates the value node that acts as the mapping origin in step 3 above. We now look at the coding to produce the mapped node required in step 2. The configuration to implement step 1 is discussed in Chapter 7.

The following functionality is simplistic in the sense that the view controller examines the context of its component controller and replicates only the independent nodes. Replicating an entire context node hierarchy is possible, but to treat this task in a completely generic manner requires coding that is much more involved.

```
public void wdDoInit() {
  //@@begin wdDoInit()
  // Get the metadata object for the context root node
  IWDNodeInfo rootNodeInfo = wdContext.getNodeInfo();

  // Get a reference to the metadata of the root node
  // in the component controller
  IWDNodeInfo compCtx =
    wdComponentAPI.getContext().getRootNodeInfo();

  // Loop around all the independent nodes in the
  // parent context replicating however many
  // independent nodes are found
  for (Iterator compCtxIt = compCtx.iterateChildren();
      compCtxIt.hasNext();)
    replicateNodeInfo((IWDNodeInfo)compCtxIt.next());
  //@@end
}
```

**Listing 9.2** Generic creation of mapped nodes in a view controller

In the `wdDoInit()` method of the view controller, the following functionality takes place:

▶ A reference is obtained to the metadata of the context root node of the view controller.

▶ A reference is obtained to the metadata of the context root node of the component controller.

▶ For each independent node in the component controller's context, call the method `replicateNodeInfo()`.

The next coding section shows the implementation of the method `replicateNodeInfo()`. Generally speaking, the mapping origin of a mapped context node can be defined in two different ways. These are:

1. Specify the mapping origin as a parameter to the method `IWDNodeInfo.addMappedChild()`.

2. The mapping origin parameter is left null in the call to `IWDNodeInfo.addMappedChild()`. The required value is set by a later call to the `setMapping(IWDNodeInfo, boolean)` method.

Of these options, SAP recommends the second.

| Important |
| --- |
| The method `setMapping()` should be called only once! Do not attempt to alter a node's mapping origin once the mapping relationship has been traversed. |
| Even mapping relationships obey the lazy data access principle. That is, until you attempt to read data from a mapped node, the link between the mapped node and the mapping origin node is not traversed and is therefore still open to modification. However, once that link is traversed, the relationship becomes unchangeable until the mapped node instance is destroyed. |

Since the differences relate to the call to the method `addMappedChild()` and the statements that immediately follow, only those statements are listed in the following code samples. Once these differences have been described, the entire `replicateNodeInfo()` method will be shown using option 2.

The method `IWDNodeInfo.addMappedChild()` is similar to the `IWDNodeInfo.addChild()` method seen in the previous example, but with several important differences. By definition, a mapped node inherits certain attributes from its mapping origin node, the most obvious of which is the node's cardinality. Since a mapped node does not maintain its own element collection (it simply points to the element collection of the mapping origin node), its cardinality value will always be equal to the cardinality of the mapping origin node.

> **Important**
>
> A mapped node is a distinct object from the mapping origin node. Do not think that a mapped node is simply a reference to the node instance in the mapping origin context. The node in the mapping context is a distinct object instance that maintains its own values. The only thing common between the two nodes is that the mapped node's element collection is a reference to the element collection found in the mapping origin node. Other than this, they are separate objects.

The parameters to `IWDNodeInfo.addMappedChild()` are as follows:

▸ The name of the mapped node. This does not need to be the same as the name of the mapping origin node, but for the sake of simplicity, we will use the name of the mapping origin node.

▸ The class of the mapping origin node (now redundant).

▸ A Boolean flag that determines whether the mapped node is a singleton or not. Since we are creating an independent node, this parameter must be set to `true`.

  ▸ A Boolean flag that determines the first part of the mapped node's selection cardinality. This is the **Mandatory Selection** flag.

  ▸ A Boolean flag that determines the second part of the mapped node's selection cardinality. This is the **Multiple Selection** flag.

▸ The path name to the mapping origin node. Without this value, the mapping reference is incomplete. The various options for mapped node creation lie in whether you specify a value here. We will look at both situations.

▸ A Boolean flag that controls whether the mapping origin's list of selected elements is mapped.

▸ A Boolean flag that controls whether the lead selection is initialized.

### 9.2.1    Technique 1

In the first technique, all the metadata required to describe the new mapped node is created in a single call to the method `addMappedChild()`. Notice the parameter in bold; this is the value required to define the path name from the mapped node to the mapping origin node.

```
public void replicateNodeInfo(IWDNodeInfo
                                    mappingOrigin) {
  //@@begin replicateNodeInfo()
<snip>

  // Create a new node in the local context based on
  // the values of the mapping reference node
  IWDNodeInfo childNodeInfo =
    wdContext.getNodeInfo().
```

```
    addMappedChild(mappingOrigin.getName(),
                   mappingOrigin.getClass(),
                   true,  // Singleton
               mappingOrigin.isMandatorySelection(),
               mappingOrigin.isMultipleSelection(),
               mappingOrigin.getPathDescription(),
                   false, // Map node selection?
                   true); // Init lead selection?
```

`<snip>`

**Listing 9.3** Specifying the mapping origin as a parameter to addMappedChild()

### 9.2.2    Technique 2

Notice in the second technique that the parameter in bold is now `null`. Since the parameter that defines the mapping origin has not been supplied, the mapped node is unusable until an additional call to `setMapping()` is made. The call to `setMapping()` is now performed by passing in the `IWDNodeInfo` object of the mapping origin node and a Boolean to indicate whether the list of *selected* elements is to be mapped.

```
public void replicateNodeInfo(IWDNodeInfo
                                          mappingOrigin) {
  //@@begin replicateNodeInfo()
<snip>

  // Create a new node in the local context based on
  // the values of the mapping reference node
  IWDNodeInfo childNodeInfo =
    wdContext.getNodeInfo().
      addMappedChild(mappingOrigin.getName(),
                     mappingOrigin.getClass(),
                     true,  // Singleton
                 mappingOrigin.isMandatorySelection(),
                 mappingOrigin.isMultipleSelection(),
                 null,  // Mapping origin def'd later
                     false, // Map node selection?
                     true); // Init lead selection?

  // Map the current node to the corresponding node of
  // the parent context
  childNodeInfo.setMapping(mappingOrigin, false);

<snip>
```

**Listing 9.4** Calling addMappedChild() with a null mapping origin parameter and then adding it by calling setMapping()

### 9.2.3    Method replicateNodeInfo()

Now that the different methods of defining a node's mapping origin have been clarified, all that remains is to show the coding for the entire method `replicate-NodeInfo()`.

```
public void replicateNodeInfo( IWDNodeInfo
                                           mappingOrigin) {
  //@@begin replicateNodeInfo()
  // Reset counters
  attrCount   = 0;
  binarySkip  = 0;
  complexSkip = 0;

  // Create a new node here in the local context based
  // on the values of the mapping reference node
  IWDNodeInfo childNodeInfo =
    wdContext.getNodeInfo().
      addMappedChild(mappingOrigin.getName(),
                     mappingOrigin.getClass(),
                     true,  // Singleton
                 mappingOrigin.isMandatorySelection(),
                 mappingOrigin.isMultipleSelection(),
                     null,
                     false, // Map node selection?
                     true); // Init lead selection
    childNodeInfo.setMapping(mappingOrigin, false);
  // Iterate around the node's attributes
  for (Iterator attIt =
                    mappingOrigin.iterateAttributes();
       attIt.hasNext();) {
    IWDAttributeInfo thisAttr =
      (IWDAttributeInfo)attIt.next();
    attrCount++;
    // Binary attributes can be bound to the
    // OfficeControl,FileUpload, and FileDownload  UI
    // elements. Even then, there is no generic
    // mechanism for determining whether the binary
    // data is suitable for such a UI element.
    // Therefore, this coding example makes no attempt
    // to visualize binary attributes, and simply
    // filters them out
    if (thisAttr.getDataType().isSimpleType()) {
      ISimpleType st = thisAttr.getSimpleType();

      // Is the data type of this attribute binary?
      if (st.getLocalName().equalsIgnoreCase("binary"))
        // Without additional MIME type information,
        // there is no generic mechanism for
```

```
        // determining the suitability of the binary
        // data.
        binarySkip++;
      else
        childNodeInfo.
          addMappedAttribute(thisAttr.getName(),
                             thisAttr.getName());
    }
    // Complex data types cannot be visualized using
    // Web Dynpro UI elements without further
    // type-specific processing
    else
      complexSkip++;
  }
  //@@end
}


//@@begin others
static int binarySkip;
static int complexSkip;
static int attrCount;
//@@end
```

**Listing 9.5** Method replicateNodeInfo() used for generic node

The method `replicateNodeInfo()`works in the following way:

1. Some static counters are reset. The purpose of these will be explained later.

2. Create a mapped child node in the view controller's context using the details found in the mapping origin node.

3. Now add the metadata describing the node attributes. This is done by creating an iterator on the mapping origin node and then looping around each attribute, creating a corresponding attribute in the local context. There is, however, a complicating factor.

4. Since we are referencing data that already exists in another context, we must examine the data type of each attribute and decide whether it can be visualized.

> **Important**
>
> Only node attributes belonging to the package com.sap.dictionary can be bound to UI elements.
>
> Within the package com.sap.dictionary, binary data can be visualized only if it contains data suitable for the OfficeControl UI element or is to be transferred using the FileUpload or FileDownload UI elements.
>
> Data types belonging to the package com.sap.dictionary are known as simple types.

5. If the node attribute is of a simple data type, it is a potential candidate for visualization. If it is not, increment the `complexSkip` counter since the data within this attribute cannot be visualized through a standard Web Dynpro UI element without further processing.

6. We will not attempt to determine the suitability of binary data for display. This basic implementation simply filters out such context attributes.

7. For each node attribute that is of a simple data type, test to see if it is `binary`. If it is, increment the `binarySkip` counter. If the attribute is of any other simple data type, create the metadata for a new attribute in the local node using the details inherited from the corresponding attribute in the mapping origin.

8. The counter variables `attrCount`, `binarySkip`, and `complexSkip` have been made static deliberately. This is so that their values can be accessed from the static method `wdDoModifyView()`. It is within this method that you will need to write the code that creates the dynamic view layout for your dynamic context nodes.[6]

9. If required, you can use these counter values to inform the user that there may be context attributes missing from the display because their data types prevent immediate visualization.[7]

---

6  See Section 10.7 on dynamic UI generation.

7  It is quite possible to write a view controller that visualizes complex data types, but such coding would need to examine the structure of the complex data type and react to whatever it finds. This form of coding needs to use reflection and is not discussed here.

# 10 Advanced Use of the UI

In this chapter, we take a look at more detailed topics concerning UI programming.

## 10.1 Working with Tree UI Elements

The Tree UI element behaves somewhat differently from other UI elements. The main difference lies in the construction of the context nodes used to supply data the UI elements.

In the case of a Table UI element, for instance, the context is structured in a way that reflects the requirements of the business data. So in previous examples, we have bound a Table UI element directly to the context node called SalesOrders. This node is structured according to the requirements of a sales order document, and its structure is unrelated to any particular UI element that might be used to display the data.

This is not the case with the Tree UI element. In this case, the context node that supplies data to the Tree must reflect the structure required by the UI element. Typically, this will result in attributes that hold values to control the Tree's properties.

### 10.1.1 Types of Tree UI Element

There are three distinct UI elements used for creating trees:

▶ **Tree**
The Tree UI element is the starting point for the tree structure. This UI element must be bound to the context node that defines the starting position for your tree data. The properties of this UI element also control the default appearance of the tree. For instance, what are the default icons used for nodes and items? Should the root node be visible or have some descriptive text?

▶ **TreeNodeType**
There should be one TreeNodeType UI element added directly below the Tree UI element to represent each node in the context hierarchy beneath the node defined for the Tree UI element. The TreeNodeType UI element is designed to represent any node in the tree structure that is permitted to have children.

This UI element has a property called hasChildren. If this property is set to false, the TreeNodeType UI element will be rendered as if it were a TreeItemType UI element.

▶ `TreeItemType`

The `TreeItemType` UI element is designed to represent any node in the tree structure that is not permitted to have children, that is, a leaf node.

Since setting a `TreeNodeType` UI element's `hasChildren` property to `false` causes it to be rendered as if it were a leaf node, it is somewhat superfluous to use the `TreeItemType` UI element at all, since its functionality is a subset of that provided by the `TreeNodeType`.

### 10.1.2 Building a Tree Whose Depth Is Known at Design Time

Let's say we want to use a tree to represent the context structure for **Sales Orders** and **Line Items** shown in Figure 10.1.

**Figure 10.1** Context for a Static Tree Definition

One `Tree` UI element is defined to point to the `SalesOrders` node, and the `TreeNodeType` UI element is defined to point to the `LineItems` node. Both of these UI elements have a `dataSource` property, and in both cases these properties must be set to the context node representing the top of the tree structure.

When you have a context hierarchy that is three or more nodes deep, you will still create a single `Tree` UI element pointing to the top level context node, and there will still be a `TreeNodeType` UI element for each of the child nodes, but the hierarchical arrangement of `TreeNodeType` UI elements will not reflect the structure of the nodes in the context. All that is necessary is that you define one `TreeNodeType` UI element directly under the `Tree` UI element for each node in the hierarchy, and the processing in the Server-Side Rendering step of the Phase Model sorts out the actual hierarchical position of the nodes relative to each other.

### 10.1.3 Building a Tree Whose Depth Is Unknown at Design Time

In Figure 10.2, the depth of the tree hierarchy is known at design time; therefore, there is no need to use recursive nodes in the context.

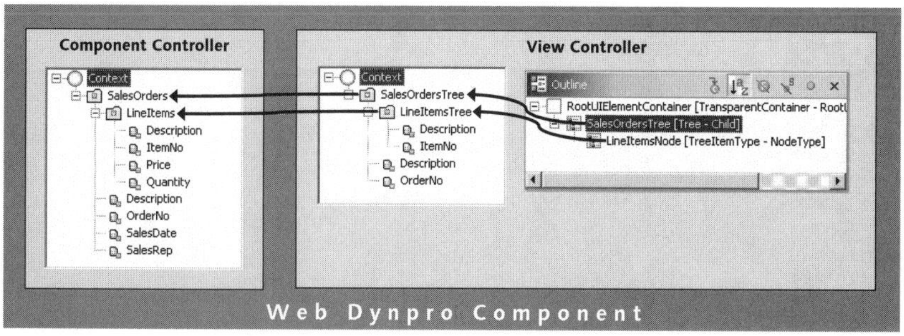

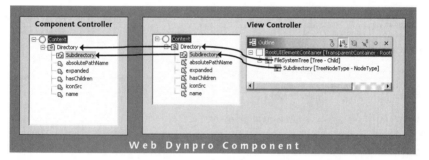

**Figure 10.2** Defining a Tree Whose Depth Is Known at Design Time

Alternatively, for tree structures whose depth is unknown at design time, the unknown depth must first be represented .in the context using recursive nodes. This allows the tree depth to grow dynamically. A good example of such a structure is the representation of a file system (see Figure 10.3).

**Figure 10.3** Dynamic Tree Definition

The only difference between the static and dynamic definitions is the use of a recursive node in the context. It is also assumed that the `TreeNodeType`'s `onLoadChildren` event will have an action event handler associated with it to calculate whether the node currently being expanded has any children.

### 10.1.4 Building a Context Node Suitable for a Tree UI Element

In Figure 10.4, you can see that a model node has been created whose attributes represent the values required for representing a file system structure (see Appendix C for the full details of how to create this example as a working Web Dynpro application).

Look closely at the attributes of node `Directory`. Not all of them are related to files or directories in a file system. Some of these attributes are present only because they are needed by the `Tree` UI element. Table 10.1 illustrates the purpose of each attribute in the node `Directory`.

**Figure 10.4** Context Structure Holding Attributes for Both a File System Structure and the Tree UI Element to Display It

| Context Attribute | What Type of Information Is It? |
|---|---|
| absolutePathName | Business data |
| dateModified | Business data |
| expanded | Tree UI element property |
| hasChildren | Tree UI element property |
| hidden | Business Data |
| iconSrc | Tree UI element property |
| leaf | Tree UI element property |
| name | Business data |
| readOnly | Business data |
| size | Business data |

**Table 10.1** Some Attributes of the Directory Context Node Are Needed to Store the Business Data and Others Are Needed by the Tree UI Element

The only attribute value that the user actually sees is the name property. This property is bound to the TreeNodeType UI element's text property and becomes the text seen next to the tree node.

In this simple case, it is acceptable to merge the so-called business data (file system information) and Tree UI element properties into a single context element, because there are only a handful of attributes related to the business data. However, when you have a large amount of business data, it is preferable to map the single attribute of business data from the non-visual to the visual controller and then supplement that mapped node with attributes required by the Tree UI element.

This will probably result in a context node that contains a mixture of model and value attributes. As you can see in Figure 10.5, the model node and single model attribute are mapped (to their data source in the context of a non-visual controller), and the attributes related to the `Tree` UI element are value attributes local to the view controller's context.

Figure 10.6 illustrates how the various properties of the `Tree` and `TreeNode` UI elements have been bound to the context nodes and attributes created in Figure 10.5.

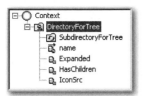

**Figure 10.5** Context Structure for a Tree UI Element Holding Both Model and Value Attributes, Which Are Both Mapped and Unmapped

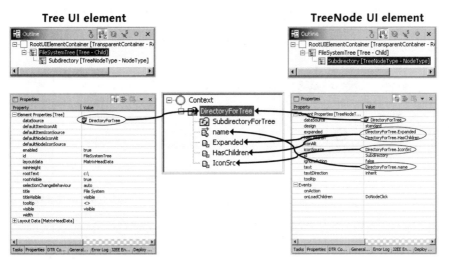

**Figure 10.6** Data Binding for Tree and TreeNodeType UI Elements

### 10.1.5 Making a Tree Node Interactive

To make the tree node interactive, it is necessary to implement at least the `onLoad-Children` event and possibly also the `onAction`.

The `onLoadChildren` event is only fired the *first* time a node is expanded. Thereafter, this event is not fired when the node is expanded. This event is very useful when the tree depth is not known until runtime. The user expands a tree node for the first time, and an action handler method can then be called to calculate whether that node has any children. Once the result has been calculated, it is stored and can be used again without needing to recalculate anything. The context structure behind a tree of this type will probably need to use recursive nodes.

The onAction event is raised every time a node is expanded; however, it only causes a round trip to the server if you have associated it with an action in the view controller. This event should only be used when the result you calculated the last time the node was expanded has become invalid.

> **Important**
>
> Remember that all child nodes used to display information through a Tree UI element *must* be non-singleton nodes.

In Figure 10.7, three steps are shown:

1. Create an action in the view controller. Here the action is called DoNodeClick.

2. Associate the action with the client-side event raised by the TreeNodeType UI element called onLoadChildren. Now, when this event is raised in the client, there is an association with a server-side action event handler method (onActionDoNodeClick); therefore, a round trip can take place to process this event.

3. Implement the required functionality in the action event handler method.

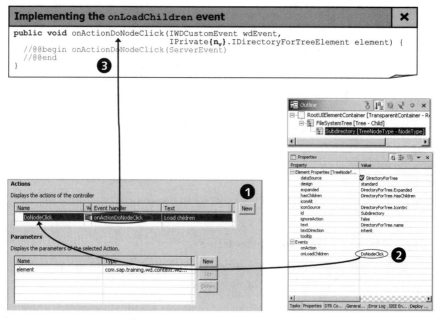

**Figure 10.7** Implementing the onLoadChildren Event

The onLoadChildren event supplies a String parameter containing the name of the context element selected by the user. The Web Dynpro Framework recognizes that although this parameter is a string, it represents the fully qualified path from the context root node to the node instance the user has just selected. It also recognizes that the data type of the parameter to the action is a context element. Therefore, it will automatically convert the string value supplied by the UI element event to the data type required by the action handler. This topic is discussed more fully in Section 7.8.3.

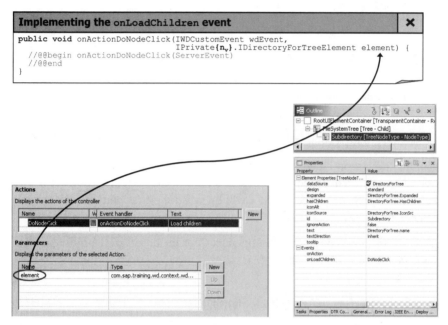

**Figure 10.8** The DoNodeClick Action Receives a Parameter Called element

One further association needs to be made before the link between the TreeNode-Type UI element and the action event handler method is complete.

The TreeNodeType UI element will raise several events, and the one we're interested in is onLoadChildren. When this event is raised (in the client), a parameter called path is made available. This parameter is the path name to the node in the context that has just been clicked on, and its value is passed back to the Web Dynpro Framework.

Figure 10.8 shows the declaration of the element parameter for the action DoNodeClick. The only issue here is that the onLoadChildren event passes a parameter called path, but we have just declared our action event handler to have a parameter called element.

Therefore, a few lines of code must be written to link the parameter value called path received from the client to the action event handler parameter element.

```
public static void
  wdDoModifyView(IPrivate${nv} wdThis,
                 IPrivate${nv}.IContextNode wdContext,
                 IWDView view, boolean firstTime) {
  //@@begin wdDoModifyView
  if (firstTime) {
    IWDTreeNodeType treeNode =
      (IWDTreeNodeType)view.getElement("Subdirectory");
    treeNode.mappingOfOnLoadChildren().
             addSourceMapping("path","element");
  }
  //@@end
}
```

**Listing 10.1** Coding to associate the client event parameter with the action event handler parameter

See Section 7.8 for a complete discussion of parameter mapping functionality.

Now that the action called DoNodeClick has been associated with the onLoadChildren client-side event raised by the TreeNodeType UI element, the action event handler method onActionDoNodeClick() will be called the first time the tree node is expanded.

Please see the worked example in Appendix C for the details of the coding needed in the method onActionDoNodeClick().

### 10.1.6 Properties of Tree UI Elements

The properties of trees and tree nodes can be found in the classes IWDAbstractTreeNodeType, IWDTreeNodeType, and IWDTree.

Table 10.2 shows the tree and tree node properties that can be bound to context attributes:

| Tree | TreeNode |
| --- | --- |
| defaultItemIconAlt | iconAlt |
| defaultItemIconSource | iconSource |
| defaultNodeIconAlt | ignoreAction |
| defaultNodeIconSource | tooltip |
| minHeight | text |
| rootText | design |
| rootVisible | dataSource |

**Table 10.2** Bindable Properties of the Various Tree UI Elements

| Tree | TreeNode |
|------|----------|
| title | expanded |
| defaultNodeIconSource | tooltip |
| titleVisible | hasChildren |
| width | |
| dataSource | |

**Table 10.2** Bindable Properties of the Various Tree UI Elements (cont.)

## 10.2 Efficient Use of Actions to Enable and Disable UI Elements

Certain UI elements trigger client-side events. For these events to be processed on the server, there must be an association between the client-side event and an action event handler on the server. This association is performed by instances of the class IWDAction.

Instances of the class are known as actions and are runtime objects that can be enabled and disabled as required by the functionality of your application. As you saw in Section 7.8.1, it is possible to have multiple client-side events all associated with the same action; thus, they will all invoke the same action event handler method. At this point, it would be worthwhile to ensure that you fully understand the difference between a primary and secondary event. If you can't remember, go back and reread Section 7.7.4.

Let's say you wish to stop a user from clicking on a Button UI element (for instance, the user has insufficient authorization), but you don't want to remove the UI element from screen. You could take one of two approaches. Either:

▶ Bind the visibility property of the button to a suitable context attribute. Then make the button disappear by setting the context attribute to WDVisibility.BLANK.

▶ Disable the action associated with the button's onSelect event. This is done by calling the action's setEnabled() method and passing it the Boolean value false.

The latter option is a very useful technique for controlling the range of tasks a user can perform based on some value such as their authorization.

Now the Web Dynpro Framework automatically disables or adapts all UI elements using this action. If the action is associated with a primary event, the entire UI element is disabled for user input. If it is associated with a secondary event, the UI element remains enabled for user interaction, but certain areas of interactivity will be non-functional. Either way, though, if an action has been disabled, the UI element event(s) to which it is associated will never be raised, thus making it is impossible for the user to trigger a round trip to the server.

As you will probably appreciate, this technique allows you to enable or disable *all* the UI elements on the screen using a single call to the setEnabled() method of the relevant action.

> **Caveat Confector**
>
> Don't fall into the trap of thinking that to disable some UI element such as a Button or a LinkToAction, you simply access the UI element object directly and disable its action explicitly. All UI elements using actions can be enabled or disabled by manipulating their associated runtime action object.
>
> You should never need to access the UI element object directly to enable or disable an associated action.

> **Important**
>
> If you disable an action associated with a secondary event, the UI element will remain enabled for user interaction. An example of this is the Table UI element. If you have disabled the action associated with the secondary event onLeadSelect, the table can still be scrolled, but now the onLeadSelect event will never be raised, and, consequently, the associated action event handler method will never be called.

## 10.3 Programmatic Assignment of Actions to UI Element Objects

If you have written a generic action event handler, it can be assigned to a UI element object at runtime.

Let's say we have created an action in a view controller called GenericEvent. This will be processed therefore by an action event handler method called onActionGenericEvent(). We must now dynamically assign this action to a Button UI element called SaveButton.

This is done using the following steps in method wdDoModifyView():

```
// Obtain a reference to the action handler called GenericEvent
WDActionEventHandler actHandler = WDActionEventHandler.GENERIC_EVENT;
```

**Listing 10.2** Get a reference to the action event handler object associated with the action

An action event handler is simply the class created at design time when you declare the action called GenericEvent. In itself, it will not do anything until it is turned into a runtime action object. So continuing from the coding seen in Listing 10.2:

```
// Create runtime action object
IWDAction genericEventAction =
  wdThis.wdCreateAction(actHandler,"Whatever event text you like");
```

**Listing 10.3** Create a runtime action object

**Figure 10.9** Now We Have a Disabled Runtime Action Object

Figure 10.9 shows that we now have a disabled runtime action object. If we were to assign this runtime action object to a UI element event, it would disable the UI element.[1] So, the runtime action object must be enabled:

```
// Enable the runtime action object
genericEventAction.setEnabled(true);
```

**Listing 10.4** Enable the runtime action object

Next we must get a reference to the Button UI element object called SaveButton.

```
// Get a reference to the button UI element
IWDButton btn = (IWDButton)view.getElement("SaveButton");
```

**Listing 10.5** Get a reference to the Button UI element object

Finally, we associate the enabled action with the Button's onAction event.

```
// Assign runtime action object to the button UI element
btn.setOnAction(genericEventAction);
```

**Listing 10.6** Assign the runtime action object to the Button UI element's onAction event

Figure 10.10 shows the complete sequence of associations performed by the coding.

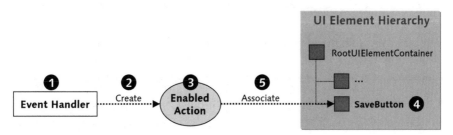

**Figure 10.10** Assign the Runtime Action Object to the Button UI Element's onAction Event

---

1 The degree of disablement is determined by whether you associate the runtime action object with a primary or secondary UI element event.

So the whole coding looks like this:

```
if (firstTime) {
  // Create a reference to the action handler called GenericEvent
  WDActionEventHandler actHandler =
    WDActionEventHandler.GENERIC_EVENT;

  // Create runtime action object
  IWDAction genericEventAction =
    wdThis.wdCreateAction(actHandler,"Event text");

  // Enable runtime action object
  genericEventAction.setEnabled(true);

  // Get a reference to the required button UI element
  IWDButton btn = (IWDButton)view.getElement("SaveButton");

  // Assign runtime action object to the checkbox UI element
  btn.setOnAction(genericEventAction);
}
```

**Listing 10.7** Complete coding for assignment of a runtime action object to a Button UI element's onAction event

Notice that the coding all takes place within an `if` statement that tests the value of the parameter `firstTime`. This indicates two things:

▶ That this coding is only required once during the view controller's lifecycle

▶ That it is implemented within the view controller's `wdDoModifyView()` method

## 10.4 Accessing Existing UI Elements in a View Layout

Before any attempt is made to construct a view layout programmatically, it is first necessary to understand how to access existing elements in a view layout.

Each view layout is constructed as a hierarchy of UI elements. Almost all UI elements form a visible part of the rendered screen; however, certain UI elements are only structural and, therefore, invisible. The most important of these structural UI elements is called `RootUIElementContainer`. This UI element has the following properties:

▶ It is always the root element in a view controller's UI element hierarchy.

▶ Its name is hard coded.

▶ It is always of type `TransparentContainer`.

All other UI elements in the view layout appear as the children of RootUIElement-Container, and each child must have a unique name. The UI element's name then becomes the easiest form of reference for locating it in the hierarchy. If you know its name, you don't need to have any knowledge of its position in the hierarchy to access it. This technique is typically used to access UI elements created at design time.

A second method of accessing UI elements is available, but it is much more involved and should be implemented only where named access is completely impossible. In this situation, not only is the name of the UI element unknown, but you will probably also have no knowledge of the hierarchical UI element structure. Under these circumstances, you must perform a depth-first traversal of the UI element hierarchy.

First, let's look at referencing UI elements by name.

### 10.4.1  Accessing UI Elements by Name

To access a UI element by name, you must know two things:

▶ The UI element's name

▶ The UI element's object type

Knowing these values, all you have to do is call the method getElement(String) of the view object and cast the returned object as the appropriate UI element type.

| Important |
| --- |
| The coding illustrated here can be only executed in the method wdDoModifyView(). This is the only method in which you have access to the view object. |

The example below retrieves the UI element called LastNameInput and then requests that it have input focus.

```
public static void
        wdDoModifyView(IPrivate${nv} wdThis,
                       IPrivate${nv}.IContextNode wdContext,
                       IWDView view,
                       boolean firstTime) {
  //@@begin wdDoModifyView
  if (firstTime) {
    // Get a reference to the UI element LastNameInput
    IWDInputField lastNameInput =
      (IWDInputField)view.getElement("LastNameInput");
```

```
    // Set input focus on this field
    lastNameInput.requestFocus();
  }
//@@end
}
```

**Listing 10.8** Referencing a UI element by name

There are several things to notice about this code sample.

▶ The class names of the input parameters to `wdDoModifyView()` have been generalized, `${nv}` being the name of this particular view controller. Obviously, you will not see this abbreviation in your code, but rather the name of your view controller.

▶ The Boolean value `firstTime` allows you to determine whether you are building the initial presentation of the view layout (`firstTime==true`) or are responding to user input (`firstTime==false`). This example only sets the focus to the input field `LastNameInput` the first time the screen is rendered.

▶ The method `view.getElement(String)` returns only a generalized `IWDViewElement` object. This must be cast to the correct object type for you to have access to the UI element's specific getter and setter methods.

---

**Caveat Confector**

Do not use this style of coding to set the value of a UI element property. Instead, you should bind the property to an appropriate attribute in the context and then write to the context, not the UI element.

When the UI element has been created dynamically, you can still bind the relevant properties to the context and then manipulate the context.

It is very bad coding style to manipulate UI element properties directly because it often leads to an increase in coding complexity yet delivers no practical benefit to the program.

You should always look to reduce the complexity of your coding — not increase it. Binding UI element properties to the context is a very effective way to reduce code complexity.

---

### 10.4.2 Accessing UI Elements Generically

To access UI elements generically, a depth-first traversal of the UI element hierarchy must be performed.

Two approaches can be taken:

▶ Approach 1 is a simple traversal mechanism and is quite straightforward to implement but has the disadvantage that it is not fully generic, as it can respond only to child elements returned by the method `IWDUIElementContainer.iterateChildren()`.

▶ Approach 2 is totally generic but is more complex to implement. You may also incur a performance overhead because Java reflection must be used.

### Approach 1: Simple Traversal Mechanism

This mechanism performs a recursive, depth-first traversal of only those UI elements returned by the method `iterateChildren()` of the class `IWDUIElementContainer`.

The important point to understand here is that the method `iterateChildren()` belongs to the class `IWDUIElementContainer`; however, this is not the only class that can hold aggregations of child UI elements. The UI tree can be spanned by other UI element aggregations belonging to non-container elements, such as the `TabStrip`. Therefore, if processing is confined only to UI elements returned by `iterateChildren()`, it is possible that certain parts of the UI tree will not be traversed.

This approach can be implemented by writing a simple recursive finite state engine, as follows:

▶ The method (in this example called `visit()`) will receive one parameter of type `IWDViewElement`; this is the base class for all UI elements.

▶ If a UI element object is received that is not a container element,[2] then a leaf node has been reached and recursion can terminate.

▶ The UI element type must now be identified, and the required processing performed.

▶ If you do not explicitly code how the presence of a certain UI element should be handled, then no action is taken.[3]

▶ It is here that a special exception can be made if you know you are going to need to handle tab strip UI elements.

▶ If the UI element is a container object, perform any processing necessary for the container and then obtain an iterator of its child elements and call yourself for each successive child.

The method described below shows the principles for implementing such a traversal.

```
public static void
      wdDoModifyView(IPrivate${nv} wdThis,
                    IPrivate${nv}.IContextNode wdContext,
```

---

2   This is a reference to a UI element that is permitted to have children.
3   This is the advantage of a finite state engine implementation — it is very robust.

```java
                    IWDView view,
                    boolean firstTime) {
  //@@begin wdDoModifyView
  // Start with the root UI element
  visit(view.getRootElement());
  //@@end
}


private static void visit(IWDViewElement e) {
  // Is this UI element a container?
  if (e instanceof IWDUIElementContainer) {
    // Yup. If necessary, do something to the container
    IWDUIElementContainer elCont = (IWDUIElementContainer)e;
    elCont.<some_method>;

    // Visit each child element
    for (Iterator it = elCont.iterateChildren(); it.hasNext();)
      visit((IWDUIElement)it.next());
  }
  // Nope, implement a finite state engine to identify each UI
  // element that needs to be processed individually
  else if (e instanceof IWDButton) {
    // Instruct all button UI elements to obtain their icon
    // source from SomeNode.SomeAttribute in the context
    ((IWDButton)e).bindImageSource("SomeNode.SomeAttribute");
  }
  else if (e instanceof <UI_element_class>) {
    // Do something to the UI element ...
  }
  // Finally, handle the special case of a tab strip
  else if (e instanceof IWDTabStrip) {
    // Do something to the tabstrip itself
    IWDTabStrip tabStrip = (IWDTabStrip)e;
    tabStrip.<some_method>;

    // Do something to each tab, then recursively process the
    // contents of tab strip
    for (Iterator it = tabStrip.iterateTabs(); it.hasNext();) {
      IWDTab tab = (IWDTab)it.next();
      tab.<some_method>;

      // Visit content using recursive call to visit()
      visit(tab.getContent());
    }
  }
}
```

**Listing 10.9** Simple traversal of a UI element hierarchy

Notice that a tab strip UI element must be handled as a special case of a UI element that contains an aggregation of child elements but is itself not a UI element container.

### Approach 2: Generic Traversal Mechanism

If you want to be able to respond in a completely generic manner to any aggregation of UI elements, the depth-first traversal mechanism must be extended. Now Java reflection must be used to determine the capabilities of each UI element in the hierarchy.

This form of implementation does not require that any UI elements be treated as special cases.

| Caveat Confector |
|---|
| Before you implement this type of coding, ask yourself, "Why am I doing this?"<br><br>If it is because you are writing some sort of utility component that must behave in a completely generic manner, fine; generic behavior is a fundamental part of your component's functionality, and therefore this style of coding is appropriate.<br><br>However, if you are simply copying the coding out of this book because you think it will make you look smart, then don't do it.<br><br>At all points in your development, you should be looking to lower the overall complexity of your application, not increase it. |

To implement coding that operates in a completely generic manner, the traversal mechanism must be neutral to the following situations. It must be able to process all UI element aggregations irrespective of:

▶ Whether the current element is a container element or not

▶ The method name by which the aggregation is returned

The required logic works as follows:

Every UI element class has methods that will return an aggregation of UI elements. If the aggregation has single cardinality, the method will be named `get<Aggregation>()`. If the aggregation has multiple cardinality, the method will be named `iterate<Aggregation>()`.

Therefore, the steps involved are required when implementing a general-purpose UI element parser:

1. Using reflection, examine each UI element class and obtain a list of its methods.

2. Examine all the method names to see if they start with the words `iterate` or `get`. This will identify which aggregation type is being returned.

3. If we have found a method that returns an aggregation of multiple cardinality, does it return UI elements or some other class? That is, are the returned objects derived from the class `IWDViewElement`?

4. All the methods satisfying the name criteria in step 2 and the return type criteria in step 3 are now invoked.

5. Recursively process the UI elements returned from each call.

The following utility class (courtesy of Armin Reichert) performs the necessary generic traversal of a UI element hierarchy.

```
// This template class provides a depth-first, generic traversal
// of a UI element hierarchy.
public class UITreeVisitor {
  private Map aggregationsByClass = new HashMap();
  private Set visited = new HashSet();

  public void beforeVisitChildren(IWDViewElement e) {
    // Do something useful before visiting the view element's
    // children
  }

  public void visitElement(IWDViewElement e) {
    // Do something useful with the current UI element.  This
    // processing is best implemented as a finite state engine
  }

  public void afterVisitChildren(IWDViewElement e) {
    // Do something useful after the view element's children
    // have been visited
  }

  // Traverse all UI aggregations under the given view element
  public final void visit(IWDViewElement e) {
    // Record visit to this element in a HashMap
    visited.add(e);

    visitElement(e);
    beforeVisitChildren(e);

    // Find all the methods of the current element that return UI
    // element aggregations. These aggregations could have single
    // or multiple cardinality.
    List aggregations = getOutgoingAggregations(e.getClass());

    // Process each method
    for (Iterator it = aggregations.iterator(); it.hasNext();) {
      // Get a reference to the next method
      Method m = (Method)it.next();
```

```java
      // Does this method return an aggregation of multiple
      // cardinality?
      if (m.getName().startsWith("iterate")) {
        // Yup, so invoke this method process all the child UI
        // elements recursively
        try {
          // Loop around the child UI elements in the iteration
          for (Iterator targets = (Iterator)m.invoke(e, null);
               targets.hasNext();) {
            IWDViewElement child = (IWDViewElement)targets.next();

            // Visit the child (as long as we haven't been here
            // before)
            if (!visited.contains(child))
              visit(child);
          }
        }
        catch (Exception x) {
          // Oh dear, we shouldn't have arrived here...
        }
      }
      else {

        // Nope, so this method must return a single UI element
        try {
          // Call the method to see what we get
          IWDViewElement child =
            (IWDViewElement)m.invoke(e, null);

          // Visit the child (as long as we haven't been here
          // before)
          if (!visited.contains(child))
            visit(child);
        }
        catch (Exception x) {
          // We shouldn't have arrived here either...
        }
      }
    }

  afterVisitChildren(e);
}

// Returns the list of outgoing aggregations for the given view
// element class. This information is cached for efficiency.
// An empty list will be returned when a leaf node is
// encountered.  This behaviour defines the termination
// condition for recursion.
```

```
    private List getOutgoingAggregations(Class clazz) {
      // Have we already encountered this class before?
      if (aggregationsByClass.containsKey(clazz)) {
        // Yup, so return the results from the cache
        return (List)aggregationsByClass.get(clazz);
      }
      else {
        // Nope, so find the methods of this class that all return
        // one or more UI elements
        List aggregations = collectOutgoingAggregations(clazz);

        // Store the method list to avoid having to repeat the
        // above processing
        aggregationsByClass.put(clazz, aggregations);

        return aggregations;
      }
    }

    // Build a list of outgoing aggregations for the given view
    // element class using reflection.
    private List collectOutgoingAggregations(Class clazz) {
      List result = new ArrayList();

      // Get a list of all the methods in this element class
      Method[] methods = clazz.getMethods();

      // Now check to see what each method does...
      for (int i = 0; i < methods.length; ++i) {
        // Does the method name start with "iterate"?
        if (methods[i].getName().startsWith("iterate"))
          // Yup, we can safely assume that this method returns an
          // aggregation of UI elements of multiple cardinality
          result.add(methods[i]);

        // Does the method name start with "get"?
        if (methods[i].getName().startsWith("get")) {
          // Yup, check the method's return type
          Class returnType = methods[i].getReturnType();

          // Is the return type ultimately derived from an
          // IWDViewElement?
          if (IWDViewElement.class.isAssignableFrom(returnType))
            // Yup, we can safely assume that this method returns
            // an aggregation of single cardinality (i.e., one UI
            // element).
            result.add(methods[i]);
        }
      }
```

```
    // Return a list of methods that, when called, will all
    // return an aggregation of one or more UI elements
    return result;
  }
}
```

**Listing 10.10** Generic traversal of a UI element hierarchy

This traversal mechanism is able to navigate through a UI element hierarchy of any arbitrary structure. All you need to implement is the finite state engine processing within the method `visitElement()` to do something useful when UI elements of a particular type are encountered.

## 10.5    Introduction to Dynamic View Generation

A Web Dynpro UI can usually be built in such a way that the whole screen layout is defined at design time. That is, you place UI elements on the view layout in the NWDS and bind their properties to context nodes or attributes. This is known as a *static* UI definition.

Once the design time declarations have been made, NWDS generates the necessary Java classes to create the declared layout. The only coding that then needs to be written is that necessary to fill the context with data. Each UI element in the hierarchy then obtains its data from the context by means of data binding.

The significant point to understand here is that the programmer is separated from the actual UI element objects by the context. At design time, you declare UI elements in your view layout and bind their properties to suitable context nodes and attributes. Then, at runtime, you place appropriate data into the context to control both the displayed data and the behavior of the UI elements. The Web Dynpro Framework is then able to render the entire screen without you needing to interact directly with any UI element object.

This is an example of where the data generator–data consumer principle has been implemented. Within the scope of a view controller, the UI elements are considered consumers of data, and the context nodes and attributes are considered generators (or suppliers, if you prefer that term).

The view controller, then, as a whole unit, is considered to be a consumer of data from some non-visual controller. This principle is implemented by means context mapping, and in order to prevent a visual controller from acting as a generator of data, its context is only ever part of its private interface — never its public interface.

> **Caveat Confector**
>
> When developers first start working with Web Dynpro, they hear the term MVC and assume it is like some other MVC-based toolset with which they are familiar. They then start to write code as if they were using that other toolset.
>
> *This can be a recipe for disaster!*
>
> Many Web Dynpro implementations have become excessively complex because developers have not understood the basic development concepts implemented in Web Dynpro. Consequently, the maintenance of such an application becomes time consuming and error prone.
>
> If you spend some time learning good Web Dynpro design principles, you will be able to create Web Dynpro applications that require *much* less effort to maintain.

> **Important**
>
> The UI element hierarchy created at design time can be modified, or even totally deleted, at runtime. The purpose of a declared view layout is to act as a starting point for any modifications that may be required at runtime.
>
> The use of the term *static* here does not indicate that the UI element hierarchy is immutable; rather, it refers to the fact that when the view controller is initialized, you start from a known, fixed layout. If the static view layout is deleted at runtime, it can be reset simply by calling the method `IWDView.resetView()`.

Dynamic UI generation stands as a direct contrast to static UI generation. A Web Dynpro view containing a dynamic UI layout has very few (if any) UI elements in its layout at design time. It is now down to the application developer to write the coding necessary to create the UI element hierarchy at design time.

> **Caveat Confector**
>
> If you want to write this type of application, you must understand several important principles. The following sections will discuss all of these principles in detail.
>
> Failure to understand these principles will result in the creation of coding that, at best, will be inefficient and, at worst, will need to be thrown away and rewritten.

## 10.6    The Principles of Dynamic View Construction

Before embarking upon an application design that uses dynamic view construction, consider carefully whether it would be possible to break up your view layout into declarative units that can be interchanged dynamically. This approach is preferable to building the entire view layout dynamically. However, if after careful consideration of your application's requirements, you conclude that it is not possible to declare your view layout at design time, it can be constructed dynamically at runtime.

### 10.6.1 Is There a Simpler Way of Doing It?

In some circumstances, a Table UI element will function as a very good "dynamic" display, without actually needing to be created at runtime. For instance, if you are displaying the line items of a sales order, and you would like the amount of information on the screen to expand and contract as the number of line items changes, then the following is a good alternative to creating UI elements at runtime:

1. Create a Table UI element on your view layout at design time.

2. Bind the table to a suitable context node.

3. Bind the visibleRowCount property of the Table UI element to a context attribute of type integer. Let's say this attribute is called VisibleRows.

4. Now, as the number of elements in the line items node varies, you can programmatically alter the context attribute that is bound to the table's visibleRowCount property. Thus, the table will expand and contract as required.

5. The value of the VisibleRows context attribute is a perfect candidate for being implemented as a calculated attribute. Once you have written the getter method, the Web Dynpro Framework will call it every time the screen is rendered, thus ensuring that the table only ever displays the correct number of rows.

Let's go back to the sales orders example that we have been using. The following code sample is the coding seen in a view controller and assumes that:

▶ The view controller contains a mapped node called SalesOrders.

▶ This mapped node has had an extra unmapped attribute added to it called VisibleRows.

▶ The attribute VisibleRows is of type integer, is read only, and is a calculated attribute.

The following code will limit the maximum number of displayed rows to 15 and the minimum number to 5.

```
public int getSalesOrdersVisibleRows(
            IPrivate${nv}.ISalesOrdersElement element) {
  //@@begin
  // How big is the node collection?
  int soSize = element.node.size();

  // Return the number of visible rows between the upper
```

```
// limit of 15 and the lower limit of 5
return (soSize > 15) ? 15 : (soSize < 5) ? 5 : soSize;
//@@end
}
```

**Listing 10.11** Calculated attribute to return the number of visible rows in a table between the limits of 15 and 5 rows

### 10.6.2 The Fundamental Principles of Dynamic View Layout Construction

The fundamental principles of constructing a dynamic view layout can be summarized as follows:

1.  Wherever possible, construct as much of the view layout as possible at design time.

2.  Place as little code as possible into the method `wdDoModifyView()`.

3.  Prior to entering the method `wdDoModifyView()`, the view controller's context must already contain the necessary nodes, attributes, and runtime data. This task must *not* be performed in `wdDoModifyView()`. Do not write to the context during `wdDoModifyView()`.

4.  In addition to the business data to be displayed, the context should also contain nodes and attributes that can be used to control the behavior of the UI elements themselves. This principle remains true irrespective of whether the context node has been declared at design time or built dynamically at runtime.

5.  Either way, by the time you build the UI element hierarchy in the method `wdDoModifyView()`, the context must have been fully prepared for read-only use.

6.  Construct the view layout in the method `wdDoModifyView()` only when the Boolean parameter `firstTime` is `true`. Assuming that some sort of user interaction will occur with the view, it is very unlikely that you will need to reconstruct the view layout after every round trip.

7.  If `firstTime` is false, try to avoid UI element hierarchy manipulation.

8.  During the construction process, you need to assign values to the various properties of each UI element. This should be done by binding the properties to relevant context attributes by calling method `${ui}.bind${uip}()`, where `${ui}` is the UI element object and `${uip}` is the bindable UI element property.

9.  It is possible to set the UI element property directly using the `${ui}.set${uip}()` method, but this approach should only be taken for assigning values to properties that will remain constant for the duration of the view controller's lifespan.

10. All subsequent modifications to UI element behavior should be controlled by manipulating the context, not the UI element object.

> **Important**
>
> ▶ The principles shown above remain true irrespective of whether the UI elements were created at design time or runtime.
>
> ▶ The call to the method `${ui}.bind${ui`p`}()` is the recommended approach because it allows UI manipulation to be performed via the context, that is, from outside the method `wdDoModifyView()`.

If you follow these principles, you will ensure that your view layout is constructed in a manner that will provide the lowest amount of support effort after the application has gone live. For instance, if you continually use the `${ui}.set${ui`p`}()` method, you'll encounter the following consequences:

▶ If multiple UI elements all share the same property value (say, the `visible` property), you need to call the `${ui}.set${ui`p`}()` method for each individual element. This is highly inefficient and makes code maintenance much harder.

▶ You can only ever alter the value of that property in the method `wdDoModify-View()`. This, again, is *really* bad coding style and demonstrates a lack of understanding of Web Dynpro coding principles.

Both of these consequences are the result of not understanding the concept of data binding and then working around your lack of understanding by putting lots of redundant coding into the method `wdDoModifyView()`.

> **Important**
>
> Two dangers are often not recognized by people writing a dynamically constructed view layout. The first has an impact on performance, and the second on code flexibility.
>
> ▶ All too often, dynamic view layouts are constructed in which the entire UI element hierarchy is rebuilt every time the method `wdDoModifyView()` is called; that is, the logic does not consider the value of the Boolean parameter `firstTime`. It is very rare to have a situation in which you *genuinely* need to reconstruct the entire view layout every time there is a round trip. Therefore, this coding style should be avoided.
>
> ▶ If you want to change the appearance of your screen, you will need to rewrite part or all of the functionality in method `wdDoModifyView()`.

> **Caveat Confector**
>
> SAP fully recognizes that not all application requirements can be fulfilled by a view layout containing a static UI element hierarchy. However, if it is necessary to construct your view layout dynamically, you must make sure you follow the principles listed above. Failure to do so could result in the creation of an application that is very difficult to maintain.

## 10.7 Dynamic Construction of a UI Element Hierarchy

The dynamic construction of a UI element hierarchy is typically required when you have to display a context of unknown structure. Under these circumstances, it is not possible to create much of a UI layout at design time, because some (or even all) of the nodes in the view controller's context have not yet been defined.

Before implementing the dynamic construction of a UI element hierarchy, make sure you understand the following restrictions:

▶ First, you are only permitted to access UI element objects in the view layout from within the `wdDoModifyView()` method of the view controller.

▶ Second, refer back to Chapter 4 and remind yourself of the point in time during which the `wdDoModifyView()` method runs in the Phase Model's request–response cycle. By the time the phase model processing has reached this step, all controller contexts should be *fully populated*. In other words, the processing performed within the method `wdDoModifyView()` should be concerned *only* with the construction of the user interface and with *not* the business processing required to obtain the data being displayed.[4]

▶ Third, `wdDoModifyView()` is a static method. This is the result of a deliberate design decision made to discourage developers from storing references to UI element objects as instance members.

Do not store references to UI element objects and then attempt to manipulate them outside `wdDoModifyView()` (in event handlers, for instance). Every time `wdDoModifyView()` is called, all references to UI element instances will be overwritten.

Now that you have an understanding of the hierarchical structure of UI elements in a view layout, the dynamic construction approach will be easier to understand. This approach is typically required when you want to create a UI element layout based on information whose structure can only be known at runtime.

> **Important**
>
> The solution documented here has its limitations. The following example deals only with a simple context structure. It is possible to write a totally generic context viewer, but to discuss such an application adequately would occupy too much space, and it is not the purpose of this book to discuss a specific application.

### 10.7.1 Implementation Example

Consider the following situation: A view controller context might contain an independent child node called `SalesOrders`. If this node exists, it needs to be displayed as a table.[5] For the purposes of this example, we will assume that if the context

---

4 Due to the Web Dynpro Framework's lazy data access mechanism, it is still possible that supply functions for context nodes could be executed during `wdDoModifyView()`. This would only happen if the node's contents were being accessed for the first time during the current request–response cycle.

5 Each node attribute becomes a table column, and each node element becomes a table row.

node is absent at design time, the corresponding Table UI element will also be absent from the view layout at design time.[6]

The task now is to create a view layout that can respond to a context of unknown structure. It is necessary, therefore, that the wdDoModifyView() method examine the structure of the context and generate UI elements according to what it finds.

> **Important**
>
> If the context node SalesOrders had been created at design time, a typed accessor method would have been created called wdContext.nodeSalesOrders(). However, in our situation, this method does not exist, so the generic accessor method wdContext.getChildNode() must be used instead. This method requires two parameters: the name of the node to be accessed and the index in the parent node's collection of the element to which the child node is related.[7]

The following example examines the context for independent nodes and places any nodes it finds in collapsible Tray UI elements. The following types of displays are constructed depending on the number of elements found in the node collection:

▶ **Zero elements**
An empty node has been found, so an appropriate text message is displayed.

▶ **One element**
The single element is displayed as a pair of label–input field columns.

▶ **More than one element**
The node is displayed as a table in which each element is a row of the table.

### 10.7.2    Implementation of the Method wdDoModifyView()

Several utility methods have been created. The first method, called showNode(),displays any node. This then examines the contents of the node and calls either show-NodeAsColumns() or showNodeAsTable() depending on the number of elements it finds.

One important point to realize is that because the method wdDoModifyView() is static, any methods it calls must also be static. Since it is not possible to declare a static method from the Methods tab in the view controller editor, any utility methods required by wdDoModifyView() have to be defined between the //@@begin others and //@@end markers found at the end of the view controller's source code.

---

6   It is possible to declare a Table UI element at design time but to leave its dataSource property unbound. The caveat here is that before the screen can be rendered, you *must* ensure that either the dataSource parameter is correctly bound or the Table UI element is removed from the view.

7   For independent nodes (i.e., nodes that have the context root as their immediate parent), this value will always be zero, because the root node has one and only one element — element zero.

Every view controller that is part of the current view assembly has its wdDoModify-
View() method called irrespective of any previous application errors that may have
taken place.

The following code is divided into different sections. Each one is discussed sepa-
rately.

```
public static void
      wdDoModifyView(IPrivate${n_v} wdThis,
                     IPrivate${n_v}.IContextNode wdContext,
                     IWDView view,
                     boolean firstTime) {
//@@begin wdDoModifyView
// It is only necessary to build the UI element hierarchy once
if (firstTime) {
  nodeCounter = 0;

    // Get a reference to the root UI element in the view layout
    // hierarchy.
    IWDTransparentContainer tCont =
      (IWDTransparentContainer)view.getRootElement();

    // Every UI element container must have a layout manager
    // assigned to it.  The layout manager defines how the child
    // UI elements will be arranged within this container.  Since
    // a layout manager cannot exist independently from a
    // container element, the act of calling the container's
    // createLayout() method both creates a new instance of the
    // layout manager and assigns it to the UI element container.
    tCont.createLayout(IWDRowLayout.class);

    // Loop around as many independent nodes as can be found in
    // the context
    for (Iterator indNodeIt =
        wdContext.getNodeInfo().iterateChildren();
        indNodeIt.hasNext();) {
      nodeCounter++;

      // Get the next independent node info from the iterator
      IWDNodeInfo indNodeInfo = (IWDNodeInfo)indNodeIt.next();

      // Call showNode() to create a visual representation of the
      // current node
      showNode(tCont, view,
        wdContext.getChildNode(indNodeInfo.getName(),0));
    }
    // If the context contains no nodes, then display an
    // appropriate message
    if (nodeCounter==0) {
```

```
        IWDTextView tv =
          (IWDTextView)view.createElement(IWDTextView.class,
                                    "EmptyContextTextView");
        tv.setText("The context is empty!");
        tv.setDesign(WDTextViewDesign.HEADER2);
        tCont.addChild(tv);
      }
    }
//@@end
  }
//@@begin others
  static int nodeCounter;
//@@end
```

**Listing 10.12** Generate a dynamic UI layout by traversing the independent context nodes

The following processing steps takes place in wdDoModifyView():

1. The processing is only to take place if this is the first time wdDoModifyView() has been called.

2. A node counter is initialized.

3. A reference is obtained to the RootUIElementContainer object. This UI element will contain all subsequent additions to the view layout.

4. A layout manager is assigned to the entire view layout.

5. Via the wdContext object, we can obtain a reference to the context root node's metadata. This is the object returned by wdContext.getNodeInfo(). From this, we can obtain an iterator on the metadata for all the independent child nodes in the context.

6. It must be stressed that this iterator returns objects that describe context meta-data — not actual data. When working with both context nodes (IWDNode objects) and context node metadata (IWDNodeInfo objects), you must not confuse the two object types.

7. Iterate around all the objects under the context root, casting each as an IWDNodeInfo object.

8. The nodeCounter variable gives a numerical value to each node. This is only necessary for making each UI element name unique.

9. The utility method showNode() is now called. This generic method examines whatever node it is passed and creates an appropriate visual representation for it. The method showNode() is passed a reference to RootUIElementContainer, the Web Dynpro Framework-defined view object, and a reference to the current node object in the iteration.

10. Once the iterator has been processed, if the nodeCounter variable still equals zero, the context was empty, and an appropriate message is displayed.

The coding of the third parameter in the call to `showNode()` requires some explanation:

Because we have no idea what any of the context nodes are called, we cannot use any of the typed accessor methods available for nodes created at design time; therefore, we must access the context generically. This requires the use of the `getChild-Node()` method. Every context node object implements this method, and it will return the instance of the named child node for the particular element of the parent collection. In general, you can retrieve an instance of any child node `${chn}` from its parent node `${cn}` by the following coding:

```
IWDNode childNode = ${cn}.getChildNode("Name of ${chn}",
                                      <element index in ${cn}>);
```

In this case, we need to reference an independent node.[8] Therefore, there are two things to note:

▶ Access to the context root node is provided through the object `wdContext`.

▶ The call to the method `getChildNode()` must specify with which element in the parent node the child node is associated. The context root node can only ever have one element (its cardinality is hard-coded to `1..1`), therefore, the element number *must* be zero.

### 10.7.3    Implementation of the Method showNode()

The logic for the method `showNode()` can been seen in Figure 10.11.

The following processing takes place in `showNode()`:

▶ We have been passed a reference to the specific node object to be displayed. This is a reference to the actual runtime data. However, we need to know about the node's metadata; therefore, we call the `getNodeInfo()` method on the node object.

> **Important**
>
> Every node object `${cn}` has an associated metadata object. This can be obtained by calling `${cn}.getNodeInfo()`. However, if you have a node info object, it is not possible to obtain an instance of the related node object because there are potentially many different objects based on this one metadata object. In other words, there is no such method as `IWDNodeInfo.getNode()`.

▶ A `Tray` UI element is created, and its design property is set.

---

8  Any node that has the context root node as its immediate parent is known as an *independent* node.

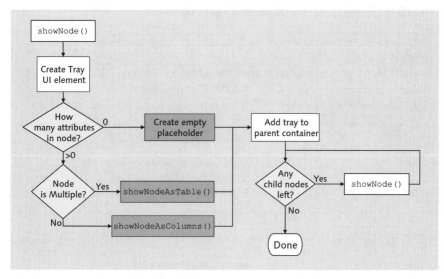

**Figure 10.11** Flow Chart for showNode() logic

► Every `Tray` UI element has a mandatory child caption object. This object is defined, its text value is assigned from the name of node info object, and then the caption is added to the tray.

► Now the number of elements in the current node is examined, and the following action taken:

   ► Zero elements: Display text message.

   ► One element: Show node element as a label–input field pair of columns.

   ► Many elements: Show node elements as a table.

► Once an appropriate visual representation has been created for the current node, another iterator is obtained on the current node's child nodes. This iterator is now processed, and `showNode()` is called recursively for each child node.

► Notice on the recursive call to `showNode()` that the same `getChildNode()` method is being used, but with two important differences:

   ► The method belongs to the current node being processed, not `wdContext`.

   ► We must obtain the appropriate child node instance for whichever element is at the lead selection of the current node. This will not necessarily be element zero. The element at the lead selection is controlled automatically by which table row the user has clicked on.

The `showNode()` method can be implemented in the following way.

```
private static void showNode(IWDTransparentContainer tCont,
                    IWDView view, IWDNode thisNode) {
  // Get the metadata for the current node
```

```
IWDNodeInfo thisNodeInfo = thisNode.getNodeInfo();

// Create a collapsible tray in which to display the node
IWDTray theTray =
  (IWDTray)view.createElement(IWDTray.class,
                              "NodeTray" + nodeCounter);
theTray.setDesign(WDTrayDesign.FILL);
// A tray UI element must have a descriptive caption in its
// header. A caption is a distinct UI element in its own right.
IWDCaption trayCaption =
  (IWDCaption)view.createElement(IWDCaption.class, "NodeTray" +
                                nodeCounter + "Caption");
trayCaption.setText("Node " + thisNodeInfo.getName());

// Add the caption to the tray
theTray.setHeader(trayCaption);

// How many elements does the context node contain?
switch (thisNode.size()) {
// Empty node collection
  case 0:
    IWDTextView tv =
      (IWDTextView)view.createElement(IWDTextView.class,
                                      "NoData" + nodeCounter);
    tv.setText("Node " + thisNodeInfo.getName() +
               " has no elements");
    theTray.addChild(tv);
    break;
// One element in node collection
  case 1:
    // Configure the Tray UI element to have a layout manager of
    // RowLayout
    theTray.createLayout(IWDMatrixLayout.class);
    showNodeAsColumns(view, thisNodeInfo, theTray);
    break;
// Many elements in node collection
  default:
    // Add table UI element to tray UI element
    theTray.addChild(showNodeAsTable(view, thisNodeInfo));
}

// Add the tray UI element to the transparent container
tCont.addChild(theTray);

// Loop around as many dependent nodes as can be found for this
// node
for (Iterator chnIt = thisNode.getNodeInfo().iterateChildren();
     chnIt.hasNext();) {
  nodeCounter++;
```

```
    // Store the next iterator object as an IWDNodeInfo
    IWDNodeInfo chnInfo = (IWDNodeInfo)chnIt.next();

    // Call showNode() to create a visual representation of the
    // current node
    showNode(tCont, view,
            thisNode.getChildNode(chnInfo.getName(),
                                thisNode.getLeadSelection())));
  }
}
```

**Listing 10.13** The method showNode() builds a UI layout appropriate for the node it has been passed

First, notice that the showNode() method is defined between the //@@begin others and //@@end comment markers found at the end of the view controller's source code. This is the only place in the controller coding where you may define a static method. This form of processing produces a sequence of tray elements down the screen that corresponds to the top-to-bottom, left-to-right traversal of the node hierarchy.

The last two methods to be discussed are the utility methods that take a node and display it either as a pair of label–input field columns or as a table.

### 10.7.4  Implementation of the Method showNodeAsColumns()

showNodeAsColumns() should be called only if the node it is to display contains a single element. The logic for the method showNodeAsColumns() can been seen in Figure 10.12.

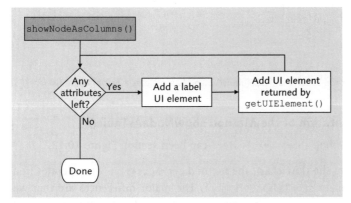

**Figure 10.12** Flow Chart for showNodeAsColumns() Logic

The getUIElement() method examines the data type of the current context attribute and returns a UI element suitable for displaying it.

The showNodeAsColumns() method can be implemented in the following way.

```
private static void showNodeAsColumns(IWDView view,
                                      IWDNodeInfo thisNodeInfo,
                                      IWDTray theTray) {
  // For each attribute, create a label/input pair of fields
  for (Iterator attrIt = thisNodeInfo.iterateAttributes();
       attrIt.hasNext();) {
    IWDAttributeInfo thisAttr  = (IWDAttributeInfo)attrIt.next();
    IWDUIElement     newElem   = null;
    String           fieldName = thisAttr.getName();

    // Create a label UI element and set its text to be name of
    // the attribute
    IWDLabel newLabel = (IWDLabel)view.
                    createElement(IWDLabel.class,
                                  fieldName+ "Label");
    newLabel.setText(fieldName);

    // Set the layout data to be the start of a new matrix row
    // and switch off the vertical bar to the left of the label
    // text
    newLabel.createLayoutData(IWDMatrixHeadData.class);
    newLabel.setDesign(WDLabelDesign.LIGHT);

    newElem = getUIElement(view, thisAttr);

    // As long as both the new label and the new element have been
    // created, append them to the group UI container
    if (newElem != null) {
      theTray.addChild(newLabel);
      theTray.addChild(newElem);
    }
  }
}
```

**Listing 10.14** The method showNodeAsColumns() displays a node as a pair of columns

### 10.7.5 Implementation of the Method showNodeAsTable()

The logic for the method showNodeAsTable() can been seen in Figure 10.13.

As you can see from the flow chart, the method showNodeAsTable() operates in a very similar manner to showNodeAsColumns(). The major differences are that we create a table column UI element instead of a label, and the UI element returned from the method getUIElement() is assigned to be the table column's cell editor.

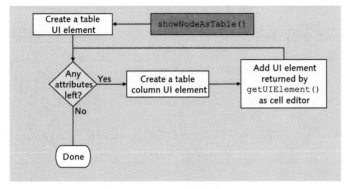

**Figure 10.13** Flow Chart for showNodeAsTable() Logic

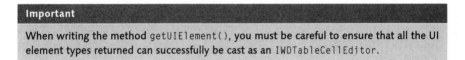

**Important**

When writing the method `getUIElement()`, you must be careful to ensure that all the UI element types returned can successfully be cast as an `IWDTableCellEditor`.

The `showNodeAsTable()` method is implemented in the following way.

```
private static IWDTable showNodeAsTable(IWDView view,
                                        IWDNodeInfo childNodeInfo) {
  IWDTableColumn tabCol;
  IWDCaption    tabColCap;
  IWDUIElement  cellEditor;

  // Create a table object and bind its dataSource property to
  // the current node info object
  IWDTable tab = (IWDTable)view.
                  createElement(IWDTable.class,
                                childNodeInfo.getName() +
                                "Table");
  tab.bindDataSource(childNodeInfo);

  // Iterate around the attributes of this node turning each one
  // into a table column
  // Each UI element object must be given a unique name
  for (Iterator attIt = childNodeInfo.iterateAttributes();
       attIt.hasNext();) {
    // Create a table column object. All table columns must have
    // a caption element as their headers and some sort of
    // element as their cell editors. A column may have only one
    // type of UI element as its cell editor.
    IWDAttributeInfo thisAttrib = (IWDAttributeInfo)attIt.next();
    tabCol = (IWDTableColumn)view.
              createElement(IWDTableColumn.class,
                            "ColumnFor" + thisAttrib.getName());
```

345

```
                // Define a column caption, set the text, and add it to the
                // column.
                tabColCap = (IWDCaption)view.
                         createElement(IWDCaption.class,
                                  "CaptionFor" +
                                  thisAttrib.getName());

                tabColCap.setText(thisAttrib.getName());
                tabCol.setHeader(tabColCap);

                // Bind cell editor to the path of the context attribute
                tabCol.setTableCellEditor(
                  (IWDTableCellEditor)getUIElement(view, thisAttrib));

                // Finally, add the column to the table
                tab.addGroupedColumn(tabCol);
        }

     return tab;
}
// static variable declarations
   static int nodeCounter;
//@@end
```

**Listing 10.15** The method showNodeAsTable() displays a node as a table

### 10.7.6   Implementation of the Method getUIElement()

The logic for the method getUIElement() can been seen in Figure 10.14.

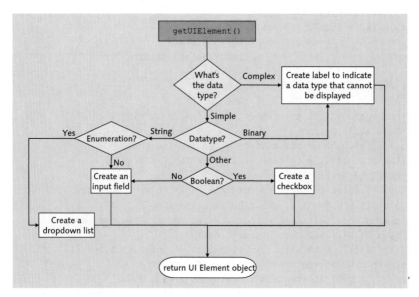

**Figure 10.14** Flow Chart for getUIElement() Logic

The getUIElement() method can be implemented in the following way:

```
private static IWDUIElement getUIElement(IWDView view,
                                IWDAttributeInfo thisAttr) {
  IWDUIElement newElem = null;
  String newID = "elementFor" + thisAttr.getName();

  // Is this attribute based on a dictionary simple type?
  if (thisAttr.getDataType().isSimpleType()) {
    // Yup. Get both the dictionary simple type and the built-in
    // type from which it is derived
    ISimpleType sType  = thisAttr.getSimpleType();
    String       biType = sType.getBuiltInType();

    // Can the built-in type be shown by some type of input field?
    if (biType.equalsIgnoreCase("string") ||
        biType.equalsIgnoreCase("date")   ||
        biType.equalsIgnoreCase("decimal")) {
      // Yup, can we get a list of possible inputs this field?
      if (sType.hasSVService() &&
          sType.getSVServices().getValues() != null) {
        // Yup. Use a drop down to display possible input values
        IWDDropDownByKey newField =
          (IWDDropDownByKey)view.createElement(
            IWDDropDownByKey.class, newID);
        newField.bindSelectedKey(thisAttr);
        newField.createLayoutData(IWDMatrixData.class);
        newElem = newField;
      }
      // No value list can be obtained
      else {
        // Display the attribute value using an input field
        IWDInputField newField =
          (IWDInputField)view.createElement(
            IWDInputField.class,
            newID);
        newField.bindValue(thisAttr);
        newField.createLayoutData(IWDMatrixData.class);
        newElem = newField;
      }
    }
    // If the field type is boolean, then use a checkbox UI element
    else if (biType.equals("boolean")) {
      IWDCheckBox newField =
        (IWDCheckBox)view.createElement(IWDCheckBox.class, newID);
      newField.bindChecked(thisAttr);
      newField.createLayoutData(IWDMatrixData.class);
      newElem = newField;
    }
```

```
  }
  else {
    // The field is not based on a dictionary simple type, and
    // cannot therefore be displayed without either further
    // examination, or knowledge of an appropriate MIME type
    IWDLabel newField =
      (IWDLabel)view.createElement(IWDLabel.class, newID);
    newField.setText("Unable to display contents of " +
                    thisAttr.getName() +
                    ". Wrong data type");
    newField.createLayoutData(IWDMatrixData.class);
    newElem = newField;
  }

  return newElem;
}
```

**Listing 10.16** The method getUIElement() returns a UI element object suitable for displaying the context attribute it is passed

## 10.8    Implementing an OVS

The purpose of an OVS is to enable the user to select one or more field values based on a search they perform. If the user is required to enter some value such as a customer id but knows only that the customer is called "Acme Industries" or that they are located in Dullsville, Nebraska, then they need some facility to search for the key value (the customer id) based on some other non-key values (the name or the location). The point here is that an OVS gives the user the ability to search for one or more field values based on a flexible set of search criteria.

This form of Value Help is derived directly from that found in an SAP system.

> **Important**
>
> The following discussion of OVSs assumes you are going to search a backend SAP system for the required values by calling a suitable remote-enabled ABAP function module (also known as an RFC module).

> **Caveat Confector**
>
> You should check whether your backend system provides you with suitable *OVS-enabled* RFC modules.
>
> OVS-enabled means that all the required input attributes are defined in a flat structure. Likewise, all attributes to be displayed in the search results table belong to a flat output structure. In other words, the generic OVS component provided by the Web Dynpro Framework cannot automatically accommodate hierarchically arranged input or output attributes.

This restriction can be worked around by declaring separate OVS input or output nodes for each level of the hierarchy. These nodes will typically be value nodes, with the required attributes defined using simple types found in the Adaptive RFC Dictionary.

The copying of data between these hierarchically related nodes must be manually implemented in the OVS listener methods `onQuery()` and `applyResult()`.

### 10.8.1 Basic Concept

The basic concept of an OVS is to extend the capability of a Web Dynpro context attribute. This at first may seem counterintuitive because we have been talking about enabling a user to find a key value based on a search performed using non-key values.

The point here is that the UI elements used to display data are just a superficial skin on top of the real information. The UI layer is simply the means by which data is presented to the user and is therefore not important when we consider how data is processed.

> **Important**
>
> When you create an OVS, you are extending the capability of a *context attribute*, and not any particular UI element!

Once a particular context attribute has had an OVS associated with it, any time that attribute is displayed; the **Advanced Search** OVS icon will appear next to the UI element to indicate that extra search functionality is available (see Figure 10.15). The search functionality belongs to the context attribute, not the UI element.

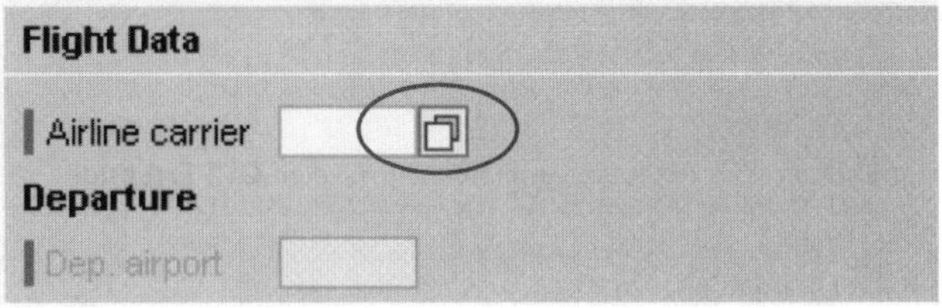

**Figure 10.15** An OVS Extension to a Context Attribute Is Available when this Icon Appears

As shown in Section 7.9.5, to implement an OVS, you must create a custom controller that will return a class implementing the `IWDOVSContextNotificationListener` interface.

Within this interface are three methods that need to be implemented and each method corresponds to a time at which user interaction can take place.

1. `applyInputValues(IWDNodeElement datafromApp,`
   `           IWDNodeElement inputToOvsQuery)`

2. onQuery(IWDNodeElement inputToOvsQuery,
        IWDNode ovsQueryResults)

3. applyResult(IWDNodeElement dataForApp,
        IWDNodeElement selectedOvsResultElement)

### 10.8.2 Assigning the OVS Extension to a Context Attribute

Before looking at the details of how the OVS is implemented, we will look at how the functionality of a context attribute can be extended. This involves assigning an OVS extension to the context attribute(s) in question. In the following example we will only be extending the functionality of a single attribute.

The example used here is taken from the SAP Developers Network (SDN) document called "Web Dynpro Valuehelp Using Object Value Selector," but the coding has been simplified to increase clarity.[9]

First, we want to extend the functionality of the AirlineId attribute found in the node FlightData of a view controller. This context structure is shown in Figure 10.16.

**Figure 10.16** View Controller Context. The Attribute AirlineId Will Have an OVS Extension Added to It

It is important to understand that the context node FlightData shown in Figure 10.16 acts as both the input to the OVS search fields and the element from which the selected search results are obtained.

In this example, the node FlightData has a cardinality of 1..1. If any values exist in its attributes at the time the OVS is invoked, these values will be copied to the OVS input fields. Similarly, when the user selects the required row from the OVS results table, the attribute values of the selected row will be transferred to this context element.

---

9 This document can be downloaded by performing a search for the above name on *http://sdn.sap.com*.

So the 1..1 cardinality node FlightData acts as both input to and output from the OVS.

The coding to associate the AirlineId context attribute with the OVS is shown below:

```
public void wdDoInit() {
  //@@begin wdDoInit()
  // Get the metadata of the context attribute to be extended
  IWDAttributeInfo airlineIdInfo =
    wdContext.nodeFlightData().
      getNodeInfo().getAttribute("AirlineId");

  // Store the metadata in an array
  IWDAttributeInfo[] ovsStartUpAttr = { airlineIdInfo };

  // Get a reference to the controller acting as the OVS provider
  IPublicOVSCust ovsProvider = wdThis.wdGetOVSCustController();

  // Tell the WDValueServices helper class to extend the
  // functionality of the context attribute by associating it with
  // the OVS listener class and the related input and output nodes
  WDValueServices.addOVSExtension("Flight Selection",
                                  ovsStartUpAttr,
                                  ovsProvider.getOVSInputNode(),
                                  ovsProvider.getOVSOutputNode(),
                                  ovsProvider.getOVSListener());
  //@@end
}
```

**Listing 10.17** The method wdDoInit() in the view controller contains the coding to add an OVS extension to one of the context attributes

In our case, the call to WDValueServices.addOVSExtension() is being made for a single context attribute. However, if more IWDAttributeInfo objects were added to the ovsStartUpAttr array, each one would be associated with the same OVS listener.

| Important |
| --- |
| If multiple context attributes are to be associated with a particular OVS, these attributes must all belong to the same context node. |

All of this coding assumes, of course, that we have already written a custom controller (in this case called OVSCust) that provides an instance of a class implementing the IWDOVSContextNotificationListener interface.

Before we look at the actual coding within this custom controller, let's first look at the sequence of events that take place when a user first invokes, and then interact with, an OVS.

### 10.8.3  OVS Processing

Once the functionality of the AirlineId context attribute has been extended to include an OVS, any UI element[10] used to display that context attribute will show the Advanced Search icon next to it.

**OVS Instantiation**

When the user clicks on the icon to the right of the input field indicated in Figure 10.15, this causes a round trip to the server, and a Value Help service event is raised. See Section 4.4.5 to remind yourself of how the Web Dynpro Framework handles this type of request during Phase Model processing.

The applyInputValues() method of the IWDOVSContextNotificationListener class is the event handler that subscribes to the Value Help service event, so after the Web Dynpro Framework has instantiated the generic OVS component, this method is called, and the pop-up window is displayed.

If you refer back to Listing 10.17, you will see that the OVS listener object is called ovsListener, and this is assigned to the AirlineId context attribute via the call to method WDValueServices.addOVSExtension().

Once the OVS has been instantiated, you will see a pop-up window containing various UI elements. These UI elements are generated automatically on the basis of the context nodes supplied to the queryInputNode and queryResultNode parameters of the addOVSExtension() method.

**OVS Query Execution**

After the user enters his input parameters, he clicks the Go button. This raises an event subscribed to by the onQuery() method. The onQuery() method is responsible for interacting with the backend system and placing the search results in the context node visualized by the table in the lower half of Figure 10.17.

**Returning the Result from the OVS**

Once the search results have been displayed in the table, the user is then able to select the required row. The action of selecting the row causes a round trip, and the applyResults() method is called. This method is then responsible for taking the

---

10  I am assuming of course that the UI element being used is capable of receiving user input.

data from the selected row and copying it back to the node element that contains the OVS enabled attribute. In other words, the current element in the node Flight-Data (see Figure 10.17) is populated with the data from the selected row of the OVS results table (see Figure 10.18).

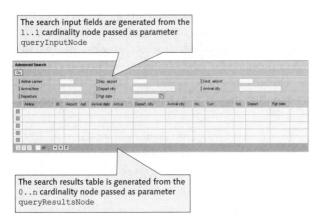

**Figure 10.17** The Input Fields and Results Table Are Generated Based on the Attributes Found in the Nodes Passed to the addOVSExtension() Method

**Advanced Search**

Go

| | Airline carrier | AA | | Dep. airport | | | Dest. airport | |
|---|---|---|---|---|---|---|---|---|
| | Arrival time | | | Depart.city | | | Arrival city | |
| | Departure | | | Flgt date | | | | |

| | Airline | ID | Airport | Apt | Arrival date | Arrive | Depart. city | Arrival city | No. | Curr. | Iso | Depart | Flgt date | Flugpreis |
|---|---|---|---|---|---|---|---|---|---|---|---|---|---|---|
| ■ | American Airlines | AA | SFO | JFK | 4/9/2004 | 5:21:00 PM | SAN FRANCISCO | NEW YORK | 0064 | American Dollar | USD | 9:00:00 AM | 4/9/2004 | 422.94 |
| ■ | American Airlines | AA | SFO | JFK | 3/12/2004 | 5:21:00 PM | SAN FRANCISCO | NEW YORK | 0064 | American Dollar | USD | 9:00:00 AM | 3/12/2004 | 422.94 |
| ■ | American Airlines | AA | SFO | JFK | 2/13/2004 | 5:21:00 PM | SAN FRANCISCO | NEW YORK | 0064 | American Dollar | USD | 9:00:00 AM | 2/13/2004 | 422.94 |
| ■ | American Airlines | AA | SFO | JFK | 1/16/2004 | 5:21:00 PM | SAN FRANCISCO | NEW YORK | 0064 | American Dollar | USD | 9:00:00 AM | 1/16/2004 | 422.94 |
| ■ | American Airlines | AA | JFK | SFO | 2/9/2005 | 2:01:00 PM | NEW YORK | San Francisco | 0017 | American Dollar | USD | 11:00:00 AM | 2/9/2005 | 422.94 |

1 of 31

**Figure 10.18** OVS Search Results

### 10.8.4 OVS Implementation

**Creating an OVS Custom Controller**

An OVS is best housed within a custom controller. This has the advantage of keeping all the OVS functionality separate from the other controllers in your component. It is particularly important to avoid the temptation to throw the OVS coding into the view controller. This architecture is wrong for two reasons:

1. The OVS functionality is not reusable across different view controllers.
2. You have caused a data consumer (the view controller) to function as a data generator.

   This is *REALLY* bad architecture and should always be avoided because it makes future maintenance of the application much harder.

If you knowingly implement coding that blurs the distinction between data consumers and data generators, *Go Directly To Jail, Do Not Pass Go, Do Not Collect £200!*

In the custom controller used for this demo,[11] a context structure and three methods have been declared. The context structure is as shown in Figure 10.19. The content of the node `OVSFlightQueryOutput` is displayed as the OVS results table. This node must have a cardinality of `0..n`. When the user selects an element from this node, that data will be used to populate the fields in the `FlightData` node in the view controller. The attributes in node `OVSFlightQueryInput` will appear as the OVS input fields. This node corresponds to the `FlightData` node in the view controller.

```
⊟─◯ Context
   ⊞─🗓 Bapi_Flight_Getlist_Input
   ⊟─🗓 OVSFlightQueryOutput
          ⬢ Airline
          ⬢ AirlineId
          ⬢ Airportfr
          ⬢ Airportto
          ⬢ Arrdate
          ⬢ Arrtime
          ⬢ Cityfrom
          ⬢ Cityto
          ⬢ Connectid
          ⬢ Curr
          ⬢ Curr_Iso
          ⬢ Deptime
          ⬢ Flightdate
          ⬢ Price
   ⊟─🗓 OVSFlightQueryInput
          ⬢ AirlineId
          ⬢ Airportfr
          ⬢ Airportto
          ⬢ Arrtime
          ⬢ Cityfrom
          ⬢ Cityto
          ⬢ Deptime
          ⬢ Flightdate
```

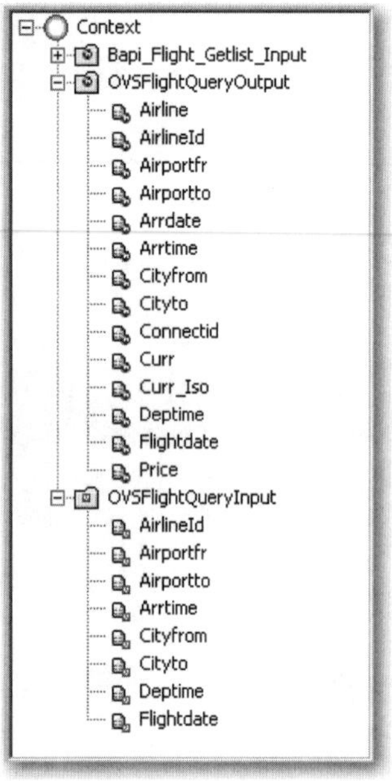

**Figure 10.19** The Context Structure Used by the OVS Custom Controller

Within this controller, three methods have been created. These methods are:

▶ `IWDOVSContextNotificationListener getOVSListener()`
Returns an instance of the OVS notification listener class. This is the object that enables the context attribute's functionality to be associated with an OVS.

▶ `IWDNode getOVSInputNode()`
Returns a reference to the context node holding the OVS input fields.

▶ `IWDNode getOVSOutputNode()`
Returns a reference to the context node holding the OVS results table.

---

11  Remember that this demo is a simplified version of the OVS demo application available from SDN.

If you refer back to Listing 10.17, you will see that each of these methods are called when passing parameters to method `WDValueServices.addOVSExtension()`.

The coding for these methods is shown below in a condensed form.[12]

```
public class OVSCust {
  <snip>

  public void wdDoInit() {
    //@@begin wdDoInit()
    Bapi_Flight_Getlist_Input bapiInput =
                              new Bapi_Flight_Getlist_Input();
    wdContext.nodeBapi_Flight_Getlist_Input().bind(bapiInput);
    //@@end
  }

  <snip>

  public IWDOVSContextNotificationListener getOVSListener( ) {
    //@@begin getOVSListener()
    return ovsListener;
    //@@end
  }

  public IWDNode getOVSInputNode( ) {
    //@@begin getOVSInputNode()
    return wdContext.nodeOVSFlightQueryInput();
    //@@end
  }

  public IWDNode getOVSOutputNode( ) {
    //@@begin getOVSOutputNode()
    return wdContext.nodeOVSFlightQueryOutput();
    //@@end
  }

  <snip>

  private IWDOVSContextNotificationListener ovsListener =
    new OVSListener("AirlineId");
  //@@end
}
```

**Listing 10.18** Bare bones of the custom OVS controller

---

12 By *condensed*, I mean that comments, generated helper variables, unimplemented standard hook methods, and the `IWDOVSContextNotificationListener` inner class implementation have been snipped.

### Creating an Implementation of the IWDOVSContextNotificationListener Interface

Now we arrive at the point where the actual OVS coding must be implemented. Our class is called OVSListener and has been implemented as an inner class of the custom controller called OVSCust shown above in Listing 10.18.

```
//@@begin others
private class OVSListener implements IWDOVSContextNotificationListener {
  private String attrName;

  public OVSListener(String attrName) {
    super();
    this.attrName = attrName;
  }

  public void applyInputValues(IWDNodeElement applicationNodeElement,
                               IWDNodeElement queryInputNodeElement) {
    Object initialValue = applicationNodeElement.getAttributeValue(attrName);
    queryInputNodeElement.setAttributeValue(attrName, initialValue);
  }

  public void onQuery(IWDNodeElement queryInputNodeElement,
                      IWDNode queryOutputNode) {
    IOVSFlightQueryInputElement input =
      (IOVSFlightQueryInputElement)queryInputNodeElement;

    Bapi_Flight_Getlist_Input bapiInput = new Bapi_Flight_Getlist_Input();
    Bapisfldst bapiDestTo              = new Bapisfldst();
    Bapisfldst bapiDestFrom            = new Bapisfldst();
    Bapisfldra bapiDateRange           = new Bapisfldra();

    if (input.getFlightdate() != null) {
      bapiDateRange.setLow(input.getFlightdate());
      bapiDateRange.setHigh(input.getFlightdate());
      bapiDateRange.setSign("I");
      bapiDateRange.setOption("EQ");
      bapiInput.addDate_Range(bapiDateRange);
    }

    if (input.getCityfrom() != null)
      bapiDestFrom.setCity(input.getCityfrom());

    if (input.getCityto() != null)
      bapiDestTo.setCity(input.getCityto());

    if (input.getAirportfr() != null)
```

```
    bapiDestFrom.setAirportid(input.getAirportfr());

  if (input.getAirportto() != null)
    bapiDestTo.setAirportid(input.getAirportto());

  if (input.getAirlineId() != null)
    bapiInput.setAirline(input.getAirlineId());

  bapiInput.setDestination_From(bapiDestFrom);
  bapiInput.setDestination_To(bapiDestTo);

  try {
    bapiInput.execute();
    queryOutputNode.bind(bapiInput.getOutput().getFlight_List());
  }
    catch (WDDynamicRFCExecuteException e) {
      IWDMessageManager msgMgr = wdComponentAPI.getMessageManager();
      msgMgr.reportException(e.getNestedLocalizedMessage(), false);
    }
  }

  public void applyResult(IWDNodeElement applicationNodeElement,
                          IWDNodeElement queryOutputNodeElement) {
    WDCopyService.copyCorresponding(queryOutputNodeElement,
                                    applicationNodeElement);
  }
}
//@@end
```

**Listing 10.19** The implementation of the IWDOVSContextNotificationListener interface

Each of the methods has various points of which you should be aware.

### The Constructor

The value of a local variable called `attrName` is set using the parameter to the constructor of the same name. This variable is used in the `applyInputValues()` method.

### Method applyInputValues()

This method is used when the OVS is first instantiated by the Web Dynpro Framework. In our case, we are associating only a single context attribute with the OVS, so the functionality implemented here is very simple.

The value of the context attribute from the view controller's context is obtained as a Java `Object` and used to set the value of the OVS's corresponding input field. Therefore, whatever value is already in the view controller's input field for `AirlineId` will appear in the corresponding field when the OVS pop-up window is seen.

This functionality can be extended for as many attributes in the parameter `applicationNodeElement` as are associated with the current OVS.

This functionality also relies on the fact that the attribute name and data type in the view controller's context are *exactly* the same as the attribute name and data type in the OVS's `OVSFlightQueryInput` node.

### Method onQuery()

This method contains the functionality that is specific to driving the actual search process. For this demo, we must take the data found in the OVS input fields and use it to drive the ABAP function module `BAPI_FLIGHT_GETLIST`. The coding here will be function module specific and therefore cannot really be generalized.

If you do not understand why the calls to the methods `bapiDateRange.set<something>()` are necessary, please look up the ABAP help on a SELECT-OPTION. A SELECT-OPTION is an ABAP table with a standardized structure for defining ranges in search parameter values.

The various input parameters of this function module are populated, and then it is invoked. The function module then returns some search results on the output side of its interface, and this information is bound directly to the context node `OVSFlightQueryOutput`.

### Method applyResult()

This is the method that takes the selected row from the OVS results table and copies the data back into the view controller element that contains the attribute that originally invoked the OVS.

If you have constructed your context attributes carefully, you should be able to make use of the `WDCopyService` helper class to do this for you.

# 11    Navigation and Error Handling

Although it may not seem obvious at first, error handling and navigation are closely linked to each other. This is because if errors are detected, they usually interrupt subsequent navigation processing. Since navigation is dependent upon all previous steps having completed successfully, it is useful to write both areas of processing to operate in conjunction with each other.

## 11.1    Navigation Processing

If you refer back to Figure 2.14 in section 2.5.2, you'll see that a component's interface view controller is conceptually similar to a view controller. The difference, however, is that a view controller manages an aggregation of UI elements, whereas an interface view controller manages an aggregation of views.

An Interface view controller does not have a view layout as such; instead it has a design time entity called a window. This is the entity within which all the views making up a particular visual interface of the component are brought together (see Figure 11.1). Then (and this is the key point for the following discussion) navigation paths are defined between the views in the window.

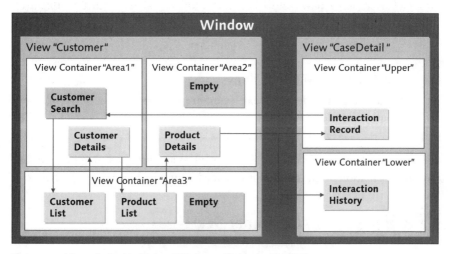

**Figure 11.1** Views Embedded into a Window with Navigation Paths

To create a navigation link, you must first embed some views into the window and then define a pair or navigation plugs. These are the exit and entry points used when you want to navigate from one view to another. These plugs are known as inbound and outbound plugs.

### 11.1.1 The View Assembly

Look at the views embedded into the window in Figure 11.1. At the highest level, there are two views called Customer and CaseDetail. These views each contain several `ViewContainerUIElement` UI elements — which have other views embedded within them. So we can see that there are views embedded within views embedded within the window.

One misunderstanding that is common among people new to Web Dynpro is that they look at the design time definition of the window and ask, "Are all those views going to be displayed in the screen at the same time?" This is a perfectly reasonable question, and the answer is that unless your window layout is very simple, only a subset of those views will ever be displayed on the screen at any one time.

At runtime, only a subset of the views seen in the window will be visible on the screen at any one time, and as the user interacts with the application, navigation requests will be raised. These navigation requests cause one or more views to disappear from the screen and be replaced with other views.

This dynamically changing subset of views seen at any one time is known as the view assembly, and navigation links are the means by which the view assembly content is rearranged.

Look back at section 2.5.2 for another description of interface view controllers, windows, and the view assembly.

### 11.1.2 Outbound Navigation Plugs

An outbound plug is a declared exit point from a view controller. For every declared outbound plug $\{P_{out}\}$ in a view controller, a method is created called `wdThis.wdFirePlug`$\{P_{out}\}$`()` (see Figure 11.2).

You may pass as many parameters as you want to an outbound plug method, but the implementation of this method is provided by the Web Dynpro Framework.

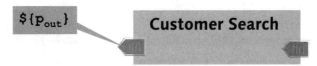

**Figure 11.2** Outbound Plug Definition

### 11.1.3 Inbound Navigation Plugs

An inbound plug is a declared entry point into a view controller. For every declared inbound plug ${p_{in}}$ in a view controller, a method called wdThis.onPlug${p_{in}}$() is created (Figure 11.3). This method receives a reference to the navigation event object that invoked it.

You may pass as many parameters as you want to an inbound plug method, and you must provide this method's implementation.

**Figure 11.3** Inbound Plug Definition

```
public void onPlug${p_{in}}(IWDCustomEvent wdEvent) {
  //@@begin onPlug${p_{in}}(ServerEvent)
  //@@end
}
```

**Listing 11.1** Generated inbound plug method

### 11.1.4 Navigation Processing

Outbound plug methods can be called at any point in the Phase Model up until the Navigation and View Initialisation step. Typically, they are called by application event handlers or in the doBeforeNavigation step as shown in Figure 11.4.

> **Important**
>
> The doBeforeNavigation step is a hook method found only in component controllers, and outbound plugs are methods specific to view controllers. Therefore, it is reasonable to ask "How can the functionality found in the wdDoBeforeNavigation method of the component controller call a private method in a view controller?"
>
> The simple answer is that it cannot be done directly, but it can be done by having the component raise an event to which a method in the view controller subscribes. The view controller's event handler method then fires the outbound plug.
>
> This topic will be dealt with in greater detail in the following sections.

Once an outbound plug has been fired, the Web Dynpro Framework treats this method call simply as a request for navigation. Since multiple outbound plugs could all be fired during a single round trip, all navigation requests need to be processed at a distinct point in time, rather than on an ad hoc basis.

Therefore, any time an outbound plug is fired, the request for navigation is placed on the navigation queue where it waits until the Navigation and View Initialisation step of the Phase Model processing (see Figure 11.5).

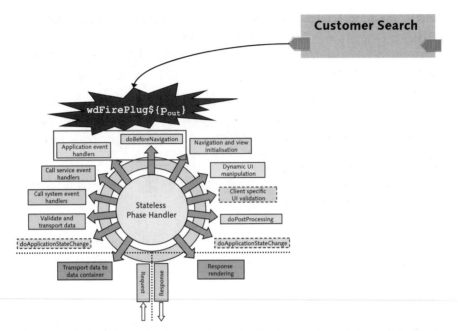

**Figure 11.4** Outbound Plugs Are Fired During Action Event Processing or in the doBeforeNavigation Step

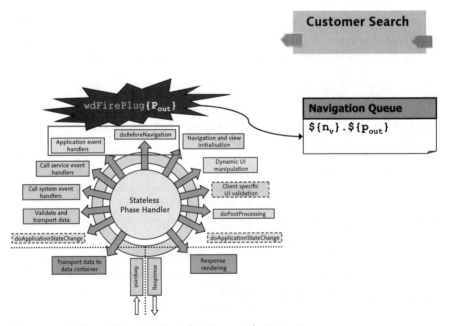

**Figure 11.5** Outbound Plugs Are Treated as Requests for Navigation

After the `doBeforeNavigation` method has been called for all controllers in the component hierarchy,[1] the Phase Model processing enters the `Navigation and View Initialisation` step. This is where the contents of the navigation queue are examined and either processed in their entirety or bypassed completely.

---

**Caveat Confector**

You cannot pick and choose which requests in the navigation queue will be processed. You either process the whole queue, or you bypass the whole queue. You cannot process navigation requests selectively, so navigation requests should only be entered into the queue if you know they will really be required.

This fact has important consequences when performing navigation and error processing within large Web Dynpro applications.

---

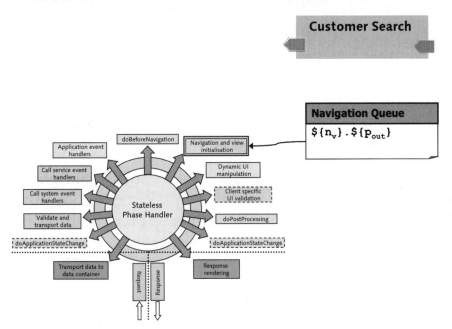

**Figure 11.6** The Navigation Step of the Phase Model Processes the Entries in the Navigation Queue

As long as a call to the `IWDMessageManager` has not been made with the `cancelNavigation` flag set to `true`, the Web Dynpro Framework will now process all the navigation requests in the queue. Entries in the navigation queue are shown in Figure 11.6, but they are not accessible to the developer.

The *basic* logic used to process the navigation queue is shown in Figure 11.7.

---

1  Remember that the Web Dynpro Framework uses a top-down approach when calling the same hook method across a component hierarchy.

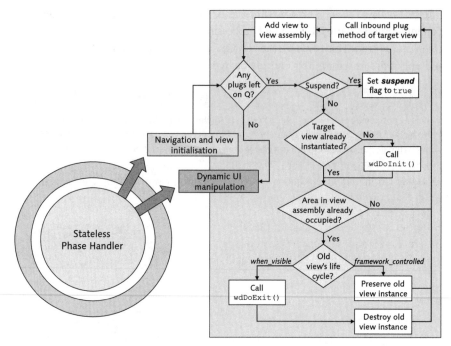

**Figure 11.7** Basic Navigation Logic

The reason Figure 11.7 shows only basic logic is to avoid the flow chart becoming very large and complex.[2] The processing has been omitted where:

▶ One outbound plug is connected to multiple inbound plugs.

▶ The outbound plug is connected to an inbound plug belonging to the interface view controller of another component. This situation could cause an entirely new component to be instantiated.

▶ Inbound plug processing immediately fires other outbound plugs.

The Navigation and View Initialisation step of the Phase Model is when view controller lifecycle management takes place. If the inbound plug points to a view controller that has not yet been instantiated, the Web Dynpro Framework first instantiates it and then calls its wdDoInit() method. Only after these steps have been completed is the inbound plug method called.

Similarly, if a view controller is being removed from the view assembly, the Web Dynpro Framework checks its lifespan property to see what to do with the old instance. The default lifespan setting is framework_controlled, which means a single view instance will be used for the entire lifespan of the component — irrespective of whether the view is a member of the current view assembly.

---

2 Also, there is not enough room on the page!

If the lifespan setting is when_visible, as soon as the view controller is removed from the view assembly, the view controller's wdDoExit() method is called, and then the instance is thrown away. If the view is later displayed again, a new instance will be created.

### 11.1.5    Re-Entrant Navigation Links

Normally, when you fire an outbound plug, you are telling the Web Dynpro Framework that the current view controller is no longer required in the view assembly and that you want its space to be occupied by a different view controller. In other words, remove the old view controller from the view assembly and put another view controller in its place.

However, there is a special type of UI element known as a ViewContainerUIElement. Much like a window, this UI element is capable of having other view controllers embedded within it. Since this UI element lives within the layout of a view controller, it allows you to nest views or even entire child components, within each other.

In this situation, it is quite possible that the parent view controller could define an outbound navigation link whose destination is some view embedded within its own ViewContainerUIElement. Such a navigation link is known as a re-entrant navigation link.

Whenever an outbound plug is fired that belongs to a re-entrant navigation link, the current view controller instance is always retained in the view assembly, but a child view instance contained within it is replaced.

In the following situation, we have a parent component called RootComp that uses two child components called ArtistComp and GunfighterComp. The purpose of RootComp is to present the user with a choice of displaying one or the other of the two child components. RootComp will then display the interface view of whichever child component the user selects.

In Figure 11.8, notice that the solid arrows indicate that the root component has a declared usage of the child component's interface controllers, and the dotted arrows indicate that the interface view controllers of the child components have been embedded into the window of the parent component.

The window of the root component RootComp has a single view embedded within it called PersonView, and within this view is a single ViewContainerUIElement (see Figure 11.9).

Next, the interface views of the ArtistComp and GunfighterComp child components are embedded into the ViewContainerUIElement. In addition to this, the default view within the UI element container is the empty view (see Figure 11.10).

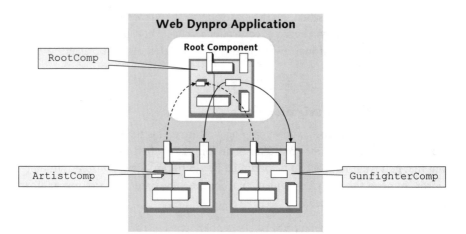

**Figure 11.8** Component Architecture of the Application Using Re-Entrant Navigation Links

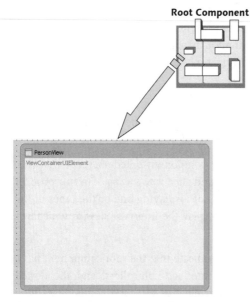

**Figure 11.9** Root Component Window Design: Part 1

Now we need to be able to control which child component is visible within the ViewContainerUIElement. To do this, first we create two *outbound* plugs on the root component's PersonView.

"Outbound plugs going out to where?" you might think. Well, that's exactly the point: They're not going *out* to anywhere. A re-entrant navigation link is simply regular navigation link that re-enters the view and connects to the inbound plug of some embedded view (see Figure 11.11).

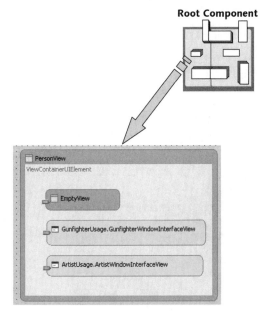

**Figure 11.10** Root Component Window Design: Part 2

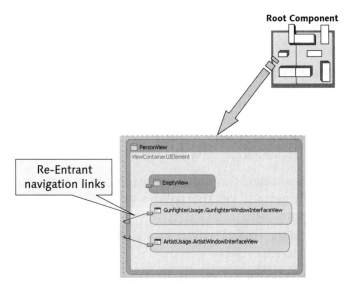

**Figure 11.11** Root Component Window Design: Part 3

Now the root component RootComp can control which child component is visible in the ViewContainerUIElement simply by calling one outbound plug or another in the view PersonView. Then at runtime the application displays one of the two child components (see Figure 11.12).

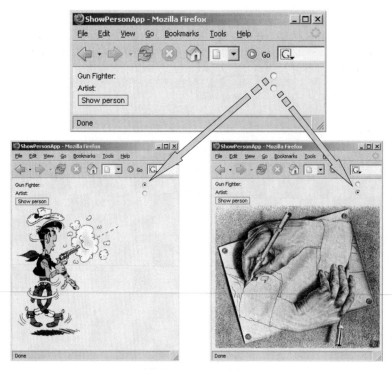

**Figure 11.12** Re-Entrant Navigation Links at Runtime

## 11.2    Suspend and Resume Plugs

Suspend and resume plugs are special types of navigation plugs that allow the Web Dynpro Framework to place an application into a dormant state and then wake it up again. The purpose of suspend and resume plugs is to allow a Web Dynpro application to perform the following sequence of processing:

1. An outbound plug of type suspend belonging to the root component's interface view controller is fired. By means of a browser redirect, the functionality found on an external website is invoked.

2. Whilst the functionality of the external website takes place, the Web Dynpro application is placed in a dormant state.

3. Upon receipt of the corresponding resume plug, the Web Dynpro Framework does the following:

   ▶ Reactivates the suspended application

   ▶ Data received from the external website[3] is made available to the application

   ▶ Business processing continues

---

3  Via an HTTP(S) GET or POST request.

### 11.2.1 Declaring Suspend and Resume Plugs

You will not find suspend and resume plugs in a regular view controller. They exist only in an interface view controller. This is the controller associated with a Web Dynpro window and is responsible for manipulating a component's entire visual interface.

#### Suspend Plugs

A suspend plug is declared in much the same way as any other outbound plug (see Figure 11.13), except for the following differences. A suspend plug:

▶ Can only exist within an interface view controller.

▶ Always has a parameter called Url of type string.

▶ Does not appear as a graphical icon in the window editor. Therefore, you cannot use it as the starting point for a navigation link.

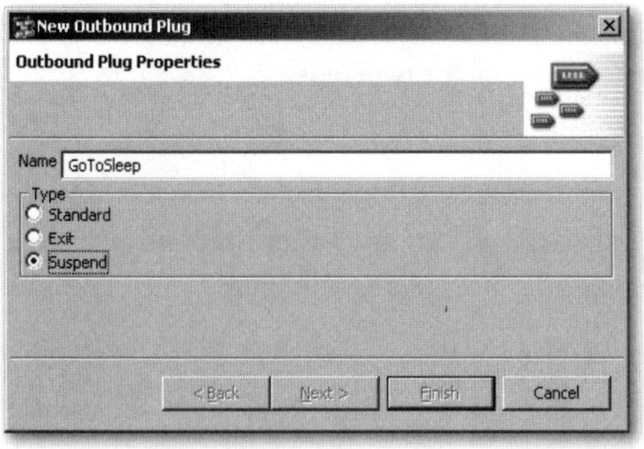

**Figure 11.13** Suspend Plug Declaration in an Interface View Controller

When you want to fire a suspend plug, the coding is exactly the same as for firing any other outbound plug except for the following two differences:

▶ The outbound plugs of an interface view controller belong to its public interface. Therefore, the suspend plug can be fired from outside the interface view controller by any other non-visual controller.

▶ You must know the exact address of the external website and supply this address (plus any required parameters) as the value of the Url parameter to the suspend plug method.

A suspend plug should be fired in the wdDoBeforeNavigation() method of the root component. Do not cut corners by firing a suspend plug directly from a view controller — this will give you a real maintenance headache.

The following code fires a suspend plug called GoToSleep defined in the interface view controller belonging to window ${w}.

```
public void wdDoBeforeNavigation(boolean isCurrentRoot) {
  //@@begin wdDoBeforeNavigation()
  if (isCurrentRoot) {
    String url =
      new String("http://www.whealy.com?p1=val1&p2=val2");
    wdThis.
      wdGet${w}InterfaceViewController().
        wdFirePlugGoToSleep(url);
  }
  //@@end
}
```

**Listing 11.2** The coding to call a suspend plug

---

**Caveat Confector**

Due to the limitations of the HTTP protocol, it is only possible to redirect the browser to the external website using an HTTP(S) GET request. This means any values that need to be passed to the external website must be added to the query string and will therefore appear in plain text.

If the external website requires user authentication, an HTTPS connection should first be opened, followed by a client certificate request from the remote server.

---

**Resume Plugs**

A resume plug is declared in much the same way as any other inbound plug (see Figure 11.14), except for the following differences. A resume plug:

▶ Can only exist within an interface view controller.

▶ Does not appear as a graphical icon in the window editor. Therefore, you cannot use it as the end point of a navigation link.

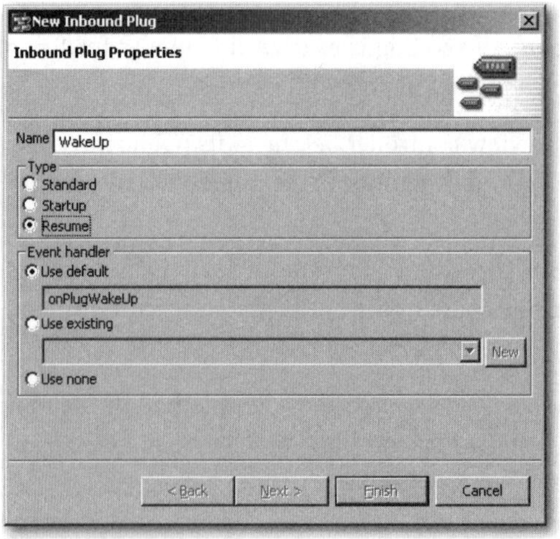

**Figure 11.14** Resume Plug Declaration in an Interface View Controller

The resume plug is called automatically when the Web Dynpro Framework receives the return URL from the external website.

As with any other inbound plug, you must implement the coding within the inbound resume plug method to process the data received from the external website.

### Making an Application Suspendible

For an application to be resumed correctly after it has been suspended, you *must* set the predefined application property `sap.suspensibility` to `true`.

> **Caveat Confector**
>
> If you forget to set the application property `sap.suspensibility` to `true`, your application will not suspend — instead, it will be terminated. Then when the resume request is received, the application will restart using the parameters received from the external website.
>
> This may not cause an application failure in a technical sense, but it will destroy the continuity of your business process.

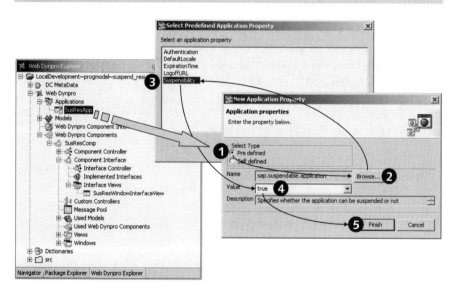

**Figure 11.15** Resume Plug Declaration in an Interface View Controller

Figure 11.15 shows the steps needed to add the suspensibility property to a Web Dynpro application:

1. By double-clicking on the application name, you can create a new application property. Click on the **New** button to bring up the illustrated pop-up window.
2. Browse for the names of the predefined properties.

3. Select **suspensibility**.

4. Set the value to **true**.

5. Click **Finish**.

### 11.2.2 Suspend and Resume Plug Processing

Look back at Sections 4.4.2 and 4.4.12 to remind yourself how the `wdDoApplicationStateChange()` hook method works. This is the method that is responsible for handling any change of state of the entire Web Dynpro application. This includes both suspend and resume processing.

The `doApplicationStateChange` step of the Phase Model is a floating step that conditionally executes either at the start or end of the processing loop.

#### Suspend Plug Processing

The simplest way to implement the coding in the method `doApplicationStateChange()` is to use a finite state engine, and the simplest way to suspend the application is simply do nothing.

If you do nothing when the application state change reason equals SUSPEND, the Web Dynpro Framework will preserve the state of the application for you. However, the application will remain suspended in the AS Java's memory, and then only for the time-out period specified either globally in the AS Java, or locally within the Web Dynpro application itself.

```
public void wdDoApplicationStateChange(
        IWDApplicationStateChangeInfo stateChangeInfo,
        IWDApplicationStateChangeReturn stateChangeReturn) {
  //@@begin wdDoApplicationStateChange()
  //Find out why we have entered the state change method
  String appChangeReason =
    stateChangeInfo.getReason().toString();
  String sessionId = stateChangeInfo.getSessionId();

  // Implement a finite state engine to process the state
  // change reason
  if (appChangeReason.
        equals(WDApplicationStateChangeReason.SUSPEND)) {
    // Implement the coding to tidy up any loose ends before
    // the application is suspended
  }
  else if (appChangeReason.
          equals(WDApplicationStateChangeReason.RESUME)) {
    // Usually, you don't need to do anything here
  }
```

```
else if (appChangeReason.
        equals(WDApplicationStateChangeReason.TIMEOUT)) {
  // The application has timed out, so try to rescue the
  // situation as best as possible.  No interaction with
  // the user is possible here.
  }
//@@end
}
```

**Listing 11.3** Implementing the doApplicationStateChange method as a finite state engine

### Resume Plug Processing

When an external website hands control back to the Web Dynpro Framework, the first thing that happens is that the method wdDoApplicationStateChange() is entered with a state change reason of RESUME.

Usually, there is nothing to do at this time, because the Web Dynpro Framework does everything for you. However, this hook exists to create a time where custom functionality can be added if you need it.

### Resume Plug Parameters

If you have defined any parameters for the resume navigation plug, the Web Dynpro Framework will check to see if these parameters exist in the data returned from the external website. If a match can be found, then the parameter value is automatically supplied to the resume plug parameter. All such resume plug parameters must be of type string.

If the parameters returned from the external website do not match those in the resume plug's signature, or are unknown at design time, then the entire request object can be obtained by calling

```
IWDRequest returnReq =
  WDProtocolAdapter.getProtocolAdapter().getRequestObject();
```

**Listing 11.4** Obtaining the HTTP request object

### 11.2.3 Requirements for an External Website

The external website visited after the Web Dynpro application has been suspended must adhere to the following standards:

▸ Accept and retain the query string parameter value sap-wd-resumeUrl in an unmodified form.

▸ Accept all query string parameters passed from Web Dynpro in the HTTP(S) GET request. Other than the parameter sap-wd-resumeUrl, these parameters are entirely negotiable

▶ It is recommended that the length of the redirect string not exceed 1,024 characters, as certain reverse proxy servers have been known to truncate URLs longer than this.

▶ If the external website requires user authentication, SAP recommends the use of an HTTPS connection followed by a client certificate request from the remote server. This is because all parameters added to an HTTP(S) query string are visible in plain text.

▶ When the user has finished his interaction with the external website, it must provide a button or hypertext link that returns all relevant information back to Web Dynpro using the URL value found in the parameter `sap-wd-resumeUrl`.

▶ The HTTP method used to return data to Web Dynpro can be either GET or POST and can contain as much information as required.

### 11.2.4 Configuring Time-Out Values

Once an application has been suspended by the Web Dynpro Framework,[4] there are three parameters that can control the duration for which an application may remain suspended. Starting from the most generic, global parameter and working to toward the most specific, these are:

▶ The `DefaultExpirationTime` property of the Web Dynpro Framework

  ▷ The default value is 3,600 seconds (1 hour).

  ▷ This is a global parameter that will affect the timeout of all Web Dynpro applications running on this server node — irrespective of whether they are in suspend mode or simply idle through user inactivity.

▶ The `sap.expirationTime` application parameter

  ▷ By default, an application will not have this parameter defined.

  ▷ This is a predefined parameter that controls the period of time for which an application may remain inactive.

  ▷ If this parameter is declared, its value takes precedence over the value of the global parameter `DefaultExpirationTime`.

▶ The `sap.suspendExpirationTime` application parameter

  ▷ By default, an application will not have this parameter defined.

  ▷ This parameter must be added as a self-defined (i.e., defined by the developer) parameter and defines the period of time for which an application may remain suspended within the Web Dynpro Framework.

  ▷ If this parameter is declared, its value takes precedence over the value of the application parameter `sap.expirationTime`.

---

4  Remember that if you suspend an application manually, it can remain timed out for as long as you please.

For applications intended to make automatic use of suspend and resume plugs, SAP recommends that the parameter `sap.suspendExpirationTime` is used so that time-out values can be managed on an application-by-application basis.

If you want to modify the global time-out value for the entire server node, the `DefaultExpirationTime` property can be configured by starting the Visual Administrator for the required server node. Once you have expanded the required the server node instance, select **Services** • **Configuration Adapter** and expand the structure on the **Display configuration** tab to **webdynpro** • **sap.com** • **tc~wd~dis-pwda** • **Propertysheet Default** (see Figure 11.16).

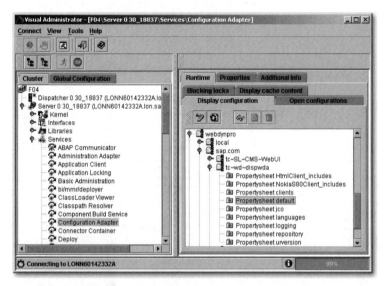

**Figure 11.16** Finding the Property Sheet Containing the DefaultExpirationTime Property

After clicking on the pencil icon in the toolbar to switch to edit mode, double-click on **Propertysheet default** and edit the property value (see Figure 11.17).

| name ▲ | value | custom |
|---|---|---|
| AccessibilityChecksEnabled | false | ☐ |
| ActivateURLParameters | true | ☐ |
| AllowUserPersonalization | true | ☐ |
| DefaultExpirationTime | 3600 | ☐ |
| DefaultServerSessionAtLeastOne... | 2 | ☐ |
| DevelopmentMode | true | ☐ |
| IGSUrl | | ☐ |
| ValidateByRendering | true | ☐ |
| ZipResponse | false | ☐ |
| sap.acf.adobe.CABFileVersion | default | ☐ |
| sap.defaultConnectionTimeOut | 30 | ☐ |

OK

**Figure 11.17** Editing the DefaultExpirationTime Property

If, however, you want to create a custom time-out value for each application, then declare the self-defined application property `sap.suspendExpirationTime` to have your required value. This can be done by following the steps shown in Figure 11.18:

1. By double-clicking on the application name, you can create a new application property. Click on the **New** button to bring up the illustrated pop-up window.

2. Enter the property name `sap.suspendExpirationTime` in the name field. Remember, this value is case sensitive.

3. Add some value appropriate for you application, for example, 1,200 seconds (20 minutes).

4. Click **Finish**.

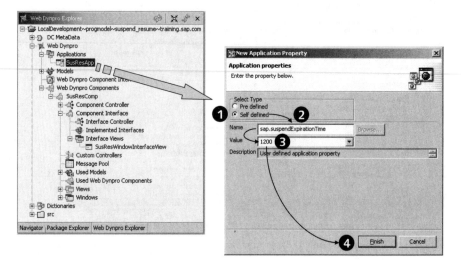

**Figure 11.18** Setting the Application Property sap.expirationTime

## 11.3 Error Handling

The way in which your Web Dynpro application handles errors must be thought about carefully during the design phase. The reason is that as your application grows in size, there will be an increase in the number of places in which errors could occur.

For small Web Dynpro applications that are built from only two or three components, the guidelines discussed in the following section will be somewhat excessive, but as the number of components in your Web Dynpro application grows, the need for centralized error management will increase.

The first thing to identify, therefore, is all the possible times during Phase Model processing at which an application error could occur (see Figure 11.19).

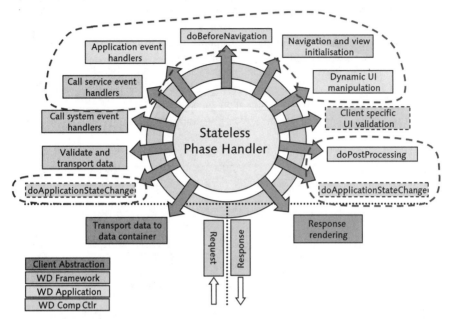

**Figure 11.19** Any Error Could Occur, Well … Almost Anywhere!

As you can see, the results are not very specific. An error could occur at virtually any step of the Phase Model processing, so let's narrow things down somewhat.

### 11.3.1 The Input and Output Halves of the Phase Model Processing

Phase Model processing is divided into two halves, and the manner in which errors are processed depends on *when* the error took place. The Navigation and View Initialisation step of the Phase Model marks the division between the input and output halves of the processing cycle (see Figure 11.20).

Since view controllers are not responsible for generating the data they display, the errors that occur after navigation should be related *only* to view initialization and UI hierarchy construction.

Calls to the IWDMessageManager should be avoided during view initialization and UI manipulation.

> **Caveat Confector**
>
> All processing on the input half of the Phase Model processing is concerned with reacting to the input just received from the user. This involves input validation followed by calls to the backend system to perform the required step(s) of the business process.

Once the Phase Model enters the Navigation and View Initialisation step, you should consider all business processing to have completed and the contexts of the various view controllers to be populated. The output half of the Phase Model processing should be concerned only with the construction of the next view assembly.

If you blur the distinction between the processing performed during the input and output halves, you will create an application that is much harder to maintain. Thus, you have increased the application's total cost of ownership. This is unnecessary and quite avoidable if these architectural principles are followed.

However, there are no wizards or code checking tools to force you to follow these guidelines. They must be followed as a matter of programmer discipline.

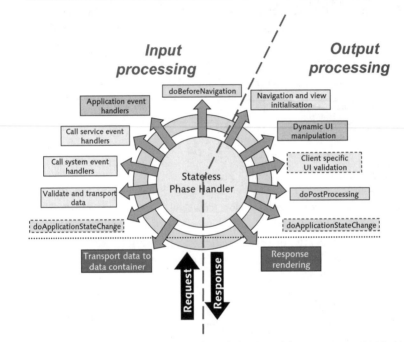

**Figure 11.20** The Input and Output Halves of Phase Model Processing are Divided by Navigation Processing

### 11.3.2 Centralized Error Handling

Each half of the Phase Model processing finishes with a special method. The input half (i.e., before the navigation queue is processed) finishes with the wdDoBefore-Navigation() method, and the output half finishes with the doPostProcessing() method.

It is within these methods that the error processing for each half of the Phase Model cycle should be located. As a result of error processing during wdDoBeforeNavigation(), it may be necessary to modify or even abort navigation processing. Therefore, you should consider the processing that handles errors before navigation and the processing that handles navigation to be closely related.

Let's say a particular view controller has determined that the user entered an invalid combination of data. Should the view controller issue a message immediately, or should the error be reported up to the component controller for centralized processing?

Well, the answer depends on the complexity of your business application. For applications that have a small number of views in a component, it might be quite acceptable to have the view controller issue the error message directly. However, in cases where data spread across multiple views (or even components) must be analyzed before navigation can take place, one view cannot know about the data in any other view (or component); therefore, in this situation, error processing and navigation should be centralized within the root component's component controller.

---

**Caveat Confector**

Error processing and navigation processing are very closely related, because if error processing fails, you will probably not want to perform any navigation until the errors have been cleared.

Consequently, the `wdDoBeforeNavigation()` method should be seen as the centralized location within a component in which all pre-navigation errors are handled. Only when the errors have been corrected should the navigation processing be allowed to proceed.

This style of coding is required because you cannot process the navigation queue selectively: It's all or nothing. Therefore, view controllers should not waste time firing their own outbound navigation plugs if errors could occur in other controllers that would then force navigation processing to be aborted.

The consequence of centralized error handling is that navigation plugs are only fired *after* all view controllers have reported that they are not in an error state.

---

### Reporting Errors from a View Controller to the Component Controller

The easiest way for a view controller to report an error state to the component controller is by creating a dedicated node in the component controller's context and then mapping it through to the view controller(s).

The context node used to report errors should contain attributes that describe the information that would be passed to the `IWDMessageManager` if the view controller were to raise the message itself.

In Figure 11.21 we have a context node called `ValidationError` that has the following attributes:

▶ `AttributeInfo` holds the metadata of the context attribute containing the invalid value.

▶ `Element` holds the element of the node collection containing the invalid value.

▶ `Message` holds the message to be displayed by the message manager.

▶ `MessageParm1..n` hold any parameters needed for the message. Four attributes have been created here, but this number is completely arbitrary.

▶ `MsgMgrInst` holds a reference to this component's message manager. This value is only needed if error information is to be passed from a child component up to a parent component.

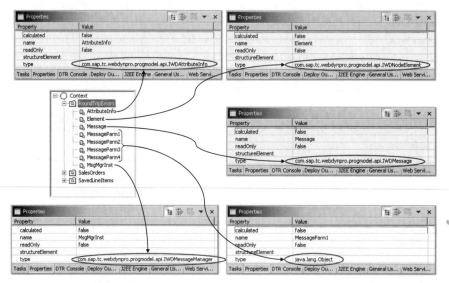

**Figure 11.21** Context Node for Error Handling

The purpose of this error node is to act as a repository for all error information. The node shown in Figure 11.21 is suitable for holding any type of error, irrespective of whether it occurred before or after navigation.

Rather than allowing each view controller to issue its own error messages,[5] they should write their error information to this context node. Then when the `wdDoBeforeNavigation()` method is reached, the component controller can analyze the situation and decide whether to proceed with navigation.

Each view controller should then have access (via context mapping) to the error node in the component controller. This is shown in Figure 11.22.

```
public void wdDoBeforeNavigation(boolean isCurrentRoot) {
    //@@begin wdDoBeforeNavigation()
    boolean errorFlag = false;

    // Only process errors if I'm the root component
    if (isCurrentRoot) {
```

---

5  This includes allowing for the possibility that a view controller could abort the processing of the entire navigation queue.

```
// Get a reference to the error node
IRoundTripErrorsNode rtErr =
  wdContext.nodeRoundTripErrors();
int i = rtErr.size();

// Is there anything in it?
if (i > 0) {
  IRoundTripErrorsElement thisEl = null;
  WDMessage thisMsg;

  // Process each error message
  for (int j = 0; j < i; j++) {
    thisEl = rtErr.getRoundTripErrorsElementAt(j);

    // Treat the message as a WDMessage object
    thisMsg = (WDMessage)thisEl.getMessage();

    // How bad is it?
    if (thisMsg.getType().equals(WDMessageType.ERROR))
      errorFlag = true;

    // Gather together any message parameters
    Object[] parms = {thisEl.getMessageParm1(),
                      thisEl.getMessageParm2(),
                      thisEl.getMessageParm3(),
                      thisEl.getMessageParm4() };

    // How should this message be displayed?
    // Is there any associated context information?
    if (thisEl.getElement()        != null &&
        thisEl.getAttributeInfo() != null) {
      // Yes, so display a context related message
      // without cancelling navigation
      thisEl.
        getMsgMgrInst().
          reportContextAttributeMessage(
            thisEl.getElement(),
            thisEl.getAttributeInfo(),
            thisEl.getMessage(),
            parms,
            false);
    }
    // No, context information was not supplied
    else
      thisEl.getMsgMgrInst().
        reportMessage(thisEl.getMessage(), parms, false);
  }

  // Since all the messages have now been processed,
```

```
      // invalidate the context node. This is necessary
      // because the same node will be used for errors that
      // happen after navigation
      rtErr.invalidate();
    }
    // Do navigation processing here
    if (errorFlag) {
      // At least one message of type ERROR was issued so
      // you'll probably not want to perform any navigation
    }
    else {
      // No ERROR messages were issued, so raise the
      // necessary events to cause navigation to occur
    }
  }
  //@@end
}
```

**Listing 11.5** doBeforeNavigation method coding to display any errors that may have occurred during action event handler processing

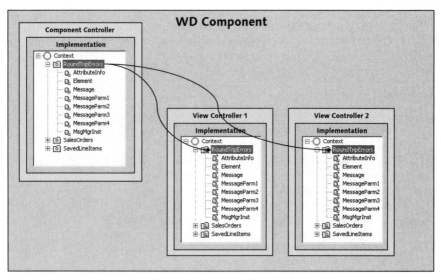

**Figure 11.22** The Context Node for Error Handling Should be Mapped Through to the View Controllers

### 11.3.3 Error Handling Across a Component Hierarchy

You may have noticed that the context node shown in Figure 11.21 contains an attribute for the message manager instance. If you are only handling the errors from a single component, this attribute is redundant. However, if you are processing the errors from multiple components, this attribute is vital.

**Message Managers and Message Scope**

Each Web Dynpro component contains its own specific instance of the class IWDMessageManager. Not only is the message manager instance specific to the component, but so are the message objects themselves (these are instances of the class WDMessage).

Let's say that a child component called DisplayOrdersComp has a message called CONNECTION_ERROR defined within it. We know that both the message and the message manager instance required to display this message are specific to the component DisplayOrdersComp. Therefore, if you were to pass a reference to the message CONNECTION_ERROR outside the scope of the component DisplayOrdersComp, it would be completely meaningless within the scope of the receiving component.

Therefore, when message references are to be passed from a child component up to a parent component, a reference to the child component's message manager must also be passed. Then, when the parent component needs to display the message, it does so by invoking a method in the child component's message manager. This is what the coding in Listing 11.5 does.

**Centralized Handling of Errors that Occur in Child Components**

In order for there to be effective management of errors across a component hierarchy, it is very important that the child components report their errors up to the root component as soon as they are detected.

The reason for this is that when the Phase Model enters the doBeforeNavigation or doPostProcessing steps, the associated standard hook methods are called starting at the top of the component hierarchy. This means the root component's wdDoBeforeNavigation() method will already have executed by the time the same hook method is called in any child component. Therefore, any functionality you place in such standard hook methods of child components will always run *after* the corresponding method has run in the parent component.

Figure 11.23 shows how a child component should report errors up to its parent component.

The following steps are performed:

1. An error is detected during action handler processing in a child component. The architecture of this application is sufficiently complex that the child component cannot know whether this error is serious enough to require navigation to be aborted; therefore, it must report the error up to the parent component for centralized processing.

2. For the child to report this error up to the parent, it must call an error handling method in the interface controller.

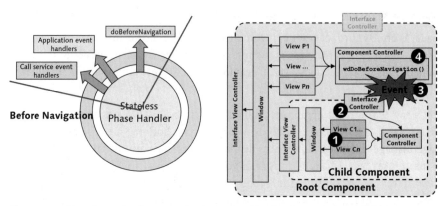

**Figure 11.23** Error Reporting Sequence During Action Handler Processing in a Child Component

3. The error handling method in the interface controller then raises an event and passes as event parameters all the information needed to describe the error. A method in the root (or parent) component then subscribes to this event and stores the error information in a dedicated context node. In this case, the event handler method that logs errors has been given the arbitrary name of handleEr-rors().

4. Only when the event handler processing for all views in the view assembly has finished, does the Phase Model then move from the Application Event Handlers step to the doBeforeNavigation step. By the time this step is entered, all child components must *already* have reported their errors up to the root component. Now, when the doBeforeNavigation step is entered, the method wdDoBeforeNav-igation() is called first in the root component. This is the only time the isCur-rentRoot parameter to wdDoBeforeNavigation() will be set to true, and this is the point at which error management should take place. See Listing 11.5 for details.

### 11.3.4 Principles for Handling Errors Trapped Before Navigation

Here are some general principles that should be followed when processing errors trapped *before* navigation.

▶ In general, there are several places where errors could occur before navigation. These are during:

  ▷ Action handler processing in view controllers

  ▷ Supply function execution

  ▷ Processing of calculated attributes

  ▷ Value Help requests (Object Value Selectors)

▶ Generally speaking, errors originating in view controller action handlers interrupt navigation, usually by postponing it until after the error has been corrected. This, of course, will not be the case if the round trip was caused by a non-validating action.

▶ Unless your application has very a simple view assembly structure, navigation decisions based upon the validity of user input should be delayed until the doBeforeNavigation step of the root component. This is particularly true for applications where the functionality is provided by a hierarchy of components. In this situation, only the root component will have a global perspective on the data spread across all the child components.

▶ If it is acceptable in your architecture for a view controller is to issue a message directly, then avoid setting the cancelNavigation parameter to true, as this will negate any subsequent navigation logic in the method wdDoBeforeNavigation().

▶ Apart from the raisePendingException() method, calls to any of the message manager's raise...() methods will *never* return control to the application code. These methods should be used for reporting fatal errors only.

▶ All standard hook methods are executed by the Web Dynpro Framework in a top-to-bottom manner. This has the following consequences:

  ▶ For pre-navigation errors to be handled centrally by the wdDoBeforeNavigation() method *in the root component*, the information must have arrived there *before* the DoBeforeNavigation step of the phase model is reached.

  ▶ This can only be achieved if the child components fire events from methods in their interface controllers during the Application Event Handlers step of the phase model. The root (or parent) component then responds to these events and accumulates the data in an error reporting node such as the one shown above in Figure 11.21.

### 11.3.5 Principles for Handling Errors Trapped After Navigation

Here are some general principles that should be followed when processing errors trapped *after* navigation.

▶ In general, there are several places where errors could occur after navigation. These are during:

  ▶ View initialization or destruction, that is, the wdDoInit() and wdDoExit() standard hook methods of a view controller.

  ▶ Component initialization — if navigation causes the interface view controller of a child component to be referenced for the first time.

  ▶ Inbound plug processing (onPlug${p_{in}}())

  ▶ UI element hierarchy processing (wdDoModifyView())

- ▸ Supply function execution

- ▸ Processing of calculated attributes

► Any attempt to call the message manager with the `cancelNavigation` parameter set to `true` will be ignored. In certain circumstances, it could lead to the Web Dynpro Framework aborting your entire application.

► Calling any one of the message manager's `raise...()` methods will immediately terminate your application, leaving the UI tree in a potentially undefined state, thus making it impossible to report the error state back to the user in a graceful manner. In other words, you'll be sending the user a stack trace.

► As with errors trapped before navigation, information about error situations detected after navigation should be written to a context node in the root component and reported by coding in the `wdDoPostProcessing()` method.

► Once the `doPostProcessing` step of the Phase Model has been entered, the entire UI element hierarchy will *already* have been rendered for browser-based users. See Section 4.4.10 to remind yourself of what happens in the `Client Specific UI Validation` step.

► Any call to the message manager from within the `doPostProcessing` step will alter the UI element hierarchy, thus forcing the entire UI tree to be re-rendered. For efficiency, therefore, you should only report serious or fatal errors during the `doPostProcessing` step.

► All standard hook methods are executed by the Web Dynpro Framework in a top-to-bottom manner. This has the following consequences:

- ▸ For post-navigation errors to be handled centrally by the `wdDoPostProcessing()` method *in the root component*, the information must have arrived there *before* the `doPostProcessing` step of the Phase Model is reached.

- ▸ This can only be achieved by the child components firing events during the `View Initialisation` and `Dynamic UI manipulation` steps of the Phase Model. The root (or parent) component then responds to these events and accumulates the data in an error reporting node such as the one shown in Figure 11.21 above.

# 12    Components at Runtime

In this chapter we take a look at some diverse topics related to the functionality and behavior of Web Dynpro components.

The first section looks at how Web Dynpro components can make use of the object-oriented principle of polymorphism.

In object-oriented design theory, any time two classes are derived from the same parent class (or interface), the behavior of any inherited methods can vary in the child classes. So, for example, let's say an interface has been defined for a `Person`, and this interface contains a `greet()` method. Now let's derive two child classes from the `Person` class called `Yorkshireman` and `Geordie`.[1]

Both of these child classes implement the `greet()` method in their own distinctive way: When you call `Yorkshireman.greet()` you'll hear "Ay up, lad!", and when you call `Geordie.greet()` you'll hear "Y'areet, pet?".

Any class operating with the `Person` class as implemented by either the `Yorkshireman` or the `Geordie` classes does not need to care about exactly *how* the `greet()` method works. All they need to know is that the method exists and it will do something specific to the child class when you call it. This principle is known as *polymorphism*.

The second section looks at the various types of pop-up window that can be used within a Web Dynpro application.

Finally, the last section looks at properties that can be assigned to Web Dynpro applications and properties that can be derived from the URL that invoked the Web Dynpro application.

## 12.1    Web Dynpro Components and Polymorphism

If you look back at Section 11.1.5, you will remember that a component called `RootComp` was created that used two child components called `GunfighterComp` and `ArtistComp`. The architecture of that example required that `RootComp` made a direct usage declaration for each of the two child components. In other words, a tight coupling relationship exists between the parent component and the two child components.

---

1  Anyone who comes from the city of Newcastle in the north of England is known as a *Geordie*.

Now go back and look at Section 3.5.2 and remind yourself about the concept of a component interface definition (CID). Here is where we can turn that theory into practice by modifying the example in Section 11.1.5 to use a CID.

To reduce how tightly the parent component `RootComp` is bound to the child components, a CID can be created that will become the child component used by `RootComp`.

Within a CID, you may define the following things:

▸ An interface controller with

    ▸ A context

    ▸ Methods

    ▸ Events

▸ An interface view definition with

    ▸ Inbound plugs

    ▸ Outbound plugs

▸ Used models

In the example in Figure 12.1, a CID called `PersonInterface` has been created. The purpose of this is to define a generic interface structure for any component that implements this interface. Within this CID, a method called `draw()` has been declared within the interface controller.

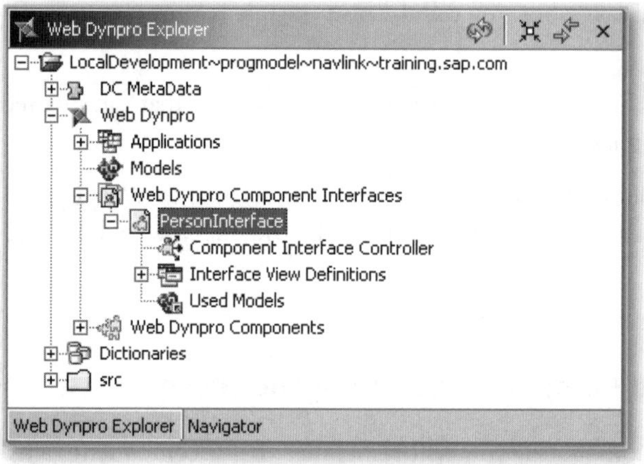

**Figure 12.1** A Component Interface Definition

The next step is to modify both the `ArtistComp` and `GunfighterComp` definitions. These two components are both examples of a type of person; therefore, we will add `PersonInterface` as an implemented interface to both of these components (see Figure 12.2).

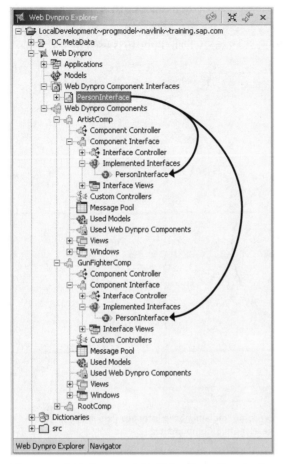

**Figure 12.2** ArtistComp and GunFighterComp Now Implement the PersonInterface

As soon as this declaration is made, the consuming components (ArtistComp and GunFighterComp) immediately have the interface structure defined in PersonInterface copied into their own interfaces. This means both ArtistComp and GunFighterComp now have a draw() method in their interface controllers.

> **Caveat Confector**
>
> When a component declares the use of a CID, the interface structure is *copied* into the consuming component and not *inherited* in the true object-oriented sense.
>
> This means that if you change the structure of a component interface definition after it has been declared for use, the changes will *not* be replicated into the consuming components. They must be implemented manually.

As a result of ArtistComp and GunFighterComp both implementing the CID PersonInterface, the top-level component RootComp no longer needs to declare a direct usage of these two child components; instead, it simply declares a single usage of PersonInterface. In Figure 12.3, you can see that both ArtistComp and GunFighterComp implement the CID PersonInterface, which, in turn, is used by RootComp.

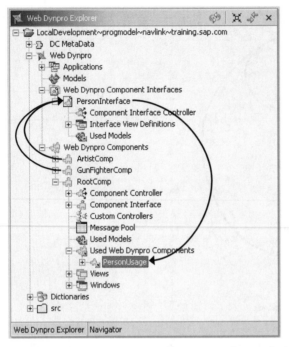

Figure 12.3 ArtistComp and GunFighterComp Implement the Interface PersonInterface, and RootComp Implements PersonInterface as a Child Component

With this architecture, RootComp need not know anything about which specific component is providing the implementation found behind PersonInterface. All it cares about is that it can call the draw() method, and *a* component will respond — be it ArtistComp or GunFighterComp.

In this example, if ArtistComp is sitting behind PersonInterface, when you call the draw() method, he'll get his pencils, but if GunFighterComp is sitting behind the interface, calling the draw() method will make him go for his guns.

For the different components to be interchangeable, it is necessary to modify the structure of RootComp's window. If you look back at Figure 11.11, you will see that it was necessary to embed the interface view controllers of both ArtistComp and GunFighterComp into RootComp's PersonView.

This structure is now no longer necessary because we can make use of the interface view defined in the CID. Now we only need one re-entrant navigation link and one interface view instead of two (see Figure 12.5).

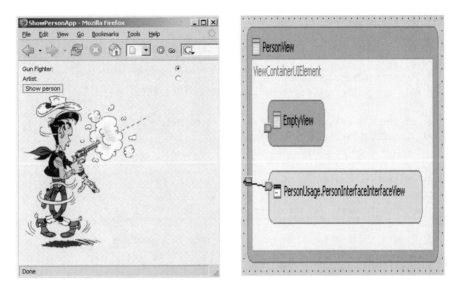

"Draw!" means one thing to a Gun Fighter,
but something completely different to an Artist!

**Figure 12.4** Polymorphism at Work Through a CID

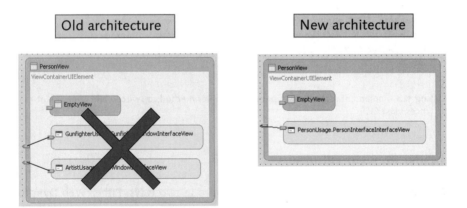

**Figure 12.5** Now Only One Interface View Needs To Be Embedded Into PersonView

The user can select which child component he wants to see by selecting the appropriate radio button and then pressing the **Show Person** button. Depending on which radio button is selected, it will write either the string Artist or GunFighter into a mapped context node called SelectedPerson.Person.

Behind the **Show Person** button is an action handler method that calls the method chooseComponent() in the component controller of RootComp. This method is implemented as follows:

```
public void ChooseComponent() {
  //@@begin ChooseComponent()
  // Get a reference to the component interface definition
  // usage
  IWDComponentUsage compUsage =
    wdThis.wdGetPersonInterfaceUsageComponentUsage();

  // If there is already an active instance, delete it
  if (compUsage.hasActiveComponent())
    compUsage.deleteComponent();

  // Which person did the user select?
  ISelectedPersonElement selPers =
    wdContext.currentSelectedPersonElement();

  // Create the component instance using the full package
  // name based on which person the user selected
  if (selPers.getPerson().equals("Artist"))
    compUsage.createComponent("com.sap.artist.ArtistComp");
  else
    compUsage.
      createComponent("com.sap.gunfighter.GunFighterComp");

  // Via the component interface definition, call the draw
  // method. This will work without needing to know which
  // specific child component is sitting behind the interface
  wdThis.wdGetPersonUsageInterface().draw();
  //@@end
}
```

**Listing 12.1** Implementation of a component controller method to switch child component instances via a CID

## 12.2    Pop-Up Windows

Pop-up windows are managed by Web Dynpro in two ways. Either Web Dynpro maintains control of the pop-up window after it has been created, or it does not. If Web Dynpro maintains control, two types of pop-up window can be presented; so in all, three types of pop-up can be created by Web Dynpro (see Figure 12.6). These can be summarized as follows:

▶ Web Dynpro maintains control by opening a pop-up window that persists for:

   ▶ Only a single round trip

   ▶ Multiple round trips

▶ Web Dynpro opens a new browser window and subsequently has no further control over the new window's content.

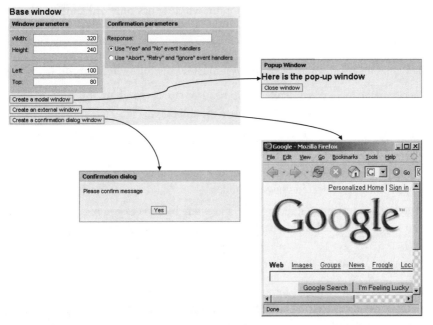

**Figure 12.6** Three Distinct Types of Pop-Up Windows

| Important |
| --- |
| In the SAP NetWeaver 7.0 version of Web Dynpro (formerly known as SAP NetWeaver 2004s), pop-up windows cannot be moved or resized. In the SAP NetWeaver 7.0 release of Web Dynpro for ABAP and the SAP NetWeaver 7.1 release of Web Dynpro for Java (known as Composition Environment), this restriction does not exist. |

### 12.2.1 Single Round-Trip Pop-Up Window

This type of pop-up window is known as a confirmation dialog, because it is present on the screen only for a single round trip. The configuration possibilities of such a pop-up window are limited to presenting some descriptive text and one or more buttons.

To create a confirmation dialog, all that is needed is for you to choose which action event handler methods will be used to process the events raised by each button in the pop-up.

**Figure 12.7** A Simple Confirmation Dialog

In Figure 12.7, you can see that the pop-up window has only one button. Therefore, only one action event handler method is needed to handle the event raised when this button is pushed.

When creating a confirmation dialog you must do the following things:

▶ Decide which view controller will be used to respond to the button push event(s) coming back from the confirmation dialog.

▶ Create as many action event handlers in the selected view controller as there are buttons on the confirmation dialog.

▶ Instruct the Web Dynpro component that it should create a confirmation dialog object using the selected view controller.

▶ Add to the confirmation dialog object as many buttons as you require (each button being associated with a particular action event handler in the view controller).

▶ Display the confirmation dialog.

Notice what is *not* required here. Even though we must choose the use of a view controller, at no time do we need to worry about the view's layout. The only role performed by the view controller is to act as a container for the action event handlers that will receive control when a particular button is pushed. The view layout of the chosen view controller will never be used in a confirmation dialog.

---

**Important**

When you create a confirmation dialog, you have no control over the layout. Remember, this type of pop-up window exists only for a single round trip, so your design should not require there to be anything more than a selection of buttons for the user to click. When creating the confirmation dialog, you simply add buttons to the pop-up window, and the Web Dynpro Framework will lay them out for you.

Each button must have a dedicated action event handler method associated with it. It is not possible to add a parameter to each button so that a single action event handler can distinguish which button was clicked. See Section 7.9 for more details on parameter mapping.

---

The code in Listing 12.2 shows a method called `createConfDialog()`. This method exists in the following situation:

▶ The method `createConfDialog()` exists in the component controller and *not* a view controller.

▶ It will be called by an action event handler in a view controller when the user needs to confirm a certain task.

▶ The view controller called `FirstView` is nominated to handle the button push events that come back from the pop-up window.

▶ We will add a **Yes** and a **No** button to the confirmation dialog. The events raised when these buttons are clicked will be handled by action event handler methods of the same name.

▶ The action event handler methods `yes()` and `no()` have already been created in view controller `FirstView`.

```
public void createConfDialog( ) {
  //@@begin createConfDialogWindow()
  // Get a reference to both the window manager and the view
  // controller's metadata
  IWDWindowManager  winMgr =
    wdComponentAPI.getWindowManager();

  IWDControllerInfo viewCntlrInfo =
    wdComponentAPI.getComponentInfo().
      findInViews("FirstView").getViewController();

  // A confirmation dialog must be created with at least one
  // button. Therefore, when the pop-up window is created,
  // the event handler for the first button must also be
  // supplied .
  IWDEventHandlerInfo    evtHndlr   =
    viewCntlrInfo.findInEventHandlers("Yes");
  IWDConfirmationDialog confDialog = winMgr.
    createConfirmationDialog("You chose \"Yes\" and \"No\"",
                             evtHndlr, evtHndlr.getName());

  // Find the event handler for the "No" option, and add it
  // as another choice to the existing dialog window
  evtHndlr = viewCntlrInfo.findInEventHandlers("No");
  confDialog.addChoice(evtHndlr, evtHndlr.getName());

  // Show confirmation dialog
  confDialog.show();
  //@@end
}
```

**Listing 12.2** Creating a confirmation dialog pop-up window

This confirmation dialog will close automatically after the user has made a single selection, and control is then passed to the nominated action event handler in the view controller in the normal way.

> **Important**
>
> There are two ways to create a confirmation dialog. In the above code, notice that the confirmation dialog is created using a call to the method `createConfirmationDialog()`. However, there is also a method called `createConfirmationWindow()`.

The difference between them is that if you call `createConfirmationWindow()`, you will not be able to add any more buttons to the pop-up. You will be limited to a single button.

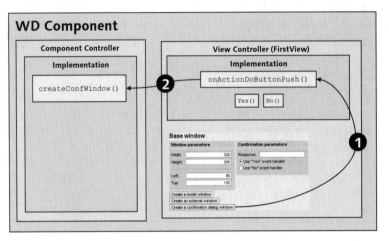

**Figure 12.8** The Process Flow to Create a Confirmation Dialog

Notice what coding has *not* been implemented in Listing 12.2. Although it is technically possible to do so, the view controller does not create the pop-up window itself. Controlling the flow of logic is not the responsibility of a view controller. Therefore, when the user clicks the button on the client (step ❶ in Figure 12.8), the action handler method in the view controller (`onActionDoButtonPush()`; step ❷) calls a method in the component controller in order for the confirmation dialog to be created (step ❸ in Figure 12.9).

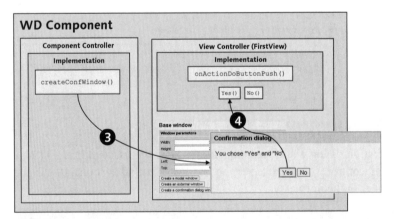

**Figure 12.9** The Process Flow After a Confirmation Dialog Button Has Been Clicked

Then when the user clicks one of the buttons in the confirmation pop-up, the appropriate action handler method is called in the associated view controller (step ❹).

## 12.2.2 Multiple Round-Trip Pop-Up Windows

We can take what we have learned about single round-trip pop-up windows and extend it to create a pop-up window that persists for multiple round trips. Such a pop-up window is known as a modal window.

From a technical perspective, there are two main differences between a confirmation dialog and a modal window. A modal window requires:

▶ A dedicated window in your Web Dynpro component to define its contents

▶ A distinct instance of the Phase Handler to process round trips originating from this window (see Figure 12.10)

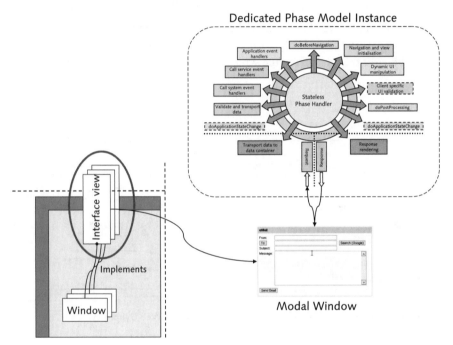

**Figure 12.10** The Round Trips from a Modal Window Are Processed in a New Instance of the Phase Model

When creating a modal window, you must first have prepared a dedicated window in your Web Dynpro component and embedded at least one view into it (see Figure 12.11). It must be understood that because this pop-up window persists for multiple round trips, a distinct event must be raised to close this window.

The code in Listing 12.3 shows how to create and destroy a modal window and exists in the following situation:

▶ The method `createModalWindow()` exists in a component controller and *not* in a view controller.

▶ It will be called by an action event handler in a view controller when the pop-up needs to be created.

▶ A window called PopupWindow has already been created and a single view called SecondView has been embedded into it.

▶ Multiple round trips can take place whilst the modal window is visible. All of the events raised by the pop-up window are handled by SecondView, since this is the only view in the currently active view assembly (i.e., the views embedded into window PopupWindow).

▶ Closing the modal window requires a distinct event to be raised. The actual event used for closing a modal window is completely arbitrary, but the point is, one must exist.

▶ In this example, the dimensions and position of the modal window are received from a context node called WindowParameters. The user can enter values into the attributes of this node from the screen that creates the pop-up window.

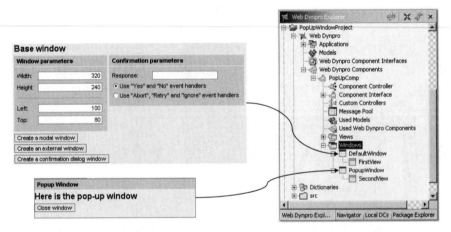

**Figure 12.11** A Modal Pop-Up Is Implemented in a Dedicated Web Dynpro Window

The coding for the method createModalWindow() is as follows. Notice that a separate method also exists for closing the modal window.

```
public void createModalWindow( ) {
  //@@begin createModalWindow()
  // Get a reference to the window's metadata
  IWDWindowInfo winInfo = wdComponentAPI.getComponentInfo().
                          findInWindows("PopupWindow");

  // Create a runtime modal window using the metadata object
  modalWindow = wdComponentAPI.getWindowManager().
                createModalWindow(winInfo);
```

```
// Set the window's dimensions and position using values
// from the WindowParameters context node
IWindowParametersElement winParms =
    wdContext.currentWindowParametersElement();

modalWindow.setWindowSize(winParms.getWidth(),
                          winParms.getHeight());
modalWindow.setWindowPosition(winParms.getLeft(),
                              winParms.getTop());

// Open modal window
modalWindow.show();
//@@end
}

public void destroyModalWindow( ) {
    //@@begin destroyModalWindow()
    modalWindow.destroyInstance();
    //@@end
}

//@@begin others
IWDWindow modalWindow;
//@@end
```

**Listing 12.3** Creating and destroying a modal window

Notice that the modalWindow object is declared outside the scope of either the cre-ateModalWindow() or destroMModalWindow() methods.

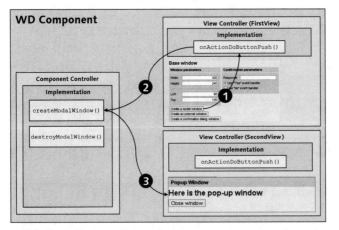

**Figure 12.12** Process Flow To Create a Modal Pop-Up Window

In Figure 12.12, the user clicks on a button to open the pop-up modal window, and this causes the associated action event handler to be called in the view controller (step ❶). The view controller method *does not* create the pop-up window itself; instead, it calls a dedicated method in the component controller (step ❷).

Once the modal window is displayed (step ❸), it persists on the screen until the user explicitly decides to close it (step ❹ in Figure 12.13). The method to close the pop-up window does not belong to the view controller; instead, the associated action event handler in the view controller calls a dedicated method in the component controller to close the pop-up window (step ❺).

While the pop-up window is visible, the screen from which it was created remains visible in the background but will not be accessible. Only one window can be active for a Web Dynpro application at any one time.

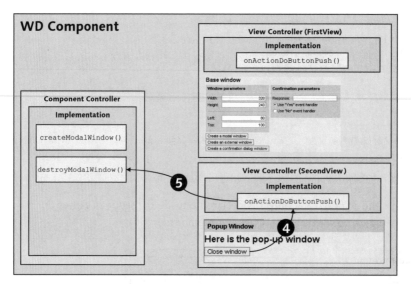

**Figure 12.13** Process Flow To Destroy a Modal Pop-Up Window

---

**Caveat Confector**

The view(s) embedded into the Web Dynpro window used for the modal pop-up must include a button of some sort to allow the user to close the window. Without this, your application will become trapped in the modal window's functionality and be unable to return to the window that created it.

---

### 12.2.3   Opening an External Window

The key difference here is that after Web Dynpro has opened a new browser window (known as an *external window*; see Figure 12.14), it looses all ability to communicate with that window. When you open this type of window, think of it as a "fire-and-forget" process: The applications running in these two windows have no communication with each other.

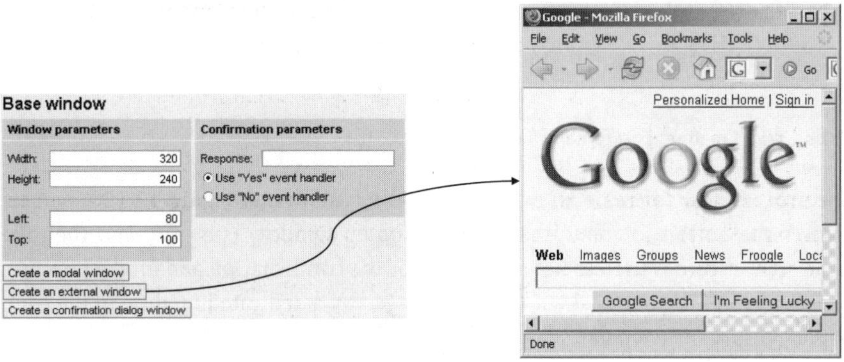

**Figure 12.14** Opening an External Browser Window

The coding to open an external window is much like the coding to open a confirmation dialog. The coding shown in Listing 12.4 has been implemented in a similar set of circumstances:

▶ The method `createExternalWindow()` exists in the component controller and *not* in a view controller

▶ It will be called by a view controller when the user wants to visit a different website without terminating the current Web Dynpro application.

▶ In this example, the dimensions and position of the modal window are received from a context node called `WindowParameters`. The user can enter values into the attributes of this node from the screen that creates the external window.

▶ An external window cannot be closed from Web Dynpro, so it is impossible to implement such a method as `destroyExternalWindow()`.

```
public void createExternalWindow( ) {
  //@@begin createExternalWindow()
  // Create a runtime external window object
  IWDWindow externalWindow =
    wdComponentAPI.getWindowManager().
      createNonModalExternalWindow("http://www.whealy.com",
                                   "External window");

  // Set the window's dimensions and position using values
  // from the WindowParameters context node
  IWindowParametersElement winParms =
    wdContext.currentWindowParametersElement();

  externalWindow.setWindowSize(winParms.getWidth(),
                               winParms.getHeight());
  externalWindow.setWindowPosition(winParms.getLeft(),
                                   winParms.getTop());
  // Open external window.  Once this method has executed,
```

```
// Web Dynpro looses all communication with the window
externalWindow.show();
//@@end
}
```

**Listing 12.4** Creating an external window

The process flow to create an external window is shown in Figure 12.15. The user presses the button to create the external pop-up window (step ❶), and then the same architecture is used as has been used for the confirmation and modal pop-ups. The creation of the external window is managed by a dedicated method in the component controller (step ❷).

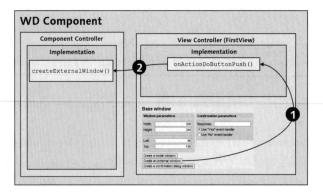

**Figure 12.15** The View Controller Calls a Method in the Component Controller To Create the External Window

Once the external window has been created, no further communication is possible between the applications running in these two windows (step ❸ in Figure 12.16).

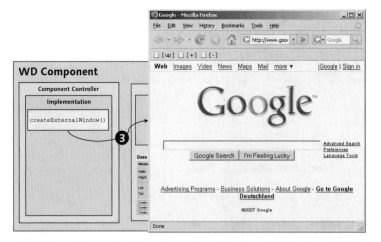

**Figure 12.16** The External Window Is Now Completely Independent of Anything Happening in Web Dynpro

The full example of the application demonstrated here can be downloaded from the SAP PRESS web pages for this book at *www.sap-press.com* and *www.sap-press.de/1243*.

## 12.3 Application and URL Properties

It is often helpful to associate certain properties with a Web Dynpro application. These properties can then be examined and used to modify the behavior of the application. Such properties are known as application properties and should not be confused with any name–value pairs that may be included in the query string used to invoke the Web Dynpro application.

### 12.3.1 Application Properties

An application property is any hard-coded value that applies to a specific Web Dynpro application. Such property values can be used to modify the behavior of a Web Dynpro component. So, for instance, you could create two applications that both use the same component as their root component. However, for the first application, you define a property called `displayMode` to have the value `false`, and for the second, `displayMode` is set to `true`.

Since both applications point to the same root component, you now have a mechanism for controlling whether the component allows the user to edit the data or not.

There are two main varieties of application property:

▶ Pre defined properties: That is, those defined by the Web Dynpro Framework (see Figure 12.17)

▶ Self-defined properties: That is, those defined by the developer

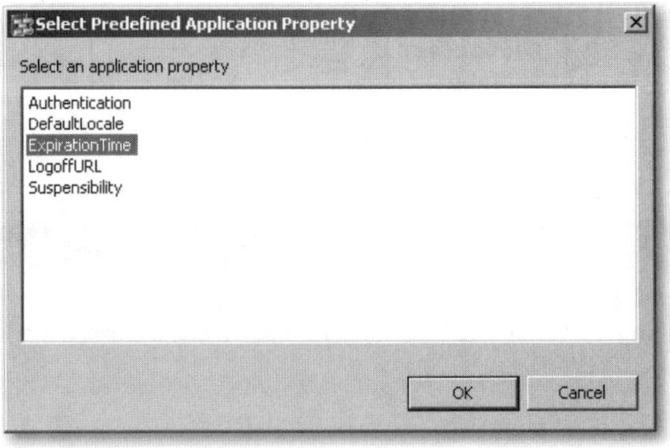

**Figure 12.17** Predefined Application Properties

If you create your own self-defined property, you can give it any valid name you choose. The value you define for this property is always stored as a `string`.

Once an application property has been defined, its value can be obtained using the following code:

```
// Get a reference to the application's metadata
IWDApplicationInfo appInfo =
  wdComponentAPI.getApplication().getApplicationInfo();

// Get the value of the authentication property using the
// name held in WDConfigurationConstants
String auth =
  appInfo().findInApplicationProperties(
            WDConfigurationConstants.
                APPLICATION_PROPERTY_AUTHENTICATION).
        getValue();

// Get the value of a self defined property
String myProp = applInfo().
                    findInApplicationProperties("myProperty").
                    getValue();
//@@end
}
```

**Listing 12.5**  Obtaining the values of predefined and self-defined application properties

### 12.3.2    URL Properties

A URL property is any value passed into a Web Dynpro application via an HTTP(S) GET or POST request. In a GET request, the parameter values are concatenated to the end of the web address and are collectively known as the *query string*. A query string uses the syntax shown in Figure 12.18.

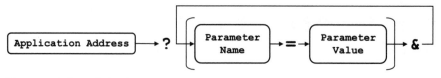

**Figure 12.18**  Query String Syntax

> **Important**
>
> Any values added to a query string will be visible in plain text in the browser's address field. Therefore, this technique should not be used for the transmission of sensitive information such as user credentials.

Two techniques are available for determining the value of a URL parameter:

▶ By creating a parameter of the same name on the inbound plug used to start the application

▶ By obtaining the parameter value from the request object via the WDProtocolAdapter

### Inbound Plug Parameter

The simplest way to work with a URL parameter value is to create a parameter of same name on the inbound plug used to start the application. By default, this plug will be called Default and is an inbound plug on the interface view controller of the root component. This is a special inbound plug of type Startup.

This is an example of one of the very few times when the Web Dynpro Framework calls an inbound plug without a corresponding outbound plug first being called.

Unless you say otherwise, when you define an application, the interface view controller used to start the application will call the start-up plug called Default (see Figure 12.19).

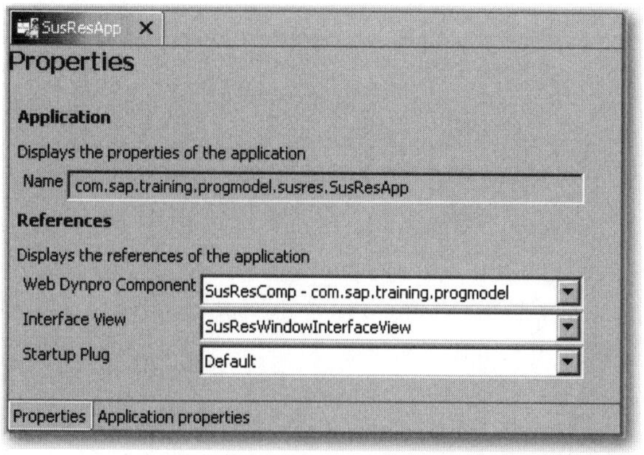

**Figure 12.19** The Start-Up Plug Called "Default" Is Used During the Declaration of an Application Unless You Say Otherwise

In the following example, we will assume that the Default start-up plug has had a property created for it called myProperty. Now, if the application that causes this root component to be invoked contains a query string value called myProperty, it will automatically be transferred into the start-up plug's parameter.

| Important |
| --- |
| A start-up plug parameter may be of any simple data type. Therefore, you must ensure that the value found in the query string can successfully be cast to the start-up parameter's data type. |

### Using the Request Object

If you do not know what parameters will be passed to you until the application is started, then declaring start-up plug parameters is not a feasible option. In this case, you can access the entire request object via the WDProtocolAdapter.

```
// First, get the protocol adapter
IWDProtocolAdapter protocolAdapter =
  WDProtocolAdapter.getProtocolAdapter();

// Then, get the request object
IWDRequest request = protocolAdapter.getRequestObject();

// Get named parameter
String myProp = request.getParameter("myProperty");

// Get map of all parameters in request object
Map propMap = request.getParameterMap();
```

**Listing 12.6** Obtaining application property values from the request object

# 13    The Adaptive RFC Layer

Many customers using Web Dynpro for Java are already users of one or more existing SAP systems; for instance, you may have an R/3 Enterprise, CRM, or BI system. For an external program to interact with the business functionality found in an SAP system, the ABAP based functionality must be invoked by means of a remote function call (RFC).

Any ABAP function module that can be called from outside the SAP system is generically known as a remote callable function module (RFM). The best known examples are the so-called BAPIs (Business Application Programming Interfaces).

## 13.1    A Brief History Lesson

Before we dive into the technical details, it is always worth understanding the sequence of events that led to the delivered SAP software being the way it currently is. So, here's a quick history lesson on how the functionality within an SAP system was made accessible to the outside world.

### 13.1.1    The Origins of RFC

External programs have been able to invoke ABAP functionality within an SAP system since version 2.0F of R/3 (circa 1994). However, the first implementation of this remote access to ABAP functionality was only available if you wrote the external interface in C.

The protocol originally used for the external invocation of ABAP function modules reveals the R/2, IBM Mainframe roots of the R/3 architecture. In the late 1960s, IBM developed a transaction processing system called CICS, and the core of this system was known as the CICS transaction server.

The predecessor to R/3 was a product called R/2 that was developed as an IBM mainframe–based application and made extensive use of a modified version of the CICS transaction server. To make their transaction server accessible to programs running on remote computers, IBM developed a programming API called Common Programming Interface for Communications (CPI-C).

When SAP was designing R/3, many of the architectural features of R/2 were brought directly from the mainframe world across to the Unix-based client-server world. Since CPI-C was already built into the R/2 architecture, extending its use into the R/3 world was a natural choice.

However, CPI-C is a very low-level API; many of the interfaces using CPI-C were written in Assembler. Therefore, to make life somewhat easier for the programmer writing the external application, SAP added the RFC layer to simplify the use of CPI-C. At its first release, the RFC interface was only available to programmers writing in C, but this layer has since been rewritten in Java — hence the JRFC.jar layer seen in Figure 13.1.

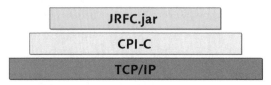

**Figure 13.1** The Java Implementation of RFC Sits on Top of CPI-C, Which Sits Directly on the Network Layer

The Java RFC (JRFC) API is still a low-level interface and requires the programmer to have a detailed understanding of both the protocol and the internal workings of the ABAP system being invoked. It does not have any concept of an abstraction layer between the business application, the underlying communication protocol, or the physical identity of the backend system. Therefore, direct use of the JRFC layer would mean that your business application must not only interface directly to a low-level communication protocol, but it must also contain (or have access to) hard-coded system information and user credentials.

This is how software was written 20-plus years ago and is no longer considered acceptable in a modern business programming environment. Therefore, SAP does not offer any support for customer applications that directly use the JRFC layer.

> **Caveat Confector**
>
> The JRFC layer is subject to internal change by SAP without notice. If you attempt to write a business application that interfaces directly with this software layer, you may find that it ceases to function correctly after an upgrade.
>
> In addition to this, you will have to spend a lot of time and effort writing such an interface, with little chance of it performing any better than, or even as well as, SAP's own software that interfaces to it.
>
> So, if you ignore this warning, you're on your own. Don't come crying to SAP about the problems if it all goes horribly wrong!

### 13.1.2   Java Connector and the Adaptive RFC Layer

There is another layer sitting on top of the JRFC interface. This is known as the Java Connector or simply JCo for short. This layer greatly simplifies the interface to the underlying JRFC layer, but it still does not provide the degree of abstraction required by modern business applications between themselves and the backend business systems.

For instance, in the JCo layer you can invoke an ABAP function module by first creating a JCO.Function object, passing it the correct input parameters, and then calling its execute() method. However, before any of this is possible, you must first have created a JCO.Client object that logs on to a specified backend system using a user id and password. This immediately ties your program down to a hard-coded set of system and user references. If you were to transport such a program from your development environment to your test environment, you would at least have to change the name of the backend system in the coding. From a quality assurance point of view, this type of modification is considered unacceptable; therefore, the business application must be decoupled from the backend system(s) with which it communicates.

As for the metadata available at runtime, JCo only provides a generic interface at the level of RFC semantics, and not a typed interface. This means the metadata available to the application at runtime was restricted to what the RFC layer could provide. This did not include any ABAP Dictionary metadata such as label texts or ValueSets. However, the limited amount of metadata present in the RFC layer allows JCo to tolerate changes in the interface structure. This is because it accesses fields using named lookup, rather than a simple offset and length.

All in all, two problems needed to be addressed: the lack of runtime metadata, and the lack of an abstraction layer to decouple the application from the backend systems. To achieve this, the Adaptive RFC layer was written (see Figure 13.2).

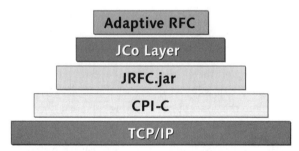

**Figure 13.2** The Adaptive RFC Layer on Top of the JCo Layer

In addition to providing the required level of abstraction, the Adaptive RFC layer incorporates a Java Dictionary and provides functionality very similar to the ABAP data dictionary.

The Adaptive RFC layer allows a proxy object to be created (known in Web Dynpro as a model), and the business application simply interacts with the proxy object.

The identity of the backend system is known only by a pair of logical system names, and even the user credentials are separated from the business application.

The proxy object holds the definition of the ABAP function module's interface. This metadata is held in a separate dictionary, and when the ABAP function module is called for the first time after the server starts up, the first thing the Adaptive RFC layer does is to check whether the interface to this particular function module has changed. If it has, its imports the new interface structure into its dictionary, and this information is then available to the consuming business application.

This is why this layer of software is known as the *Adaptive* RFC layer: because it can dynamically react to certain changes in the ABAP function module's interface. This topic will be discussed in much greater detail later on in this chapter.

Any Java program running in the AS Java — not just Web Dynpro — can make use of the Adaptive RFC layer.

### 13.1.3 The Enterprise Connector

As a slight digression, a product called the Enterprise Connector (formerly known as the Java Connectivity Builder) was designed to simplify the use of the JCo layer. This product created proxy objects that gave a one-to-one representation of the corresponding RFC function with all of its parameters.

The Enterprise Connector worked on the basis of a static interface definition created via the import of metadata at design time. This meant that within the external program, there was a static representation of the RFC module's interface containing only the offset, length, and primitive data type of each field *as it was defined at the time the interface was imported*.

The byte stream exported from the SAP system was then subdivided using this hard-coded offset and length information.

This type of interface seriously restricted the flexibility of the external program because not even the named look-up capability available in the underlying RFC layer was available; neither was there the concept of extracting metadata from the ABAP Dictionary. This produced the following limitations:

▶ ABAP Dictionary fields and data structures could only be represented by primitive data types. This created the possibility of data corruption. For instance, in ABAP you can declare a 1 byte, unsigned integer; whereas, Java has no concept of *unsigned* integers.

▶ There was no support for standard extensibility features found in the ABAP Dictionary such as the .APPEND[1] structure.

---

1  Pronounced "dot append."

- There was no support for different versions of dictionary structures found in different versions of SAP systems.
- There was no availability of interface metadata at runtime.

Consider the ABAP Dictionary structure in Figure 13.3.

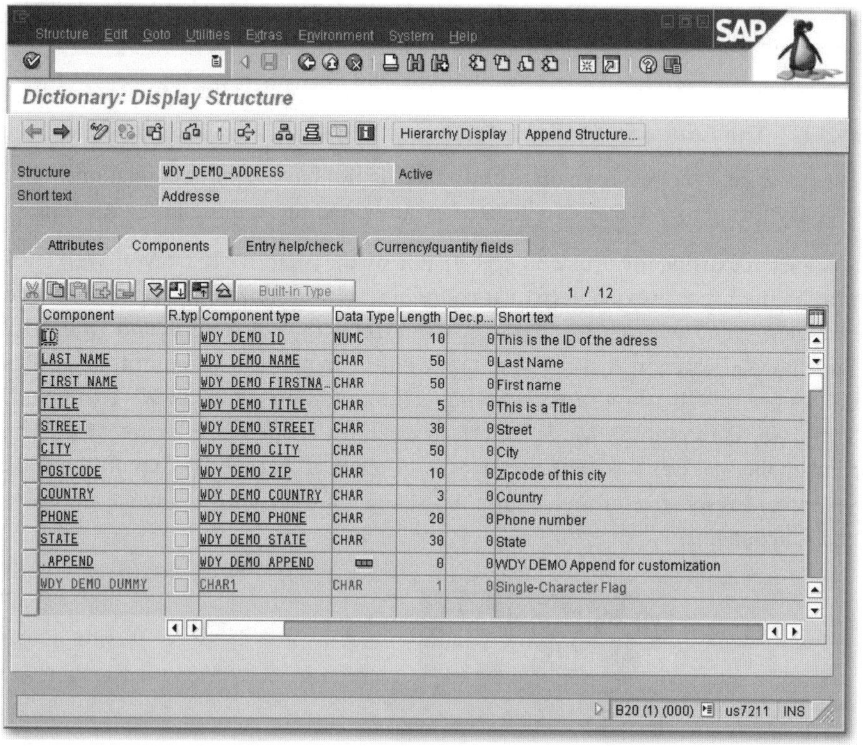

**Figure 13.3** A Typical ABAP Dictionary Structure

If this structure appeared in the interface of an RFC module, the Enterprise Connector would have generated a set of getter methods using static offset and length values, such as those shown in the following pseudo-implementation.

```
String getId()        { return bytesAsString(0,10); }
String getLastName()  { return bytesAsString(10,50); }
String getFirstName() { return bytesAsString(60,50); }
```

**Listing 13.1** A pseudo-implementation of the getter methods typical of the older static Enterprise Connector interface

If the interface to the ABAP function module was changed in *any* way, the static Enterprise Connector object became incompatible with the new byte stream, and the external program would typically suffer a fatal runtime error.

This meant that because the Enterprise Connector was not aware of any new fields in the interface, it was unable to keep running after the interface changed. The underlying JCo layer contains the ability to access any part of the interface structure, but because the Enterprise Connector made no use of this functionality, it was unable to react to modifications that took place after design time.

The shortcomings of the Enterprise Connector layer were what prompted the development of the Adaptive RFC layer.

### 13.1.4 The Common Model Interface

The software layers we have discussed so far do not have any direct relationship to Web Dynpro. Indeed, they can be used by any program running in the AS Java.

In addition to using the proxy objects created by the Adaptive RFC layer, Web Dynpro can use other proxy objects that communicate with different types of backend system. A Web Dynpro program can also interact with Web services and Enterprise Java Beans. However, it would be inefficient to implement three different API's that varied only because the underlying communication protocols were different. Therefore, the Common Model Interface has been created (see Figure 13.4). The fundamental task of this software layer is to make all backend proxy objects look the same, irrespective of the communication technology used to invoke the backend functionality.

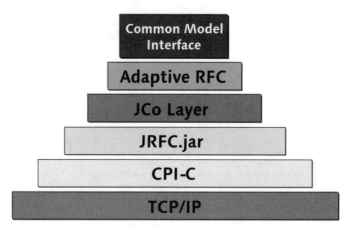

**Figure 13.4** The Common Model Interface on Top of the Adaptive RFC Layer

An end-to-end view of these different layers of communication software can be seen in Figure 13.5.

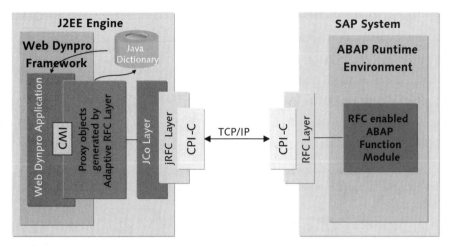

**Figure 13.5** End to End RFC Communication Architecture Between Web Dynpro and a Backend SAP System

## 13.2 General Introduction to BAPIs

For readers not familiar with the internal workings of an SAP system, a BAPI is a unit of ABAP coding known as a function module. Each function module is a member of an aggregation known as a function group. All function groups are designed in such a way that their member function modules perform tasks related to the same business process.

In addition to each function module having its own private variable declarations, function modules can share information with each other by means of variables common to the function group. Standard SAP function modules make frequent use of this technique.[2]

The average SAP system contains approximately 50,000 function modules belonging to around 8,000 function groups. Of these 50,000 function modules, some 9,500 are callable from outside the SAP system, with a variable proportion of these being BAPIs.[3]

### 13.2.1 What Is a BAPI?

From a superficial point of view, a BAPI is simply an ABAP function module that can be invoked from outside the SAP system. However, a much stricter set of criteria must be met before a function module can truly be described as a BAPI. It must:

---

2  This information sharing feature only applies when function modules are called from the same ABAP session.

3  The proportion of function modules in an SAP system that are BAPIs varies with the type of system — BI, CRM, APO, etc.

1. Have its **Remote callable** flag switched on

2. Run to completion without the need for any secondary user interaction

3. Handle all errors gracefully

4. Not cause an ABAP session change

5. Have a name that starts with `BAPI_`

6. Implement the method of an SAP Business Object

7. Maintain a static interface through different versions of the SAP system

Criteria 1 to 4 must be met for a customer-developed remote function module. All seven criteria must be met for an SAP-developed remote function module to be called a BAPI.

Unfortunately, it is my experience that many ABAP developers have either forgotten, or never knew about, some of the criteria listed above. From a technical development perspective, the criteria that are of particular importance are the ones about error handling and not causing an ABAP session change.

The principles of RFC programming in ABAP are well known and well documented in the SAP help files and other literature, yet many ABAP developers have either forgotten or never knew that such principles exist. Consequently, they find themselves in a situation where their ABAP function modules work fine when tested within the ABAP development environment but behave differently when called over the RFC interface.

Such situations can introduce bizarre bugs into the Web Dynpro applications that call them and cause unnecessary delays to the development process. All of these problems are avoidable if the principles of RFC programming are known and followed when custom ABAP function modules are written.

> **Caveat Confector**
>
> All ABAP developers involved in writing function modules for use with Web Dynpro Java must understand and adhere to the design principles documented in the SAP Online Help (*http://help.sap.com*) under the heading "BAPI Programming Guide" (Component CA-BFA) and "RFC Programming in ABAP" (Component BC-MID-RFC).
>
> Failure to adhere to these BAPI design principles will result in your Web Dynpro application being unable to manage the data in the SAP system correctly. For instance, you might experience problems with Web Dynpro's ability to manage ABAP lock objects if you are not aware of the association between a JCo session and an ABAP session.

### 13.2.2    ABAP Function Module Interface

Figure 13.6 shows that within the set of all ABAP programs is the subset of coding entities known as ABAP function modules. Within this subset is a further subset of RFC modules; these ABAP function modules can be invoked from outside the R/3 system. Within the set of RFC modules is a further subset of RFC modules that conform to the BAPI design criteria. See points 1 to 7 in the above list.

SAP R/3 System

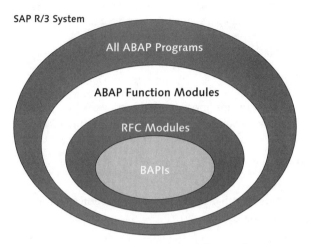

**Figure 13.6** BAPIs Are an Inner Subset of the Set of ABAP Function Modules

Irrespective of its functionality or visibility, the interface of every ABAP function module within an SAP system conforms to a standardized design. Therefore, the following explanation of the interface of an ABAP function module holds true irrespective of whether it can be called from outside the SAP system or not.

All ABAP function modules can make use of five distinct types of parameter. Some are used only for input, some are used only for output, and some are bidirectional. These parameter types are:

▶ IMPORTING **parameters**
As the name implies, IMPORTING parameters define values that are only used on the inbound side of the interface. These parameters are either single fields or scalar structures.

▶ EXPORTING **parameters**
As the name implies, EXPORTING parameters define values that are only used on the outbound side of the interface. These parameters are either single fields or scalar structures.

▶ TABLES **parameters**
TABLES parameters define any tabular structure in the function module's interface. The structure of these parameters is defined using an ABAP Dictionary structure and at runtime may contain zero or more rows.

All TABLES parameters are bidirectional. This means you may pass data into a function module in one of the TABLES parameters, and the function module can then modify the contents and pass the same table back containing completely different data.

> **Important**
>
> For this reason, when you use a Web Dynpro model object, you will find that two copies of a TABLES parameter will be maintained. One holds the data sent to the inbound side of the interface, and the other holds the data received from the outbound side of the interface.
>
> In other words, you will have a before- and after-execution version of the table.

▶ **CHANGING parameters**

CHANGING parameters define the function module's bidirectional scalar parameters. That is, a CHANGING parameter behaves like it was both an IMPORTING and EXPORTING parameter.

Standard SAP BAPIs tend not to use CHANGING parameters.

▶ **EXCEPTIONS**

EXCEPTIONS are labels used to identify that an abnormal termination situation has occurred within the function module.

Exceptions are triggered by using the ABAP statement RAISE followed by the name of the exception to be raised. The use of this statement has been explicitly excluded from SAP's definition of a BAPI. This is because upon executing a RAISE statement, the function module terminates immediately, thus violating the principle that a BAPI should run to completion, handling all errors gracefully.

If an external program (such as Web Dynpro for Java) calls an ABAP function module that raises an exception, the external program is passed the name of the exception that was raised, but the output side of the function module's interface (typically, the EXPORTING and TABLES parameters) contains values that reflect whatever state they were in at the time the exception was raised. This could be an inconsistent state that means nothing to the external program.

Therefore, SAP recommends that remote callable function modules should trap all but the most severe (i.e., fatal or unrecoverable) errors and run to completion. Thus, the external program receives the error message *and* the output data in as consistent a state as is possible given the nature of the error.

> **Important**
>
> Whilst it is not necessary for a Web Dynpro Java programmer to be able to program in ABAP, it is very important that the interface presented by an ABAP function module is understood. The different parameter types will be represented as proxy objects within the generated model, and to understand the generated objects, you must understand the interface of the underlying ABAP function module.

> **Important**
>
> If you are a Java developer with no prior experience with an SAP system, then to have a full understanding of the interface with which you are working, you should learn how to do the following in an SAP system:

- ► Logon to an SAP system[4]
- ► Use transaction SE80 (ABAP Workbench) to:
  - – Examine the interface structure of a function module, run the function module with appropriate test data, and then examine the output from the test run (alternatively, use transaction SE37).
  - – Examine the fields in a Data Dictionary table or data structure (alternatively, use transaction SE11).
- ► Use transaction SE16 to display the contents of a database table.

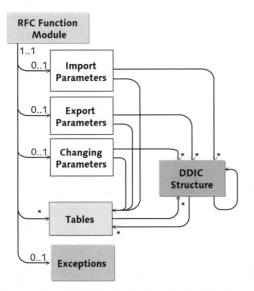

**Figure 13.7** The Interface Structure of All ABAP Function Modules

The above skills should be considered the minimum level of SAP competence required by all Web Dynpro developers. (These skills are very basic and can be taught in a matter of hours.)

Beyond this, extra knowledge related to the actual SAP application area in which you are working probably also needs to be acquired.

## 13.3 Custom-Written RFC Modules

During the course of the analysis phase of your Web Dynpro project, it is likely that you will encounter situations in which the required functionality cannot be supplied by a standard BAPI. Under these circumstances, a decision must be made on how to proceed. Various options are available, and each has its own advantages and disadvantages:

---

4  The user ID used in this situation must have at least S_RFC and S_DEVELOP authorization.

1. Adjust the functional requirements of your application to fit the functionality delivered by the standard BAPIs.

   ▶ **Advantages:** Your custom-written Web Dynpro application will only make use of standard SAP-delivered functionality and will therefore be free from any side effects after an upgrade.

   ▶ **Disadvantages:** The missing functionality may be of fundamental importance to the success of your Web Dynpro development; therefore, it cannot be excluded from the project scope.

2. If a standard BAPI can be identified that partially delivers the required functionality, this can be used as the starting point for a customer-developed wrapper RFM.

   ▶ **Advantages:** You are already half way to a solution. The wrapper RFM has an interface that is a superset of the BAPI's interface, the extra fields being those necessary to drive the enhanced functionality found in the wrapper RFC module.
   The wrapper RFC module should first call the standard BAPI. Once this has completed successfully, the extra functionality is performed.

   ▶ **Disadvantages:** More development effort is required. ABAP development skills are required in addition to Java Web Dynpro development skills.

3. If no standard BAPI can be identified that even comes close to the required functionality, a custom-written RFC module must be developed.

   ▶ **Advantages:** You have complete control over the delivered functionality.

   ▶ **Disadvantages:** More development effort is required. ABAP development skills are required in addition to Java Web Dynpro development skills.

   Your custom developments are not guaranteed to work after an SAP upgrade. The burden of responsibility for migrating custom developments to an upgraded SAP system lies entirely with the customer.

A Web Dynpro application is not concerned about whether the RFC module it invokes is a standard BAPI, an SAP-delivered RFC module, or a custom-written RFC module. In addition, because the set of BAPIs in an SAP system is a subset of all RFC modules, from this point onwards, we will refer to all ABAP function modules invoked by Web Dynpro as *RFC modules* rather than restricting the discussion to BAPIs.

## 13.4    Introduction to the Adaptive RFC Layer

As already stated, the purpose of the Adaptive RFC layer is to provide a dictionary-based, adaptive interface to the functionality found in an ABAP-based SAP system. This interface has been built in such a way that it can automatically adapt to certain modifications in an RFC module's interface.

This dictionary-based access to one or more RFC module interfaces is encapsulated within a generated class hierarchy known as a *model*. An Adaptive RFC model may contain as many RFC module interfaces as you require. Whilst no technical limits exist on the number of RFC modules that may be encapsulated within a model, there are certain practical and functional limits that you should impose upon the size of a model. These will be discussed in the following sections.

---

**Important**

Notice that the Adaptive RFC layer is called *adaptive* — not dynamic.

If you add a new field to an IMPORTING parameter or a new column to a TABLES parameter, the Adaptive RFC layer will be able to accommodate this, and the metadata describing the function module's interface will be adapted at runtime.

However, if you add a whole new TABLES or IMPORTING parameter into the function module's interface, this is too large a change to be accommodated by the Adaptive RFC layer at runtime, and it will be necessary to re-import the model in your Web Dynpro DC.

---

What the adaptive RFC interface can handle is the arrival of a new field within an existing structure. The Adaptive RFC layer can adapt to modifications such as:

▶ Addition of new fields to .APPEND structures in standard SAP tables[5]

▶ Field length changes

▶ Label text changes

▶ Value set changes

Each Web Dynpro model has its own dictionary in which are held the unique set of structures that define the interfaces of all the RFC modules in the model. When a Web Dynpro model is generated for an RFC module that uses structured parameters in its interface, the ABAP Dictionary structures are replicated as Java Dictionary Simple Types within the model's dictionary. This means almost all the metadata defined in the ABAP Dictionary is available via the model's dictionary both at design time (through the Web Dynpro Perspective of the NWDS) and at runtime. You now have runtime access to such metadata as the:

▶ Field label

▶ Column heading

▶ Tool tip

▶ Value set

▶ Field length

---

5 The use of .APPEND as a field name within an ABAP dictionary table allows another dictionary structure to be included at that point in the table definition. This mechanism allows customers to extend SAP standard tables without having to register the change as a modification to an SAP-delivered object. The structure being .APPENDed is considered free for modification by the customer.

Notice that I said *almost* all the ABAP dictionary metadata is available. There are two metadata properties that cannot be transferred into the Java Dictionary:

▶ **The contents of an ABAP dictionary domain's value table**
Within the ABAP data dictionary, you can define that the value set of a particular dictionary domain[6] will be held in a database table instead of a static list. Since it is possible for a value table to contain many thousands of rows, there is a significant risk of creating a performance problem if all value tables are imported into the Java dictionary.

In addition, any time an SAP database table is exported out of the system for use by another runtime environment (Java in this case), the whole issue of table synchronization needs to be addressed, and this is a topic for which there is currently no general solution.

▶ **Support for ABAP conversion routines other than ALPHA**
All SAP systems have been designed to be operating system and database neutral. This immediately means the SAP system must operate in a manner that is independent of any codepage used by the underlying operating system. Consequently, all SAP systems use their own internal codepage.

In addition to the codepage conversion that happens automatically as data travels in and out of an SAP system, there is the additional concept of format conversion. There are many examples of data types in which the format used for screen presentation is different from the format used for internal storage. Format conversion is performed by the ABAP data dictionary using something called a conversion routine.

A conversion routine is not a single program, but a pair of ABAP function modules called CONVERSION_EXIT_xxxxx_INPUT and CONVERSION_EXIT_xxxxx_OUTPUT, where xxxxx is the routine name. These function modules are called when data crosses the SAP system boundary.

Conversion routines (other than ALPHA) are not invoked when data is transported across the RFC interface. This means that when data arrives from the external program (Web Dynpro Java in this case) into the SAP system via the RFC interface, the external format seen by the user will not have been converted to the internal format required by the ABAP function module. The net result is that that particular input field will fail a validation test, and the ABAP function module will reject the value. If you don't know about conversion routines, you might wonder why you are getting an error message for a perfectly "good" value.

---

6 A domain is the low-level, technical definition of a field. It defines the most basic properties such as data type and length and can hold values ranges or value sets.

In an RFC interface any time you use dictionary fields that have conversion routines assigned to them in the ABAP data dictionary, you must implement the ABAP coding to call the conversion function modules yourself.

Support for conversion exits is provided in the next release of Web Dynpro (version 7.1) by means of an `IBroker` class. Using this class, any dictionary simple type can declare that the data it contains must pass through a conversion routine as it crosses an SAP system boundary.

## 13.5 Creating Adaptive RFC Models

An Adaptive RFC model is created for you by the Model Wizard in the NWDS. Very often, it is beneficial to create a Web Dynpro DC that contains only models (see Section 3.5.4 to remind yourself of the benefits), so the example here shows such a situation.

The Model Import Wizard is opened by right-clicking on the Models node in the Web Dynpro Explorer view and selecting **Create Model**. Many different types of model can be created, but the one we're interested in is the Adaptive RFC model (see Figure 13.8).

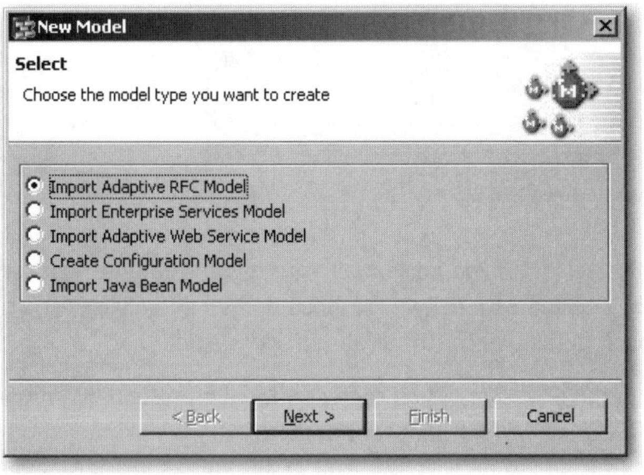

**Figure 13.8** Model Import Wizard: Select Model Type

After selecting the type of model you want to create, on the next screen you must enter the name and package of your new model and the names of the logical destinations that will be used by the Adaptive RFC layer (see Figure 13.9).

The logical destination names can be any meaningful values you choose; however, they should *not* include the name of the backend system.

Let's say your development SAP system is called DEV, your test system is called TST, and the production system is called PRD. If you create your model with a logical destination name that includes the system name (say, AddressDataDEV), this will be fine as long as you never transport that software to any other system in your landscape.

As soon as this software is transported to the test or production environments, the logical destination names are also transported. Now you have the illogical situation that the AddressDataDEV logical destination must be configured to point to the TST or PRD systems — even though the name contains the string DEV. This is counterintuitive and will lead to confusion and administrative errors.

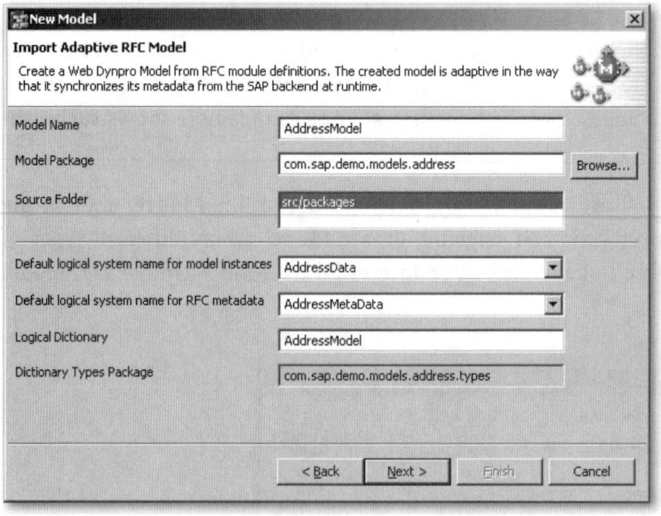

**Figure 13.9** Model Import Wizard: Enter Model Details

On the next screen (see Figure 13.10) you must enter your logon credentials for the backend SAP system from which the model will be created. If you do not have such credentials, you must speak to the administrator of that SAP system.

After you have logged on, the next screen you see intentionally presents no information. This is because there are several thousand remote callable function modules in an SAP system, and it would be very wasteful of system resources to send the entire list to your screen and then have only one or two selected. Therefore, you should enter a search string in the **Function Name** field and press the **Search** button.

In this case, we want to search for the function modules that are involved in address management, so the search has been performed using the string wdy_*_ address,[7] and this returns seven hits (see Figure 13.11). For a basic demo, we are interested in the four selected function modules.

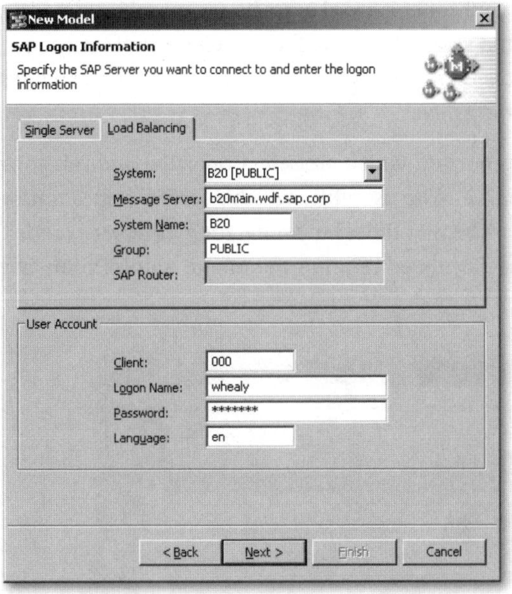

**Figure 13.10** Model Import Wizard: Log On to the Backend SAP System

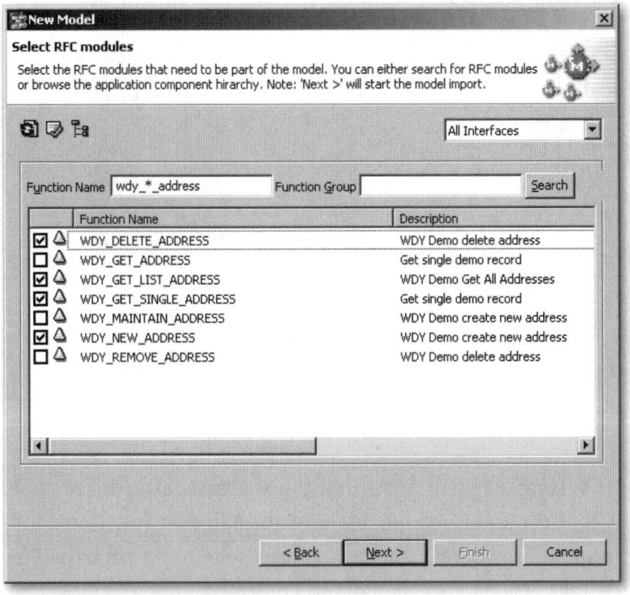

**Figure 13.11** Fourth Screen of the Model Import Wizard: Select Function Modules

7   Don't go looking for these function modules in your SAP system. They are not standard function modules and are not shipped as part of a customer system.

When the **Next** button is clicked, the Model Wizard extracts the interface metadata of the selected function modules and stores it in XML files. The length of time taken for the metadata extraction process depends on the number of function modules selected and the size of their interfaces.

Finally you are presented with a report on which classes, properties, and relations have been extracted (see Figure 13.12). The usefulness of this screen comes not so much when you import a model for the first time, but when you re-import a model. The log will tell you which entities have been re-imported due to modification and which have been ignored.

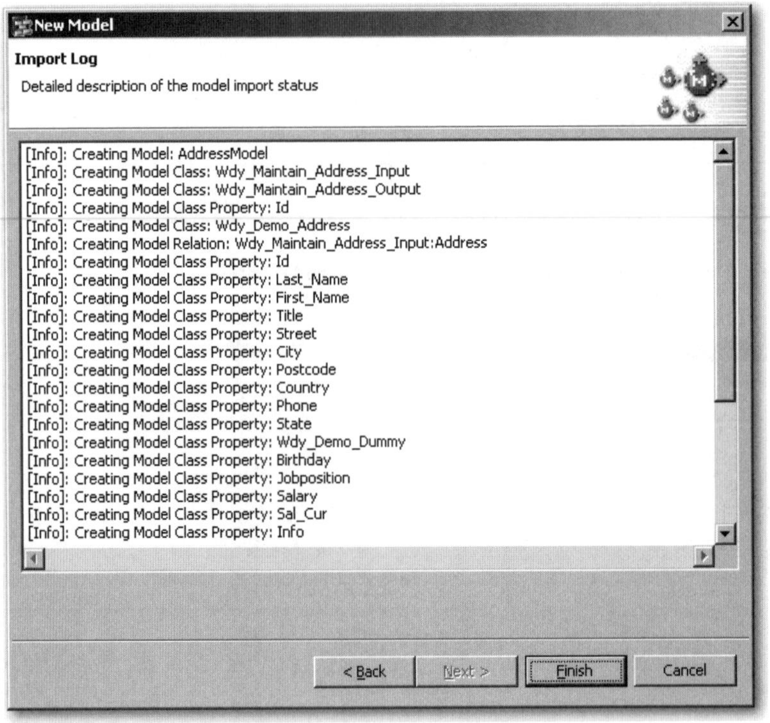

**Figure 13.12** Model Import Wizard: Metadata Extraction Log

So far, the Model Import Wizard has still not created any actual Java source code. All that has happened is that the interface metadata of the selected function modules has been extracted and stored in XML form. It is only when you click the **Finish** button that the actual Java classes are created and compiled.

Once the model has been generated, its hierarchical structure will be visible in the Web Dynpro Explorer view of your DC (see Figure 13.13).

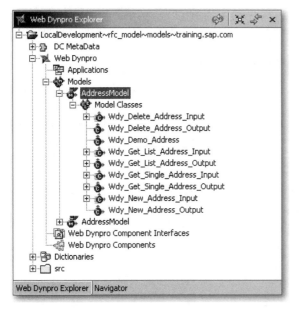

**Figure 13.13** A Generated Model

## 13.6 Structuring a Model

A frequently asked question is, "How many function modules should be put into a model?"

This question does not have a single correct answer, but there is one answer that is always wrong.

Unless you are working with a *very* simple business scenario, never create models that contain only one function module each. At runtime, such an architecture would result in an excessive number of connections to your backend system being opened. This not only will lead to an inefficient use of system resources, but could also lead to transactional problems when processing business data.

In general, all function modules that are related to performing a single business process should be grouped together into a model. In this way, you create a unit of reuse that relates to the business process, and not some lower-level technical unit.

The rule of thumb here is to think about reuse. The whole of Web Dynpro architecture is focused on getting the best level of software reuse from a *business perspective* — not a technical perspective.

In Figure 13.14, you can see that the model object is called ServiceOrderModel and that it contains the respective $\{rfm\}$_Input and $\{rfm\}$_Output classes for 11 function modules (plus various other interface classes). These function modules have

425

been grouped together according to their functionality, and therefore, the `Ser-viceOrderModel` object has a good degree of reuse from a business perspective.

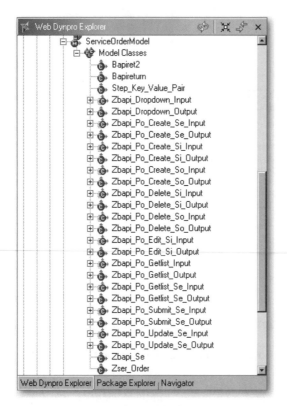

**Figure 13.14** Contents of a Model Object

| Important |
| --- |
| Do not create models containing only one function module each, as this will make very inefficient use of connections to the backend system.<br><br>Also, do not create a specific logical destination for each model. This again will make highly inefficient use of JCo connections into your backend system.<br><br>See Section 14.3 for more details on this topic. |

## 13.7 Explanation of Generated Model Classes

As a result of using the Model Wizard, a variety of classes are created; some appear under the Web Dynpro DC you are building, and others appear in a separate dictionary. It is therefore worth explaining the purpose of these generated classes.

### 13.7.1 Model Naming Convention

The name of an Adaptive RFC model is user definable. According to the SAP naming convention for such objects, the model name ${nm} should consist of the desired model name ${m} followed by the suffix Model.

${nm} = **${m}**Model

In the example shown in Figure 13.13 above, the model name is AddressModel. This naming convention must be adhered to manually, as it is not enforced by the NWDS.

### 13.7.2 Executable and Non-Executable Model Objects

If you look back at Figure 13.11, you will remember that we imported four ABAP function modules:

► WDY_GET_LIST_ADDRESS
Return a table of all known addresses

► WDY_GET_SINGLE_ADDRESS
Return details of a single address

► WDY_NEW_ADDRESS
Create a new address

► WDY_DELETE_ADDRESS
Delete an address

For each of these function modules, at least two model objects have been created.

These two model objects are created as a result of a fundamental principle in RFC programming:

► You always start an RFC call with an executable proxy object representing the *input* side of the function module's interface.

► As a result of calling the input object's execute() method, you are passed back an instance of an object that represents the *output* side of the function module's interface. The output object is *never* executable.

You can see this principle at work by looking at the objects listed in Figure 13.13. For every ABAP function module ${rfm}, a pair of model objects has been generated ending in _Input and _Output, respectively.

These two object types can be identified by the different icons:

► ![icon]: A non-executable model class

► ![icon]: An executable model class

The icon for the executable model object has some speed lines to the left of it.

427

> **Important**
>
> The executable model object acts as the parent for all other model objects in the hierarchy, and it is the only object in which you will find an execute() method.

### 13.7.3 Model Structures

If you take another look at Figure 13.13. You'll notice that there is an extra model object called Wdy_Demo_Address. This object does not obey the naming convention described above. The reason for this is that at least one of the ABAP function modules uses a structured parameter. In this case, the structured parameter is called ADDRESS and is defined using the ABAP dictionary structure called WDY_DEMO_ADDRESS. Therefore, this structure has been exported in its own right and will be used by as many function modules as require it.

In this case, this structure is used by multiple function modules:

▶ WDY_NEW_ADDRESS uses it to define its IMPORTING parameter called ADDRESS.

▶ WDY_GET_SINGLE_ADDRESS uses it to define its EXPORT parameter called ADDRESS.

▶ WDY_GET_LIST_ADDRESS uses it to define its TABLES parameter called ADDRESS_LIST.

The use of this structure for function module WDY_NEW_ADDRESS can be seen in the screenshot in Figure 13.15.

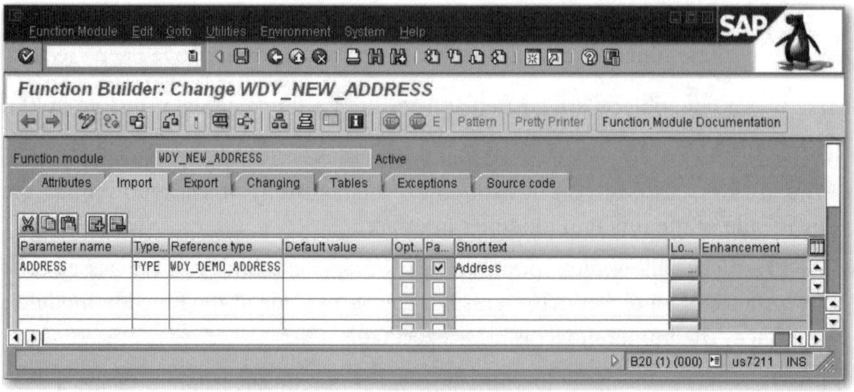

**Figure 13.15** ABAP Dictionary Structure WDY_DEMO_ADDRESS Defines the Structure of the RFC Module's IMPORTING Parameter Called ADDRESS

In the NWDS, you can see the individual fields in a data structure by double-clicking on the model structure name and then selecting the **Properties** tab. In Figure 13.16, you can see the individual fields that make up this data structure. The green tag icon 🏷 indicates that this is a scalar parameter.

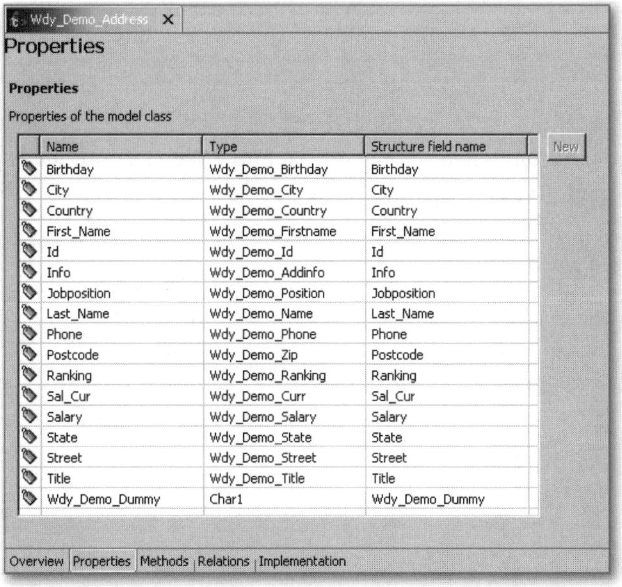


| Name | Type | Structure field name |
|---|---|---|
| Birthday | Wdy_Demo_Birthday | Birthday |
| City | Wdy_Demo_City | City |
| Country | Wdy_Demo_Country | Country |
| First_Name | Wdy_Demo_Firstname | First_Name |
| Id | Wdy_Demo_Id | Id |
| Info | Wdy_Demo_Addinfo | Info |
| Jobposition | Wdy_Demo_Position | Jobposition |
| Last_Name | Wdy_Demo_Name | Last_Name |
| Phone | Wdy_Demo_Phone | Phone |
| Postcode | Wdy_Demo_Zip | Postcode |
| Ranking | Wdy_Demo_Ranking | Ranking |
| Sal_Cur | Wdy_Demo_Curr | Sal_Cur |
| Salary | Wdy_Demo_Salary | Salary |
| State | Wdy_Demo_State | State |
| Street | Wdy_Demo_Street | Street |
| Title | Wdy_Demo_Title | Title |
| Wdy_Demo_Dummy | Char1 | Wdy_Demo_Dummy |

**Figure 13.16** Generated Model Object for the Structure WDY_DEMO_ADDRESS

### 13.7.4 The Model Dictionary

All structured parameters are represented as distinct classes (each constructed from fields defined as Dictionary Simple Types). Each time a remote callable function module `${rfm}` uses a parameter defined by one of these structures, that structure class will appear as a "relation" under the corresponding **`${rfm}`**`_Input` or **`${rfm}`**`_Output` class (or both if the parameter is bidirectional).

If you look back at Figure 13.9, you will see that when the model object was created, one of the fields was called Logical Dictionary. The purpose of this is to have all the metadata for this model stored in a single dictionary. The structures in this dictionary can then be used for defining all manner of coding entities in your application (e.g., context nodes).

Using the example in Figure 13.3 above, notice that the fields of the ABAP structure `WDY_DEMO_ADDRESS` are based on the following ABAP dictionary components (the last of which is a `.APPEND` structure):

- `WDY_DEMO_ID`
- `WDY_DEMO_NAME`
- `WDY_DEMO_FIRSTNAME`
- `WDY_DEMO_TITLE`
- `WDY_DEMO_STREET`
- `WDY_DEMO_CITY`
- `WDY_DEMO_ZIP`

- ▶ WDY_DEMO_COUNTRY
- ▶ WDY_DEMO_PHONE
- ▶ WDY_DEMO_STATE
- ▶ WDY_DEMO_APPEND

When these ABAP dictionary components are imported into a Web Dynpro model object, they appear as **Simple Types** in the Java dictionary AddressModel.

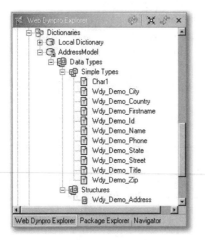

**Figure 13.17** Dictionary Simple Types and Structure Generated for WDY_DEMO_ADDRESS

If you look back at Figure 13.3 and Figure 13.17, you will see how the model generator takes the ABAP Dictionary Component Types and creates a corresponding Simple Type in the Java Dictionary. These are then aggregated into the structured type of the same name as the ABAP dictionary structure.

Therefore, the ABAP dictionary structure Wdy_Demo_Address appears under the Structures node, and the different ABAP component types (upon which the fields in Wdy_Demo_Address are based) appear under the Simple Types node.

The .APPEND structure WDY_DEMO_APPEND contains a single field of type CHAR1 called DUMMY. This is because a .APPEND structure is not permitted to contain zero fields.

---

**Important**

- ▶ A model should be designed to represent a self-contained unit of business functionality. The business functionality is frequently broken into discrete steps,[8] with each step providing an atomic unit of processing.

- ▶ In database terms, you should design a model to contain only processing steps that form a single logical unit of work. Once the functionality of a model has completed (using as many steps as necessary), a database commit (or rollback) should be issued. This topic will be discussed in greater detail in Section 14.9.

---

8  In the case of an Adaptive RFC model, each step corresponds to an RFC module.

▶ You cannot construct a Web Dynpro model from RFC modules that live in *different* SAP systems.

▶ RFC modules should be grouped into Web Dynpro models according to their common functionality.

### 13.7.5  Model Object Hierarchies and Relation Roles

Within the hierarchy of objects in a model, there is not always a simple parent–child relationship. Some classes appear multiple times under different branches because they appear on both the input and output sides of the interface. Therefore, the concept of relation roles exists.

A relation role describes the role played by a particular object when used by (or in relation to) another object.

For instance, the structure defined by WDY_DEMO_ADDRESS is used multiple times by the various function modules we have imported into our model. For instance, the function module WDY_GET_ADDRESS_LIST can receive input through its TABLES parameter called Address_List — which is defined using the structure Wdy_Demo_Address. However, since Address_List is a TABLES parameter, it can be used for both input and output of data, so you'll see the structure Wdy_Demo_Address performing different relation roles depending on which side of the interface you're looking at (see Figure 13.18).

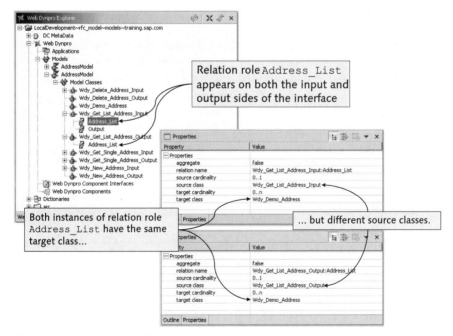

**Figure 13.18** Relation Role Address_List

431

Because the CHANGING and TABLES parameters of an RFC module are bidirectional, you will see duplicate relation role names on the input and output sides of the interface.

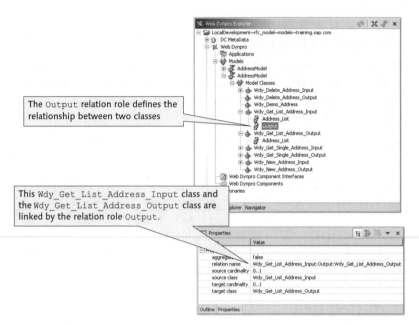

The Output relation role defines the relationship between two classes

This Wdy_Get_List_Address_Input class and the Wdy_Get_List_Address_Output class are linked by the relation role Output.

**Figure 13.19** Relation Role Output: Part 1

The Output relation role under ${rfm}_Input is always present (see Figure 13.19). Remember the fundamental principle of RFC programming mentioned in Section 13.7.2? You always start with an instance of the RFC module's input proxy class, then you call its execute() method, and as a result, you receive an instance of the output proxy class. Therefore, under the ${rfm}_Input class, you will always see the Output relation role, and this relationship is always fulfilled by the class ${rfm}_Output (see Figure 13.20).

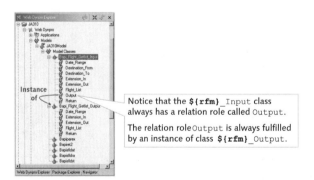

Instance of

Notice that the **${rfm}_Input** class always has a relation role called Output.

The relation role Output is always fulfilled by an instance of class **${rfm}_Output**.

**Figure 13.20** Relation Role Output: Part 2

## 13.8    Web Dynpro Models and Development Components

It is always a good idea to place Web Dynpro model objects into a dedicated development component. The reason for doing this is simply to speed up the compile time. Model objects tend to be large, take longer to compile, and do not change very often. Therefore, it makes no sense to place the model object in the same development component as your frequently changing Web Dynpro components because if you did, every time you compiled the DC, you would additionally have to recompile the models (which haven't changed). Therefore, a DC structure like that shown in Figure 13.21 is recommended.

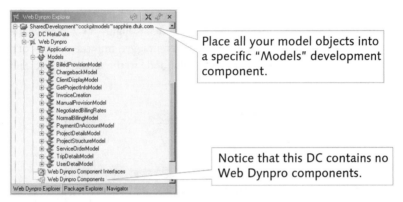

**Figure 13.21**  A Model Development Component Contains Only Model Objects

Once the model objects have been created, you should add each one to a Public Part in order for it to be publicly accessible (see Figure 13.22).

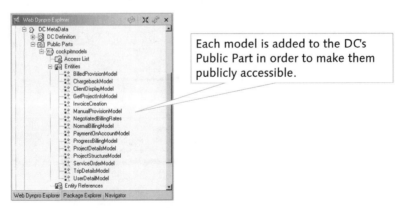

**Figure 13.22**  Add Each Model to a Public Part

Each DC that then requires the use of these models should add the Model DC as a "Used DC" under its DC Metadata node.

## 13.9 Using Model Objects in a Web Dynpro Controller

A model is declared for use within the scope of a DC of type Web Dynpro. When you want to make use of the model objects within the model, the first task is to declare the use of the model in the component's Used Models list. When this is done, all controllers in that component will have access to the model objects within the model.

### 13.9.1 Model Objects and the Context

Model nodes should be declared within the context of a non-visual controller — typically the component controller. The easiest way to declare a context model node and bind it to a model is through the Data Modeler. Figure 13.23 shows the Data Modeler screen once various models have been dragged into the context of a non-visual controller. This action creates the model node in the target context and invokes the model binding functionality.

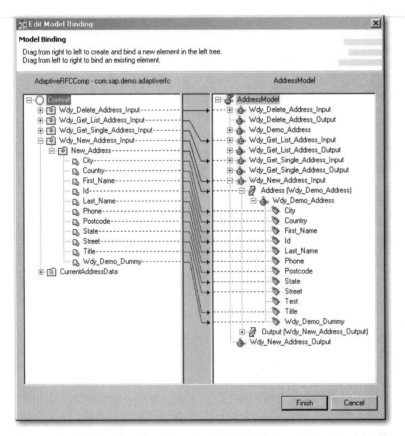

**Figure 13.23** The Data Modeller Shows the Binding Between a Context Model Node and a Model Object

> **Important**
>
> Notice that the context node `Wdy_New_Address_Input` has a child node called `New_Address`. However, this child node is bound to a model class called `Address`, not `New_Address`. This is an example of a context node having to be renamed manually to avoid a name clash. All node names in a context must be unique, irrespective of their position in the hierarchy.

Using the model classes shown in Figure 13.13 and Figure 13.16, you will end up with a context that looks similar to Figure 13.24.

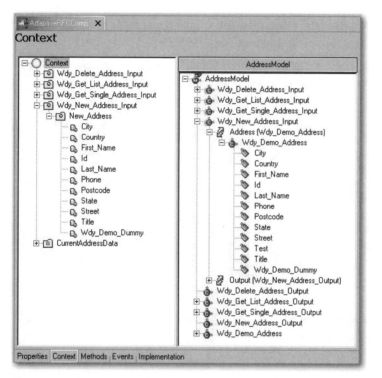

**Figure 13.24** A Model Object and Its Corresponding Context Model Node

In the context editor of the controller, you will see your context hierarchy on the left and the available model objects on the right. Figure 13.24 shows the context editor after the model nodes have been created and bound to their corresponding model classes.

Because many RFC modules use bidirectional parameters, when you bind a model node to such a model class, you will often have to rename one or more of the generated node names manually. It is common practice to append the strings `_Output` or `_Out` to node names on the output side of the interface.

**Important**

This is a general principle that must be followed when binding a context model node to a model object. Bidirectional parameters (i.e., TABLES or CHANGING parameters) always occur twice in the model object hierarchy, and one of those occurrences always needs to be renamed manually during the node mapping process. The need to rename these nodes is caused by a combination of factors:

▶ First, all node names must be unique within the scope of the entire context.

▶ Second, the Model Binding Wizard creates a context node name to have the same name as the class to which it is bound.

### 13.9.2 The Relationship Between the Contents of a Model Object and Its Corresponding Context Model Node

The basic concept here is that your business data *does not* live in a model node. The elements in a model node's collection do not contain that actual business data, but rather references to the corresponding fields in an instance of the model object.

**Caveat Confector**

It's easy to fall into the trap of thinking about a model node as if it were a value node. Each element in a value node holds the actual runtime data, but the elements in a model node only hold *references* to the runtime data. The actual runtime data live in a model object instance (see Section 5.6).

Therefore, when you add elements to a model node, you must first create an instance of the model object, and then you must bind it to the model node collection. The action of binding the model object instance to a node collection creates the required node element in the collection. Alternatively, you can call the create${mn}Element() method and pass a reference to the relevant model object. This creates a regular context model element that must then be added to the node's collection in the normal manner (see Section 6.1.4).

If a hierarchical relationship needs to exist between two or more model objects, the association between the parent and child model objects must be created by calling the appropriate setter methods of the *parent model object*.

The act of binding a model object instance to a model node is the simplest way of providing your Web Dynpro application with a standardized API into the model object's data. In other words, you are making a model object look as if it is just like any other element in a context node (see Figure 13.25).

The following coding scenario demonstrates not only the use of model objects and context model nodes at runtime, but also the importance of the above caveats.

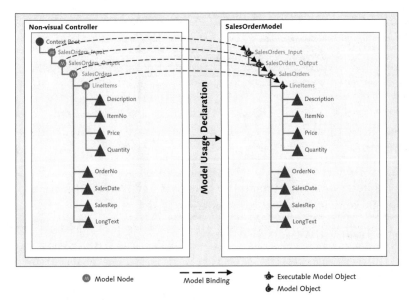

**Figure 13.25** Binding a Context Model Node to a Model Object

## 13.10 Altering a Model Object's Logical System After It Has Been Created

Once you have created a model object, it would appear that the logical system names disappear into the bowels of the model declaration, never to be seen again. Fortunately, this is not true. If you want to alter the name of a model's logical system name, you can do the following:

1. An overview of all the logical systems being used by your Web Dynpro DC can be obtained from the project properties screen. Right-click on the Web Dynpro DC name and select **Properties**. In the pop-up window, select **Web Dynpro References** from the list on the left, and then select the tab called **JCO References**. Here you will see all JCo logical systems referenced by your project or DC (see Figure 13.26).

2. If you want to change the references used by your model objects, don't try to change them in the screen in Figure 13.26; instead, you need to modify the model object definitions themselves.

3. To change the logical system for the RFC metadata, select the Dictionaries node under your Web Dynpro DC and then select the Model node for the relevant model object. Now select the **Properties** tab and you will see the name of the logical system as in Figure 13.27. The value can be overwritten here.

4. To change the logical system for model instances, open the Models node under your Web Dynpro DC and then the appropriate Adaptive RFC model object.

437

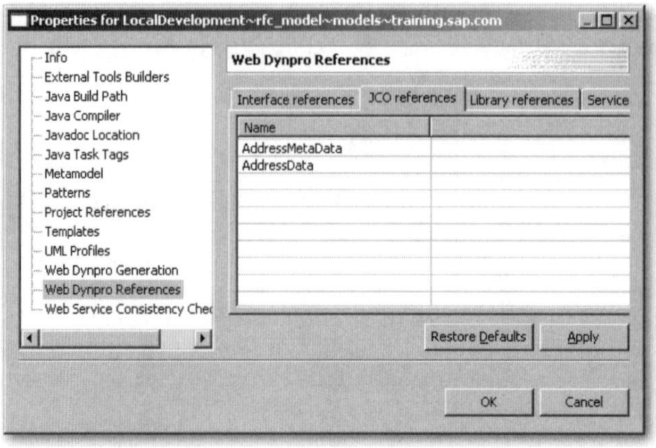

**Figure 13.26** JCo References Within a Web Dynpro DC

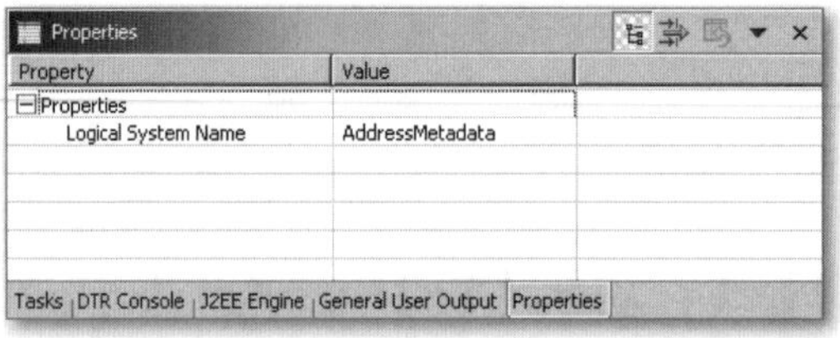

**Figure 13.27** Model Object Property Showing the Logical System for RFC Metadata

5. Then double-click on *any* of the subordinate model classes and again select the **Properties** tab. You will see two sets of properties: those that are specific to the individual model class you selected and those that are specific to the model object in general. Under **Model Settings** you will see the name of the logical system, and this can also be overwritten (see Figure 13.28).

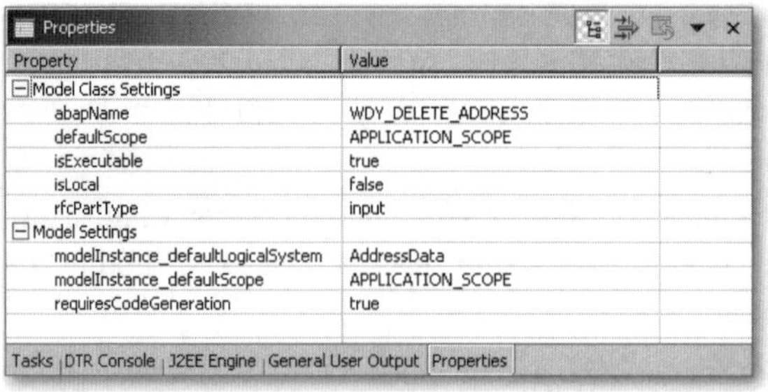

**Figure 13.28** Model Object Property Showing the Logical System for Model Instance Data

After you have made these modifications, re-display the screen shown in Figure 13.26, and you will notice that now both the old and new JCo destination names are listed. It is a good idea to remove the old names from this list. Otherwise, when you deploy this application, the AS Java will think your application has a dependency on the old JCo destination name(s), when in reality it doesn't. This is just a matter of good housekeeping.

## 13.11   A Simple Example Using Context Model Nodes at Runtime

This sample application is one in which basic address maintenance is performed. This application lives in a DC called `AdaptiveRFC` and has a single application called `AdaptiveRFCApp` and a single component called `AdaptiveRFCComp`.

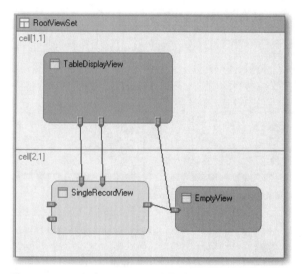

**Figure 13.29** Window Diagram of the AdaptiveRFC Application Showing the Navigation Paths Between the Different View

Figure 13.29 shows that the screen is composed from a viewset of one column and two rows. In the first row, the view `TableDisplayView` has been embedded, and this uses a table UI element to display the address details. In the bottom view, the default view is `EmptyView`. The business process is that the user is displayed a list of addresses in the table UI element in `TableDisplayView`. The user can either select a row from the table or create a new address. Either way, an outbound plug is fired that causes the address details view `SingleRecordView` to appear in the viewset row as shown in Figure 13.30.

If the user clicks the **Create new address** button, the view shown in Figure 13.31 will appear. The same view is reused for display purposes when the user clicks either the **Display previous address** or **Display next address** button (see Figure 13.32).

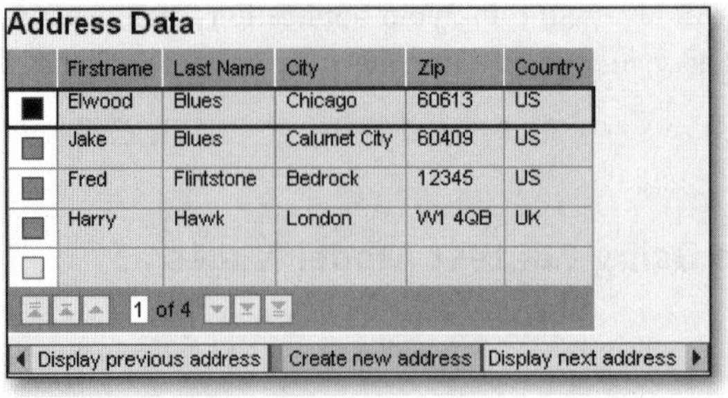

**Figure 13.30** Layout of TableDisplayView

**Figure 13.31** SingleRecordView Used for Creating a New Address

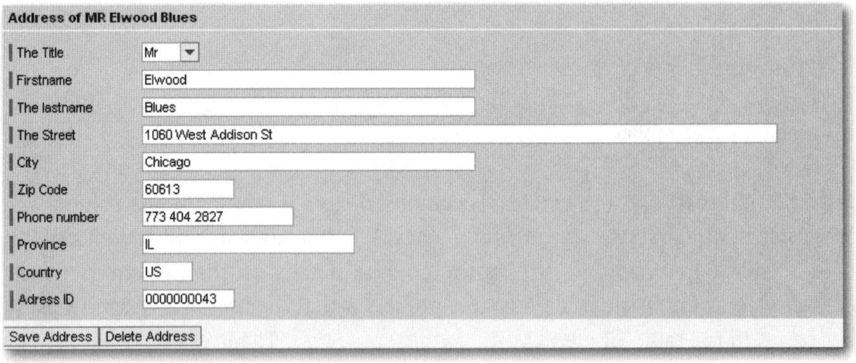

**Figure 13.32** SingleRecordView Used for Displaying or Editing an Existing Address

### 13.11.1 Preparing the Context at Design Time

The context of the component controller for `AdaptiveRFCComp` is shown above in Figure 13.24. The model nodes have been created in the Data Modeler by dragging each `${rfm}_Input` class from the model on the right-hand side and dropping it on the context structure shown on the left-hand side. All duplicate node names have been renamed manually. (Incidentally, why do the output classes Wdy_Delete_ Address_Output and Wdy_New_Address_Output have no "plus" icons next to them?)[9]

The context also contains a value node called CurrentAddressData, which is of type Wdy_Demo_Address. This means its metadata is identical to the structured parameters returned by the RFC modules. The purpose of this value node is to act as a holding area for the address data currently being either displayed or created.

### 13.11.2   Component Controller Coding

When the component AdaptiveRFCComp is instantiated, the first task that must be performed is the preparation of the model objects for use via the context. This preparation need only occur once per component lifecycle; therefore, it can be placed in the method wdDoInit() of the AdaptiveRFCComp component controller.

---

**Caveat Confector**

When programming with context model nodes and model objects, you must make a clear distinction between coding that manipulates the context model node and coding that manipulates the model object bound to the node.

If you get the two types of object muddled up, you can get some very confusing results.

---

```
public void wdDoInit() {
  //@@begin wdDoInit()
  // Create the reference to the component's message
  // manager
  msgMgr = wdComponentAPI().getMessageManager();

  // Create instances of the RFC module proxy objects
  // These objects always describe the input side of
  // the RFC module's interface. The output side of the
  // interface is always represented as a child of the
  // input side.
  getAddressListInput   =
    new Wdy_Get_List_Address_Input();
  getSingleAddressInput =
    new Wdy_Get_Single_Address_Input();
  deleteAddressInput    =
    new Wdy_Delete_Address_Input();
  newAddressInput       = new Wdy_New_Address_Input();
  // Bind model objects to the corresponding context
  // model nodes
  wdContext.nodeWdy_Get_List_Address_Input().
          bind(getAddressListInput);
  wdContext.nodeWdy_Get_Single_Address_Input().
          bind(getSingleAddressInput);
```

---

9   This is because these RFC modules do not return any data.

```
wdContext.nodeWdy_Delete_Address_Input().
        bind(deleteAddressInput);
wdContext.nodeWdy_New_Address_Input().
        bind(newAddressInput);

// Create an instance of the specific model object
// to hold new address information. This corresponds
// to the IMPORTING parameter ADDRESS for RFC module
// WDY_NEW_ADDRESS
Wdy_Demo_Address theAddress = new Wdy_Demo_Address();

// Associate the model object for the new address
// information with the model object representing the
// input side of the WDY_NEW_ADDRESS RFC module.
// This correctly establishes aparent/child
// relationship between these objects
newAddressInput.setAddress(theAddress);

// Read all available addresses
readAddressData();
//@@end
}

//@@begin others
private Wdy_Get_List_Address_Input getAddressListInput;
private Wdy_Delete_Address_Input   deleteAddressInput;
private Wdy_New_Address_Input      newAddressInput;
private Wdy_Get_Single_Address_Input
                                  getSingleAddressInput;

private IWDMessageManager          msgMgr;
//@@end
```

**Listing 13.2** Coding to prepare the context model nodes of component Adaptive RFC

Notice that three principal tasks are being performed here:

1. The proxy objects for each RFC module are first instantiated. These proxy objects are executable model objects and represent the entire input side of each RFC module's interface.

   Notice that the proxy object variables are declared between the //@@begin others and //@@end markers that occur at the end of the source code. In this application, we only need one instance of each RFC module proxy object; therefore, to avoid having to pass object references around as parameters, we can declare class-wide objects for use throughout the entire instance.

2. Each of the model object instances created in step 1 are then bound to the corresponding context model nodes. This action completely replaces the model node's element collection with the object being bound. See the class reference entry for IWDNode.bind() for more information on the behavior of this method.

3. Of the four RFC modules called by this application, only one (WDY_NEW_ADDRESS) requires input in the form of a data structure. Therefore, it is also necessary to create a model object for the structured input parameter ADDRESS of the RFC module WDY_NEW_ADDRESS.

Once the model object representing the structured field ADDRESS has been created (called theAddress), it is associated with the parent model object (called newAddressInput). The executable model object for the RFC module WDY_NEW_ADDRESS now knows that it has a child object representing the IMPORTING structure called ADDRESS. See Figure 13.24 and Appendix D (ABAP Coding) to compare the structure of the context and the structure of the RFC module interface.

### Avoid Making an Easy Mistake

If you do not have a good understanding of the relationship between model objects and the context model nodes to which they are bound, it is likely that you will fail to spot the error in the following code.

The wdDoInit() method shown in Listing 13.2 has been repeated below, with a couple of small, but highly significant, changes.

```
public void wdDoInit() {
  //@@begin wdDoInit()
<snip>
  newAddressInput = new Wdy_New_Address_Input();
  wdContext.nodeWdy_New_Address_Input().
                               bind(newAddressInput);
<snip>
  // Create an instance of the specific model object to
  // hold new address information. This corresponds to
  // the IMPORTING parameter ADDRESS for RFC module
  // WDY_NEW_ADDRESS
  Wdy_Demo_Address theAddress = new Wdy_Demo_Address();

  // Add a new element to the ADDRESS model node to hold the
  // input parameters
  INew_AddressElement newAddrEl =
    wdContext.nodeNew_Address.
      createNew_AddressElement(theAddress);
  wdContext.nodeNew_Address.addElement(newAddrEl);
  // Read all available addresses
  readAddressData();
  //@@end
}
```

**Listing 13.3** Incorrect coding attempting to add structured parameter information to a model object

Whilst this coding may seem plausible, it will result in a runtime error. This error is due to a misunderstanding of how the elements of a model node's collection relate to the actual model objects. The following line of reasoning is usually the cause:

1. The object `newAddressInput` is an executable model object that represents the entire input side of the RFC module `WDY_NEW_ADDRESS`. This object has a mandatory structured `IMPORTING` parameter called `ADDRESS`.

2. The model object `theAddress` represents the `IMPORTING` parameter `ADDRESS` of this RFC module.

3. The model object representing the `IMPORTING` parameter `ADDRESS` (`theAddress`) must be recognized as the child of the model object `newAddressInput`.

4. In the context, the model node `Wdy_New_Address_Input` has had the model object `newAddressInput` bound to it.

5. The model node `New_Address` is the child node of the model node `Wdy_New_Address_Input`.

6. Therefore, if I add the model object `theAddress` to the element collection of the model node `New_Address`, it will become the child of the model object `newAddressInput` because the parent model object lives in the parent model node `Wdy_New_Address_Input`.

Oops! NO!

The logic is fine up until the last step, when an illogical conclusion is drawn from otherwise logical information. The fault lies in the failure to realize that context model nodes only hold references to model objects. You cannot establish a parent–child relationship between two model objects simply by binding them to the corresponding context nodes.

Therefore, for a parent–child relationship to exist between two model objects, the setter method in the parent model object must be called and passed a reference to the child model object. Only then will the two objects be hierarchically related.

In our example, the vital missing statement is:[10]

```
newAddressInput.setAddress(theAddress);
```

Syntactically, the highlighted code in Listing 13.3 is perfectly correct and will genuinely add an element to the child model `New_Address`. However, if you were then to populate `newAddrEl` with data and execute the RFC module, you would get a runtime error saying that the mandatory parameter `ADDRESS` has not been supplied.

---

10   Once this association has been made between the model objects, the context can be synchronized with the model objects by calling the `invalidate()` method of the relevant context model node.

The consequence of all this is that the highlighted statements in Listing 13.3 serve no useful purpose and should be replaced by the single statement shown above.

### Using Model Objects at Runtime

The following stages are required to prepare the model objects and context model nodes for use:

1. Instantiate the executable model objects (in this case, these are the `${rfm}_Input` objects).

2. Bind these objects to the correct model nodes in the context.

3. Associate all parent and child model objects with each other.

Steps 2 and 3 do not necessarily need to be done in this order.

When a model object's `execute()` method is called (see Figure 13.33, step ❶), the input parameter values are passed to the backend system, and the ABAP functionality is invoked. As soon as the ABAP function module has performed its task, the output data is returned to Web Dynpro, and the model object is updated. However, the context node to which the model object is bound must be told to resynchronize itself with the model object. This is performed by calling the context node's `invalidate()` method (step ❷). After this has completed, the context node points to the new data in the model object.

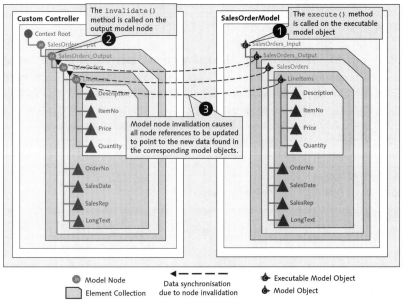

**Figure 13.33** After a Model Object Has Been Executed, the Associated Context Model Node Must Be Synchronised by Calling the Node's invalidate() Method

To show the use of the model objects, we will go through the coding that first displays a list of all the addresses, and then we will look at the coding to create a new address.

Based on the principles discussed in Section 3.4, all interaction with the model objects is confined to the component controller. In turn, the data supplied by the model objects is available to the view controllers through context mapping.

As you can see from the component diagram in Figure 13.34, both view controllers have declared that they require the use of the component controller. This means both TableDisplayView and SingleRecordView have access to all the data in the component controller's context and it methods.

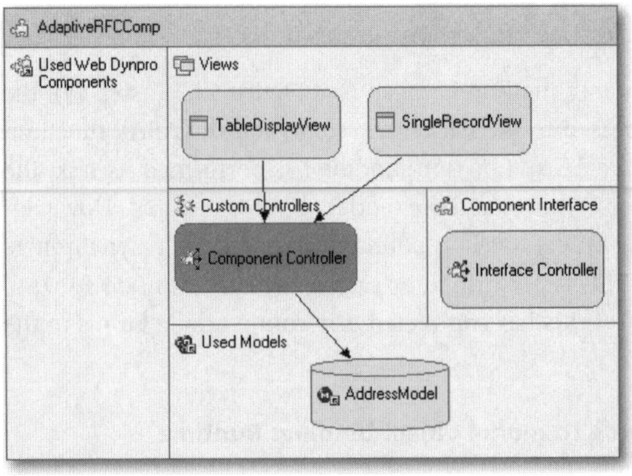

**Figure 13.34** Diagram View of the Component AdaptiveRFCComp

The coding in Listing 13.4 to Listing 13.8 follows immediately after that in Listing 82. Standard methods such as wdDoExit() and wdDoPostProcessing() have been omitted from these listings because they have not been implemented. The following user-defined methods have been declared:

- readAddressData()
  Reads all available addresses
- readSingleAddress()
  Reads the address data for the given address id
- createNewAddress()
  Creates a new address using the data in node currentAddressData
- deleteAddress()
  Deletes the address data for the given address id
- doErrorMsg()
  Utility method to handle any model object execution errors

```
public void readAddressData( ) {
  //@@begin readAddressData()
  try {
    // Invoke the RFC module to return a list of
    // addresses
    getAddressListInput.execute();
    // Synchronise the context node representing the
    // output side of the RFC interface with updated
    // model object
    wdContext.nodeAddressList_Output().invalidate();
  }
  catch (WDDynamicRFCExecuteException e) {
    doErrorMsg(e);
  }
  //@@end
}
```

**Listing 13.4** The method readAddressData()

```
public void readSingleAddress(java.lang.String id) {
  //@@begin readSingleAddress()
  // Store the address id in the inbound side of the
  // model object's interface.  This could be done via
  // the context, but the coding is shorter and easier
  // to understand if the model object is accessed
  // directly.
  getSingleAddressInput.setId(id);

  try {
    // Invoke the RFC module to return a single address
    getSingleAddressInput.execute();
    // Synchronise the context node representing the
    // output side of the RFC interface with updated
    // model object
    wdContext.nodeSingle_Output().invalidate();

    // Copy the returned address information from the
    // context
    // model node to the value node acting as a
    // temporary holding area
    WDCopyService.
      copyCorresponding(
        wdContext.currentAddressElement(),
        wdContext.currentCurrentAddressDataElement());
  }
  catch (WDDynamicRFCExecuteException e) {
    doErrorMsg(e);
  }
    //@@end
  }
```

**Listing 13.5** The method readSingleAddress()

```
public void createNewAddress( ) {
  //@@begin createNewAddress()
  // Get references to the current (only!) element in
  // the temporary holding area, and the current
  // element in the New_Address node
  ICurrentAddressDataElement addrSrcEl =
    wdContext.currentCurrentAddressDataElement();
  INew_AddressElement addrDestEl        =
    wdContext.currentNew_AddressElement();

  // Copy the data from the holding area to the RFC
  // module input parameter called ADDRESS
  WDCopyService.
    copyCorresponding(addrSrcEl, addrDestEl);

  try {
    // Invoke the RFC module to create an address
    newAddressInput.execute();
    // Synchronisation is not necessary here because
    // this particular RFC module produces no output

    // Re-read address data to refresh display
    readAddressData();
  }
  catch (WDDynamicRFCExecuteException e) {
    doErrorMsg(e);
  }
  //@@end
}
```

**Listing 13.6** The method createNewAddress()

```
public void deleteAddress(java.lang.String id) {
  //@@begin deleteAddress()
  // Store the address id in the inbound side of the
  // model object's interface.  This call could be made
  // via the context, but the coding is shorter and
  // easier to understand if the model object is
  // accessed directly.
    deleteAddressInput.setId(id);

  try {
    // Invoke the RFC module to delete the address
    deleteAddressInput.execute();
    // Synchronisation is not necessary here because
    // this particular RFC module produces no output

    // Re-read address data in order to refresh display
    readAddressData();
  }
```

```
  catch (WDDynamicRFCExecuteException e) {
    doErrorMsg(e);
  }
  //@@end
}
```

**Listing 13.7** The method deleteAddress()

```
public void
  doErrorMsg(WDDynamicRFCExecuteException e ) {
  //@@begin doErrorMsg()
  // Get the error message for the current locale
  String msg = e.getLocalizedMessage();

  // If there isn't one, then get the locale
  // independent message
  if (msg == null || msg.length() == 0)
    msg = e.getMessage();

  // If there isn't one of these either, then get the
  // string representation of the exception
  if (msg == null || msg.length() == 0)
    msg = e.toString();

  // Issue the exception message as a warning through
  // the message manager
  msgMgr.reportWarning(msg);
  //@@end
}
```

**Listing 13.8** The method doErrorMsg()

Notice that a common set of steps exists in each method that invokes a model object's functionality. The RFC module ${rfm} is represented by the class ${rfm}_Input. This class is then instantiated as the model object ${mo}. Using these abbreviations, the following steps can be seen in each method:

1. Supply data to the correct instance of the class ${rfm}_Input. This can be done either by manipulating the context model node to which the model object is bound[11] or by direct manipulation of the model object. Direct access to the model object makes the coding easier to read.

2. Within a try/catch construct, invoke the RFC module either by calling wdContext.node${mn}().modelObject().execute()[12] or directly by calling ${mo}.execute().

---

11  This is only possible after the model object ${mo} has been bound to the context model node.
12  Again, invoking an executable model via the context can take place only if the model object has been bound to the context model node.

3. After the model functionality has completed, the model node representing the output side of `${rfm}`'s interface must be invalidated.

4. Calling the method `wdContext.node${mo}_Output.invalidate()` causes all references in the model node's element collection to be discarded and resynchronized with the new data found in the model object. This process is performed recursively down the context hierarchy, starting from the invalidated node, so you do not need to call the `invalidate()` method for each node in a hierarchy.

5. The exception processing implemented in the `catch` clauses is simplistic in this example but is illustrative of the use of a message manager object. The message manager displays as many error messages as required when the component's view assembly is next rendered.[13] See Section 11.3 for more information on error handling in large applications.

### 13.11.3 View Controller Coding

One of the most frequently made mistakes in Web Dynpro programming is to place business functionality within the coding of a view controller. Remember the data consumer–data generator principle? Is a view controller a generator or consumer of data? If you didn't answer "data consumer," then you've missed a fundamental design principle.

The only coding that should be placed in a view controller is that responsible for managing the user interface and responding to user input. Interacting with a backend system is not the responsibility of a view controller, because that would turn it into a data generator. Just because it is technically possible to call an ABAP function module from a view controller does not mean your application is well designed.

The coding here implements the correct design principles. Any time a view controller handles a user action that requires a call to the backend system, that call is always handled by a non-visual controller.

#### Coding for the View TableDisplayView

The functionality of the view shown in Figure 13.30 is very simple. Consequently, the context is simple, and very little coding is required in the controller's implementation.

Notice in Figure 13.35, that context mapping has only been performed for the `Address_List` node on the output side of the RFC module `WDY_GET_ADDRESS`'s interface. This is the only information required in the view layout; therefore, no other node mappings are required.

---

13  The message manager is a singleton with respect to a Web Dynpro component.

**Figure 13.35** Context for the View TableDisplayView

The only methods that have been implemented in this view controller are the following four UI action handlers:

▶ `New`
Create a new address entry

▶ `Previous`
Skip to previous address

▶ `Next`
Skip to next address

▶ `SelectionChange`
User clicks on row in table UI element

These action handlers are responsible for firing the following outbound plugs (see Figure 13.29):

▶ `DisplayNewOut`
Trigger navigation to an initialized `SingleRecordView`

▶ `DisplaySingleOut`
Trigger navigation to a populated `SingleRecordView`

```
public void onActionNew( IWDCustomEvent wdEvent ) {
  //@@begin onActionNew(ServerEvent)
  wdThis.wdFirePlugDisplayNewOut();
  //@@end
}
```

**Listing 13.9** Event handler for new address

This event handler simply fires an outbound plug to invoke the display of view Sin-gleRecordView in an initialized state.

```
public void onActionNext(IWDCustomEvent wdEvent ) {
  //@@begin onActionNext(ServerEvent)
  int thisEl = wdContext.nodeAddress_List().
             getLeadSelection();
  int elCnt = wdContext.nodeAddress_List().size();
  // Prevent variable jumpTo from going off the end
  // of the element collection
  int jumpTo = (thisEl == -1)
             ? 0
             : ((thisEl + 1 == elCnt)
                ? thisEl
                : ++thisEl);

  wdContext.nodeAddress_List().
    setLeadSelection(jumpTo);
  wdThis.wdFirePlugDisplaySingleOut(
          wdContext.currentAddress_ListElement().
             getId());
  //@@end
}
```

**Listing 13.10** Event handler to show next address

When attempting to display the next element in a collection, it is very important that the value of the lead selection is not incremented off the end of the node's element collection. Hence, the ternary operator has been used to provide a compact range check for the new index value jumpTo.

Once the lead selection of the node Address_List has been correctly incremented, the outbound plug is fired to invoke the display of the view SingleRecordView in a populated state.

```
public void onActionPrevious(IWDCustomEvent wdEvent ) {
  //@@begin onActionPrevious(ServerEvent)
  int thisEl = wdContext.nodeAddress_List().
             getLeadSelection();
  // Prevent variable jumpTo from going off the
  // beginning of the element collection
  int jumpTo = (thisEl == -1)
             ? 0
             : ((thisEl - 1 < 0)
                ? 0
                : --thisEl);

  wdContext.nodeAddress_List().
    setLeadSelection(jumpTo);
```

```
wdThis.wdFirePlugDisplaySingleOut(
        wdContext.currentAddress_ListElement().
            getId());
//@@end
}
```

**Listing 13.11** Event handler to show previous address

When attempting to display the previous element in a collection, it is very important that the value of the lead selection is not decremented below zero. This is because a lead selection value of -1 means that no element is currently selected. Again, the ternary operator has been used to provide a compact range check for the new index value jumpTo.

Once the lead selection of node Address_List has been correctly decremented, the outbound plug is fired to invoke the display of the view SingleRecordView in a populated state.

```
public void
  onActionSelectionChange(IWDCustomEvent wdEvent ) {
  //@@begin onActionSelectionChange(ServerEvent)
  if (wdContext.currentAddress_ListElement() != null)
    wdThis.wdFirePlugOutDisplaySingle(
            wdContext.currentAddress_ListElement().
                getId());
  //@@end
}
```

**Listing 13.12** Event handler to show previous address

Whenever a user clicks on a row in a table UI element, it is possible to trap this event by assigning an action to the table's onLeadSelect event. In this case, the action is called SelectionChange, so the event handler method is called onAction-SelectionChange().

As long as there is an element to display (this could also be determined by testing that wdContext.nodeAddress_List.getLeadSelection() != -1), fire the outbound plug to display the details of the selected table row. This invokes the display of the view SingleRecordView in a populated state.

### Coding for the View SingleRecordView

The context of the view SingleRecordView (see Figure 13.36) is just as simple as the context of TableDisplayView, except this time a mapped *value* node is used instead of a mapped *model* node. If a UI element is bound to an attribute of a mapped node, that UI element can receive data from and supply data to the mapping origin node.

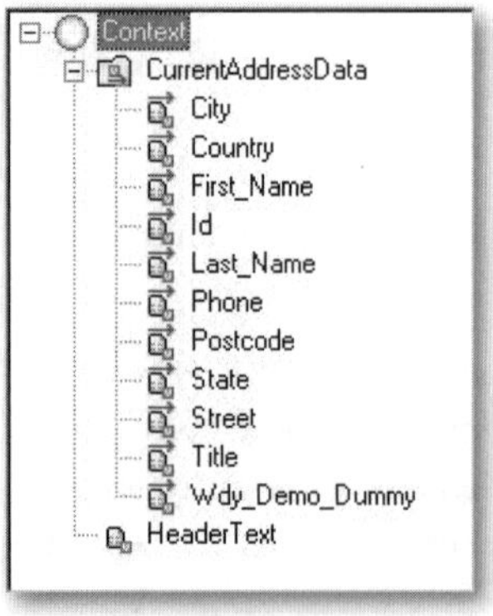

**Figure 13.36** Context for the View SingleRecordView

The independent attribute HeaderText is a calculated attribute that supplies the text seen at the top of the Group UI element in Figure 13.31 and Figure 13.32 (see Section 5.11). This means no data is stored in HeaderText at runtime; instead, its associated getter method (getHeaderText()) is called every time the attribute's value is required.

Because context mapping is being used here, no action is required at component initialization time. Consequently, the standard hook method wdDoInit() contains no coding.

The view controller SingleRecordView has two declared actions:

▶ **Save**
Save the current address details

▶ **Delete**
Delete the current address details

```
public void onActionSave(IWDCustomEvent wdEvent ) {
  //@@begin onActionSave(ServerEvent)
  wdThis.wdGetAdaptiveRFCCompController().
    createNewAddress();
  //@@end
}
```

**Listing 13.13** Event handler for the action Save

In keeping with the design principle that a view controller should not interact directly with a model object, the address details are saved by calling the appropriate method in the component controller. Context mapping ensures that the data entered by the user through the view's UI elements is automatically available to the component controller.

```
public void onActionDelete(IWDCustomEvent wdEvent ) {
  //@@begin onActionDelete(ServerEvent)
  String id = wdContext.
          currentCurrentAddressDataElement().getId();

  wdThis.wdGetAdaptiveRFCCompController().
    deleteAddress(id);
  wdThis.wdFirePlugHideMeOut();
  //@@end
}
```
**Listing 13.14** Event handler for the action Delete

The Delete action handler must conform to the same design principle as the Save action handler. The action handler in the view controller does not interact directly with the model object; instead, it calls the appropriate method in the component controller to delete the address details. After this has completed, the outbound plug is fired to hide the view SingleRecordView.

The view controller SingleRecordView has the following inbound plugs:

▶ **CreateNewIn**
   Cause the view layout to be initialized

▶ **DisplaySingleIn**
   Read the address details for the specified address id.

```
public void onPlugCreateNewIn(IWDCustomEvent wdEvent ) {
  //@@begin onPlugCreateNewIn(ServerEvent)
  initAddressData();
  //@@end
}
```
**Listing 13.15** Initialize the view when the CreateNewIn inbound plug is fired

This plug is fired in response to a user's request to create a new address. Therefore, each element in the context node to which the UI elements are bound must be initialized (see Figure 13.36):

```
public void onPlugDisplaySingleIn(IWDCustomEvent wdEvent,
                                  String id ) {
  //@@begin onPlugDisplaySingleIn(ServerEvent)
  wdThis.wdGetAdaptiveRFCCompController().readSingleAddress(id);
  //@@end
}
```
**Listing 13.16** Inbound plug DisplaySingleIn

This plug is fired in response to a user's request to display the details of a specific address. This address is identified by the parameter id. As before, the view controller does not interact directly with the model object, but calls the appropriate method in the component controller to read the address data.

Two other methods must briefly be shown: initAddressData() and the getter method for the calculated attribute HeaderText, called getHeaderText().

```
public void initAddressData() {
  //@@begin initAddressData( )
  IWDNodeInfo     nodeInfo =
    wdContext.nodeCurrentAddressData().getNodeInfo();
  IWDNodeElement elem      =
    wdContext.currentCurrentAddressDataElement();

  // Initialise attribute values using the default
  // value of the simple type
  for (Iterator iter = nodeInfo.iterateAttributes();
    iter.hasNext();) {
    IWDAttributeInfo attrInfo =
      (IWDAttributeInfo)iter.next();

    elem.setAttributeValue(attrInfo.getName(),
      attrInfo.getSimpleType().getDefaultValue());
  }

  // The ABAP data type NUMC is currently represented
  // as a Java String. The only drawback is that in
  // ABAP, NUMC fields have an initial value of "all
  // zeroes", whereas a string has the initial value
  // of "" (empty string).  Therefore, the
  // getDefaultValue() method will not return the
  // correct initial value for this data type.
  wdContext.currentCurrentAddressDataElement().
            setId("0000000000");
  //@@end
}
```

**Listing 13.17** The method initAddressData()

In order to initialize a context node in a generic manner, it is necessary to examine the data type of each attribute and then assign the appropriate initial value for that data type. This functionality assumes that all the attributes of the context node are based on dictionary simple types.

An iterator is obtained to return the metadata of the node's attributes, and then each attribute in the element is reset to the default initial value for its data type. This coding does not require a nested loop, because there will only ever be at most one element in the node (cardinality = 0..1).

Last, since the id field is of data type String, its initial value is the empty string, but this field is interpreted by ABAP as a numeric character value (type NUMC). Therefore, the correct initial value is to pad the field with zeroes.

```
public String getHeaderText(IPrivateSingleRecordView.
             IContextElement element) {
  //@@begin
  String msg;
  ICurrentAddressDataElement addrEl =
    wdContext.currentCurrentAddressDataElement();

  if (wdContext.nodeCurrentAddressData().isEmpty())
    msg = "Address entry not possible";
  else if(addrEl.getFirst_Name() == null)
    msg = "Enter new address";
  else
    msg = "Address of "          + " " +
          addrEl.getTitle()      + " " +
          addrEl.getFirst_Name() + " " +
          addrEl.getLast_Name();

  return msg;
  //@@end
}
```

**Listing 13.18** Getter method for calculated attribute HeaderText

This getter method first checks that the node actually has an element in it. If it does not, it will be impossible for the user to enter any data through the UI, because there is no element in the context node in which the information can be stored. Under these circumstances, any UI elements bound to context attributes that do not exist at runtime will be disabled for user input.

If there is an empty element, we must be entering a new address — hence the "Enter new address" message. Otherwise, construct the header text from the title, first name, and last name.

### 13.11.4 Look at What Has Not Been Done

Do you notice what type of coding is missing from all of these methods? Someone with a JSP coding background will probably have noticed that at no time has any interaction with specific UI element objects taken place.

By now, you should be able to answer the following question: How do the data get from the model object onto the screen without any code being written?

Well, you have written some code — you just did it declaratively rather than explicitly. Three declarations have been made that create the required chain of connections. This chain is built and operates as follows:

1. The model object is bound to a context model node in the component controller.

2. The component controller then invokes the model's functionality.

3. After the `invalidate()` method has been called for the `${rfm}_Output` model node, the data within the model object is available to the context.

4. The data in the component controller's context acts as the mapping origin for the mapped nodes in both view controllers.

5. The context nodes in the view controller have UI elements directly bound to them. Therefore, the data in the context attributes act as the suppliers, and the UI element properties act as consumers.

6. The Web Dynpro Framework then handles the screen rendering for you based on the following chain of connections (this is also shown in Figure 13.37):

   Model object → component controller's context → view controller's context → UI element property.

In this example, only a single line of code needs to be written, namely the call to the `invalidate()` method. This synchronizes the references in the model node's element collection, with the new data in the model object. After that, the Web Dynpro Framework automatically transports the data from the model object through to the UI elements on the screen.

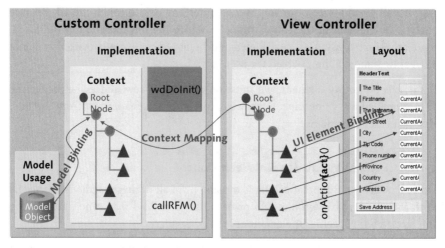

**Figure 13.37** The Data Flow from a Model Object to a UI Element

## 13.12   Adapting to Changes in an RFC Interface

In this situation, we have two view controllers, both of which are displaying information derived from a model object. Since TableDisplayView is only showing a tabular overview, it is unnecessary to modify this view layout when the RFC module's interface changes.

However, SingleRecordView displays all the details of the selected address. Therefore, we have to add some coding to this view controller to handle any changes in the RFC module's interface. As with all the other areas of Web Dynpro programming that we have dealt with, some fundamental principles must be understood.

► The view layout is composed of UI elements that are handled in two ways:

  ▸ A static set of UI elements is declared at design time and requires no programmatic adjustment.

  ▸ A dynamic set of UI elements is known only at runtime. The UI element hierarchy needs dynamic modification to account for these new fields.

► Adaptation can only take place for fields within .APPEND structures of ABAP tables.

► The static view layout created at design time must be built in such a way that the area used for field display can expand in response to changes in the RFC module's interface.

If you refer back to Figure 13.3, you will notice that the last field in the structure WDY_DEMO_ADDRESS is a .APPEND field called WDY_DEMO_APPEND.[14] Also notice that the only field in this structure is a CHAR1 field called WDY_DEMO_DUMMY. This field was omitted from the static UI layout in Figure 13.32 because it carried no useful information. This field cannot be dropped from the structure of WDY_DEMO_APPEND, so we have to implement coding that suppresses its display.

> **Important**
>
> The Adaptive RFC layer assumes that all interfaces changes are additive.

Now the .APPEND structure WDY_DEMO_APPEND has been modified to include six new fields (see Figure 13.38).

To account for these changes in the RFC module's interface, we do not need to re-import the model object; we do need to write some code that generically handles additional fields. When the function module is called for the first time,[15] the Adap-

---

14 The .APPEND syntax appearing in an ABAP table definition indicates that the fields found in the dictionary structure (in this case WDY_DEMO_APPEND) are to be included at this point in the table.

15 The first time that is, since this node of the AS Java has started.

tive RFC layer will query the SAP system, and discover that the structure of the interface has changed. It will then adapt the relevant dictionary structures to reflect the new interface. The modified definitions will then be available to the Web Dynpro application through the Java dictionary.

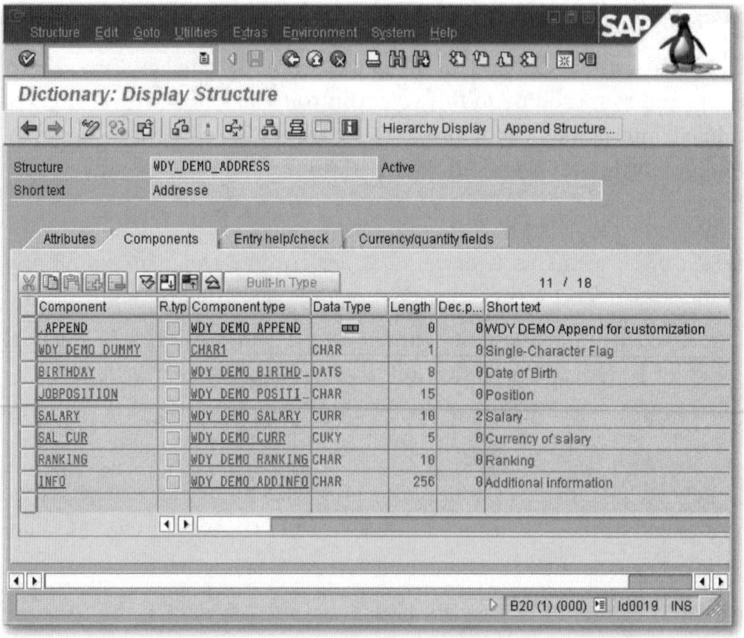

**Figure 13.38** New Fields Added to the .APPEND Structure WDY_DEMO_APPEND

It is now your responsibility to check for new fields and adapt the UI layout accordingly. The code to do this must be executed from within the method wdDoModify-View(), and can be implemented in the following way:

```
public static void
    wdDoModifyView(IPrivate${nv} wdThis,
                   IPrivate${nv}.IContextNode wdContext,
                   IWDView view,
                   boolean firstTime) {
//@@begin wdDoModifyView
boolean appendFound = false;

// Find out what dictionary structure is used to
// define context node CurrentAddressData
IWDNodeInfo nodeInfo =
  wdContext.nodeCurrentAddressData().getNodeInfo();
IStructure structure = nodeInfo.getStructureType();

// Is the context node based on a dictionary
```

```
    // structure and are we building the screen for the
    // first time?
    if (structure != null && firstTime) {
      // Loop around all the attributes in the
      // dictionary structure
      for (Iterator iterator = structure.fieldIterator();
        iterator.hasNext();) {
        IField field = (IField)iterator.next();

        // Does the current field belong to an
        // append structure?
        if (!appendFound)
        // Nope, check the current field
          appendFound = field.belongsToAppend();
        else
          // Add the next .append field to the UI
          addFieldToLayout(view, wdContext,
                           nodeInfo, field.getName());
    }
  }
  //@@end
}
```

**Listing 13.19** wdDoModifyView() coding to check for additional fields in a model node's metadata

Notice that the class names of the parameters to the method `wdDoModifyView()` have been generalized.

The coding now starts to make use of the dictionary structure classes `IStructure` and `IField`. These classes can be found in the package `com.sap.dictionary.runtime`. The processing is very straightforward here:

▶ Get a reference to the metadata of the context model node that may have changed.

▶ From the metadata object, get a reference to the dictionary structure that defines this model node.

▶ Check that the model node is defined on a dictionary structure and that this is the first time the view has been processed.

▶ Loop around the iterator of fields supplied by the dictionary structure.

▶ Since we don't want to display the dummy field in the .APPEND structure, the coding should always skip the first field. This is achieved by switching on the flag `appendFound` after the first .APPEND field has been found. This allows all subsequent .APPEND fields to be processed and avoids the need for any explicit reference to the field `WDY_DEMO_DUMMY`.

▶ If the current field belongs to a .APPEND structure, call the method `addFieldToLayout()` to include this field in the UI element hierarchy.

Since the method `addFieldToLayout()` is called from the static method `wdDoModify-View()`, it must be created between the `//@@begin` and `//@@end` comment markers.

So far, we have had no need to know about the structure of the static UI element hierarchy, but now that we are going to extend this hierarchy, some structural details need to be known. The static UI element hierarchy of `SingleRecordView` is shown in Figure 13.39. Compare this hierarchy with the rendered screen in Figure 13.32.

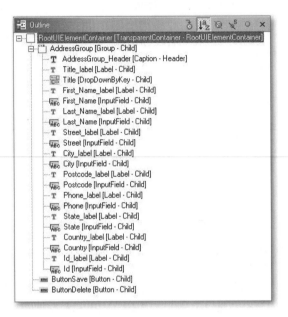

**Figure 13.39** Static UI Element Hierarchy of SingleRecordView

Since the static label-input field pairs live in the Group UI element `AddressGroup`, any additional label-input field pairs ought also to live within this UI element container.

```
//@@begin others
private static void
  addFieldToLayout(IWDView view,
                   IPrivate${nv}.IContextNode wdContext,
                   IWDNodeInfo nodeInfo,
                   String fieldName) {
  // New element for user input — we don't know what
  // type it will be yet
  IWDUIElement newElem = null;

  // New element identifier
  String newID = "elementFor" + fieldName;
```

```
// Create a new label element
IWDLabel newLabel = (IWDLabel)view.
                    createElement(IWDLabel.class,
                            "labelFor" + fieldName);
newLabel.setLabelFor(newID);
newLabel.createLayoutData(IWDMatrixHeadData.class);

// Get the metadata of the current field
IWDAttributeInfo thisAttrib =
                    nodeInfo.getAttribute(fieldName);

// Get reference to group UI container
IWDUIElementContainer container =
  (IWDUIElementContainer)view.
                            getElement("AddressGroup");

// Is this attribute based on a dictionary simple
// type?
if (thisAttrib.getDataType().isSimpleType()) {
  // Yup. Get both the dictionary simple type and
  // the built-in type from which it is derived
  ISimpleType sType = thisAttrib.getSimpleType();
  String      biType = sType.getBuiltInType();

  // Can the built-in type be represented by some
  // type of input field?
  if (biType.equalsIgnoreCase("string") ||
      biType.equalsIgnoreCase("date")   ||
      biType.equalsIgnoreCase("decimal")) {
    // Yup, can a list of possible inputs be derived
    // for this field? I.E., Does a simple value
    // (SV) service exist for this field, and will
    // the SVService actually return something?
    if ((sType.hasSVService()) &&
        (sType.getSVServices().getValues() != null)){
      // Yup. Use a drop down to display possible
      // input values
      IWDDropDownByKey newField =
        (IWDDropDownByKey)view.
        createElement(IWDDropDownByKey.class, newID);
      // Bind drop down key to context field having
      // the SVService
      newField.
        bindSelectedKey("CurrentAddressData." +
                        fieldName);
      newField.createLayoutData(IWDMatrixData.class);
      newElem = newField;
    }
    // No SVService exists (or can be obtained),
    // so check if this field is longer than 128
    // characters?
```

```
            else if (sType.getMaxExternalLength() > 128 ||
                    sType.getMaxLength()            > 128) {
              // Yup, so display the value in a text edit UI
              // element with wrapping turned on
              IWDTextEdit newField = (IWDTextEdit)view.
                      createElement(IWDTextEdit.class, newID);
              newField.bindValue("CurrentAddressData." +
                                fieldName);
              newField.setWrapping(WDTextWrapping.SOFT);
              newField.createLayoutData(IWDMatrixData.class);
              newElem = newField;
            }
            // No SVService exists (or can be obtained), and the field
            // is < 128 characters in length
            else {
              // Display the value using an input field
              IWDInputField newField = (IWDInputField)view.
                  createElement(IWDInputField.class, newID);
              newField.bindValue("CurrentAddressData." +
                                fieldName);
              newField.createLayoutData(IWDMatrixData.class);
              newElem = newField;
            }
          }
          // If the field type is boolean, then use a
          // checkbox UI element
          else if (biType.equals("boolean")) {
            IWDCheckBox newField = (IWDCheckBox)view.
                      createElement(IWDCheckBox.class, newID);
            newField.bindChecked("CurrentAddressData." +
                                fieldName);
            newField.createLayoutData(IWDMatrixData.class);
            newElem = newField;
          }

          // As long as both the new label and the new
          // element have been created, append them to the
          // group UI container
          if (newLabel != null &&
              newElem   != null) {
            container.addChild(newLabel);
            container.addChild(newElem);
          }
        }
      }
    }
//@@end
```

**Listing 13.20** Coding to incorporate new Adaptive RFC fields to an existing UI element hierarchy

The coding in Listing 13.20 above does not rigorously test all possible data types that could be returned for a given dictionary simple type. However, if you know that the Adaptive RFC interface only adds fields of the types shown in the coding, then the implementation above is sufficient.

The logic of the above coding is very similar to that illustrated in Figure 13.13 to Figure 13.16 in Section 13.10.

Once you have changed the ABAP dictionary structure and activated your changes, all the RFC modules that use the structure WDY_DEMO_ADDRESS in their interface will be updated.

---

**Important**

The J2EE engine contains several caches of all the model objects contained in all the deployed applications. These caches are optimized by technical system. This means that if several different Web Dynpro applications call RFC modules in the same SAP system, and they also share the same ABAP dictionary structures in their interfaces (as often happens with the structure BAPIRET2), then only one copy of that dictionary structure will be held in the model cache.

Two options are available for flushing these caches:

▶ Restart your AS Java

▶ Follow the instructions in the SDN document called "Metadata Cache Invalidation for Webdynpro Adaptive RFC Models," written by Arun Bhat.

---

When the application is now restarted, the view layout will adapt to the new structure as shown in Figure 13.40.

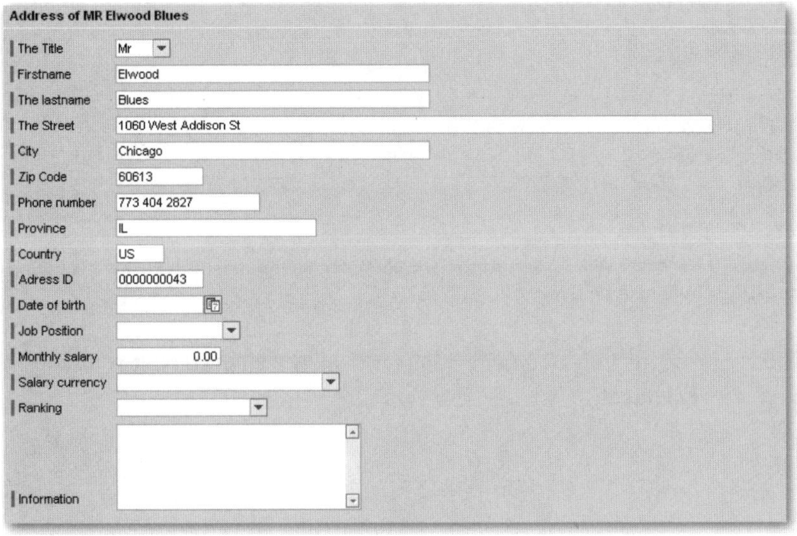

**Figure 13.40** The view SingleRecordView After It Has Adapted to the New RFC Module Interface

There are a couple of things to notice here:

▶ The field `WDY_DEMO_DUMMY` does not appear (see Listing 13.19 for why this is so).

▶ If the data types of the new dictionary fields indicate that possible input values are available, these are obtained and associated with the input field.

▶ Overall, the view `SingleRecordView` has reacted intelligently to the new fields in the dictionary structure.

The Simple Value service automatically provides the possible information that could be entered into a particular field. Three fields on this screen have an associated Simple Value service (see Figure 13.41).

**Figure 13.41** View Drop-Down Lists Whose Values Are Supplied by the Simple Value Service

The Date Picker shown in Figure 13.42 appears automatically because the `Input-Field` UI element has been bound (dynamically) to a context field of type `Date`.

**Figure 13.42** A Date Picker Will Appear Automatically When an InputField UI Element Is Bound to a Context Attribute of Type Date

Since the `WDY_DEMO_APPEND-INFO` field is longer than 128 characters, it is displayed in a `TextEdit` UI element.

# 14 JCo Connection Management

In all the discussion in Chapter 13, one very important subject was not mentioned — that is, how does your Web Dynpro application log on to the back end SAP system?

## 14.1 Connecting to an SAP System

Any time a connection to an SAP system is required, the user or program must supply the correct logon parameters. All SAP systems have a variety of methods for accepting user credentials such as explicit names and passwords or digital certificates. Here we take a look at the basic authentication technique in which a user id and password are supplied.

### 14.1.1 Logon Parameters

To invoke an RFC module in an SAP system, it is necessary for the invoking program to log on to the SAP system. The logon process for a program is identical to the logon process performed by an online user. Four pieces of information are always required:

▶ A user id

▶ A password

▶ The SAP client

▶ A logon language

There is a variety of techniques for supplying these values (for instance, single sign on using a Single Sign-On 2 [SSO2] cookie), but irrespective of the specific technique, without these four identifying values, no connection can be made with an SAP system.

For readers not familiar with an SAP system, the user id and password will be familiar values, but you may not have encountered the need for a language, and you almost certainly will not know what a "client" is.

### 14.1.2 Language

Since SAP systems are multilingual, the logon process requires the two-character ISO code for the language in which you want to operate. The only languages available by default are English (EN) and German (DE). The text for any additional languages must be explicitly imported, which is a process usually performed when the SAP system is installed. This has an important influence when creating model objects.

When you are using the Model Wizard to extract the interface metadata of an ABAP function module, part of this process involves the wizard logging on to the backend system using the four values mentioned above. Here's where you must be careful.

> **Important**
>
> If you have created your Web Dynpro DC in one language (say, Spanish), but then using the Model Wizard, you log on to the backend system in a different language (say, English), to which language will the exported text strings belong?
>
> Well, the language used by the Model Wizard, of course.
>
> But what's the default language for your project?
>
> Oops! You've just stored English text in fields that are assumed to contain Spanish.[1] Web Dynpro will assume that the text strings belong to the DC's default language when in fact they don't. At runtime, therefore, the user would log on in Spanish but be presented with English text on the screen.
>
> You must ensure that all language references in your DC refer to the same language at design time.

### 14.1.3 Client

A term *client* is used to describe a subdivision of an SAP system. These subdivisions do not represent legal entities of your business, but rather, administrative areas within which different data and configurations can be held.

Traditionally, the client value is any three-digit number (with the exceptions of 000, 001, and 066[2]), but it is technically possible to identify an SAP client using any three alphanumeric characters.

All transactional data created by SAP business applications and almost all configuration settings are *client specific*. This means the information exists in only one client of the SAP system. If you were to log on to a different client, you would find a totally different set of configuration and application data.[3]

> **Important**
>
> All SAP user ids are client specific.

---

1 This is called "Spanglish."
2 Client 000 is the system client and is of fundamental importance to the normal running of your SAP system. Don't even think about deleting this client. Client 001 is only present in SAP Enterprise and R/3 systems, and Client 066 is reserved for the SAP EarlyWatch health check service.
3 Technically, all client-specific SAP data is stored in database tables that have the client value as the first field of the primary key.

There is also data in an SAP system that is client independent.[4] Certain areas of application configuration are client independent, but the most important types of data in this category are all ABAP source code and the entire data dictionary. This has the very important consequence that when a program or a dictionary structure is changed and then activated, *all users in all clients will be affected by this change.*

> **Caveat Confector**
>
> Since ABAP programs are client independent, and the business data upon which they operate is client specific, it is entirely possible that when the same program is run by the same user logged on in different clients, the program will produce totally different results.
>
> Therefore, when setting up the JCo destinations in your AS Java, you must know exactly which client you should connect to.

## 14.2    Identifying the Correct Backend System

To ensure that a business application remains decoupled from any specific backend system, the concept of logical JCo destinations is used. For readers familiar with SAP systems, this is exactly the same concept as that provided by transaction SM59.

### 14.2.1    Logical JCo Destinations

When a model object is created for the first time in the NWDS, in addition to the names of the RFC modules to be imported, two other pieces of information must be specified. These are the names of the JCo destinations that will be used for calling the RFC modules found in this model.

> **Important**
>
> You must always specify two JCo destinations for each model. The reason for this is that one will be used for obtaining metadata about the RFC module interfaces, and the other will be used for the actual invocation of the RFC module's functionality.

In Figure 14.1, you can see the information specified for the AddressModel model object used in the previous section.

There are two important things to notice here:

▶ The model object lives in its own Java package.

▶ The names for model instances and RFC metadata can be anything you like. However, as mentioned before, do not include the SAP system name in the logical destination name because of the confusion that will be created after the software has been transported.

---

4   That is, the database table in which this information is stored does not use the client value in its key.

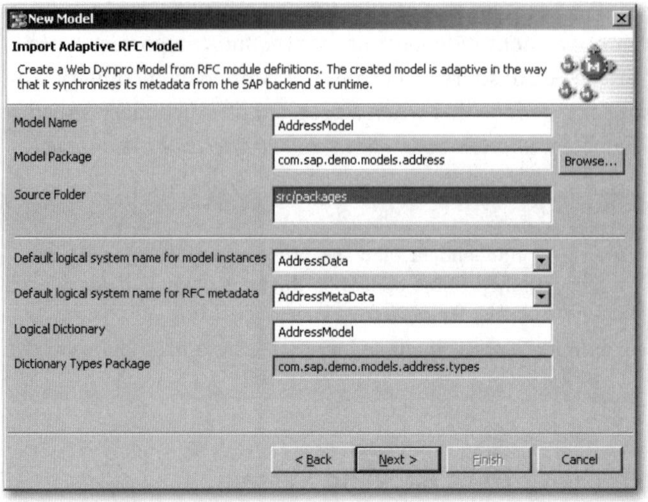

**Figure 14.1** Information Required for the Definition of the AddressModel Model Object

The logical system names specified for the model instances and the RFC metadata do not need to exist before the model is imported. You can even deploy your application to the AS Java before these destinations have been configured; obviously, however, you need to have configured them by the time you execute your application.

As their description implies, these names refer to logical systems, not physical SAP systems, but before we can set up these logical system names, some configuration must first be performed in the System Landscape Directory (SLD) of your AS Java.

### 14.2.2 Prerequisites for Creating a Technical System

It is not the intention of this book to provide a detailed discussion of the configuration and administration procedures required to make your AS Java functional. These tasks are fully documented in the related SAP documentation and will only be dealt with here in overview. For the purposes of this overview, the following assumptions have been made:

▶ You will be connecting to a stand-alone AS Java installed on your local development machine.

▶ The default HTTP port of 50000 has not been changed during installation.

▶ The AS Java has had the latest Common Information Model (CIM) data imported into it.

▶ You have a user ID for the AS Java with administration authority.

▶ You have installed, or at least have access to, the latest version of the SAP client software SAP GUI.

▶ In the backend SAP system, you have a valid user id with sufficient authority to perform a remote function call. For a productive environment, you also need a valid SAP system user with the authority to perform a remote function call.[5]

### 14.2.3    Creating a Technical System

The first task is the creation of a technical system. The technical systems defined in your SLD hold the physical information about all the external systems with which the AS Java can communicate. Only once the physical information has been entered for a given system can you then create a logical JCo destination.

▶ Connect to the SLD of your AS Java using the URL *http://localhost:50000/sld*.

▶ Enter your administrative user id and password.

▶ Use the Technical System Wizard to supply the necessary information to describe your SAP system. This includes entering the installation number of your SAP system, which can be obtained from the **System • Status** pop-up window in SAP GUI.

Once you have created the technical system, you will see a screen that is similar to Figure 14.2.

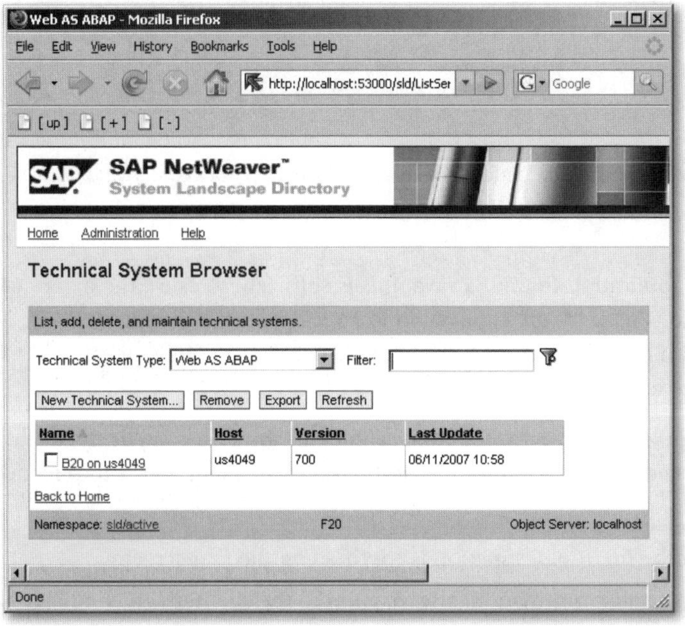

**Figure 14.2**  Technical System Browser

---

5  SAP users come in various categories (Dialogue, Communication, System, Service, and Reference). For online use with SAP GUI, you must have a Dialogue user, but for programmatic access, a System user should be used.

Here, we can see that a technical system called B20 has been defined. Using the configuration in this SLD, when any logical JCo destinations are created, only this one system will be available for selection.

Make sure that a technical system has first been defined for every external system with which you want to communicate.

### 14.2.4 Creating a JCo Destination

Now that at least one technical system is available, the logical JCo destinations used in the Web Dynpro model object can be created.

Connect to the Web Dynpro Content Administrator using the URL *http://local-host:50000/webdynpro/welcome* and then press the **Maintain JCo Destinations** button. Figure 14.3 shows what this screen could look like.

**Figure 14.3** JCo Destinations in the Web Dynpro Content Administrator

If you deploy an application to the AS Java, this is sufficient to cause the names of any JCo destinations used by the application to appear in the list in Figure 14.3. If the JCo destination has been correctly configured, a green icon will appear next to the name, else the icon will be red.

A JCo destination can either be created by specifying all the values explicitly, or the details can be copied from an existing JCo destination. The main points to remember are these:

▶ The client used by the JCo destination is specified on the first screen.

▶ For the model instance destination, always point to the client in which the business data lives.

▶ The RFC metadata destination will request information from the ABAP data dictionary. Because this information is not client specific, your only consideration is that the user assigned to this logical destination can log on in the specific client.

▶ For simplicity, it is advised to use the same client for each pair of JCo destinations.

▶ When security information needs to be specified, your values will vary depending on the environment you are configuring. Four options are available, each with their relative merits:[6]

▷ **User/Password**

Advantages: Quick and easy to set up. Good for a development environment setup.

Disadvantages: No user audit trail or user-specific authorization. All RFC modules are executed under the identity of this one user irrespective of the identity of the client-side user. This is good for testing but is not recommended for productive use.

▷ **Ticket**

Advantages: User management can be handled by another SAP NetWeaver product such as the NetWeaver Portal.

Disadvantages: Requires the use of another SAP NetWeaver-compatible product that can generate SSO2 cookies.

▷ **Client Certificate (X.509)**

Advantages: User management can be handled by any software layer that issues trusted X.509 certificates.

Disadvantages: Without extra security procedures in place, client certificates can only authenticate the client device — not necessarily the user operating the client device.

▷ **User Mapping**

Advantages: User management can be handled by the SAP NetWeaver User Management Engine, which can reference a Lightweight Directory Access Protocol (LDAP) server.

Disadvantages: Extra configuration required.

▶ In addition to this, communication between the AS Java and the SAP backend system can be encrypted using the Secure Network Communication (SNC) Layer.

▶ The user id used for the RFC metadata destination can only be specified as a user–password combination. This user should be created to be of type System within transaction SU01 in the backend SAP system. Users of type System are not permitted to log on using SAP GUI.

Once the JCo destinations have been set up, press the **Test** button to ensure that a connection can be made.

---

6 These four options are only available for the model instance destination (i.e., the JCo destination that actually invokes the RFC module).

## 14.3    The JCo Pool Concept

Within the JCo software layer (see Figure 14.4), the concept of connection pooling has been implemented. This concept has been available for many years but is frequently overlooked or misunderstood.

The concept of a connection pool in itself is not new and needs no explanation, but its implementation within the JCo layer does require some explanation because it has a critical effect both on the architecture of your model objects (i.e., how many function modules are contained within a single model object) and the number of RFC connections that the Web Dynpro Framework will open into the backend SAP system. The principle to follow here is that you want your application to consume the minimum possible number of connections into the backend SAP system.

First, the Adaptive RFC layer (which sits on top of JCo) will create the connection pool for you. Then, all the Web Dynpro application need do is to make a request to the Adaptive RFC layer for the next available connection from the pool (see Figure 14.4).

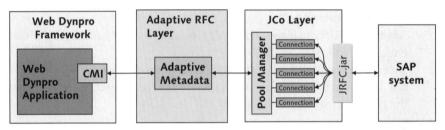

**Figure 14.4**  JCo Pools Exist Within the JCo Layer but Are Managed by the Adaptive RFC Layer

### 14.3.1    Pool Allocation

A JCo pool is created automatically by the Adaptive RFC layer, but only after a request has been received for a connection. In other words, until the first call to `${mo}.execute()` is made, the pool will not even exist.

Within a JCo connection object, certain values can be preconfigured such as the user id, password, and logon language. Other values cannot be known until after a connection has been opened (e.g., the number of bytes the backend system uses per character).

To create a pool of connections, all these values must be known up front. So what the JCo Pool Manager does is log on once to the backend system, obtain all the necessary values for a connection object, and then store these in a *master connection* object. This object is then cloned every time a new connection is requested from the pool. This speeds up the logon time when the new connection is first used.

### 14.3.2 Pool Naming Conventions

Many software layers within the AS Java use the JCo Layer, and each has its own standards for naming connection pools. In the case of the Adaptive RFC Layer, connection pools are named using the following four values:

▶ Logical destination name

▶ User ID

▶ Language

▶ Connection type

So if someone with a user id of `HarryHawk` runs a Web Dynpro application that logs on in English to the backend system defined by the JCo logical destination `Address-Data` using an SSO cookie, then the connection pool will be called:

```
AddressData_HarryHawk_EN_useSSO
```

> **Caveat Confector**
>
> The creation of connection pools is completely automatic, and the application developer should not attempt to implement his own version of the Adaptive RFC layer. Apart from being a redundant exercise, it is my experience that customers who have attempted this have achieved little more than the introduction of performance problems into their business applications.

As you can see, one pool will exist per user, per logical destination. In theory, it is possible that the same user could log on in different languages using different logon methods (e.g., named user ID–password or SSO cookie or X.509 certificate), so these variables are included in the pool name.

From a practical perspective, it unlikely that the logon language and connection type will actually act as unique identifiers; therefore, for the remainder of this discussion, we will assume that pools can be uniquely identified on a per-destination, per-user basis.

### 14.3.3 Pool Definition

The size of a JCo pool is determined when you create the JCo destination. Four values can be configured (see also Figure 14.5):

▶ **Maximum Connections**
The Maximum Connections value determines the upper limit for the number of connections this pool may contain.

▶ **Maximum Pool Size**
Once an application has finished with a connection, the connection is not closed immediately; instead, it is returned to the pool. This parameter defines the max-

imum number of connections left open after they have been returned to the pool.

▶ **Connection Timeout**
Once a connection has been returned to the pool, it will remain open for this time-out period (in seconds). In other words, if another application does not request a connection within this time-out period, the connection will be closed.

▶ **Maximum Wait Time**
The Maximum Wait Time defines the length of time (in seconds) that the JCo layer will wait when trying to open a new connection.

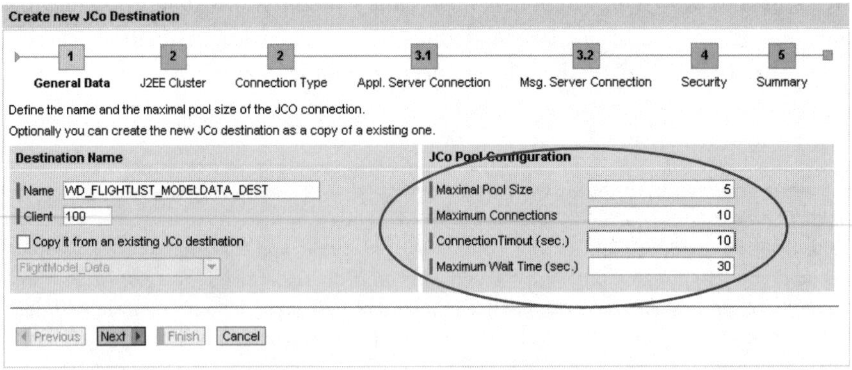

**Figure 14.5** JCo Pools Are Configured When the JCo Destination Is Created

I have seen many situations in which administrators have found that the default value of 10 for the Maximum Connections parameter appears not to be large enough, so they increase it to something like 100. This appears to fix the problem, so they conclude that the problem has been solved.

Unfortunately, this rather shallow approach to problem solving tends to create more problems than it solves. It is very unlikely that a JCo pool will need to contain as many as 100 connections.

Think about how pools are allocated: one pool per user per JCo destination. Do you really have a situation in which one user will be running enough applications connecting to the same backend system via the same logical connection to require 100 concurrent connections? I think this situation is very unlikely.[7]

This type of problem usually occurs when developers are testing their Web Dynpro application and running it over and over again. Under these circumstances, they run their application and find that it does not work, so they modify it and rerun it. However, they do not close the browser window containing the first or subsequent

---

7 Unless of course you are having all users of an application log on as the same user and share the same logical destination.

test runs. As far as the Web Dynpro Framework is concerned, the old application instances are still active, so the JCo connections they use from the connection pool remain allocated.

If you test your Web Dynpro applications this way, you will quickly exhaust the number of available connections in the connection pool. The problem is easy to solve, however. Just close the browser window containing the old application instance. The action of closing the browser sends an unload service event to the Web Dynpro Framework,[8] and the application is then closed down. This causes all JCo connections to be released and returned to their respective pools.

## 14.4 Pool Usage at Runtime

Since JCo pools are allocated on a per-user per-destination basis, the pool dimensions should be configured so that at any one time, the JCo pool will have sufficient capacity for all the connections required by one user, connecting to the same backend system, running a realistic number of applications.

### 14.4.1 Correct Design of Web Dynpro Applications

Figure 14.6 shows a correctly designed Web Dynpro application. This application uses two models (M1 and M2), each of which makes use of its own JCo destination (DEST1 and DEST2). These two destinations point to different backend systems, so at runtime this Web Dynpro application requires a connection into each backend system.

Notice that even though we have a single application being executed by a single user, two JCo pools have been created. This is because each of the model objects (M1 and M2) has been defined to use different logical destinations. Consequently, using our assignment of one pool per user per destination, two pools will be created.

If we extend this scenario, Figure 14.7 shows the pool allocation created when the same user has two Web Dynpro applications running. The second application uses two model objects (M3 and M4) that use the same logical destinations as models M1 and M2, respectively.

Here, you can see that even though two Web Dynpro applications are running, each using a different set of model objects, the combination of user name–logical destination has not changed. Therefore, rather than creating new JCo pools for the second application, the existing pools are used and they simply supply a further connection from their capacity.

---

8 See Section 4.4.5 for more information on service events.

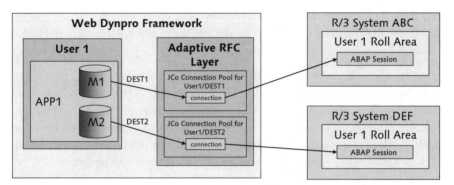

**Figure 14.6** A Correctly Designed Web Dynpro Application Consumes the Minimum Number of JCo Connections at Runtime

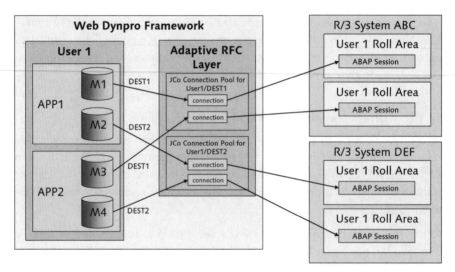

**Figure 14.7** One User Running Two Web Dynpro Applications

The next logical step is to scale up the above situation from one user to two users running the same two applications (see Figure 14.8). As you can see, now that a second user name is involved, new connection pools must be created.

Notice also that in each of the backend SAP systems, the same user has logged on twice. This is not an error. It is necessary because each user roll area[9] corresponds to the functionality being performed in a distinct Web Dynpro application instance. Therefore, the business data being manipulated in the backend system must be kept separate.

---

9  A *user roll area* is the name given to the memory space allocated to a user within the SAP system. This memory space contains all the information for the user's session and application data currently being processed.

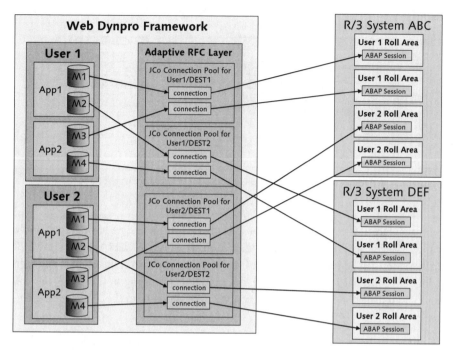

**Figure 14.8** Two Users Running Two Web Dynpro Applications

### 14.4.2 Incorrect Design of Web Dynpro Applications

So what happens when the applications are not designed correctly? The simplest way to show this is by modifying the example shown in Figure 14.6. Originally, we had an application that required information from two backend systems. Consequently, models M1 and M2 used logical destinations DEST1 and DEST2, respectively. This is a perfectly acceptable architecture.

Now let's do it wrong.

Let's say APP1 has been modified. Instead of using M1 and M2, it now uses M1 and M3. Recall from Figure 14.7 that models M1 and M3 both use the logical destination DEST1. What effect will this change have at runtime? How many connections will now be consumed from the connection pool?

As you can see from Figure 14.9, now that models M1 and M3 are being used by the same application, the default situation is that each model will consume its own connection from the connection pool. Since each JCo connection corresponds to a distinct user roll area in the backend SAP system, we now have a situation in which a single Web Dynpro application has logged on to the same backend system twice.

Is this efficient? Nope! Under certain circumstances, it can cause apparently self-contradictory errors in your application.

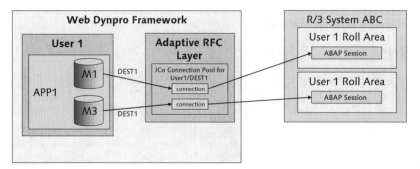

**Figure 14.9** A Poorly Designed Web Dynpro Application: Two Models that Both Use the Same Logical Destination

In certain areas of SAP application processing the business data has its own, application-specific locking mechanism (e.g., human resources [HR]). Before any HR information can be modified, it must first be locked. However, once a lock has been taken out for a particular HR record, only programs running in the same user roll area can update the information. Now apply this situation to the application architecture in Figure 14.9.

Let's say model M1 contains the proxy objects for the function modules that lock and unlock HR data. Model M3 contains the proxy objects for the function modules that perform the HR updates. We now have the strange situation in which USER1 runs this application, model M1 calls the function module to lock the HR data, and then M3 tries to update the locked information. The update function module will return an error message saying something to the effect of "USER1 cannot update this HR record, because it is locked by USER1."

This apparently self-contradictory message is known as a *lock conflict*, and it happens simply because the two model objects are using different connections from the JCo pool, and consequently, the function modules they call are executed in separate user roll areas.

### 14.4.3 Correcting a Poor Model Architecture

There are two approaches to correcting the problem described above. Either the function modules in the two models should be combined into one, or you should add a line of code to your program.

**Combining Models**

There is no specific tool to combine the proxy objects from two models. The only option is to choose the **Re-import model** option for one model and then select the function modules that need to be included. This is not a particularly elegant solution, and it may affect the reusability of the model that is being enhanced.

**Coding Optimization**

It is usually unfeasible to combine model objects within a specific application because this will affect their reusability in other applications. Therefore, a simple coding option is available.

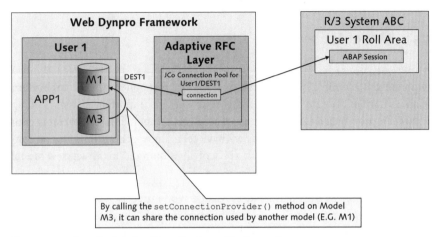

**Figure 14.10** Two Models Can Share the Same JCo Connection

By calling the `setConnectionProvider()` method for one model, you can cause it to share the connection used by another model (see Figure 14.10). This is a far simpler and more elegant solution, as it does not affect the reusability of either model. However, you must remember to add this line of coding.

As soon as you do this, the strange error messages will disappear because both models are sharing the same JCo connection, which means that any function modules they call will run in the same ABAP session.

In the following example, let's say we have two models: `AddressModel` and `PersonnelModel`. Both of these models contain proxy objects to call ABAP function modules, but at the moment we are concentrating on the models themselves, not the proxy objects they contain.

```
// Create an AddressModel instance
AddressModel addrModel =
  (AddressModel)WDModelFactory.
    getModelInstance(AddressModel.class,
                WDModelScopeType.APPLICATION_SCOPE);

// Create a PersonnelModel instance
PersonnelModel persModel =
  (PersonnelModel)WDModelFactory.
    getModelInstance(PersonnelModel.class,
                WDModelScopeType.APPLICATION_SCOPE);
```

```
// Make sure the PersonnelModel instance and the
// AddressModel share the same JCo connection
persModel.setConnectionProvider(addrModel);
```

**Listing 14.1** Code sample to create two model instances and then make sure they use the same JCo connection

## 14.5 Model Scope Type

Let's say we have a larger application in which there are multiple Web Dynpro components. It is entirely possible that two or more components in the application declare a usage of the same model. In this situation, it is important to avoid having a separate model instance per component, because this could lead to problems with the application's functionality, and as we have seen, more connections will be consumed from the connection pool than are actually required. This is where a model object's scope type needs to be examined.

When a model object is instantiated, the scope type property (WDModelScopeType) determines the scope that the model instance will occupy. The default value here is WDModelScopeType.APPLICATION_SCOPE, and this is the correct value for about 95 % of your programming requirements.[10] This class has already been used in the code sample in Listing 14.1 above.

There are four scope type values, but as stated, you'll hardly ever need to use a non-default value:

▶ WDModelScopeType.APPLICATION_SCOPE
One instance of the model will be shared by all component instances within the application. This is the default value and is correct for 95 % of your coding requirements.

▶ WDModelScopeType.COMPONENT_SCOPE
One instance of the model will be shared by all controllers within a single component.

▶ WDModelScopeType.TASK_SCOPE
The instance of the model will only persist for a single round trip, after which, it will be discarded. This effectively makes the connections into the backend system stateless.

▶ WDModelScopeType.NO_SCOPE
The model instance will not be controlled by any scope existing within Web Dynpro. This is useful when you want multiple *applications* to be able to share the same model instance — even if one application shuts down before the next one is started.

---

10 This is also why many people do not know about manipulating this value — simply because the default is almost always the correct value.

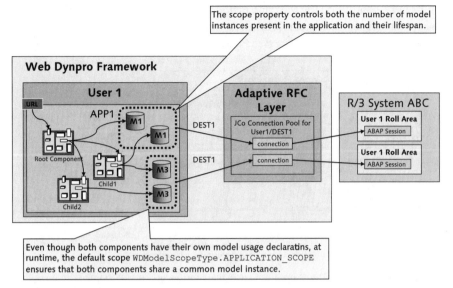

The scope property controls both the number of model instances present in the application and their lifespan.

Even though both components have their own model usage declaratins, at runtime, the default scope `WDModelScopeType.APPLICATION_SCOPE` ensures that both components share a common model instance.

**Figure 14.11** The Model Scope Type Determines How Many Instances of a Model Object Will Exist Within a Given Scope

As you can see from Figure 14.11, the components in the application APP1 all declare model usages. Table 14.1 below shows the declared model usages.

| Component | Uses Model |
|---|---|
| Root component | M1 |
| Child1 | M1 and M3 |
| Child2 | M3 |

**Table 14.1** Model Usage Across Multiple Components in the Same Application

Since the root component and the component Child1 both declare a usage of model M1, the default model scope type of APPLICATION_SCOPE ensures that both these components share the same model instance. This immediately means that only one connection is consumed from the JCo connection pool (because there's only one instance of the model). Similarly, the components Child1 and Child2 share the same instance of model M3.

However, we're back in the same situation as we were in Figure 14.9. Two model instances both require a connection to the same backend SAP system, but because of potential problems with transactional processing (e.g., lock conflicts), both model instances should share the same JCo connection.

This can be done by calling the same method that was used before: call the `setCon-nectionProvider()` method to cause one model instance to share the connection used by another model instance (see Figure 14.12).

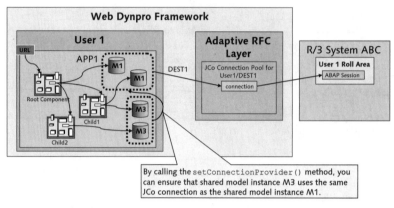

**Figure 14.12** The Shared Model Instances Now Share the Same JCo Connection from the Connection Pool

## 14.6 Calculating JCO Pool Size

The question of how to calculate JCo pool sizes is one I am frequently asked, but it is not one for which there is a general answer. When you are building your Web Dynpro application, you should be aware of the following things:

▶ The number of model objects your application uses

▶ How many logical destinations are required

▶ Whether or not the model objects within your application share JCo connections

In Figure 14.13, the calculation looks at the number of connections required by a single user across all the applications he is expected to run. This total is then split up according to the number of logical destinations required by all the applications. This first step in the calculation will give you the expected number of connections required per user per pool. Since this total is not a precise figure, you should allow your JCo connection pool to have between one-third and one-half more connections than this calculation tells you. Some fine-tuning will probably also be required here. The pool consumption can be monitored in the Web Dynpro Console (**Monitor • JCo Connection Pools**), and you can then assess the true runtime consumption of connections.

If you now multiply the total number of connections per logical destination by the expected number of users on your system, you will arrive at the expected number of RFC connections each backend system has to support.

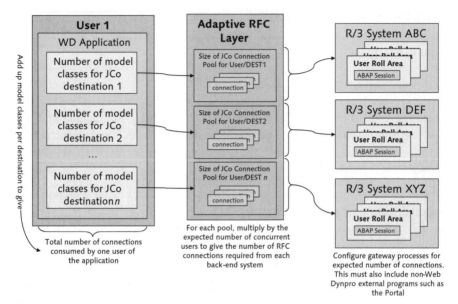

**Figure 14.13** A Basic Approach to Calculating JCo Pool Size

This method of calculating JCo pool size takes only a basic approach and has made some generalizing assumptions. In reality, you should examine each application and take into account:

▶ The number of model objects it uses

▶ Whether or not connections are shared

▶ The number of logical destinations used across all the models

As you probably can appreciate by now, it is not possible to condense this calculation down to a simple equation.

## 14.7 Metadata Connections

*Why are metadata connections needed?* Good question. As you will recall, every model object requires the use of two logical destinations: one for calling the actual function modules, and the other for checking the structure of the interfaces.

### 14.7.1 Pool Optimization

Look back at Section 14.3.2 and remind yourself about the naming convention used by the Adaptive RFC layer for JCo connection pools.

If you have created a logical destination called AddressMetadata, which logs on in English with a user called METADATA[11], then the JCo Pool created for these connections will be called:

```
AddressMetadata_METADATA_en_useDefinedUser
```

Since this type of connection is concerned with dictionary information and not business information, there is no particular need to have a dedicated metadata connection per application connection. The only thing you must ensure is that the technical system is consistent.

So it is possible to optimize your own metadata connections by creating only one logical destination per backend system.[12] This logical destination is then used by all models that obtain any kind of data from that backend system. This in turn means you have only one connection pool created for all metadata connections across all your models.

### 14.7.2 Metadata Connection Usage

The metadata connection for a particular model object is used only once per lifecycle of the AS Java. The first time a function module is called, the metadata connection will be used to load a description of the function module's interface into the various caches in the AS Java. The metadata caches are volatile, so after the server node is restarted, the caches must be refilled.

If the same function module is called a second time, the metadata connection is not used. The interface data is simply read from the cache.

## 14.8 Impact of JCo Connections on the SAP Gateway Process

All SAP systems are built using a process-based architecture. An SAP system is not a single process, but rather a collection of interrelated processes — each of which performs a fixed task. These processes can be distributed across multiple servers and, taken together, form a single SAP system.

An SAP system is composed of the following processes (in varying numbers):

▶ **Dialogue**
Processes online user requests from the SAP GUI client software.

---

11  Remember, the user created in the backend system for metadata connections should be of type System. This user type is reserved for program to program communication only.
12  Remember not to put the backend system name into the logical destination name.

- **Update**
  Manages database updates. Updates are divided into two categories:
  - V1: Primary updates (time critical)
  - V2: Secondary or statistical updates (not time critical)

- **Enqueue**
  Handles the locking and unlocking of business objects before and after database updates.

- **Batch**
  Handles all programs running as background tasks.

- **Message**
  Handles inter-process communication and messaging.

- **Gateway**
  Handles connections to and from external systems. This includes other SAP systems.

- **Spool**
  Handles printed output.

These processes occur in varying combinations in different system scenarios, but every time an external program needs to communicate with functionality inside an SAP system, the remote function call must pass through the backend system's Gateway process (see Figure 14.14).

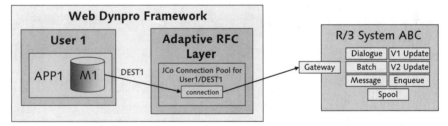

**Figure 14.14** The Gateway Process of an SAP System Handles All Incoming and Outgoing Communication with External Systems

Every time a connection is made into an SAP system, the Gateway process allocates a block of memory (~200Kb per connection) to hold the connection details (see Figure 14.15).

Within the configuration parameters for your SAP system (transaction RZ10) is a parameter called gw/max_conn. By default, this value is set to 500, which means there can be at most 500 concurrent external connections open in the gateway.

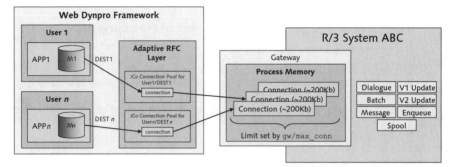

**Figure 14.15** Each Connection in the Gateway Process Requires About 200Kb of Memory

> **Caveat Confector**
>
> In SAP systems with a kernel version of 6.40 or less, there is a hard-coded limit of 2,000 connections. Even if you set the `gw/max_conn` parameter to some higher value, the 2000-connection limit cannot be exceeded.
>
> This limitation is not present in SAP systems with kernel versions 7.0 or higher.

The active connections in an SAP Gateway process can be monitored using transaction SMGW shown in Figure 14.16.

| Nu... | Local LU Name | Local TP Name | Remote LU N... | Remote TP N... | Users | Status | Dest | ConvID | Protocol | Last Request | SAPEr | APPC |
|---|---|---|---|---|---|---|---|---|---|---|---|---|
| 0 | bsw6026 | sapgw21 | gtadmain.wdf.... | sapdp21 | HEINKE | Connected | GTADIR_S | 78566404 | Internal Communi... | Tue Feb 20 13:37:22 2007 | 0 | 0 |
| 1 | bsw6026 | sapgw21 | gtadmain.wdf.... | sapdp21 | HEINKE | Connected | GTADIR_S | 30154663 | Internal Communi... | Fri Feb 23 11:35:27 2007 | 0 | 0 |
| 2 | bsw6026 | sapgw21 | gtadmain.wdf.... | sapdp21 | ROUSSEAUB | Connected | GTADIR_S | 26518204 | Internal Communi... | Fri Feb 23 10:31:30 2007 | 0 | 0 |
| 5 | bsw6026 | sapgw21 | bsw6026 | sapgw21 | BRECHTMI | Connected | SAPLOG... | 26427824 | Internal Communi... | Fri Feb 23 11:31:45 2007 | 0 | 0 |
| 6 | pwdf1398 | sapdp24 | bsw6026 | sapgw21 | C5034964 | Connected | CWBAD... | 22507162 | Internal Communi... | Fri Feb 23 09:30:25 2007 | 0 | 0 |
| 7 | bsw6026 | sapgw21 | gtadmain.wdf.... | sapdp21 | EYERMANN | Connected | GTADIR_S | 63580816 | Internal Communi... | Thu Feb 22 17:34:54 2007 | 0 | 0 |
| 8 | bsw6026 | sapgw21 | gtadmain.wdf.... | sapdp21 | TIGHZERTW | Connected | GTADIR_S | 27036928 | Internal Communi... | Fri Feb 23 10:34:17 2007 | 0 | 0 |
| 9 | bsw6026 | sapgw21 | gtadmain.wdf.... | sapdp21 | DJOMO | Connected | GTADIR_S | 30529824 | Internal Communi... | Fri Feb 23 11:40:00 2007 | 0 | 0 |
| 11 | bsw6026 | sapgw21 | gtadmain.wdf.... | sapdp21 | HEINKE | Connected | GTADIR_S | 85215988 | Internal Communi... | Mon Feb 19 11:42:57 20... | 0 | 0 |
| 12 | bsw6026 | sapgw21 | 10.21.82.172 | sapdp21 | UHRIG | Connected | b20main_ | 28611083 | Internal Communi... | Fri Feb 23 11:38:52 2007 | 0 | 0 |
| 13 | bsw6026 | sapgw21 | %%SAPGUI%% | gnetx.exe | LAKSHMANANS | Connected | EU_SCR... | 58233805 | External Commun... | Wed Feb 21 12:03:57 20... | 0 | 0 |
| 17 | bsl8005 | sapgw26 | bsw6026 | sapgw21 | KIMCHO | Connected | B20_STAU | 20319292 | Internal Communi... | Thu Feb 22 05:02:32 2007 | 0 | 0 |
| 19 | bsw6026 | sapgw21 | 10.66.32.78 | sapdp21 | LIENERTM | Connected | bsw6028_ | 51239222 | Internal Communi... | Thu Feb 22 13:45:49 2007 | 0 | 0 |
| 20 | bsw6026 | sapgw21 | gtadmain.wdf.... | sapdp21 | C5034988 | Connected | GTADIR_S | 65595021 | Internal Communi... | Tue Feb 20 10:48:23 2007 | 0 | 0 |
| 21 | bsw6026 | sapgw21 | gtadmain.wdf.... | sapdp21 | ROSENKRANZD | Connected | GTADIR_S | 28904289 | Internal Communi... | Fri Feb 23 11:20:21 2007 | 0 | 0 |
| 22 | bsw6026 | sapgw21 | %%SAPGUI%% | gnetx.exe | DJOMO | Connected | EU_SCR... | 26319088 | External Commun... | Fri Feb 23 10:39:01 2007 | 0 | 0 |
| 23 | pwdf1533 | sapdp24 | bsw6026 | sapgw21 | D042454 | Connected | CWBAD... | 26942318 | Internal Communi... | Fri Feb 23 10:31:28 2007 | 0 | 0 |
| 24 | bsw6026 | sapgw21 | gtadmain.wdf.... | sapdp21 | KRETSCHMER | Connected | GTADIR_S | 29187042 | Internal Communi... | Fri Feb 23 11:20:20 2007 | 0 | 0 |
| 25 | LONN6014 | jlaunch | bsw6026 | sapgw21 | LONN60142314 | Connected | <Java | 29861097 | Internal Communi... | Fri Feb 23 11:42:24 2007 | 0 | 0 |
| 27 | bsw6026 | sapgw21 | %%SAPGUI%% | gnetx.exe | MANOT | Connected | EU_SCR... | 30728888 | External Commun... | Fri Feb 23 11:43:11 2007 | 0 | 0 |
| 31 | bsw6026 | sapgw21 | gtadmain.wdf.... | sapdp21 | HEINKE | Connected | GTADIR_S | 63241445 | Internal Communi... | Thu Feb 22 16:57:15 2007 | 0 | 0 |
| 34 | bsw6026 | sapgw21 | gtadmain.wdf.... | sapdp21 | KUMARPRAK | Connected | GTADIR_S | 23137309 | Internal Communi... | Fri Feb 23 10:24:20 2007 | 0 | 0 |

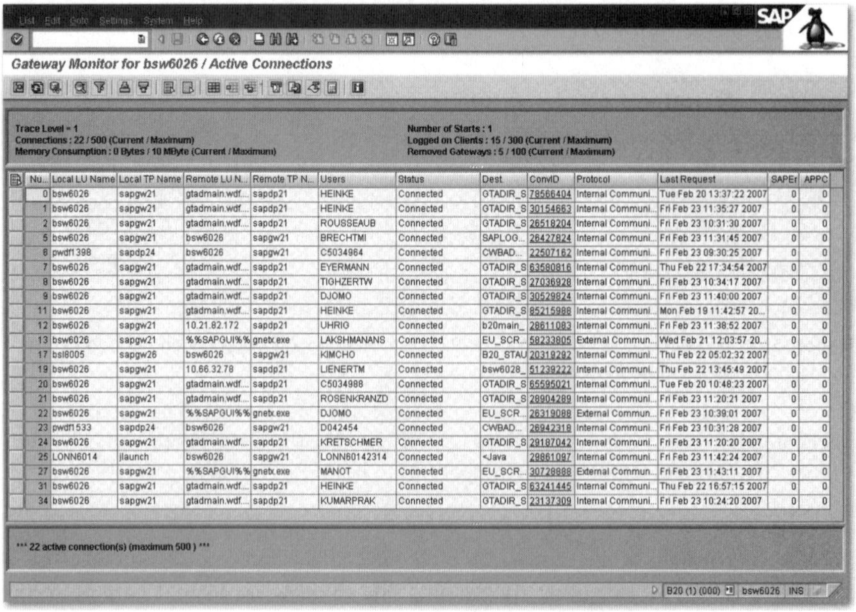

**Figure 14.16** The Active Connection in a Gateway Process Can Be Monitored Using Transaction SMGW

## 14.9 Relationship Between JCO Destinations and ABAP Sessions

The documentation that follows is a brief overview of the standard SAP documentation that describes the procedures to be followed when writing RFC modules. Please refer to the standard SAP documentation for a complete discussion of the topic. The information contained here only covers the main points in summary form from a Web Dynpro point of view.

### 14.9.1 Logging on to an SAP System

When an external program needs to invoke any functionality within an SAP system, that program must first log on to the SAP system. Since all SAP systems are client/server-based applications, not only must the external program supply valid user credentials, but it must identify to which application server it needs to connect. All this information is held within the JCo connection object described above.

### 14.9.2 ABAP Sessions

Once you have successfully logged on to an SAP system, you are allocated an area of memory within the application server called a user roll area. The user roll area contains all the data related to your activity on that SAP system. This includes all the data used by all the programs you are currently executing.

The user roll area is subdivided into areas called ABAP sessions. Each ABAP session holds the current state of a logical unit of work (LUW) for a single program. Once an online user has logged on to SAP using the SAP GUI client software, he may create multiple sessions within his roll area by opening new SAP GUI windows. All the windows together belong to a single user (and therefore a single user roll area), but each SAP GUI window can be executing a different transaction. The current execution state of each transaction within each window is maintained in a distinct ABAP session (see Figure 14.17).

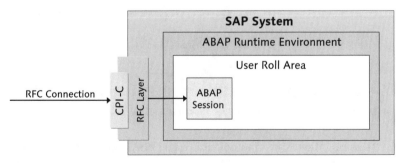

**Figure 14.17** An Incoming RFC Connection Is Attached to an ABAP Session

When an RFC connection is established into an SAP system, not only is a user roll area created for that user, but an ABAP session is created. Then within this session, the required function module is executed.

If the ABAP statement COMMIT is issued, you are instructing the ABAP runtime that the current logical unit of work has finished and that all database updates should be committed to the database (see Figure 14.18). This formally terminates the ABAP session, and a new ABAP session is started automatically (see Figure 14.19).

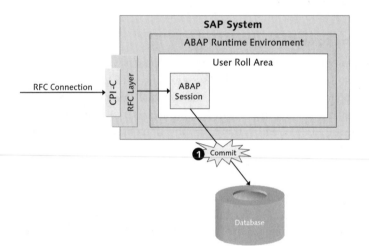

**Figure 14.18** When a Database Commit Is Issued, the ABAP Session Is Considered Closed

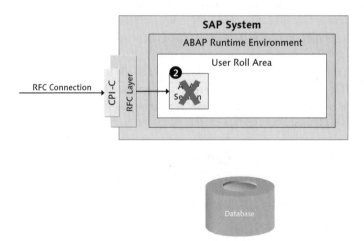

**Figure 14.19** The ABAP Session that Has Just Been Closed Is Destroyed

A new ABAP session is then started automatically, and ABAP processing continues. Notice that the existing RFC connection is automatically associated with the new ABAP session (see Figure 14.20).

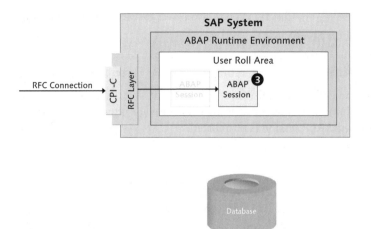

**Figure 14.20** A New ABAP Session Is Started Automatically

| Important |
| --- |

The Adaptive RFC layer does not currently support SAP's transactional RFC (tRFC) interface.

### 14.9.3 Performing ABAP Database Updates Without Causing an Unwanted Session Change

Again, this is a well-known situation in ABAP programming and is well documented in the standard help pages, but in summary, the basic principles are as follows:

▶ The functionality to perform the actual database update should be encapsulated within a function module. In our example, we'll give this function module the simplistic name of ZUPDATE_DATABASE.[13] This function module *cannot* be called from outside the SAP system.

▶ We perform our Web Dynpro business processing accumulating all the necessary information for the database update. This information can be accumulated in either the Web Dynpro application memory, or in the ABAP session. Which option you choose depends on how many backend function modules need to be called as preprocessing steps before the update takes place and whether the function modules you are calling are custom-written.

▶ Finally, when the Web Dynpro application is ready to perform an update, it calls some RFC module — say, ZWD_UPDATE_PREPARE.[14] This function module is

---

13  Any customer-written function module must start with the letter Z or Y.

14  This function module does not really exist. Its name is illustrative of what you would need to write if you were custom writing a real business application.

responsible for calling the function module ZUPDATE_DATABASE with the *critical* parameter of IN UPDATE TASK.

This extra directive to the ABAP CALL FUNCTION statement causes the execution of the function module to be delayed until the end of the current LUW — that is, when the database COMMIT takes place.

▶ Now that the call to ZUPDATE_DATABASE is held in the update queue, it will only be executed when the ABAP session is terminated.

▶ Finally, the LUW must be explicitly terminated by calling BAPI_TRANSACTION_ COMMIT.

I have frequently found custom-written ABAP function modules that contain direct database updates. The ABAP code (in itself) is perfectly correct and works perfectly well when tested within the ABAP test environment, but apart from being really bad coding style, an implicit COMMIT can seriously interfere with any transactional processing you are trying to perform.

Function modules that contain direct database updates cannot be used as part of a transactional group and are therefore of limited value to Web Dynpro business applications.

### 14.9.4  Statements to Avoid in an RFC Module

*So, can I use any ABAP statements I like in an RFC function module?* The short answer is no. The number of ABAP statements that cannot be used in an RFC module is small, but should you use them, then they will forcibly terminate an RFC connection. These statements are:

▶ LEAVE TO

▶ SUBMIT

▶ CALL FUNCTION ... DESTINATION ...

The type of RFC error you will get from the use of these statements is documented in SAP Note number 174306.

## 14.10  Avoiding the Read–Write–Read Problem

If custom ABAP function modules are written without a good understanding of ABAP session management,[15] it is possible that the following problem can occur. This is related both to the time taken by the SAP system to complete a database update, and the way in which the custom RFC modules have been written.

---

15  As happens all too often!

Consider the steps in the following (simplistic) business scenario:

1. An RFC module is called to obtain some information from an SAP system. This data is presented to the Web Dynpro user in the form of an editable table. For the purposes of this discussion, we shall give this RFC module the fictional name ZREAD_DATA_FOR_WD.[16]

2. The user makes certain modifications to the data and clicks the **Save changes** button.

3. The modified data is passed to another RFC module with the fictional name of ZUPDATE_DATA_FOR_WD. This program has been coded in such a way that it performs an immediate database update (which is acceptable in this situation since our demo business process is effectively stateless).

4. As soon as ZUPDATE_DATA_FOR_WD returns control to the Web Dynpro application, ZREAD_DATA_FOR_WD is called a second time to reread the updated information.

5. Oops! The Web Dynpro application now displays the old, *unmodified* data.

The problem here is caused by two factors:

1. The two RFC modules have not been written to function as a coordinated pair.

2. The time taken for an SAP system to complete a database update depends upon the workload it is currently under. In high-load situations, there will be a slight delay between the completion of the LUW in ABAP and the *actual* update of the database table(s).

In our example, this delay could sometimes be greater than the interval between the call to ZUPDATE_DATA_FOR_WD and the subsequent call to ZREAD_DATA_FOR_WD. This is known as the Read–Write–Read problem, and it can be avoided in the following manner. First, it is important to state what assumptions have been made about this solution. These are:

▶ Data is supplied to Web Dynpro from an SAP system by calling the RFC module ZREAD_DATA_FOR_WD.

▶ Modified data from Web Dynpro is updated within the SAP system by calling the RFC module ZUPDATE_DATA_FOR_WD.

▶ Both of these function modules live in the same ABAP function group called ZWD_INTERFACE.

▶ Both of the executable model objects that represent these RFC modules live in the same adaptive RFC model. Therefore, they implicitly share the same JCo connection and the same ABAP session.

---

16 The ABAP function module and function group names used in this example do not represent any functionality delivered by SAP. They are merely used as illustrations of what could be developed.

ZREAD_DATA_FOR_WD should be written such that it maintains a set of internal tables. These act as a cache for the data that could potentially be modified. The read process therefore amounts to the steps shown in Figure 14.21.

1. The RFC module ZREAD_DATA_FOR_WD is called with the parameters identifying the desired data.

2. Do the internal cache tables hold the required information?

   (Since these internal tables live in the function group's global memory area, the data they contain persists for the lifespan of the user roll area, not just the lifespan of the RFC module call.)

3. If the information is not in the cache, read the database and update the internal cache tables. If the required information is found in the cache, this step is omitted.

4. The required data is then taken from the internal tables and placed into the outbound side of the RFC module's interface.

5. Control is returned to the calling program.

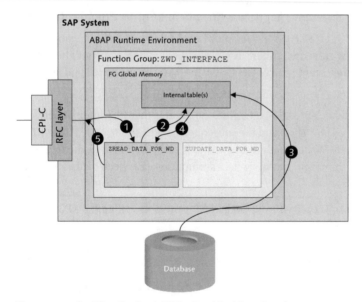

**Figure 14.21** Avoiding the Read–Write–Read Problem: Part 1

Now when ZUPDATE_DATA_FOR_WD is called, the data being updated must, by definition, already exist in the function group's cache tables. This is a safe assumption to make because the RFC module ZUPDATE_DATA_FOR_WD will only ever be used in conjunction with ZREAD_DATA_FOR_WD, which performs the steps shown in Figure 14.22.

1. The RFC module ZUPDATE_DATA_FOR_WD is called with all the data to be modified.

2. Update the appropriate rows in the internal cache. This is a synchronous update.

3. Update the database. This is an asynchronous update — it doesn't matter if the actual database update is delayed slightly since subsequent reads of the modified data will always be returned from the cache

4. Control is returned to the calling program.

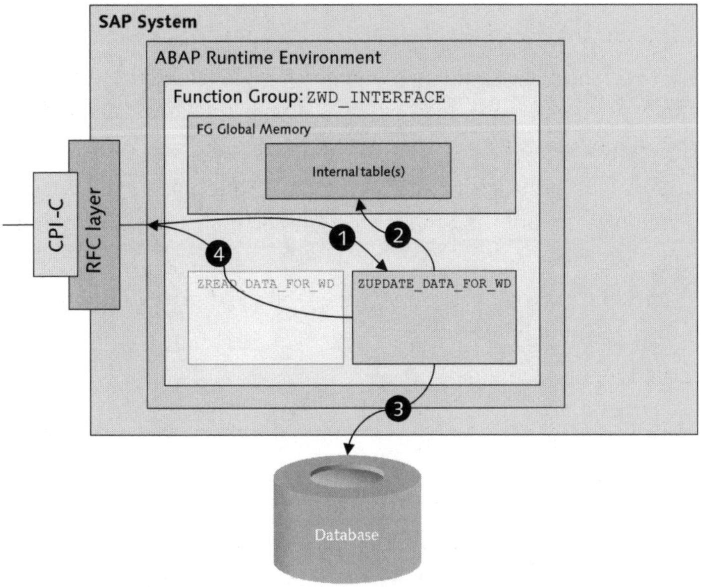

**Figure 14.22** Avoiding the Read–Write–Read Problem: Part 2

The RFC module ZREAD_DATA_FOR_WD can now be called to reread the data irrespective of whether the database update has completed or not. The database will only be accessed for data that cannot be found in the internal cache tables. Such data cannot have been updated during the lifespan of this JCo connection; therefore, the database must contain the latest version.

# Appendix

# A   Web Dynpro Naming Placeholders

Since the NetWeaver Developer Studio (NWDS) generates a lot of Java source code using the various entity names declared at design time, it is possible to generalize the names that will be created. Throughout this book, the following set of variables has been used to identify various named entities in Web Dynpro. The value of these variables is defined when you declare the particular entity at design time. These values are then combined to form composite names that obey the SAP recommended naming convention for Web Dynpro coding entities.

These names are presented in boldface when they appear within coding entity names.

## A.1   Web Dynpro Component Architecture

The following variables are related to the creation of Web Dynpro components.

| ${a} | Application |
|------|-------------|
| ${c} | Component |
| ${cc} | Custom controller |
| ${cid} | Component interface defintion |
| ${msg} | Message |
| ${v} | View |
| ${w} | Window |

## A.2   Web Dynpro Controllers

The following variables relate to the entities within view controllers.

| ${act} | Action |
|--------|--------|
| ${pin} | Inbound plug |
| ${pout} | Outbound plug |
| ${ui} | Any UI element object |

| ${ui_p} | The property of any UI element |
|---------|-------------------------------|
| ${ui_evt} | Any client-side event raised by a UI element |

## A.3    Model Objects

The following variables relate to the entities within or related to models.

| ${m} | Model (which will contain one or more model objects) |
|------|------------------------------------------------------|
| ${mo} | Model object (typically referred to by a context model node) |
| ${rfm} | Remote callable ABAP function module |
| ${st} | Dictionary Simple Type |

## A.4    NetWeaver Development Infrastructure Entities

The following variables relate to the entities within the NWDI.

| ${dc} | Development component |
|-------|----------------------|
| ${sc} | Software component |

## A.5    Context Entities

The following variables relate to the entities within a Web Dynpro context.

| ${ca} | Any context attribute |
|-------|----------------------|
| ${chn} | Any context child node |
| ${cn} | Any context node |
| ${ctx} | Context name; always equals the controller name to which it belongs |
| ${mn} | Model node |
| ${ma} | Model attribute |
| ${rn} | Recursive node |
| ${vn} | Value node |
| ${va} | Value attribute |

## A.6 Generic and Composite Abbreviations

The following variables relate to a variety of entities used during Web Dynpro development.

| | |
|---|---|
| ${dt} | Any data type defined in the Java dictionary. |
| ${dt_p} | The data type of the UI element property p. |
| ${dt_{ca}} | The data type of the context attribute ca |
| ${l} | Locale value. |
| ${n_x} | The name that is formed by the combination of one of the listed placeholders and a naming convention suffix. <br><br> This value forms a composite placeholder embedded into the names of the generated coding entities. The subscript x indicates the type of composite name. |
| ${p} | Component usage purpose. This is part of a child component usage name in which you should describe the purpose for which this child component instance is being created. |
| ${pkg_n} | Any part of a Java package name. These parts are used to form the directory names in the deployed application and are concatenated to form the full package name used by an import statement. <br><br> Therefore, if: <br><br> ▶   ${pkg_1}=com <br> ▶   ${pkg_2}=sap <br> ▶   ${pkg_3}=tc <br> ▶   ${pkg_4}=webdynpro <br><br> then the package name ${pkg_1}.${pkg_2}.${pkg_3}.${pkg_4} will become com.sap.tc.webdynpro. |
| ${pkg_{sap}} | The standard SAP Java package within which all internal Web Dynpro Framework classes live. <br><br> This is currently com.sap.tc.webdynpro.* |
| ${vnd} | The Java vendor name formed from reversing the order of the first m of the n parts of the package names (where m < n). <br><br> Using the example given for the ${pkg_n} placeholder above, the vendor could be formed from reversing the order of the first two parts of the package name to give <br><br> ${vnd} = ${pkg_2}.${pkg_1} = sap.com. |

## A.7 Subscripts for Composite Placeholders Using the SAP Recommended Suffixes

The following variables show how the SAP recommended naming convention for Web Dynpro development entities can be constructed. These are the design time names created during the development of your application.

| ${n_a}$ | Application | = ${a}$+ "App" |
|---------|-------------|-----------------|
| ${n_c}$ | Component controller | = ${c}$ + "Comp" |
| ${n_{cc}}$ | Custom controller | = ${cc}$ + "Cust" |
| ${n_{civ}}$ | Component interface view | = ${w}$ + "InterfaceView" |
| ${n_{ctl}}$ | A controller of any type | |
| ${n_m}$ | Model | = ${m}$ + "Model" |
| ${n_{pi}}$ | Inbound plug | = ${p_{in}}$ + "In" |
| ${n_{po}}$ | Outbound plug | = ${p_{out}}$ + "Out" |
| ${n_{cid}}$ | Component interface definition | = ${cid}$ + "CompI" |
| ${n_u}$ | Component usage | = [${n_c}$\|${n_{cid}}$]${p}$ + "Inst" |
| ${n_v}$ | View | = ${v}$ + "View" |
| ${n_{vs}}$ | Viewset | = ${vs}$ + "Viewset" |

## A.8    AS Java Placeholders

The following variables are used to identify entities or services within the AS Java:

| | |
|---|---|
| `<SID>` | The system ID is a three-character identifier for an installed SAP system and is an alphanumeric value that must start with a letter, for example, CE1, J2E, or PRD. |
| `<instance_id>` | The instance ID is a combination of letters and numbers that is defined when your SAP Server is installed. The specific combination of letters used in the instance ID is determined by which processes are installed for that particular server.<br><br>For example, the first instance of a Java Server would be called JC00. "JC" indicates that a Java engine has been installed, and "00" indicates that this is the first instance.<br><br>If a second instance of a Java Server were installed on the same machine, it would typically have an instance ID of JC01. |
| | For an AS ABAP, the instance ID could be something like DVEBMGS00, where each letter indicates that a particular type of process has been installed, and "00" indicates that this is the first instance on this machine.<br><br>D = Dialogue<br>V = Update<br>E = Enqueue<br>B = Batch<br>M = Message<br>G = Gateway<br>S = Spool |

# B  Naming Conventions

Coding generated by the NWDS is easier to understand if the following naming convention is used consistently. This convention is designed to provide you with information about the function of each generated coding entity and will help when the structure of a large project needs to be understood.

## B.1  General Rules for Naming

Since all the Web Dynpro coding described in this book is implemented in Java, the standard naming rules that apply for Java also apply for Web Dynpro, but with certain important restrictions.

Since Java is a Unicode-compliant language, it is possible to create variables that use characters such as ä, é, and ñ, or characters from a non-Roman alphabet. Within Web Dynpro, such characters must not be used! This is because when the Java variable names are included in both the generated form definition (typically HTML) and the embedded scripting language (e.g., JavaScript), the names are not escaped or encoded.

**Caveat Confector**

Web Dynpro coding entity names must use only the characters A..Z, a..z, 0..9, or _. Digits are allowed from only the second position onward.

**Important**

You should never use the prefixes wd, WD, or IWD, as these prefixes are used by the NWDS during the generation of internal coding entities. It is likely that you will create a name conflict if you use one of these prefixes.

## B.2  Naming Conventions for Coding Entities

### B.2.1  Applications: ${n_a} = ${a}App

The actual application name ${n_a} should consist of the desired application name ${a}, followed by the suffix App. ${a} should describe the business process being delivered.

### B.2.2 Components: ${n_c} = ${c}Comp

The actual component name ${nc} should consist of the desired component name ${c} followed by the suffix Comp. ${c} should describe the (reusable) unit of functionality delivered by this component.

### B.2.3 Component Interface Views: ${n_{civ}} = ${w}InterfaceView

The creation of the window ${w} automatically causes the component interface view ${nciv} to be created, where ${nciv} = **${w}**InterfaceView. Since this name is created automatically, you are not permitted to change it.

### B.2.4 Component Usage: ${n_u} = ${n_c}${p}Inst or ${cid}${p}Inst

For component *A* to be able to use the data and functionality within component *B*, component *A* must first declare the use of component *B*. The name of the component usage is the instance name of the particular component class.

Component usage is defined for two situations:

1. When a component is being used
2. When a component interface definition is being used

The usage instance name ${nu} should therefore consist of either the component name ${nc} or the component interface definition name ${cid}, followed by the usage purpose ${p} and the suffix Inst.

### B.2.5 Custom Controllers: ${n_{cc}} = ${cc}Cust

The actual custom controller name ${ncc} should consist of the desired controller name ${cc} followed by the suffix Cust.

### B.2.6 Inbound Plugs: ${n_{pi}} = ${p_{in}}In

The actual inbound plug name ${npi} should consist of the desired inbound plug name ${pin} followed by the suffix In. ${pin} should start with an uppercase letter.

The inbound plug should be named according to the reason for which the target view is being entered.

All inbound plugs have a corresponding event handler in the view controller. By default, this method is named onPlug**${np1}**(), but you are free to modify this name if required.

### B.2.7 Models: ${n_m}$ = ${m}$Model

The actual model name `${n_m}` should consist of the desired model name `${m}` followed by the suffix `Model`.

Each Web Dynpro model *must* live in its own Java package; for example, the package name should conform to a pattern such as `${pkg_1}.${pkg_2}.${pkg_3}.models.${n_m}`.

If you attempt to force two models to cohabit within the same package name, then this could result in erroneous behavior of the models at runtime and possible data loss.

### B.2.8 Outbound Plugs: ${n_{po}}$ = ${p_{out}}$Out

The actual outbound plug name `${n_{po}}` should consist of the desired outbound plug name `${p_{out}}` followed by the suffix `Out`. `${p_{out}}` should start with an uppercase letter.

The outbound plug should be named according to the reason for which the current view is being left, not the reason for which the target view is being entered.

All outbound plugs have a corresponding method in the view controller. This method is always called `wdFirePlug${n_{po}}()`. You may not modify either its name or its implementation.

### B.2.9 Component Interface Definition: ${n_{cid}}$ = ${cid}$CompI

The actual component interface definition name `${n_{cid}}` should consist of the desired name `${cid}` followed by the suffix `CompI`.

### B.2.10 Component Interface View Definition: ${n_{civ}}$ = ${n_{cid}}$<any_name>

If only one interface view is defined for a component interface definition, no manual action is needed because the suffix `InterfaceView` is added automatically to the window name `${w}` by the NWDS.

Should multiple interface views be required, subsequent component interface definition view names should consist of the component interface definition name `${n_{cid}}` followed by some distinguishing name.

### B.2.11 Views: ${n_v}$ = ${v}$View

The actual view name `${n_v}` should consist of the desired view name `${v}` followed by the suffix `View`.

### B.2.12    Viewsets: ${n_{vs}}$ = ${vs}$Viewset

The actual viewset name ${n_{vs}}$ should consist of the desired viewset name ${vs}$ followed by the suffix Viewset. ${vs}$ should describe the area of the screen delimited by the viewset.

The use of viewsets is to be discouraged because a more flexible mechanism is available through the use of the UI element called ViewUIElementContainer.

### B.2.13    Windows: ${w}$ = ${n_c}$ or ${n_c}$Window or <any_name>Window

By default, whenever you create a component ${n_c}$, a window ${w}$ will be created of the same name. It is usually helpful to add the suffix Window to the window name so that:

    ${w}$ = **${n_c}$**Window

instead of simply

    ${w}$ = ${n_c}$

If more windows need to be created (for instance for modal pop-up windows), you should add the suffix window to some distinguishing name.

    ${w}$ = **<any_name>**Window

# C  Exercise to Display a File System Using a Recursive Context Node Structure

Here are all the steps necessary to build a small application that will display a file system structure on the screen like the one shown in Figure C.1.

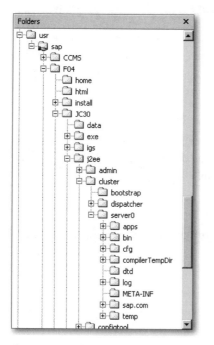

**Figure C.1** A File System Structure Can Be Represented Using Tree UI Elements

## C.1  Create a New Web Dynpro DC

The following values should be supplied:

▶ Software component: MyComponents under Local Development

▶ Vendor: `training.sap.com`

▶ Name: `ui/tree`

▶ Language: `<your_language>`

▶ Type: Web Dynpro

## C.2    Create a Web Dynpro Component

The next step is to create a Web Dynpro component with the following properties:

▶ Name: `FileSystemComp`
▶ Package: `com.sap.training.ui.tree`
▶ Window: `FileSystemWindow`
▶ View name: `FileSystemTreeView`

## C.3    Create a Java Bean to Represent a Directory Entry

To have a standardized representation of a directory entry, we can create a small Java Bean. This will be imported as a model object and can then be used to define a context model node.

1. Switch to the Navigator view.

2. Fully expand the `src/packages` branch hierarchy.

3. Underneath the lowest-level directory (tree), create two new subdirectories called `filesystem` and `xmimodel`. This can be done by right-clicking on the tree directory and selecting **New • Other • Simple • Folder**. Enter the folder name in the field provided.

4. Create a file called `DirectoryEntry.java` in the `filesystem` directory.

5. Edit `DirectoryEntry.java` and enter the stub coding for a bean with the following attributes:

   ▶ `Name`: String
   ▶ `AbsolutePathName`: String
   ▶ `IconSrc`: String
   ▶ `Size`: long
   ▶ `DateModified`: java.sql.Date
   ▶ `Hidden`: Boolean
   ▶ `ReadOnly`: Boolean
   ▶ `IsExpanded`: Boolean
   ▶ `HasChildren`: Boolean
   ▶ `IsLeaf`: Boolean

6. Give the class an empty constructor.

7. Now use the **Generate Getter and Setter** tool from the right-click menu to create getter and setter methods for each property.

> **Warning!**
>
> You need to modify the names of the getter methods created for any Boolean properties. The Web Dynpro Java Bean importer assumes that all getter methods (irrespective of type) start with the word *get*, but the **Generate Getter and Setter** tool creates a getter method starting with the word *is* for Boolean properties.
>
> Therefore, change the names of all getter methods for Boolean properties from `is<property_name>` to `get<property_name>`.

Here is a suitable implementation. Note the corrected Boolean getter method names.

```
package com.sap.training.ui.tree.filesystem;

import java.sql.Date;

public class DirectoryEntry {
  private String Name;
  private String AbsolutePathName;
  private String IconSrc;
  private long Size;
  private Date DateModified;
  private boolean Hidden;
  private boolean ReadOnly;
  private boolean IsExpanded;
  private boolean HasChildren;

  public DirectoryEntry() { }

  public String getAbsolutePathName() {
    return AbsolutePathName;
  }
  public Date getDateModified() {
    return DateModified;
  }
  public String getIconSrc() {
    return IconSrc;
  }
  public String getName() {
    return Name;
  }
  public long getSize() {
   return Size;
  }
  public boolean getHasChildren() {
    return HasChildren;
  }
```

```java
public boolean getHidden() {
  return Hidden;
}
public boolean getExpanded() {
  return IsExpanded;
}
public boolean getReadOnly() {
  return ReadOnly;
}

public void setAbsolutePathName(String s) {
  AbsolutePathName = s;
}
public void setDateModified(Date d) {
  DateModified = d;
}
public void setIconSrc(String s) {
  IconSrc = s;
}
public void setName(String s) {
  Name = s;
}
public void setSize(long l) {
  Size = l;
}
public void setHasChildren(boolean b) {
  HasChildren = b;
}
public void setHidden(boolean b) {
  Hidden = b;
}
public void setExpanded(boolean b) {
  IsExpanded = b;
}
public void setReadOnly(boolean b) {
  ReadOnly = b;
}
}
```

Listing C.1 Java Bean to represent a directory entry

## C.4    Import the Java Bean as a Model

Switch back to the Web Dynpro Explorer view and create a new Java Bean model with the following properties:

▶ Name: DirectoryModel

▶ Package: com.sap.training.ui.tree.xmimodel

Make sure the **Project(Source folder)** radio button is selected and click **Next**. Then add the DirectoryEntry class to the model list and click **Finish**.

## C.5    Component Controller Configuration

The following steps relate to the tasks performed on the component and the component controller.

### C.5.1    Declare Model Usage

In the component FileSystemComp, add DirectoryModel as a used model.

### C.5.2    Context Configuration

In the context of the component controller FileSystemComp do the following:

1. Create a model node in the context called Directory. Bind the node to the class DirectoryModel.DirectoryEntry and select all attributes.

2. Create a recursion node under the node Directory called Subdirectory. Configure its repeatedNode attribute to point to the node Directory.

The context structure shown in Figure C.2 is going to be used to represent a simple file system hierarchy. The node Directory has a cardinality of 0..n, and each element within it represents either a file or a directory. The root node of the context is analogous to the root directory of the file system.

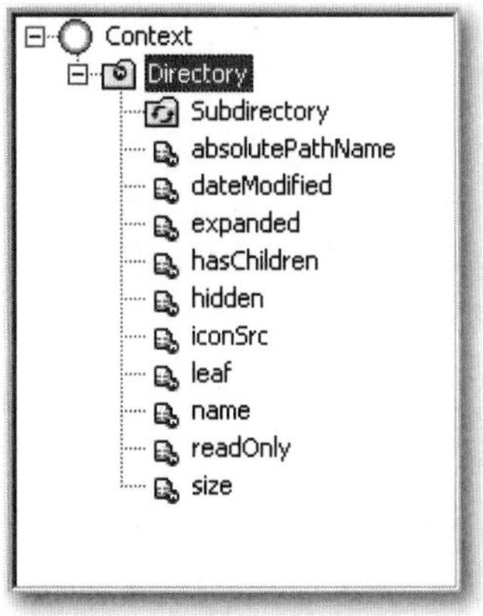

**Figure C.2** A Context Node Suitable for Representing a File System Structure

If an element of the node Directory represents a file, the recursive node Subdirectory will be null; however, if the element represents a subdirectory, the recursive child node Subdirectory will be created as a non-singleton child node of type

Directory. The whole recursive process can now be repeated in the new child instance of Directory.

## C.5.3 Method Declarations and Coding

You need to declare the existence of two methods in the component controller of component FileSystemComp. These are called readDirectory() and expandNode().

### Declaration of the Method readDirectory()

This method receives a parameter called parentDir of type java.io.File and returns an object of type java.util.Vector.

### Declaration of the Method expandNode()

This method receives a parameter called element of type IDirectoryElement and returns void.

**Warning!**

Two packages contain the IDirectoryElement class. When selecting which package the IDirectoryElement class belongs to, you must specify the component controller's package.

### Implementation of the Method readDirectory()

The following logic should be implemented in the method readDirectory().

▶ Check that the File object it has received is:

  ▶ Not null

  ▶ Contains children

▶ If both of these conditions are true, then for each child in the File object, create a new object of type DirectoryEntry, set its parameters using the values from the current child file object, and then add it to the output vector.

A suitable implementation is shown below:

```
public java.util.Vector
  readDirectory(java.io.File parentDir) {
  //@@begin readDirectory()
  Vector v = new Vector();

  // As long as neither the parent file or the parent node
  // are null
  if (parentDir != null) {
    File[] children = parentDir.listFiles();
```

```
    // Does the current directory have any children?
    if (children != null) {
      int numChildren = children.length;

      for (int i = 0; i < numChildren; i++) {
        File thisFile = children[i];

        DirectoryEntry d = new DirectoryEntry();
        d.setAbsolutePathName(thisFile.getAbsolutePath());
        d.setDateModified(new
                          Date(thisFile.lastModified()));
        d.setExpanded(false);
        d.setHasChildren(thisFile.isDirectory());
        d.setHidden(thisFile.isHidden());
        d.setIconSrc((thisFile.isDirectory())
                     ? "~sapicons/s_clofol.gif"
                     : "~sapicons/s_x__htm.gif");
        d.setName(thisFile.getName());
        d.setReadOnly(!thisFile.canWrite());
        d.setSize(thisFile.length());

        v.add(d);
      }
    }
  }

  return v;
  //@@end
}
```

**Listing C.2**  The method readDirectory() will read the contents of any directory

There are several things to notice about this method:

▶ It relies on the fact that we have stored the absolute path name for any particular directory in the context. This is because the Java `File` class is used to read a directory's contents, and this requires an absolute path name.

▶ The class `DirectoryEntry` is the Java Bean class that has been used to define the context model node

▶ The two GIF files `s_clofol.gif` and `s_x__htm.gif` are SAP standard icon files that can be accessed using the shortcut prefix `~sapicons/`.

**Implementation of the Method expandNode()**

Within the method `expandNode()`, implement code to do the following:

▶ Obtain a reference to the element's child node `Subdirectory`.

► If the node is empty, the user has never visited this directory. Call readDirectory() to read the files in the subdirectory named in AbsolutePathName.

► Bind the resulting vector to the empty subdirectory node.

The coding for expandNode() is shown here:

```
public void expandNode(IDirectoryElement element) {
  //@@begin expandNode()
  IDirectoryNode nextNodeDown = element.nodeSubdirectory();

  // Only rebuild the next node down if we have never
  // visited it before
  if (nextNodeDown.size() == 0) {
    Vector v =
      readDirectory(new File(element.getAbsolutePathName()));
    nextNodeDown.bind(v);
  }
  //@@end
}
```

**Listing C.3** The method readDirectory() is called to populate a node that has never been visited

### Implementation of the Method wdDoInit()

For the user to see any information in the screen when the application starts, we must populate the first level of the Directory node. This corresponds to all the files and directories under the file system root. Once the user has seen this information, he is able to select a particular subdirectory, and the application then reads the selected directory on demand.

Here is the coding to give the user a starting point. Notice that this coding is in the wdDoInit() method (of the component controller). Therefore, it will be executed once and only once during the lifecycle of the component.

Add the following code to the wdDoInit() method:

► Call the readDirectory() method passing a reference to the root directory of your file system.

► Store the resulting Vector object in a variable.

► Bind the Vector object returned from the previous step to the Directory context node.

A suitable implementation is shown below:

```
public void wdDoInit() {
  //@@begin wdDoInit()
  // Start at the root directory
  File f = new File("c:\\");
```

```
// Read all the files and store as a vector
Vector v = wdThis.readDirectory(f);

// Bind the vector to the context node
wdContext.nodeDirectory().bind(v);
//@@end
}
```

**Listing C.4** Populate the first level of the recursive node structure by calling readDirectory()

Now the user can actually see something when the Tree UI element displays the file system. However, no use has yet been made of the recursive context nodes. This part of the functionality only happens when the user explicitly wants to expand a particular subdirectory.

## C.6 View Controller Configuration

The following steps relate to the tasks performed on the view controller.

### C.6.1 Context Configuration

Open the view controller FileSystemTreeView and do the following:

▶ Declare the component controller to be a required controller.

▶ Create a model node in the context called Directory.

▶ Create a recursion node under the node Directory called Subdirectory. Configure its repeatedNode attribute to point to the node Directory.

▶ Edit the mapping of the node Directory in the view controller to point the node Directory in the component controller.

### C.6.2 Create an Action

Create an action called DoNodeClick. This action requires a parameter called element of type IDirectoryElement.

> **Warning!**
>
> Two packages contain the class IDirectoryElement. You must choose the package belonging to the view controller; otherwise the coding in Section C.6.4 will not work.

The TreeNodeType UI element supplies a parameter called path of type String. This parameter describes the full context path name to the exact tree element clicked on by the user. However, the action handler method has a parameter of type IDirectoryElement. In this situation, we are going to rely on the Web Dynpro Framework's ability to convert action parameter data types to prevent a type mismatch.

### C.6.3 Editing the View Layout

In the view layout, add a `Tree` UI element with the following properties:

| | |
|---|---|
| dataSource: | Directory |
| defaultNodeIconSource | Directory.iconSrc |
| id | FileSystemTree |
| rootText | "c:\" |
| title | "File System" |

Add a `TreeNodeType` UI element under `FileSystemTree` with the following properties:

| | |
|---|---|
| dataSource | Directory |
| expanded | Directory.expanded |
| hasChildren | Directory.hasChildren |
| iconSource | Directory.iconSrc |
| id | Subdirectory |
| text | Directory.name |
| onLoadChildren | DoNodeClick |

The `onLoadChildren` event is a special client-side event that the `Tree` UI element raises only when a node is expanded for the first time. Thereafter, subsequent expansions of the same node do not cause the event to be raised, and consequently, there will be no round trip to the server.

### C.6.4 View Controller Implementation

**Implementation of the Method wdDoModifyView()**

Open the view controller's implementation tab and in the method `wdDoModify-View()`, associate the UI element parameter `path` with the action handler parameter `element`. The Web Dynpro Framework handles data type conversion for us.

You can do this with the following coding:

```
public static void
  wdDoModifyView(IPrivateFileSystemTreeView wdThis,
                 IContextNode wdContext,
                 IWDView view, boolean firstTime) {
  //@@begin wdDoModifyView
  if (firstTime) {
```

```
    IWDTreeNodeType tn = (IWDTreeNodeType)view.
                                getElement("Subdirectory");
    tn.mappingOfOnLoadChildren().
                        addSourceMapping("path", "element");
  }
  //@@end
}
```

**Listing C.5** Associate the UI element parameter path with the action handler parameter element

### Implementation of the Method onActionDoNodeClick()

In the method `onActionDoNodeClick()`, we receive as a parameter, the element from the `Directory` context node selected by the user. However, this object belongs to the context of the view controller. Remember that the context of a view controller is never part of its public interface; therefore, if we were to pass a reference to this object outside the scope of the view controller, it would cease to have any meaning.

In general, any object reference that belongs to a controller's private interface is unsuitable to be passed as a parameter to another controller.

We need to call the `expandNode()` method in the component controller and pass it a reference to the element the user selected. However, the context of the view controller is mapped to the component controller. Therefore, instead of passing the view controller's private object `element`, we will pass a reference to the corresponding element in the mapping origin node. A suitable implementation is shown below:

```
public void onActionDoNodeClick(IWDCustomEvent wdEvent,
                                IDirectoryElement element ) {
  //@@begin onActionDoNodeClick(ServerEvent)

  wdThis.wdGetFileSystemCompController().
    expandNode(element.mappedDirectoryElement());
  //@@end
}
```

**Listing C.6** The action handler method in the view controller calls the expandNode() method in the component controller when a directory entry is selected for the first time

## C.7    Create an Application

Create an application called `FileSystemApp` and deploy and run your application.

The data to build the tree structure you see on the screen is only read on demand. Therefore, when the application is first executed, only the files immediately under the root directory are read and displayed. Then, as you navigate through the tree's hierarchy, each time you visit a subdirectory for the first time, the `onLoadChildren` event is raised, which causes the directory's files to be read.

Notice that if you expand a subdirectory node for the first time, a round trip to the server takes place and the node is populated. Then, if you collapse this node and expand it again, there is no round trip to the server. Not only is the data for this recursive node held in a non-singleton node (i.e., each subdirectory has its own distinct node instance), but the `Tree` UI element caches the data in the client, thus removing the need to transfer the data a second time.

## C.8    Comment on the Use of Standard SAP Icons

A complete listing of all SAP icons is available from the SAP Design Guild website (*http://www.sapdesignguild.org*). Click on the link for **Resources** and under the heading **Visual Design and Icons**, you will find a list of all the icons used by SAP, complete with a description of their purpose.

Within Web Dynpro, any icon can be accessed using the shortcut path name ~sapi-cons/ followed by the icon file name. In the example above, the `CLOSED_FOLDER` icon was used to represent a directory in the file system. This icon is identified using the shortcut file name ~sapicons/s_clofol.gif.

Please read the standard help files for further information on using standard SAP icons.

# D  ABAP Coding

The following ABAP function modules are used in the coding example in Chapter 13.

```
FUNCTION WDY_GET_LIST_ADDRESS.
*"----------------------------------------------------------------
*"*"Local Interface:
*"  TABLES
*"      ADDRESS_LIST STRUCTURE  WDY_DEMO_ADDRESS
*"----------------------------------------------------------------
data:
  wa      type WDY_DEMO_ADDRESS,
  all_ids type standard table of WDY_DEMO_ADDRESS-id,
  id      type WDY_DEMO_ADDRESS-id.
field-symbols <fsaddr>.

  clear address_list.

  select addr_key from WDY_DEMO_CUSTOM
    into id
   where name = 'ID'.
    append id to all_ids.
  endselect.

  loop at all_ids into id.
    CALL FUNCTION 'WDY_GET_SINGLE_ADDRESS'
        EXPORTING ID      = id
        IMPORTING ADDRESS = wa.
    append wa to address_list.
  endloop.

  sort address_list ascending by last_name first_name id.
ENDFUNCTION.
```

**Listing D.1** ABAP function module WDY_GET_LIST_ADDRESS returns a list of addresses

```
FUNCTION WDY_GET_SINGLE_ADDRESS.
*"----------------------------------------------------------------
*"*"Local Interface:
*"  IMPORTING
*"      VALUE(ID) TYPE  WDY_DEMO_ID
*"  EXPORTING
*"      VALUE(ADDRESS) TYPE  WDY_DEMO_ADDRESS
```

```
*"----------------------------------------------------------------
data WA type WDY_DEMO_CUSTOM.

   CALL FUNCTION 'WDY_DEMO_FILL_REC_FROM_CUST'
        EXPORTING ID      = id
         CHANGING ADDRESS = address.
ENDFUNCTION.
```

**Listing D.2** ABAP function module WDY_GET_SINGLE_ADDRESS returns a single address identified by an Address id

```
FUNCTION WDY_DEMO_FILL_REC_FROM_CUST.
*"----------------------------------------------------------------
*"*"Local Interface:
*"  IMPORTING
*"     REFERENCE(ID) TYPE  WDY_DEMO_ADDRESS-ID
*"  CHANGING
*"     REFERENCE(ADDRESS) TYPE  WDY_DEMO_ADDRESS
*"----------------------------------------------------------------
data wa type WDY_DEMO_CUSTOM.
field-symbols <fs>.

   select * from WDY_DEMO_CUSTOM
     into wa
    where ADDR_KEY = id.
      assign component wa-name of structure address to <fs>.

     if sy-subrc eq 0.
       <fs> = wa-value.
     endif.
   endselect.
ENDFUNCTION.
```

**Listing D.3** ABAP function module WDY_DEMO_FILL_REC_FROM_CUST populates the address parameter with the relevant details

```
FUNCTION WDY_DELETE_ADDRESS.
*"----------------------------------------------------------------
*"*"Local Interface:
*"  IMPORTING
*"     VALUE(ID) TYPE  WDY_DEMO_ADDRESS-ID
*"----------------------------------------------------------------
   delete from WDY_DEMO_CUSTOM where addr_key = id.
ENDFUNCTION.
```

**Listing D.4** ABAP function module WDY_DELETE_ADDRESS deletes an address identified by an Address id

```
FUNCTION WDY_NEW_ADDRESS.
*"----------------------------------------------------------------
*"*"Local Interface:
*"  IMPORTING
```

```
*"      VALUE(ADDRESS) TYPE  WDY_DEMO_ADDRESS
*"----------------------------------------------------------------
data:
  highestID type I value 0,
  currentID type I,
  wa        type WDY_DEMO_ADDRESS,
  id        type WDY_DEMO_CUSTOM-VALUE.

  currentID = address-id.

  if currentID eq 0.
    select addr_key from WDY_DEMO_CUSTOM
      into id
     where name = 'ID'.
      currentID = id.

      if currentID gt highestID.
        highestID = currentID.
      endif.
    endselect.

    currentID = highestID + 1.
  endif.
  address-id = currentID.

  CALL FUNCTION 'WDY_DEMO_FILL_CUST_FROM_REC'
      EXPORTING ADDRESS = address.
ENDFUNCTION.
```

**Listing D.5** ABAP function module WDY_NEW_ADDRESS creates a new address

```
FUNCTION WDY_DEMO_FILL_CUST_FROM_REC.
*"----------------------------------------------------------------
*"*"Local Interface:
*"  IMPORTING
*"      REFERENCE(ADDRESS) TYPE  WDY_DEMO_ADDRESS
*"----------------------------------------------------------------
data
  wa        type WDY_DEMO_CUSTOM,
  values    type standard table of WDY_DEMO_CUSTOM,
  dfies_tab type standard table of DFIES,
  dfies_wa  type dfies,
  length    type I.
field-symbols <fs>.

  CALL FUNCTION 'DDIF_FIELDINFO_GET'
      EXPORTING TABNAME   = 'WDY_DEMO_ADDRESS'
         TABLES DFIES_TAB = dfies_tab.

  loop at dfies_tab into dfies_wa.
```

```
      assign component dfies_wa-fieldname
          of structure address to <fs>.
      if not <fs> is initial.
        wa-value = <fs>.
        wa-name = dfies_wa-fieldname.
        wa-addr_key = address-id.
        append wa to values.
      endif.
    endloop.

    describe table values lines length.

    if length > 0.
      CALL FUNCTION 'WDY_DELETE_ADDRESS'
          EXPORTING ID = address-id.
      insert WDY_DEMO_CUSTOM from table values.
    endif.
ENDFUNCTION.
```

**Listing D.6** ABAP function module WDY_DEMO_FILL_CUST_FROM_REC interrogates the data dictionary and populates the address parameter according to its current definition

# E   Dictionary Structures

The following ABAP dictionary structures are used by the function modules listed in Appendix D.

| Component | Component Type | Data Type | Length | Decimal Places | Short Text |
|---|---|---|---|---|---|
| ID | WDY_DEMO_ID | NUMC | 10 | 0 | Address ID |
| LAST_NAME | WDY_DEMO_NAME | CHAR | 50 | 0 | Last name |
| FIRST_NAME | WDY_DEMO_FIRSTNAME | CHAR | 50 | 0 | First name |
| TITLE | WDY_DEMO_TITLE | CHAR | 5 | 0 | Title |
| STREET | WDY_DEMO_STREET | CHAR | 30 | 0 | Street |
| CITY | WDY_DEMO_CITY | CHAR | 50 | 0 | City |
| POSTCODE | WDY_DEMO_ZIP | CHAR | 10 | 0 | Zip code |
| COUNTRY | WDY_DEMO_COUNTRY | CHAR | 3 | 0 | Country |
| PHONE | WDY_DEMO_PHONE | CHAR | 20 | 0 | Phone number |
| STATE | WDY_DEMO_STATE | CHAR | 30 | 0 | State |
| .APPEND | WDY_DEMO_APPEND | | 0 | 0 | Append for customization |

**Table E.1** Dictionary Structure WDY_DEMO_ADDRESS

| Component | Component Type | Data Type | Length | Decimal Places | Short Text |
|---|---|---|---|---|---|
| WDY_DEMO_DUMMY | CHAR1 | CHAR | 1 | 0 | Single-character flag |
| BIRTHDAY | WDY_DEMO_BIRTHDAY | DATS | 8 | 0 | Date of birth |
| JOBPOSITION | WDY_DEMO_POSITION | CHAR | 15 | 0 | Position |
| SALARY | WDY_DEMO_SALARY | CURR | 10 | 2 | Salary |
| SAL_CUR | WDY_DEMO_CURR | CUKY | 5 | 0 | Currency of salary |

**Table E.2** Dictionary Structure WDY_DEMO_APPEND after New Fields Have Been Added

| Component | Component Type | Data Type | Length | Decimal Places | Short Text |
|---|---|---|---|---|---|
| RANKING | WDY_DEMO_RANKING | CHAR | 10 | 0 | Ranking |
| INFO | WDY_DEMO_ADDINFO | CHAR | 256 | 0 | Additional information |

**Table E.2** Dictionary Structure WDY_DEMO_APPEND after New Fields Have Been Added

| Field | Key | Initial Value | Data Element | Data Type | Length | Decimal Places | Short Text |
|---|---|---|---|---|---|---|---|
| ADDR_KEY | ✓ | ✓ | WDY_DEMO_ID | NUMC | 10 | 0 | Address ID |
| NAME | ✓ | ✓ | CHAR30 | CHAR | 30 | 0 | Short text |
| VALUE | | | | STRING | 0 | 0 | |

**Table E.3** Transparent Table WDY_DEMO_CUSTOM

# F    The Author

Chris Whealy started his professional IT career in 1986 as a PL/1 and Assembler programmer in the UK Retail Banking Industry. After 6 years, he started working on SAP R/2 systems making assembler modifications to the RV and RF modules. It's at this point, that he learned ABAP on R/2 systems.

With the launch of SAP R/3 version 2.0A, he started working in the Basis area performing installations, upgrades, and system administration. This work went hand in hand with his ongoing ABAP work.

Joining SAP UK in May 1995, Chris has always had an interest in custom interfaces into and out of the R/3 system, so in 1996 when the Internet boom started to take hold, he began to focus on browser-based interfaces to R/3 using SAP's Internet Transaction Server.

Right from the start, Chris has worked with SAP's web-based technology as it has grown and matured, and in late 2002 he turned his attention to Web Dynpro and spent a significant proportion of 2003 working closely with the Web Dynpro development team in Walldorf both learning the new technology and documenting its inner workings.

In October 2003, Chris was able to put his knowledge into practice when he started work as the lead technical consultant for a large Web Dynpro-based project at the UK subsidiary of a major international tax and audit firm.

Since then, Chris has written numerous articles and web presentations about various aspects of Web Dynpro technology, often speaks at TechEd, and is the author the following SAP training courses:

- ▶ JA310: Introduction to Web Dynpro for Java
- ▶ JA312: Advanced Web Dynpro for Java
- ▶ JA314: The Internet Graphics Server (E-Learning)

# Index

## X

**A developer's guide to new technologies and techniques in SAP NetWeaver 7.0 (2004s)**

**Discusses the new ABAP Editor, ABAP Unit testing, regular expressions, shared memory objects, and more**

485 pp., 2007, with CD, 69,95 Euro / US$ 69,95
ISBN 978-1-59229-139-7

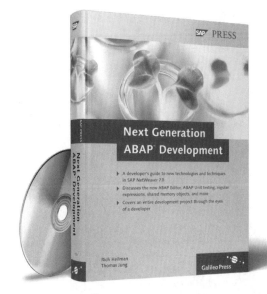

# Next Generation ABAP Development

**www.sap-press.com**

Rich Heilman, Thomas Jung

### Next Generation ABAP Development

This book takes advanced ABAP programmers on a guided tour of all the new concepts, technologies, techniques, and functions introduced in the new ABAP release 7.0. The unique approach of the book gives you a front row seat to view the entire process of design, development, and testing — right through the eyes of a developer. You'll quickly learn about all of the new ABAP programming options at your disposal, while virtually experiencing a detailed series of actual scenarios that could easily be encountered in your own upcoming projects.

**Insights on the architecture and tools of SAP Web AS Java 6.40**

**Sample application for Web Dynpro and SAP NetWeaver Development Infrastructure**

**Includes 180-day trial version of SAP Web AS Java 6.40 on DVD**

514 pp., 2005, with DVD, 69,95 Euro / US$ 69,95
ISBN 978-1-59229-020-8

# Java Programming with the SAP Web Application Server

www.sap-press.com

K. Kessler, P. Tillert, P. Dobrikov

## Java Programming with the SAP Web Application Server

Without proper guidance, the development of business oriented Java applications can be challenging. This book introduces you systematically to highly detailed concepts, architecture, and to all components of the SAP Web Application Server Java (Release 6.40), while and equipping you with all that's needed to ensure superior programming. First, benefit from an SAP NetWeaver overview, followed by the authors' guided tour through the SAP NetWeaver Developer Studio. After an excursion into the world of Web services, you then learn about the different facets of Web Dynpro technology, with in-depth details on user interfaces. This information is further bolstered with insights on the SAP NetWeaver Java Development Infrastructure and the architecture of SAP Web AS Java.

**Examples of dynamic programming, componentization, integration of applications, navigation, and much more**

**Essential and practical knowledge about installation, configuration, and administration of the Web Dynpro runtime**

497 pp., 2006, 69,95 Euro / US$
ISBN 1-59229-077-9

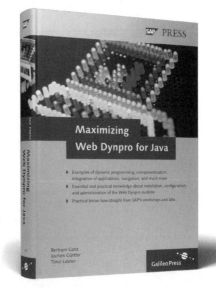

# Maximizing Web Dynpro for Java

B. Ganz, J. Gürtler, T. Lakner

## Maximizing Web Dynpro for Java

Standard examples of Web Dynpro applications can leave SAP developers with many questions and severe limitations. This book takes you to the next level with detailed examples that show you exactly what you need to know in order to leverage Web Dynpro applications. From the interaction with the Java Developer Infrastructure (JDI), to the use of Web Dynpro components, to the integration into the portal and the use of its services—this unique book delivers it all. In addition, readers get dozens of tips and tricks on fine-tuning Web Dynpro applications in terms of response time, security, and structure. Expert insights on the configuration and administration of the Web Dynpro runtime environment serve to round out this comprehensive book.

Basic principles, architecture, and configuration

Development of dynamic, reusable UI components

Volumes of sample code and screen captures for help you maximize key tools

360 pp., 2006, 69,95 Euro / US$
ISBN 1-59229-078-7

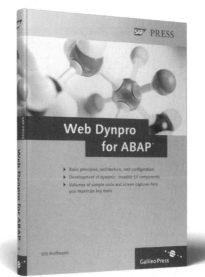

# Web Dynpro for ABAP

www.sap-press.com

U. Hoffmann

## Web Dynpro for ABAP

Serious developers must stay ahead of the curve by ensuring that they are up-to-date with all of the latest standards. This book illustrates the many benefits that can be realized with component-based UI development using Web Dynpro for ABAP. On the basis of specifically developed sample components, readers are introduced to the architecture of the runtime and development environment and receive highly-detailed descriptions of the different functions and tools that enable you to efficiently implement Web Dynpro technology on the basis of SAP NetWeaver 2004s. Numerous code listings, screen captures, and little-known tricks make this book your indispensable companion for the practical design of modern user interfaces.

**Complete reference chapters for all SAP UI libraries and their usage**

**Development, testing, and system configuration**

**Legal standards and how to apply them**

371 pp., 2007, with CD, 79,95 Euro / US$ 79.95
ISBN 978-1-59229-112-0

# Developing Accessible Applications with SAP NetWeaver

**www.sap-press.com**

Josef Köble

## Developing Accessible Applications with SAP NetWeaver

This comprehensive reference book is a developer's complete guide to programming accessible applications using SAP NetWeaver technology. Readers get step-by-step guidance on the requirements and conceptual design and development using ABAP Workbench and NW Developer Studio. The authors provide you with a detailed presentation of all relevant design elements for Dynpro, Web Dynpro (ABAP and Java), and SAP Interactive Forms by Adobe. In addition, you'll learn the ins and outs of testing applications, as well as configuration techniques for both front-end interfaces and back-end apps. With this unique approach, developers get a thorough introduction to all interface elements along with best practices for how to use them, and QA managers gain exclusive, expert insights on testing accessibility features.

Comprehensive guide to end-to-end process integration with SAP XI—from a developer's perspective

Practical exercises to master system configuration and development of mappings, adapters, and proxies

341 pp., 2007, 69,95 Euro / US$ 69,95
ISBN 978-1-59229-118-2

# SAP Exchange Infrastructure for Developers

www.sap-press.com

V. Nicolescu, B. Funk, P. Niemeyer, M. Heile

## SAP Exchange Infrastructure for Developers

This book provides both experienced and new SAP XI developers with a detailed overview of the functions and usage options of the SAP NetWeaver Exchange Infrastructure. The authors take you deep into the system with a series of practical exercises for the development and configuration of mappings, adapters, and proxies: RFC-to-File, File-to-IDoc, ABAP-Proxy-to-SOAP, and Business Process Management. Each exercise is rounded off by a description of relevant monitoring aspects and is combined in a comprehensive case study.